The
Professional Practice
of
Psychology

Developments in Clinical Psychology

Glenn R. Caddy, series editor
Nova University

MMPI-168 Codebook, by Ken R. Vincent, Iliana Castillo, Robert I. Hauser, H. James Stuart, Javier A. Zapata, Cal K. Cohn, and Gregory O'Shanick, 1984

Integrated Clinical and Fiscal Management in Mental Health: A Guidebook, by Fred Newman and James Sorensen, 1985

The Professional Practice of Psychology, edited by Georgiana Shick Tryon, 1986

Clinical Applications of Hypnosis, edited by Frank A. DePiano, 1986

In Preparation:

Advances in the Treatment of Addictive Behaviors, edited by Ted D. Nirenberg

The Behavioral Management of the Cardiac Patient, by D. G. Byrne

Language and Psychopathology, by Stephen Schwartz

The
Professional Practice
of
Psychology

Georgiana Shick Tryon, Editor
Fordham University

ABLEX PUBLISHING CORPORATION
NORWOOD, NEW JERSEY 07648

Library of Congress Cataloging-in-Publication Data
Main entry under title:

The Professional practice of psychology.

(Developments in clinical psychology)
Includes bibliographies and index.
1. Psychology—Practice. I. Tryon, Georgiana
Shick. [DNLM: 1. Professional Practice. 2. Psychology
BF 76 P964]
BF75.P7 1986   150′.23   ^ 85-13433
ISBN 0-89391-163-1

Ablex Publishing Corporation
355 Chestnut Street
Norwood, New Jersey 07648

Contents

v

Preface

The idea for this volume resulted from years of working with graduate students and beginning professionals in psychology and from my own experience in these two roles. Most graduate students have questions about professional practice which are unanswered, and sometimes unasked, in the classroom. After graduation, new professionals often learn what the practice of professional psychology is like through experience and occasional consultation with senior members of the field. Over the years, I and other contributors to this volume have received numerous calls from former students asking for information regarding everything from ethics to professional organizations.

Therefore, this book is designed to provide practical information concerning the functions of professional psychologists; the settings in which they work; and legal, ethical, and insurance issues affecting professional practice. This volume is suitable for introductory courses as well as advanced graduate seminars dealing with professional psychologists. Chapter contributors have included reference materials which the reader may pursue for indepth examinations of specific issues.

The editor is appreciative of the typing and copyediting done by Mary Conetta and Janet Carlson.

PART I

THE TRAINING OF PROFESSIONAL PSYCHOLOGISTS

Chapter 1

The Training of Professional Psychologists: Historical Developments and Present Trends

Glenn R. Caddy
Lora L. LaPointe

Nova University

Hickson and Thomas (1969), in their exploration of the nature of professions, abstracted an array of 14 criteria which they considered the essence of professional practice. Of these criteria, some were substantive in nature and dealt with issues such as educational requirements and curricula matters, others dealt with normative considerations such as ethical conduct, others with professional relationships, and still others addressed organizational and legal matters such as the establishment of professional associations and licensure. Such efforts notwithstanding, perhaps still the best guidelines developed to describe a profession are those articulated by Abraham Flexner (1915, 1925), who steered the development of modern medical education in the United States.

According to Flexner, a discipline may achieve recognition as a profession if it meets the following criteria: (a) its objectives are definite and immediately practical; (b) it has available educationally communicable techniques for the attainment of these objectives; (c) it employs techniques involving essentially intellectual operations, and its practitioners exercise responsible discretion in matching their techniques to individual problems; (d) the techniques of the profession are related to a systematic discipline whose substance is large and complex, and hence, normally not accessible to laymen; (e) its members are organized in some kind of society, with rules for membership and exclusion based, in part, upon professional competence; and (f) the aims of the professional organization are at least in part altruistic, rather than merely self-serving, and entail a code of ethics whose sanctions also are invoked in determining membership in the society and, therefore, the legitimate practice of the profession (see also Whitehead, 1929).

Flexner's definition of "profession" is not the definition of an art or a trade. As Peterson (1976a) points out:

> It is not based on the creative intuitions and expressions of the practitioner, and it is not made up of the mechanical application of unvarying techniques to human objects. Professional work requires the intelligent disciplined design of complex services to serve a clientele whose needs and resources differ from one case to another and for whom the most helpful services may change from one occasion to another. For the most part, the fundamental attitude of the professional practitioner, though not the product of his work, resembles that of the scientist (p. 573).

Within psychology, ambiguity regarding the definition of professional psychology has been and continues to be a fundamental problem. In both the American Psychological Association (APA) Standards for Providers of Psychological Services (APA, 1977) and in the accreditation guidelines for training programs (APA, 1979), for example, the various practitioner specialities have been defined. Yet there is no simple generic definition of the profession. The terms "professional psychology" and "clinical psychology" often have been used interchangeably, presumably because clinical psychology has always occupied such a large part of the practitioner psychology arena. More recently, we have seen the emergence of the title and field of Health Care Psychology (DeLeon, 1979; Iscoe, 1982; Singer & Krantz, 1982, Tanabe, 1982; Wright, 1976), which is conceptualized as including and expanding clinical psychology. But the term "professional psychology" clearly does not include the fields of counseling, school, or industrial psychology, each of which has been variously defined and contains major practitioner components. Psychology, as Fox, Barclay, and Rodgers (1982) have articulated, has grown through the development of its parts, without a clear specification of its core. These authors point to the APA accreditation process as exemplary of the lack of definitional clarity within the discipline. Quoting Fox et al.:

> Accreditation criteria were originally developed for clinical psychology programs as an applied arm of what was basically an academic discipline. Subsequently, school and counseling programs were added to the list. The consequence of this piecemeal process is that, instead of accrediting professional psychology programs, APA accredits specialty programs or subfields of psychology. (p. 306)

These same authors go on to note the fact that psychology licensing laws in the United States (like those of the other major professions) are in most instances generic in nature, while the accreditation procedures are for specialities. Such a situation, Fox et al. suggest, adds to confusion both in the public perception and within psychology.

The essential question of definition, it seems, is tied to the question of whether or not the profession of psychology can represent an identifiable field that can be defined and regulated to serve the best interests of the public. In 1981, the faculty of the School of Professional Psychology at Wright State University adopted the following definition of professional psychology:

> Professional psychology is that profession which is concerned with enhancing the effectiveness of human functioning. Therefore, a professional psychologist is one who has expertise in the development and application of quality services to the public in a controlled, organized, ethical manner; based on psychological knowledge, attitudes and skills, in order to enhance the effectiveness of human functioning.

Quite similar definitions have been offered by authors such as Dorken and Rodgers (1976), Peterson (1976b), and Rodgers (1980). The central concept within such definitions is that practicing psychologists define their profession by the field of need which they service, not by the specified knowledge base from which they function nor by the organizational setting within which their service is delivered. There is little question but that such a definition can be considered too broad, the result being that it encompasses the work of other professions. Such a definition, however, is intended neither to be monopolistic nor exclusionary. Rather, it specifies the primary focal area of the practice of psychology.

We will turn now to present some of the major themes in the evolution of professional psychology. While each of the practitioner-oriented specialties will be presented en passant, the clinical specialty area will be examined in greater detail.

THE EMERGENCE OF PSYCHOLOGY AS A PROFESSION

As early as 1904, James McKeen Cattell made the prediction that eventually there would be a profession as well as a science of psychology (Cattell, 1937). The origins of professional activity in psychology, and in clinical psychology in particular, have been traced in the United States to the period 1895 to 1925 (Watson, 1953). If self-determined control of its members is the hallmark of a profession, the first stirrings of attempts at control arose in the American Psychological Association in 1895, and took the form of considering control of clinical procedures through evaluation of test data. It was not until 20 years later, however, that the APA went on record formally to discourage the use of mental tests by unqualified individuals. Then, inevitably, in 1917 a committee to consider the qualifications appropriate for psychological examiners was appointed, and 2 years thereafter another committee was charged with considering the certification of consulting psychologists. Also in 1919, a special interest group known as the Section of Clinical Psychology was formed within APA, and after much maneuvering the certification of clinical psychologists finally was begun. Only 25 psychologists applied for certification, however, and in 1927 a policy committee concluded that certification was not practical. A vote of the APA membership followed, and the policy of certifying clinical psychologists was discontinued. The APA, founded as it had been to advance psychology as a science, did not show any particular commitment during the first quarter of the twentieth century to reflecting the professional aspirations of those of its members who were interested in the practical applications of psychological knowledge.

The first formal proposal for the establishment of a professional psychology training program was made by Loyal Crane in 1925. Crane reflected concern that the scientific training of the doctoral (Ph.D.) psychologist seemed inappropriate for the practicing clinician, and he noted too the limited prestige accorded psychologists both by members of related professions and by the public in general. He suggested that relevant substance must be placed into the education of psychologists, and he proposed both a distinctive degree, the Doctor of Psychology (Psy. D.), and a specific 4-year medically-related curriculum as the most appropriate manner for achieving an education of such relevance. Interestingly, during this same period, there existed impressive support for Crane's commitment to the emergence of practitioner-oriented psychology. This support came from powerful ideological contributors such as Freud and Menninger, although, of course, these leaders did not address the details of psychology, such as the specific degree or curricula matters, that were raised by Crane. As early as 1923, Karl Menninger (see Reisman, 1966) had reflected the view that medicine provided an inadequate basis for understanding personal and interpersonal disorders. Similarly, Freud (1927) had argued, in his unfortunately titled manuscript *The Problem of Lay Analysis,* that psychology and not medicine was the discipline on which the practice of psychoanalysis should be based.

Eminently reasonable as these perspectives are when viewed today, in their time they produced little effect of substance. As Peterson (1982) has remarked:

> Clinical psychology had not yet established the principles nor developed the methods needed to qualify as an independent profession. It was functionally ancillary and administratively subordinate to medicine . . . (it) did not have the force to be regarded even as a significant upstart by well-established medical professionals. (p. 21)

According to Fernberger (1932), the twenties was a period of little action within APA as far as the movement towards the professionalizing of psychology was concerned, though in 1930 the Association of Consulting Psychologists was formed from a still earlier group founded in 1921. Gradually, the Association of Consulting Psychologists extended its membership and became one of the more important elements, later to merge into the American Association for Applied Psychology (see English, 1938; Fryer, 1946). The first organizational meeting of this new association was held in 1937.

By the start of the Second World War, there existed two major psychological societies in the United States. The APA continued to devote its efforts to the advancement of psychology as a science, while the American Association for Applied Psychology committed itself to advancing the application of psychology. In 1945, however, these two societies and others, like the Psychometric Society and the Society for the Psychological Study of Social Issues, combined into what Wolfle (1946) referred to as the reorganized APA. Both in spirit and practice, this new APA committed itself to represent psychology both as a science and as a profession.

It is also significant that 2 years after the close of the Second World War, the American Board of Examiners in Professional Psychology was formed and began the process of individually certifying psychologists in the practice of clinical, counseling, and industrial/organizational psychology.

THE EDUCATION OF PROFESSIONAL PSYCHOLOGISTS

Historically, the precursors of professional training in clinical settings in the United States were internships at the Vineland Training School in New Jersey, the Illinois Juvenile Psychopathic Institute, the Boston Psychopathic Hospital, the Western State Penitentiary in Pennsylvania, and the New York Institute for Child Guidance. But the professionally oriented training provided at these institutions was entirely the responsibility of the pioneer professional psychologists who practiced within them. Certainly, no formal relationship existed during these early days between such professional training facilities and academic settings or departments of psychology. An academic model of professional training that provided for both didactic preparation within a department of psychology, and practical or internship experience, did not emerge until the report of the Shakow Committee (APA,1947). This committee proposed both a set of general principles and a model program for professionally oriented graduate education. This program would include 2 years of study in the area of general psychology, dynamics of human behavior, related disciplines, diagnostic methods, therapy, and research methods. Within that program, the internship would be offered during the third year; and, during the fourth year, final work on the dissertation would be conducted. Also included in the fourth year would be seminars on professional problems and cross-discipline issues, and additional courses in psychology, as needed, would be offered in order to round off the individual student's program (see also APA, 1948, 1949).

Two years after the Shakow Committee Report, the first in a series of conferences on graduate education in clinical psychology was held.

The Boulder Conference. In August 1949, a Conference on Graduate Education in Clinical Psychology was held in Boulder, Colorado (see Raimy, 1950). The primary impetus for this conference was the requests to the APA from the Veterans Administration and the United States Public Health Service to provide these agencies with names of universities deemed to have competent educational programs in clinical psychology, to develop a procedure for accrediting such institutions, and, finally, to produce recommendations of the type of program considered by APA to provide the most satisfactory training for clinical psychologists.

Before 1949, the responsibility for any kind of professional training in clinical psychology had been placed almost exclusively on the student. As Shakow (1978) remarked, it consisted essentially of do-it-yourself programs. Given the lack of experience within psychology with professionally oriented educational activities, and given also the unprecedented post-war demand for persons professionally trained in the mental health field, the Boulder Conference gave clinical psychologists the unique opportunity to consider just what kind of profession they wanted, and to determine how their profession could best meet some of the needs for mental health services.

During those 2 weeks at Boulder, the conferees examined and attempted to establish positions on issues such as the social needs to be addressed in the training of clinical psychologists, the kinds and levels of training required by psychologists in this changing society, ethics and problems of training, background preparation for clinical psychologists, training for research and for psychotherapy, selection and evaluation of students, accreditation of training institutions, and licensing and certification. Some of the most significant issues and conclusions of the Conference were as follows.

Firstly, the conferees asserted that the title "clinical psychologist" should be used only by persons with a doctoral degree in clinical psychology received from a recognized university. Secondly, the conferees concluded that there were three primary social needs to be addressed by clinical psychologists: the provision of direct services, the prevention of conditions which require such services, and the enhancement of the concept of positive mental health. Thirdly, it was agreed that research should be given a place of equal and coordinate importance with practice in the education of clinical psychologists.

The so-called Boulder model was to produce a scientist-professional who would be trained to be a scientist first and a professional second. According to Raimy (1950), it was this issue rather than any other that created the greatest polarization among the conference participants. There were several points that seemed basic to the conflict that this issue provoked: (a) It was felt that students should receive training in both research and practice so that they could work in either one or both. (b) It was argued that the general lack of dependable knowledge about personality demanded greater research. (c) It was believed that, while it would be difficult to achieve interest and competence in both research and service, the careful selection of high quality students would make such an achievement possible. (d) It was felt that, in the course of the provision of effective services, clinical psychologists would find themselves confronted with significant research problems. (e) It was believed inevitable that effective service also would provide the basis for much of the clinical research in psychology. By adopting the scientist-professional concept, of course, the conferees endorsed the basic training model that first had been made explicit in the Shakow Committee Report.

The Conference also found general agreement in supporting the core curriculum, oriented toward the tripartite goals of teaching content, developing skills, and evaluating attitudes, that had been recommended by the Shakow Committee. However, the Boulder conferees did reflect some concern for professional orientation, in that they recommended that all students receive training in the theory and practice of psychotherapy, and that a graded sequence of field training experiences be an integral part of their preparation.

In contemplating the evaluation of professional training, the conferees sought to evolve an encouragement of both diversity and uniformity. The diversity was seen as necessary because of the process of rapid development and change, which was occurring both in the society and within the discipline of psychology. Uniformity was desired in order to provide a particular meaning to clinical psychology. It was felt that uniformity could be achieved best by setting minimum standards for training. Diversity could be achieved in relationship to these standards, depending upon how training departments sought to develop their particular programs beyond the standards established.

The Conference agreed to give serious consideration to the role within clinical practice of individuals with other than doctoral training in clinical psychology. It was resolved that such individuals could carry out many activities that would contribute to the provision of professional psychological services. It was recommended that APA undertake a study of the proper functions and titles of such people, and also that an estimate of the extent of the relative and absolute need for both psychologists and such assistants be developed.

The issues of professional ethics and the further development of ethical standards for psychologists also were given particular prominence by the conferees, for it was recognized that the discipline was beginning to inject relatively large numbers of newly trained people into roles of increasing public responsibility. Thus, it was agreed that departments of psychology should ensure that graduate programs include information about ethical problems and professional responsibility in their curricula, and that they require the highest ethical standards from their faculty and students.

Finally, the Conference participants were in general agreement regarding licensure and certification. Such issues were seen as inevitable in clinical psychology, and probably also in other applied psychology areas as well. (Interestingly, private practice was seen as a relatively minor, but developing, outlet for clinical psychologists, and an outlet that the conferees did not generally favor.) While it was recognized that licensure and certification were issues for states to regulate, it was recommended that the APA increase its efforts, through advisory services and financial support to state groups, in the furtherance of licensure and/or certification enabling legislation for the practice of psychology.

There can be little question but that the Boulder Conference, and the scientist-practitioner concept that it confirmed, were to have a profound impact on the profession of clinical psychology. Certainly, most of the 42 university-based clinical training programs existing in 1949 adopted the scientist-practitioner model, and in so doing taught whatever general diagnostic and treatment methodologies were known by their faculties. Most faculty, however, were both better equipped and better prepared to teach a research framework which was widely seen to be crucial to the development of more effective clinical assessment and intervention technologies. While over the subsequent years the limitations of the scientist-practitioner model would become ever increasingly apparent, the fact that virtually all of the major clinical training conferences since Boulder have been preoccupied with the model sanctioned there attests to its significance, both conceptual and operational.

What of the education of the more practitioner-oriented counseling and school psychologists? The development and clarification of training programs for these two specialty professional groups would be achieved at the Northwestern and Thayer conferences, respectively.

The Northwestern Conference. The 1951–52 annual meeting of the Executive Committee of the then Division of Counseling and Guidance of APA (subsequently renamed the Division of Counseling Psychology) approved a statement that was, in fact, a product of a conference held at Northwestern University in Chicago during August, 1951. This statement established a set of recommended standards for the training of doctoral level counseling psychologists (APA, 1952). This statement, too, was a product of the same social forces that were spawning the awakening of a practitioner orientation in clinical psychology. The statement aimed to communicate the Division's views on the training of counseling psychologists throughout the discipline generally; to aid university departments engaged in training counseling psychologists; to facilitate discrimination by foundations, government agencies, and the like regarding the allocation of support to doctoral training programs; and to heighten the awareness within society generally of the competence of counseling psychologists.

The recommendations adopted subsequent to the Northwestern Conference addressed the following areas: the roles and functions of counseling psychologists, the selection of students, breadth of training versus specialization, and curriculum. With the exception of the matters of curriculum, the issues of the Conference and the recommendations which flowed from it were quite straightforward and so will not be presented here. In fact, the curriculum matters too were clearly presented and eminently predictable given the goals of counselor training articulated at the conference. Unlike their clinical brethren, however, counseling psychologists of the day were more singularly committed to the practitioner-oriented product of their training programs, and so curriculum matters which included counseling, professional orientation, practica, and internship training, accounted for more than two-thirds of the recommended time commitment of the program. Research, on the other hand, which was still considered important to the training of counseling psychologists, was proportionately offered only approximately one-eighth of the program curriculum. Without question, the model of training proposed for counseling psychologists was much more clearly and unambiguously drawn than was the model preferred by academic clinicians of the day.

The Thayer Conference. In August 1954, a conference addressing School Psychology at Mid-Century (Cutts, 1955) was held at the Hotel Thayer in West Point, New York. The conference was sponsored by APA's Education and Training Board and funded, in part, by the then U.S. Department of Health, Education, and Welfare. It was called to provide a forum within which to discuss the functions, qualifications, and training of school psychologists.

The Thayer conferees attempted to specify the functions of school psychologists, and in so doing they surveyed both the literature and many of the professionals in the field. In a similar vein, they sought to address the dual questions of what sort of individuals should be school psychologists, and how individuals with the desired characteristics could be encouraged to enter the profession. As might be expected, the very complexity of the above specified issues produced a somewhat indeterminate outcome.

On the matter of training (and functioning), the conferees did recommend two levels as being appropriate for providing competent psychological services within the schools.

> The position of *school psychologist* involves such broad comprehensive preparation at a high level that these responsibilities can be met only with doctoral training or its equivalent. This training should consist of four years of graduate study, one of which should be a year of internship. The position of *psychological examiner* is considered essential. The training for this position should be a two-year graduate program, of which one-half year should be an internship. Such training should equip the examiner to perform many psychological services. (Cutts, 1955, p. 31)

Focusing on the doctoral training recommendations made for the school psychologist function, a number of issues were discussed. There was a general recognition that no best educational model had been developed to train school psychologists, and there was a recognition of the need for program experimentation. No attempt was made to suggest the most advantageous program features in terms of courses or semester hours. Considerable discussion, however, did address topics such as promoting mental health; working with groups, individuals, and exceptional children; methods of changing behavior; and practicum training.

While clearly, too, the conferees saw themselves as primarily having a service provider/practitioner function, they also proved to be committed to the need for ongoing evaluative research within their profession. Thus, they unanimously approved a statement recommending that school psychologists be adequately trained in research.

There were a number of other issues raised by the Thayer participants (matters of school service ethics, questions and problems of professional status, working conditions, salary, and other guild issues). Perhaps the two other topics of greatest importance addressed during the conference, however, were certification and accreditation.

Certification of school psychologists was endorsed, and it was recommended that the legally constituted state authorities should be encouraged to provide certification for school psychologists. (It also was noted that, at the time of the conference, only 20 states and the District of Columbia had any such regulations, and that these varied widely from state to state.) It was further agreed that certification in school psychology should be developed by the American Board of Examiners in Professional Psychology, and that the APA Division of School Psychology should promote both State and Board certification.

Finally, on the matter of accreditation of school psychology training programs, the Thayer conferees unanimously supported the need for accreditation. It was agreed that APA should be requested to inaugurate a process of accreditation for school psychology training programs similar to the accreditation provided to clinical and counseling psychology training programs.

Having addressed briefly the status of the professional training of both counseling and school psychologists of the time, we will now return to a review of the developments within the more controversial clinical specialty.

The Palo Alto Conference. In August 1955, the Institute on Education and Training for Contributions to Mental Health was held at Stanford University (see Strother, 1956). The Palo Alto Conference was not a policies-oriented conference as the Boulder proceedings had been. Rather, the Conference was held to permit an examination of the views and opinions that existed within psychology regarding the mental health field, and to permit representatives of universities and of federal agencies to discuss some of the implications for psychology of the mental health movement. The Palo Alto Conference was a product of essentially three major forces: (a) the trend toward specialization that was manifested in the Boulder Conference, and subsequently in the Northwestern and Thayer Conferences; (b) the desire to follow up on the recommendations of the Boulder conferees regarding the need for a review of the policies and procedures which were developed at Boulder; and (c) the particularly rapid growth of the mental health movement.

The conferees at Palo Alto found unanimous agreement for the proposition that the mental health movement would hold even more far reaching consequences for the entire discipline of spychology than had the post-war events that brought with them such a great demand for clinical psychologists. Despite the conviction that there would be an increasing demand for highly trained clinical practitioners as the mental ehalth movement unfolded, it was the general opinion of the conferees that research on the nature and treatment of mental illness and the development of preventive programs deserved the highest priority. The decision of the Boulder conferees to attempt to integrate professional and scientific training was reviewed and found almost unanimous support. At Palo Alto, there appeared virtually no support for proposals that would separate professional from scientific training.

On the topic of specialization, the Conference supported strongly the concept of a common core curriculum for professional training, yet the intention was in no way to limit the prospects for subsequent special education. It was recognized, however, that adequate competence in any specialty area would require at least some post-doctoral training.

The other major issues examined at Palo Alto involved concerns about the quality of practicum training and of training in psychotherapy. It was recommended that a closer coordination between universities and practicum facilities and, perhaps even accreditation of practicum agencies, would be valuable. On the concern about psychotherapy training, it was agreed that: (a) training in psychotherapy is absolutely essential for psychologists who will work in a mental health setting; (b) the provision of initial psychotherapy training should be the responsibility of all graduate clinical training programs; (c) psychotherapy training should be largely experiential in nature, and should be introduced fairly early in the graduate program; and (d) postdoctoral training is necessary for the development of professional competence in therapy.

The Miami Beach Conference. The Miami Beach Conference on Graduate Education in Psychology was convened during the winter of 1958 (see Roe, Gustad, Moore, Ross, & Skodak, 1959). Unlike the Boulder Conference, and to a lesser extent the Palo Alto Conference, the Miami Conference focused on the entire field of graduate education in psychology. The issues of the Conference were organized into five major and by now rather familiar domains, involving: (a) the roles of psychologists in the various segments of society and the extent to which the education of psychologists was in keeping with these various roles; (b) the ways various parts of the curricula of psychology training programs fit together, and the function and relevance of common core curricula; (c) the nature of specialization training; (d) the nature and significance of sub-doctoral training programs; and (e) the significance of standards, accreditation, and control.

As occurred at the previous conferences, the Miami conferees recognized the continued rapid growth and presumably continuing discrepancy between demands for psychologists and the number currently or potentially available to provide service. This brought forth, yet again, the realization of the need to reevaluate the most appropriate roles for psychologists. The issue was seen in terms of the question of how best to deploy the limited manpower resources in psychology in the interests of both the society and the profession. It also was asserted, however, that the roles of psychologists should not be derived solely from society's demands for services, but that psychologists should determine what roles to emphasize, to change, and to abandon.

It was widely agreed that doctoral education should continue to train psychologists as broadly as possible. Further, it was asserted that, in order to ensure maximum utilization in psychology, training programs should continue to emphasize research. This focus was seen as especially important, for it was believed that research training would facilitate greatly the prospect for more innovative approaches to service, and that such innovation likely would increase the efficiency of the service delivery systems.

Again, as previously, the Miami conferees agreed that there is a common basic subject matter of psychology, and that it is this core that defines the discipline. Despite this general commitment to a core curriculum, the conferees did not specify the components of this core. Rather, they suggested that, in the interests of promoting innovation in training, each graduate program should select a core curriculum in such a way as to best meet the goals of the program, the needs of its students, and the capacities of its faculty. In this regard, it was recognized that psychologists engaged in the professional specialities may require a common core curriculum not shared by other specialities.

Considerable concern also was expressed by many of the conferees regarding the adequacy of doctoral level training as the sole preparation for a career in psychotherapy, and, again, it was concluded that post-doctoral training for this role is essential.

The Miami conferees continued to define psychology training in terms of the scientist-professional model. They did conclude, however, that research should be defined broadly in terms of a continuum of methodologies and not limited to rigorous hypothesis testing, and that some relaxation of the traditional specifications for the doctoral dissertation might be desirable. While the issue of granting a professional degree was raised, it met with little enthusiasm.

Finally, on the matter of controls, the Conference agreed that some form of accreditation was necessary, that the APA was the most appropriate agency to undertake such accreditation, and that extension of accreditation to postdoctoral centers should occur.

The dust had hardly settled from the Miami Conference, and it was 1960. Psychology appeared to be expanding even more rapidly than before. Membership within APA had grown rapidly from 1950, and this expansion brought diversity and many suggestions for change. There were many issues. Firstly, the number of psychologists being produced from the then 56 accredited clinical programs (and the 26 accredited programs in counseling psychology) was far too small to meet the identified public need for mental health service providers. Even the largest training programs were producing no more than 10 doctorates annually. Secondly, for a significant number of Boulder model program students, there appeared an unfortunate discrepancy between the aims of the programs and the goals of the trainees. Thorndike (1955) had suggested that clinical psychologists tended not to be interested equally in research and practice, and that these joint program goals, generally with the priority given to research, did not serve well the desires of the students within them. Moreover, as two contemporary surveys indicated (Kelly & Goldberg, 1959; Levy, 1962), given that the modal number of publications by clinical psychologists was zero, Boulder-model-trained psychologists were, in the main, simply not functioning to serve in support of the scientific endeavor. Increasingly it was being asserted that Boulder-model-trained psychologists were unproductive as scientists and incompetent as professionals. Against this growing discontent, of course, was the fact that, for academic faculty, the incentives still lay in doing research and in educating students in their own image. Walsh (1979) addressed the conflict of the time this way:

> Academic psychologists tended to be unsympathetic with students who wished to become practitioners and students often saw their mentors as wrapped up in narrow, academic interests that were sterile as far as the students were concerned. The result was that clinical psychologists trained during this period made neither good researchers nor very competent practitioners. (p. 339)

In a similar vein, Stricker (1975) looked back on the period of the mid-sixties and suggested that the education of professionally oriented clinical psychologists was actually being restricted in many universities. The events at Miami notwithstanding, Stricker suggested that many psychology departments had not in fact implemented the scientist-professional model. Rather, he said, many departments chose a heavy emphasis on scientific training with almost no attention given to practitioner training.

Irrespective of exactly what was occurring in individual programs, a call was made by Rodgers (1964) to benefit psychology as a whole by a more definitive separation of academic and professional training than that espoused by most practitioner training proponents. He made this plea in the following terms:

> Rather than impoverishing psychology, separation of professional from academic training so that each group could focus efficiently and in terms of its own criteria for excellence on its own goals should result in a more rapid progress in both areas and a more productive, less conflictual, amount of cross-fertilization. (p. 680)

In 1963, the Board of Directors of APA appointed an ad hoc committee to examine "the problems associated with the growing diversity within psychology." The Committee on Scientific and Professional Aims of Psychology (generally referred to as the Clark Committee) was asked to recommend ways in which APA could deal with these many faceted issues.

An Interim Report of the Clark Committee was published in 1965 (APA, 1965), the same year that the Chicago Conference was convened. This report argued strongly for experimentation in graduate education, even to the point of using a degree other than the Ph.D. as the designation of a person with excellent professional preparation in psychology. The 1965 report also recommended that training programs be established under administrative auspices other than university departments of psychology, and that such programs be built around an interdisciplinary faculty. Finally, this report recommended that the paradigm of psychotherapy training (the apprenticeship model) be utilized in professional preparation. While, as Clark remarked, "It is fair to say that this report did not meet with enthusiastic acceptance" (see APA, 1967), it surely foreshadowed many of the major concerns of the National Council on Graduate Education in

Psychology, and was in concert with many of the discussions within, if not the official recommendations of, the Chicago Conference.

The Chicago Conference. The Conference on the Professional Preparation of Clinical Psychologists was held in Chicago during August 1965. The overall problem with which this conference struggled was a two-edged one. To quote Hoch, Ross, and Winder (1966):

1. On the one hand, clinical psychology is still busily putting its own house in order. There is the painful and urgent problem of identity. There is widespread concern that ours be a fully independent profession. There is a need to produce enough Ph.D.'s to meet the social need which even now outstrips the numbers being trained.

2. Quite apart from internal pressures, developments in the community are already creating newer, bigger problems to be confronted. (a) A live concern with mental health keeps demands for psychological services mounting, (b) an even newer concern—the prevention of pyschological disorders—has added further problems and opportunities, (c) now it turns out that the newest concern of all, that of "community psychology," the more effective utilization of human potential—calls for clinical psychologists to fill still newer and more unaccustomed roles while not yet having resolved some of the present dilemmas. (pp. 79–80)

By 1965, psychologists in the applied area in particular seemed increasingly to be feeling a sense of social commitment. Clinical psychology was seeking greater recognition and was pressing for more and better genuine training in clinical practice. The universities appeared either to be reassessing the present training programs or were acturally planning variations, some of which appeared quite radical. Compounding all this was the general manpower problem that the Joint Commission on Mental Illness and Health had taken pains to point out, and of which the Chicago conferees were acutely aware.

Confronted with such an array of issues within the discipline, as well as the multitude of social developments, each holding its own implications for psychology, the problem as seen by Hoch et al. (1966) was to decide which challenges to accept and how to prepare psychologists to act responsibly, effectively, and flexibly to meet human need in such a rapidly changing society.

In some respects the processes and the products of the Chicago Conference proved to be similar to those of the previous training conferences. In other respects this was not the case. The previous conferences, for example, had neglected the issues associated with undergraduate preparation in psychology. A significant number of the Chicago conferees, however, believed that improved and more comprehensive undergraduate preparation in psychology deserved to be considered both in its own right and as part of a solution to problems of better graduate education, and also as part of an overall strategy for dealing with the manpower problems. On the topic of subdoctoral training, the conferees generally reflected encouragement to university departments to reexamine some of their previous assumptions and to consider experimentation with new modes of training.

While these diversions into undergraduate and subdoctoral education were significant, the focus of the Conference was most definitely on doctoral training. Yet, unlike the previous conferences, the matter was approached quite differently. Rather than listing the characteristics of a good doctoral program, the conferees chose to consider the conditions important to the implementation of good doctoral education. Similarly, in exploring curriculum issues, the conferees chose not to discuss courses per se, but rather to specify amounts of knowledge and the subject matter that required mastery. A translation of this knowledge into course terms was to be left to the university departments.

Having examined and established for themselves the nature of good doctoral training, the Chicago conferees then sought to assess the various models of doctoral programs that had been proposed for consideration in the preconference materials (see Zimet & Throne, 1965). In the course of the orienting discussions dealing with models of training, two facets required recognition. Firstly, it was noted that the scientist-professional model often had failed to produce a research orientation that graduates of such programs would carry with them in all their professional activities. Secondly, it was noted that many graduates of the traditional model programs did not conduct themselves on the job as scientist-professionals, but rather as psychotherapists, and that this latter role seemed to better meet the expectations found in the settings in which these clinicians worked. It was within this context that the various proposed models of doctoral training were examined.

The conference addressed the *psychologist-psychotherapist* and the *research-clinician* model in short order. Of the former, the conferees took the position that, in its very narrow conception of the psychologist's role, such a model seemed to do justice neither to the psychologist nor the setting in which he/she would function. The conferees did take a positive stand regarding the possible development of a new doctoral level profession of psychotherapy, but also stated that any single professional function, whether psychotherapy, research, or psychodiagnosis, does not reflect the scope of the skills of the clinical psychologist. The *research-clinician* model was rejected for different reasons. In essence, it was rejected because it seemed to add little to the scientist-professional model. The *professional-psychologist* model, as presented by Cook, Bibace, Garfield, Kelly, and Wexler (1965), provoked much discussion. Mindful of the problems that had been noted in the traditional training model, and of the pressing social need to educate greater numbers of clinical service providers in psychology, the Conference did recognize the merits of the professional model and suggested that it might serve well as an additional model within which clinical psychologists could be trained. However, in the end the Chicago conferees, like their predecessors, provided their ultimate endorsement for the scientist-professional educational approach. They felt, however, that the time had come to broaden the scope of clinical training and to diversify training opportunities so that students could build on their various special interests in the course of their professional preparation. In discussing the options for such diversification, the issue of whether programs oriented toward service rather than toward research should offer a degree other than the Ph.D. received particular attention. In the final analysis, the conferees concluded that the scientist-professional model was the form of training in clinical psychology that they would endorse, but that, if university departments chose to explore other approaches, that would be their prerogative. Either way, psychology would do well to keep an open mind on such matters and let the results speak for themselves.

The Chicago Conference contributed to the advancement of the professional model of education essentially in two respects. In the first place, it highlighted many of the issues surrounding this increasingly controversial approach. Secondly, it suggested that modifications be made within the scientist-professional model. These included increasing the proportion of practicing clinicians on the faculties of clinical training programs, and proposing that professional activities and clinical practice be accorded the same recognition and rewards previously extended to other aspects of academic endeavor. Additionally, it was suggested that the research requirement of the scientist-professional programs be broadened.

While the Chicago Conference brought the issues of professional training in psychology into greater prominence and sharper focus, there was a sense of dissatisfaction expressed by significant numbers of psychologists at what they saw as the indeterminate outcome of the Chicago meeting. (In fact, the recommendations of the Chicago Conference were not adopted as official policy by APA until September 1970.) In 1966, therefore, less than 1 year after the establishment of the first School of Professional Psychology at Fuller Theological Seminary, a group of psychologists seeking to facilitate the development of professional schools, as well as to bring about change in existing programs, organized the National Council on Graduate Education in Psychology (NCGEP). This new organization drew support from within divisions of APA, state psychological associations, and professional societies, as well as receiving the enthusiastic backing of many individual psychologists. In addition to advocating the formation of professional schools, the NCGEP published an annual listing of innovative psychology training programs with a professional orientation. This listing was based on the self-descriptions of programs, and was made available to the public at a nominal fee as a source of information about educational opportunities in psychology.

In fact, the NCGEP was challenging the APA to take the initiative in bringing about what its members regarded as needed change. A specific example of just such a challenge by the NCGEP appeared with the publication by Rothenberg and Matulef (1969) of a series of conclusions reached within the NCGEP. This article offered one of the first organized comprehensive critiques of contemporary graduate education from the perspective of professional psychologists. Rothenberg and Matulef offered the view that the atmosphere in graduate programs still was disparaging of professional practice, that clinical experience was sorely lacking in the training of most clinical graduate students, and that, overall, the expectations and needs of psychology doctoral students were still not being met.

In April 1969, just 7 months after the University of Illinois began the first Doctor of Psychology Program,[1] the APA Education and Training Board and the Board of Professional Affairs jointly formed an Ad Hoc Committee on Professional Training. This new committee was charged with meeting a variety of objectives including: the identification of innovative training models or programs, the provision of consultation and assistance to institutions seeking to develop such programs, and the planning of a national conference on professional education. In addition, this committee also became concerned with the issue of the recruitment into professional training of economically and culturally disadvantaged students. Unfortunately, because of the conflicting forces present within the committee that had been chosen to represent the various positions on the issue of professional training, and probably because of the inherent complexities of some of the resistances to change within the structure of APA, the Ad Hoc Committee on Professional Training was able to achieve only one of its major objectives, that of planning for a national conference on professional training (what became known as the Vail Conference).

There were a number of other events which preceded the Vail Conference that are noteworthy as representing milestones in the development of professional training programs in clinical psychology. In 1969, the California State Psychological Association announced its plans to sponsor the first state chartered, degree-granting, free-standing professional school. (Interestingly, the founders of this proposed school, despite their firm practitioner commitment, chose to employ the Ph.D. rather than the Psy.D. as the credential to be awarded. These individuals felt that the relatively new degree involved additional risk which, when added to the unconventional nature of the program, was unnecessary.) In 1969 also, individual certification of doctoral level school psychologists was introduced by the American Board of Professional Psychology.[2] The following year, the California School of Professional Psychology accepted its first students on campuses in both Los Angeles and San Francisco (see Dorken & Cummings, 1977). In this same year, Hahnemann Medical College (now Hahnemann University) and Biola Roesmead Graduate School both introduced Psy.D. programs. These programs were followed in 1971 by the establishment of a similar program

---

[1] In fact, the first serious attempt to establish a doctoral level professional psychology degree (other than the Ph.D.) was undertaken in the early 1950s at the McGill University, Montreal, Canada. Critics referred to the Doctorate of Psychological Science (DPsSc) as the "dipsy." While a number of Master of Psychological Science degrees were awarded at McGill, no DPsSc degree was ever awarded.

[2] In November 1968, the name American Board of Examiners in Professional Psychology was changed to the American Board of Professional Psychology.

at Baylor University. In 1971, also, a Council for a College of Professional Psychology was founded by the Nassau County (Long Island) Psychological Association, and an educational model was outlined, though, in this case, not implemented (Pusar, 1976). It was during the period 1970-1973 also that the Organizing Council for a College of Professional Psychology was incorporated in New Jersey, and began the process of evolving the professional programs that would be offered within the School of Applied and Professional Psychology at Rutgers University. Relevant also, of course, was the fact that the universities were having to realistically face changes in the society which supported them. No longer were the more esoteric research ventures receiving a high level of support, the expansion in academia had ceased, consumer satisfaction had to be addressed in attracting new students, and doctoral psychology students could no longer anticipate entering academic or research positions after completing their degrees. All this was evident at a time when the public need for psychological services was seen to be well outpacing the supply of competently educated psychological practitioners.

During this same period, a more powerfully felt criticism of the scientist-professional training model was heard from influential voices such as Peterson (1969), Albee (1970), Albee and Loeffler (1971), and Meehl (1971). These critics argued variously that it was inefficient, perhaps even unethical, to train future practitioners in research skills they would probably never employ, while failing to provide a truly comprehensive preparation for professional practice. Under ideal circumstances, the argument seemed to go, a research student should be freed from excessive coursework to develop particular areas of scholarly and methodological expertise. The practitioner student, by contrast, needed to achieve acceptable levels of competence in all areas of knowledge and skill deemed essential for clinical practice. Meehl (1971) put the point this way: ". . . the very idea of a professional degree involves the repudiation of the traditional freedom of the Ph.D. degree" (p. 60).

The critics also noted that the curricula of other professions such as law and medicine were organized to provide a broad coverage of professionally relevant knowledge, and they maintained that professional psychology, too, needed a similar format of training. Further, there appeared to be evidence (Adler, 1972; Busch, 1969; Hoch et al., 1966) that the majority of the then existent research oriented clinical training programs were opposed to further curriculum standardization or regimentation.[3] It is not surprising, therefore, that what was being ad-

---

[3] It is noteworthy that by comparison with the requirements for the Ph.D. degree in other countries, the requirements for the Ph.D. in American universities are far more standardized and involve extensive coursework demands. Equally, from a historical perspective, Harris, Troutt, and Andrews (1980) have pointed out that, in this century, higher education in the United States has been marked by a continued series of increasingly structured requirements for the doctoral degrees (see also Berelson, 1960). While there may be benefits from such standardization and structure, the movement toward this structure has not been without its critics. As far back as 1911, for example, William James had argued that "the Ph.D. octopus" would crush the true spirit of learning in the universities. James favored en-

vocated by those committed to professional psychology was an explicitly practitioner-oriented training approach, in which a more highly structured and comprehensive coursework sequence would be integrated with an extensive series of graded practicum and internship experiences.

The Vail Conference. In July 1973, with support from the National Institute of Mental Health, a Conference on Levels and Patterns of Professional Training in Psychology was held at Vail, Colorado (Korman, 1976). Most basic of all, this conference specifically endorsed the professional educational model as one type of heuristic model to guide those programs defining themselves by a basic service orientation. It did so, as Korman said, *"without* abandoning comprehensive psychological sciences as the substantive and methodological root of any educational or training enterprise in the field of psychology, and *without* depreciating the value of scientist-professional training programs for certain specific objectives" (p. 19).

Unlike any of the previous conferences, the conferees at Vail were cognizant of the reality of professional programming, and they recognized also that psychology was ready to support the existence and development of unambiguously professional programs. It was obvious that the emerging professional programs were developing in a variety of organizational settings (in medical schools, psychology departments, free-standing schools of professional psychology, autonomous professional schools in academic settings, and so on), and that these various settings could influence differentially the effectiveness and the quality of the educational programming instituted within them. Nevertheless, rather than recommend the type(s) or organizational setting(s) that the conferees considered to be most suitable for such programming, it was decided to examine the criteria that any setting should meet in order to provide high quality professional training in psychology.

The issue of program quality control, especially given the reality of the emergence of educational programs in nontraditional organizational settings, was considered especially important by the conferees. In the spirit of the redefinition of professionalism that the Conference saw as emphasizing multiple levels and several models of training, it was recommended that a new and expanded accrediting process should be created to include not only the traditional representation from relevant groups within APA, but also representatives from state psychological associations, students, and consumers.

The issue of the most appropriate professional degree label (Ph.D. versus Psy.D.) was given particular attention by the Vail conferees. It was recom-

---

couraging capable students to bypass the degree when it interferred with independent study, and asked if individuals would "count for nothing unless stamped and licensed and authenticated by some title-giving machine" (James, 1911, p. 347).

While James's views may even appear naive in the context of the current business of academia and the professionalizing of psychology, nevertheless the value of curriculum flexibility vis a vis maximizing the potential for research within the Ph.D. experience should not be ignored. Unfortunately, in our view, this is largely what has been accomplished in the evaluation of the Boulder model educational process.

mended that, in those programs in which the primary educational emphasis was on direct delivery of psychological services, and evaluation and improvement of those services, the Psy.D. degree would be particularly appropriate. In those programs that stressed educational experience designed to maximize research and the acquisition of new knowledge within psychology, the Ph.D. degree would be the doctorate of choice. Further, the conferees did recognize that the use of the Psy.D. designation might be both administratively and politically difficult in many existing programs. Thus, it was recommended that the use of the Psy.D. degree should be encouraged mainly in new programs, and in those where a change from a traditional form to an explicity professional program identity was sought.

Issues of multi-level training also absorbed much of the energies of the Vail conferees. The Conference came out strongly in favor of the view that, in the development of professional educational programs, priority must be given to those that either address multiple levels of education, or at least demonstrate clear articulation with degree programs at other levels. Planning to develop multiple levels of training within one institutional setting, and to coordinate local or regional programs at various levels, was considered to be especially important. The notion of portability of credit for work completed also was seen as particularly important, as it applied both to movement from one educational level to another and from one geographical region to another.

It was recommended that the concept of a *career ladder* should be replaced by the far more inclusive concept of a *career lattice*. This lattice structure was favored by the conferees as encouraging a broader skills acquisition at any given level, as well as encouraging upward professional movement. It was recognized, however, that the endorsement of multi-level training had some risks to it, for such a training system could be particularly prone to relegating the all too typically disenfranchised groups to the lower levels of the lattice. Thus, it was seen to be particularly important that upper level programs establish definite policies for the recruitment of individuals from such groups.

The other major theme that emerged from the Vail Conference involved a recognition of the responsibility of educational programs to be concerned with consumer and social needs. It was recognized that a comprehensive task analysis was needed to match the competencies for which workers are educated, at each point on the service lattice, with the various roles and functions that these people will be called on to provide. It also was considered particularly important that current information about the numerous and expanding demands for psychologists be translated into appropriate curricular changes. Further, it was recommended that the APA assume a more aggressive posture in exploring the developing potential career markets for individuals with various levels of training in psychology.

There were other issues raised and debated at Vail. Issues such as the content of training programs, continuing professional development, human resources, minority training, sexism, service delivery models and approaches, and legal, administrative, and structural considerations in psychology, were discussed in detail. All these issues were in keeping with the trends within psychology, as it reflected the priorities of the society of which it was a part. Whatever else this action oriented conference achieved, however, it surely provided recognition and support for professional and professional-scientist models as alternatives to the Boulder model in the education of psychologists. Yet this was less a mani-festo for change than it was a ratification of what already had occurred (see Shakow, 1978).

In the year following the conference at Vail, professionally oriented (and mainly clinical) psychologists received a further boost with the formation of the Council for the National Register of Health Service Providers in Psychology (Zimet & Wellner, 1977). The Council was formed with the assistance of the American Board of Professional Psychology following a request from the Board of Directors of APA. The stimulus for the development of the National Register was the press for information that began to be felt, from federal agencies and others, regarding psychology as an independent health profession. In creating the National Register, the aim was to establish a mechanism that would facilitate the identification of health service providers from among all licensed/certified psychologists.

Also in 1974, the Graduate School of Applied and Professional Psychology at Rutgers University admitted its first class of students. The existent Ph.D. pro-gram in clinical psychology was continued, and two new Psy.D. programs, one in school psychology and the other in clinical psychology, were introduced. The Rutgers programs were unique, for they were the first programs offered in a graduate school of psychology, independent of but coordinate with a university, and offering post-masters the Psy.D. degree (Schaar, 1974). Soon thereafter, in 1976, the National Council of Schools of Professional Psychology (NCSPP) was established with support from APA. The formation of the NCSPP provided an official voice for the professional school movement. Its aims included the gathering and exchanging of information, participation in the development of education and training policy, and providing consultation and fostering research on social problems of human welfare relevant to professional psychology. Also in 1976, after 5 years of political effort, professional schools of psychology be-came eligible for inclusion in Title VIII of PL 94-484, the Health Professions Educational Assistance Act of 1976. Clearly, professional training as well as the professional role for psychologists had become well established.

So rapid had been the development of programs in professional psychology that a need to address the issue of standards in the education of professional psychologists began to be heard (Polonsky, Fox, Wiens, Dixon, Freedman, & Shapiro, 1979). Certainly, too, there were cases being made against the intro-duction of more professional schools and new practitioner-oriented programs (Perry, 1979; Sundberg, Lowe, & Wiens, 1979). The practitioner-model pro-grams were graduating about a third as many professional psychologists as the scientist-practitioner-model clinical programs in 1978, and the data suggested that they might well produce a substantial number of the professional psychologists within a few years. This, then, was the context for the Virginia Beach Conference.

The Virginia Beach Conference. A Conference on Education in Professional Psychology was convened in April 1978 at Virginia Beach, Virginia (Caddy, Rimm, Watson, & Johnson, 1982). A rapid proliferation of professional programs had been seen within psychology, and this had resulted in concern that large numbers of inadequately educated practitioners might be produced. Outside the profession there was, in the state and federal legislation and elsewhere, a growing recognition that professional psychology was capable of producing autonomous mental health service providers. The conveners at Virginia Beach above all else saw their conference as a response to the need for the control of educational programs in professional psychology. The Conference considered both the issues involved with educational standards, and facilitated communication among practitioner-model programs about how best to educate their students.

On the topic of standards several areas were explored: the assessment and prediction of professional competence, the curricula of practitioner-model programs, the administrative structure of the programs, and practitioner-model accreditation criteria. The conferees at Virginia Beach reached agreement in adopting a total of six resolutions (see also, Watson, Caddy, Johnson, & Rimm, 1981). In summary these resolutions addressed the following.

The first resolution addressed the need to markedly increase the opportunities for well-qualified applicants to obtain doctoral level education in professional psychology. The question of an actual manpower shortage in mental health was being reevaluated by the time of the conference. The documentation of a shortage of practitioner-psychologists in the late 1970s was based on estimates that between 15,000 and 18,500 such practitioners were engaged in part-time or full-time service (Gottfredson & Dyer, 1978; Mills, Wellner, & VandenBos, 1979). In comparison to the estimate that 15% of the American population, or 34 million individuals, were in need of some type of mental health service (U.S. President's Commission on Mental Health, 1978), the number of professional psychologists appeared to be inadequate. However, the assessment of the need for services has been a complex problem (Liptzin, 1978), and estimates have varied from 1% to 60% depending on the criteria of need employed (Dohrenwend & Dohrenwend, 1974). Since the Conference, several reports have addressed the issue of manpower requirements in mental health. VandenBos, Nelson, Stapp, Olmedo, Coates, and Batchelor (1979) have estimated a shortage of between 12,000 and 20,000 professional psychologists. Utilizing more conservative criteria of need, Liptzin (1978) projected a shortage of about 8,500 professional psychologists by 1981. On the supply side of a supply/demand analysis, Richards (1979) has reported that there were at that time 18,659 doctoral students in professional psychology training programs, concluding that the number of students appears to meet or exceed the manpower requirement estimated by VandenBos et al. (1979). Contrary to the first Virginia Beach resolution, these reports indicate that there may be no need for an increase in educational opportunities in professional psychology. However, because of the disparities among the various estimates of need, it would seem that close attention should be given to monitoring manpower requirements in the near future.

The second resolution noted the need for professional programs to employ criteria for admission that give adequate attention to both inter and intra-personal attributes of applicants, as well as standard achievement measures. Also relevant here were several interrelated issues concerning the need for research to evaluate the effectiveness of current practices in the education of professional psychologists. The central issues were, of course, the need for research to provide data to guide the development of admissions policies.

The third resolution pointed up the need for the curriculum in professional psychology to ensure the mastery of a comprehensive, empirically based body of knowledge and skills delivered in an orderly, sequential fashion designed to meet accepted standards of professional competence (APA, 1977). Further, this resolution noted that training programs must create a sense of professional identity and responsibility for client welfare, and include a commitment to the ongoing evaluation of the efficiency and effectiveness of services. The essence of this resolution is self-evident. To meet the standards imposed by the ongoing evaluation consideration, however, it was widely acknowledged that practitioner-model programs must provide a thorough training in evaluative research.

The fourth resolution proposed that competent training in professional psychology can be provided best in university-based schools of professional psychology. Under special circumstances, free-standing professional schools and university psychology departments also may provide such quality training. It was noted, however, that proprietary schools and external degree programs bear a special responsibility in demonstrating that they are capable of providing quality education.

The concern about the organizational structure of programs in professional psychology stemmed from the quality assurance issue of whether each of the then-existing programs had adequate academic and clinical resources to educate competent practitioners. The issue of adequate resources had been raised in particular by psychologists concerned about the prospects of the appearance of independent schools in their states (Polonsky et al., 1979). The Council of Graduate Departments of Psychology also had adopted a resolution stating that the development of programs in professional psychology should be restricted to regionally accredited colleges and universities (M. Meyer, personal communication, February 22, 1980).

The fifth resolution addressed the standards of accreditation for professional psychology programs. It was resolved that such standards should include, in addition to generic standards, specific standards for the several professional specialties (i.e., clinical, counseling, school, and industrial-organizational psychology). While, of course, the accreditation criteria that were adopted by the APA remained only generic in nature (APA, 1979), and the conferees at Virginia Beach acknowledged that the development of specific criteria can be based on only "best guesses" until evaluative research could offer data-based guidelines, nevertheless, there was a general consensus that specific criteria can provide more rigorous quality control than generic criteria, and should be encouraged.

The sixth and final resolution pointed up the need for standards of excellence in professional programs. It was believed to be essential that training in professional psychology be as rigorous and demanding as that associated with traditional research-oriented programs. This final resolution, of course, was a statement of intent regarding all of the preceding resolutions.

The final major training conference to be outlined, the so-called Spring Hill meeting, shifts the focus of developments in professional psychology back to school psychology.

The Spring Hill Conference. A symposium on the Future of Psychology in the Schools was held at the Spring Hill Conference Center in Wayzata, Minnesota in June, 1980 (Ysseldyke, 1982; Ysseldyke & Weinberg, 1981). Like all of the conferences outlined previously, the Spring Hill Symposium was a conference set in the context of the then-current events. There were important changes that were occurring in social values, not the least of which was the fact that society increasingly was expecting the schools to function as *the* major agent of social change. Within this context, school psychologists, both individually and professionally, were expressing their frustration at not being able to influence adequately the system within which they functioned. The continued intrusion of government into educational affairs and policy was an issue of great concern to school psychologists in 1980. Significant developments included the recognition of the reality of a multi-ethnic and multi-racial educational system. Additionally, the pull away from an Anglo-dominant model had permitted both educational and psycho-evaluative judgments to be made against a normative standard which did not focus on cultural, ethnic, and racial differences. Of course, there were the concerns and issues of racism, and there were questions about the extent to which psycho-evaluative procedures may be racially discriminatory. There were also the economic pressures of a period of high unemployment, high inflation, and wide taxpayer dissatisfaction with education, which showed education and especially school psychology to be particularly vulnerable. Finally, there were the concerns regarding legislation and litigation. Over the decade of the seventies, school psychologists had seen the introduction of legislation such as Public Law 94-142, the Education of All Handicapped Children Act of 1975, and they had seen the courts impose themselves very firmly in the school psychologist's vocation (e.g., Diana v. Board of Education; Hobson v. Hansen; Larry P. v. Riles).

Within the aforegoing context, the main concerns of the Spring Hill participants were: (a) goals and roles for school psychology practice, (b) ethical and legal issues, (c) the continued professionalization of school psychologists, (d) the content of training programs, and (e) accountability. We will present an outline of the two of the above concerns that appeared most important and also are most relevant to the present discussion.

Addressing the goals and roles for the practice of school psychology, and reminiscent of the Thayer Conference, the Spring Hill participants struggled with the dilemma of serving the largest number of students and still providing the best possible services. Bardon (1981) asked, "Are our goals and purposes best expressed as those of improved mental health in the schools or as improved education?" (p. 301). The conferees at Spring Hill discussed the need to document models of exemplary school psychological practice and to communicate those best practices to the professions which work with school psychologists. Lambert (1981) noted the specialty guidelines just recently published by APA as a model for service delivery, while Hodges (1981) presented the need to conduct research contrasting alternative models for the delivery of services. There also was much dialogue regarding the essential competencies required to practice as psychologists in schools. Here, as in the earlier clinical training conferences, the issue of diversity versus specificity in curricula was again debated.

Turning now to the professionalizing of school psychology, the Spring Hill conferees examined the extent to which school psychology is a unique professional discipline, the role that school psychology organizations should play, the school psychologist's roles in influencing policy and legislation, credentialing, etc. Peterson (1981) ended the symposium by pressing school psychologists to work to mold public policy and to place primary attention on how public policy can benefit children and schools, and secondarily on how to benefit the profession.

RECENT DEVELOPMENTS

By the end of 1978, there existed 14 Psy.D. programs and at least 15 Ph.D. clinical programs that were explicitly based on a practitioner model. Of these, four had achieved APA accreditation. These programs were housed variously within graduate departments of psychology (e.g. the University of Illinois and the University of Denver), medical centers (as was the Hahnemann program), and University-based schools of professional psychology with separate administrative structures (e.g. Adelphi, Rutgers, and Wright State Universities). There were also autonomous (free-standing) schools (e.g., the California Schools of Professional Psychology), and even a consortium involving three universities and a medical school (The Virginia Consortium for Professional Psychology).

In fact, the development of practitioner-model clinical programs was proceeding at such a pace that the then APA president, Nicholas Cummings, was predicting that such programs would be producing 95% of the graduates in professional psychology by 1985 (quoted by Freeman, 1979). As of late 1982, the number of explicitly professional clinical programs had increased to at least 40, of which 11 were APA accredited.

To place these statistics into some national perspective, a review of the most recently available (1983-1984) *Graduate Study in Psychology* (APA, 1982a) showed a total of 142 doctoral listings under the "clinical" designation (including 14 Canadian programs and approximately 20 programs that are most definitely practitioner oriented). Of this total, 121 were APA accredited. Under the combined designations "clinical-adult, adult/child, personality, behavior therapy, child, community, counseling, evaluation, phenomenological, and neuropsychology" are listed an additional 17 doctoral programs (including two offered in Canadian universities). Interestingly, this listing of clinical programs is not complete, for it does not contain a number of the programs which are listed in Table 1 (e.g. California Graduate Institute, Wright Institute, the Fielding Institute, etc.). To add further perspective, *Graduate Study in Psychology* (1983-1984) also listed a total of 38 doctoral programs under the designations of "industrial," or "industrial-gerontological or organizational" (19 of which were APA accredited), a further 54 under the designation "counseling psychology" (30 of which were APA accredited), 52 under the listings "school" and "school psychology" (17 of which were APA accredited), and a further 2 programs designated "behavioral medicine," (1 was APA accredited; see Belar, 1980). There also were 2 doctoral programs that had received APA accreditation based on what was stipulated to be a combined professional-scientific model (APA, 1982b).

Ultimately, just how many programs there are throughout the country that direct their energies to producing practitioner-oriented psychological professionals is very difficult to determine. One can be confident, for example, that at least some of the Ph.D. programs listed in the graduate study guide as "clinical," but not listed in Table 1, are oriented to training students who will be practitioners. Certainly too, there are a number of similarly listed programs, probably the majority, that continue to be based on the Boulder training model, but are graduating students who will, nevertheless, focus on a career in clinical practice. Moreover, most assuredly the majority of the programs graduating doctoral recipients under the various industrial designations, and in counseling psychology, school psychology, and the like are infusing practitioner-oriented-and-educated psychologists into the society. And, of course, both within the clinical, school, and counseling psychology specialty areas, there are large numbers of masters level students who ultimately will function either as licensed/certified school psychologists or as mental health counselors. Finally, there are effects that are yet to be noted from the development of new programs that most definitely are professionally oriented. Some of these programs may help expand the scope of psychology quite substantially, though their impact, numerically, may be very slight at the present time. (For example, the law and psychology programs at Johns Hopkins University, the University of Arizona, the University of Nebraska, and Hahnemann University, see Grisso, Sales & Bayless, 1982; the Behavioral Medicine programs at the University of Miami and the Uniformed

Services University of the Health Sciences, see Belar, 1980; and the Public Health Psychology Program of the University of Hawaii, see Tanabe, 1982.) In other instances, we see the emergence of a large number of programs at the masters level, and several new doctoral programs also, which have responded to what appears to be the veritable boom in the training, and perhaps even the practice, of marriage and family therapy, principally in California. Stricker's (1975) prediction, that professional psychology would some day extend well beyond clinical psychology and into more settings in which appropriate training could be obtained, appears certainly to be reflecting the current state of affairs. (See also Sarason's 1981 commentary on what he regards as the historical narrowness and misdirection of clinical psychology, and DeLeon's 1979 recommendation that psychology alter its present identification as a mental health discipline in favor of a more generic health care identification.)

A comprehensive listing of the doctoral level clinical and other programs that clearly identify themselves as professional psychology training programs, together with some data regarding them, is presented in Table 1. The best estimate of the growth and potential impact of practitioner model programming can be determined from an examination of the numbers of students enrolled in and graduating from these programs. Figures 1 and 2 provide such a perspective. Clearly, as indicated in Figure 1, the pattern of expansion of professional programs in psychology has been strong and consistent since 1968, although there is an indication that, in the 1980s, this rate of growth is decelerating. In fact, though not available from Figure 1, by 1983 a plateauing of the curve describing the growth in professional psychology programs was beginning to occur.

The data on the number of students enrolled in and graduating from professional psychology programs (see Figure 2) offers perhaps the best indication of the growth of the influence of such programs. These data were developed from figures obtained by surveying the registration and graduation statistics of the programs listed in Table 1. (It should be noted that these data are not complete: as is indicated in Table 1, four programs did not respond.) Obviously, however, by 1982 the 44 programs listed in Table 1 were educating some 4,990 students and graduating a minimum of 430.

The picture painted by the data presented in Figures 1 and 2 is brought into even clearer focus when these data are set against the data obtained from sources beyond the professional psychology movement. For example, contrasting the data from the practitioner-oriented programs with that obtained from the clinical programs which do not describe themselves as explicitly practitioner-oriented, in 1978 the average number of students enrolled in each of the then-existing clinical professional model training programs was 102. This same figure, calculated across the then 107 APA accredited clinical programs during the same year, was 46. Further, during that year, the 16 professional programs that had been in existence long enough to graduate students at the doctoral level each produced an average of 25 graduates. The same figure calculated for the APA accredited clinical programs in 1978 was 5.7. By 1982, the average number of students

Table 1. Practitioner-Model Training Program Statistics

School	Year Established Degree(s)	Specialization	Faculty (Part-time)	Total 1982 Enrollment (% Full-time)	Percentage Females / Ethnic Minorities		Credits Required	Total Graduates (to 1982)
Adelphi University Long Island, N.Y.	1951 Ph.D.	Clinical	13(7)	186(100)	60	30	3 years + Internship	296
Fuller Theological Seminary* Pasadena, CA	1965 Ph.D.	Clinical	13(12)	176(99.4)	27.8	13.6	314 Quarter	169
University of Illinois* Urbana-Champaign, IL	1968 Psy.D.	Clinical	Program discontinued in 1980.					
California Graduate Institute Los Angeles, CA	1968 Ph.D.	Clinical MFT Behavioral Medicine	22(38)	Not available	60.0	1.5	78 Trimester	Not Available
Wright Institute Berkeley, CA	1969 Ph.D.	Social/ Clinical	Did not respond.					
California School of Professional Psychology* Los Angeles, CA	1969 Ph.D.	Clinical	18(40)	295(90)	64.7	14.2	180 Quarter	430
California School of Professional Psychology Berkeley, CA	1970 Ph.D.	Clinical (Post doctoral/ forensic & psycho-analysis)	9(57)	302(80)	66.0	9.5	90–120 Semester	574
Hahnemann University* Philadelphia, PA	1970 Psy. D.	Clinical (Post doctoral/ psychoanalysis)	26(250)	99(100)	56.0	6.9	120 Quarter	56
Biola Rosemead Graduate School*	1970 Psy.D.	Clinical	20(5)	125(68)	32	0	131 Semester	104

Institution	Year / Degree	Specialty							
La Mirada, CA									
Baylor University* Waco, TX	1971 Psy.D.	Clinical	12(4)	38(100)	51	4	98	Semester + Internship	90
California School of Professional Psychology* San Diego, CA	1972 Ph.D.	Clinical I/O (1983)	7(62)	250(80)	54	8	90–120	Semester	321
California School of Professional Psychology Fresno, CA	1973 Ph.D.	Clinical	4(33)	141(96)	36	12	90–120	Semester	183
Rutgers University* New Brunswick, NJ	1974 Psy.D.	Clinical, School	17(61)	88(46)	58	21	75	Semester	160
The Fielding Institute Santa Barbara, CA	1974 Ph.D. Psy.D.	Clinical Counseling, Organizational	(42)	375(100)	67	2.5	12	Knowledge areas	233
University of California at Davis Davis, CA	1974 Ph.D.	Clinical	5(25)	22(100)	50	20	Not Specified		16
California Institute of Transpersonal Psychology Menlo Park, CA	1975 Ph.D.	Transpersonal	6(15)	118(100)	60	2	102	Quarter	13
United States International University LaJolla, CA	1976 Ph.D. Psy.D.	Clinical MFT, I/O	Did not respond.						
Pacific Graduate School of Professional Psych. Palo Alto, CA	1976 Ph.D.	Clinical	2(16)	170(25)	62	6	176	Quarter	27

Table 1. Practitioner-Model Training Program Statistics (continued)

School	Year Established Degree(s)	Specialization	Faculty (Part-time)	Total 1982 Enrollment (% Full-time)	Percentage Females Ethnic Minorities		Credits Required	Total Graduates (to 1982)
Illinois School of Professional Psychology Chicago, IL	1976 Psy.D.	Clinical	8(27)	83(50)	47	3	108 Trimester	56
University of Denver School of Professional Psychology* Denver, CO	1976 Psy.D.	Clinical	3(47)	95(65)	57	12	135 Quarter	115
Massachusetts School of Professional Psych. Newton, MA	1977 Psy.D.	Clinical	2(31)	161(77)	57	3	132 Semester	30
Palo Alto School of Professional Psychology Palo Alto, CA	1977 Ph.D.	Clinical	(22)	39(10)	62	3	144 Quarter	5
Central Michigan University Mt. Plesant, MI	1977 Psy.D.	Clinical School, I/O	15	32(100)	40	10	100 Semester	15
Wright State University School of Professional Psychology* Dayton, OH	1977 Psy.D.	Clinical	15(56)	104(100)	61	41	207 Quarter	42
Virginia Consortium for Professional Psychology Norfolk, VA	1978 Ph.D.	Clinical	45(3)	45(100)	53	24	116 Semester	3
Nova University School of Professional Psychology Fort Lauderdale, FL*	1978 Psy.D.	Clinical (Post doctoral/ Psychoanalysis)	9(42)	183(45)	55	13	113 Semester	25
Columbia Pacific University Mill Valley, CA	1978 Ph.D.	Did not respond.						

School	Year / Degree	Specialization					
Chicago School of Professional Psychology, Chicago, IL	1979 Psy.D.	Clinical	0(25)	100(65)	40 / 4	90 Semester	4
Oregon Graduate School of Professional Psychology, Portland, OR	1979 Psy.D.	Clinical	11(19)	68(20)	49 / 3	133 Trimester	0
California Institute of Integral Studies, San Francisco, CA	1979 Ph.D.	Clinical, Counseling, East-West	11(7)	77(70)	45 / 5	Masters + 60 quarter	5
Pace University, New York, NY	1979 Psy.D.	School/Community	9(9)	91(50)	60 / 3	96 Semester	3
Forest Institute of Professional Psychology, Des Plaines, IL	1979 Psy.D.	Clinical	10(17)	132(70)	50 / 6	142 Semester	0
Florida Institute of Tech*, Melbourne, FL	1980 Psy.D.	Clinical, Counseling	8(50)	145(68)	50 / 5	132 Quarter	22
New York University, New York, NY	1980 Psy.D.	School	5(29)	28(50)	80 / 15	90 Semester	0
Yeshiva University*, New York, NY	1980 Ph.D. Psy.D.	Clinical, School	Did not respond.				
The Professional School for Humanistic Studies, San Diego, CA	1980 Ph.D.	Counseling, MFT, I/O (1983)	10(40)	794(100)	50 / 10	110 Quarter	53
American Institute of Psychotherapy/Graduate School of Professional Psychology, Huntsville, AL	1980 Psy.D.	Clinical	15	26(80)	40 / 0	108 Trimester	0

Table 1. Practitioner-Model Training Program Statistics (continued)

School	Year Established Degree(s)	Specialization	Faculty (Part-time)	Total 1982 Enrollment (% Full-time)	Percentage Females Ethnic Minorities		Credits Required	Total Graduates (to 1982)
Wisconsin School of Professional Psychology Milwaukee, WI	1980 Psy.D.	Clinical	(26)	25(50)	39	0	Masters + 60 Semester	0
Hawaii School of Professional Psychology Honolulu, HI	1981 Ph.D. Psy.D.	Clinical	7	12(59)	50	17	192 Quarter	0
Indiana State University Psychology Department Terre Haute, IN	1981 Psy.D.	Clinical	14(3)	39(100)	40	0	96 Semester	0
California Graduate School of Marital and Family Therapy San Rafael, CA	1981 Ph.D.	Clinical MFT	(49)	225(40)	70	10	147 Quarter	25
Antioch New England Graduate School Keene, NH	1982 Psy.D.	Clinical	2(18)	29(100)	45		108–128 Semester	0
George Mason University Fairfax, VA	1982 Psy.D.	Clinical, School, I/O	26	18(61)	77	6	96 Semester	0
Spalding College Louisville, KY	1982 Psy.D.	Counseling	5(7)	22(32)	73	3	72 Semester	0
Cambridge Graduate School of Professional Psychology Los Angeles, CA	1982 Ph.D'	Clinical	10(10)	34(20)	45	10	156 Quarter	0

*Accredited by the American Psychological Association

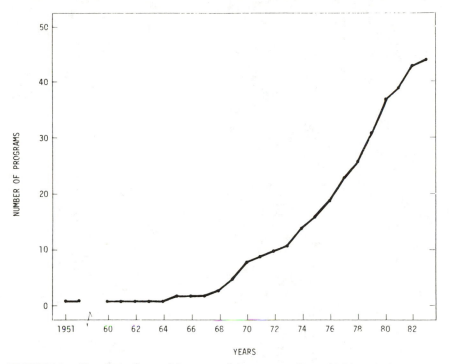

FIGURE 1.   Number of practitioner-model programs from 1951 to 1983.

enrolled in each of the explicitly professional programs was 113. The same statistic derived from the then 121 APA accredited clinical programs (which includes only a very small number of programs which identified themselves specifically as practitioner oriented) was 62. During 1982 also, whereas a mean of 8.2 graduates were produced from those clinical programs not identifying themselves as specifically practitioner-oriented, this same statistic taken across the professional programs which had been in existence long enough to produce graduates was 17. (This figure was 24 for the professional clinical APA approved programs.)

Another perspective on the impact of practitioner oriented training programs may be gleaned from an examination of overall statistics showing doctoral production throughout the country. Table 2 provides data showing doctoral production in psychology for the period 1970–1982, generated from the annual surveys of United States universities conducted by the National Research Council (NRC). It should be noted that the NRC data are derived only from surveying the Ph.D. programs listed in *Graduate Study in Psychology*. Up until the present time, these surveys have excluded not only the data available for the various Psy.D. programs, but also those for Ph.D. programs which offer professionally oriented training but are not listed in the graduate study guide.

Table 2. Doctorate Production in Psychology, 1970, 1975, 1980, and 1982

Psychology Specialty	1970	1975	1980	1982	Average Annual 1970 to 1975	Percent Change 1975 to 1980
Clinical	549	811	1106	1165	+8.2%	+6.5%
Counseling	113	231	298	346	+15.9%	+5.6%
Developmental	83	180	205	192	+17.2%	+2.8%
Educational	87	134	136	140	+9.8%	+0.9%
School	45	103	176	166	+20.2%	+13.4%
Experimental	366	351	307	240	-0.6%	-2.5%
Comparative/Physiological	138	145	116	102	+5.2%	-14.1%
Industrial/Organizational	75	63	66	83	-1.0%	+2.4%
Personality	50	62	43	36	+4.7%	-6.0%
Psychometrics	18	17	21	8	+8.2%	+11.8%
Social	157	232	190	179	+8.3%	-18.4%
General	120	245	213	240	+16.1%	-1.8%
Other	82	175	221	257	+19.6%	+5.7%
Total	1883	2749	3098	3154	+7.9%	+2.4%

Source: National Research Council. *Summary report 1982. Doctorate recipients from United States universities.* Washington, D.C.: National Academy Press, 1983. Also summary reports for 1970, 1975, and 1980.

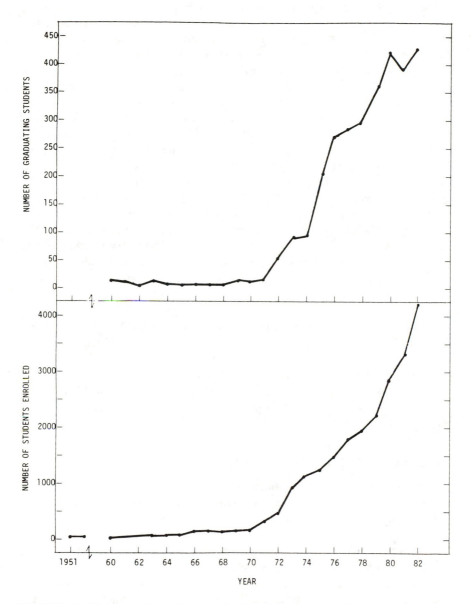

FIGURE 2. Number of students graduating from and enrolled in practitioner-model programs from 1960 to 1982.

Given the aforementioned limitiations of the NRC data, Table 2 nevertheless indicates that overall doctoral production in psychology grew quite rapidly during the first half of the 1970s, with an average annual increase of 7.9%. This growth appears to have all but leveled out during the period 1975 to 1980, during which this same annual percentage change index was only 2.4%. Of course, as a closer examination of Table 2 reveals, the most consistent growth rates across the various subfields of psychology are to be found in the practice-oriented specialties of school, clinical, and counseling psychology. The industrial/ organizational area appears to have undergone a more sedate pattern of growth, a pattern that was not apparent until after 1975. Moreover, given the general growth patterns of psychology doctorates, and the fact that total doctorate production throughout the United States in all of science, engineering, education, and the humanities peaked in 1973 at 33,727 doctorates (NRC, 1974), declined to 30,982 in 1980 (NRC, 1981), and has remained at about that level (31,048 doctorates in 1982; NRC, 1983), psychology has increased its contribution to the total doctoral production statistics by going from 6.4% in 1970 to 10.0% in 1980 to 10.2% in 1982. However, none of these figures showing the absolute and the relative growth of psychology doctoral production provide the most accurate index of the growth of psychology. As indicated previously, these statistics do not include data from some of those professional programs which currently are graduating quite substantial numbers of psychology doctorates. In fact, adding data from the professional programs listed in Table 1 that are not listed in *Graduate Study in Psychology,* the total psychology doctoral production statistics for 1980 would be approximately 1,530, and for 1982 would be approximately 1,595. (Approximately 424 and 430, respectively, above the statistics provided by the NRC.) Clearly, the role that the professional psychology movement is playing in the production of practitioner-oriented psychologists is substantial and provocative.

EVALUATING THE PRESENT SITUATION

The present situation in professional psychology can be evaluated within the context of developments within the discipline more generally over the last 20 years. Additionally, we may examine the present circumstances for professional psychologists with regard to the educational programming designed to train them as practitioners, and, ultimately, with regard to their capacity to function effectively as psychological service providers.

Reviewing the past 20 years in terms of production and employment of doctoral level psychology graduates, the National Research Council statistics indicate a context in which the annual percentage increase in the number of psychology doctorates awarded fell from a figure of 14.6% between the years 1965 and 1970 to approximately 2.4% between 1975 and 1980. Paralleling this trend was the general decline in total university enrollment at the undergraduate level, especially in the later half of the 1970s. That decade also saw the publication of numerous articles reflecting concern for the possibility of a shortage of employment opportunities for what some were seeing as the overproduction of doctoral level psychologists (see for example, Bron, 1979; Cates, 1973; Cuca, 1975b; Kessler, McKenna, Russell, Stang, & Sweet, 1976). There were others who attempted to be optimistic about the so-called "Ph.D. glut," but these were few and far between (e.g., Stern, 1976). The concern, of course, was directed primarily at the deteriorating state of the academic job market, the setting that traditionally had employed the vast majority of the new doctorates in psychology.

In order to monitor the status of the employment of psychologists, in 1971 the APA began a series of surveys, initially of chairs of graduate departments of psychology, and, after 1975, of new doctorate recipients directly (see Boneau, 1974; Boneau & Cates, 1972; Cates, 1973, Cuca, 1975b). In general, these surveys concluded that there was a definite decline in the academic job market, and that up to approximately 20% of the new doctorates in psychology were experiencing special difficulties finding suitable employment. Stapp, Fulcher, Nelson, Pallak, and Wicherski (1981) reported data from the APA doctorate employment surveys of the period 1975 to 1978, inclusive. These authors noted that, while only 2.2% of those surveyed across the 4 years reported that they were unemployed and seeking work, there was a general lack of optimism regarding the job market, and there were substantial difficulties reported even by those who had obtained satisfactory employment. Stapp et al. also observed a steady decline in the proportion of those newly employed in academic settings, especially universities. Of the men, 47.6% of those surveyed were employed in academia in 1975, compared with 34.8% in 1978. Of the women, 54.3% were employed in academic settings in 1975; this percentage declined to 44.6% in 1978. Overall, 31.0% of the men and 26.3% of the women were employed in human service settings. Here, there had been a combined sex total increase from 26.1% in 1975 to 32.4% in 1978. There also had been an overall increase in the percentage of placements of doctoral recipients in business, government, and other settings. Employment figures in this employment grouping were 15.0% in 1975 and 20.7% in 1978. (See also the studies reported by Schneider, 1981.)

There can be no question that the past 2 decades have seen a steady increase both in the percentage and in the total number statistics of psychologists who identify themselves as providing health services. In fact, the most recent data available from the NRC (Syverson, 1983) indicates that 53.7% of psychology doctoral recipients in 1982 were planning to engage in professional services in their primary employment. (The remaining options of research and development, teaching, administration, and other, attracted 14.8%, 19.0%, 7.2%, and approximately 5.4%, respectively.) Yet even these figures understate both the ratio statistics and the total number of psychology doctorates entering professional service. As noted previously, the NRC data include neither Psy.D. graduates nor some of the Ph.D. graduates from several of the programs listed in

Table 1. While the practitioner movement in psychology may not be faring as well in other countries (see the reviews by Fichter & Wittchen, 1980; and Rosenzweig, 1982), in the United States the movement has matured, and professional psychology is taking its place in the society which supports it alongside the other major professions.

There are data also from a number of other surveys that offer further perspective, specifically, on the current status and employment of practitioner-oriented psychologists. Clinical psychologists have been studied regarding their practices, attitudes, orientations, and the like, over the last 20 or so years (Garfield & Kurtz, 1974, 1975a, 1975b, 1976; Kelly, 1961; Kelly & Goldberg, 1959). More recently, a number of reports have offered data broadly addressing health service providers in psychology (Gottfredson & Dyer, 1978; Mills, Wellner, & VandenBos, 1979; VandenBos, Stapp, & Kilburg, 1981), the private practitioner more specifically (Dorken, 1977), the geographic distribution of service providers throughout the United States (Richards & Gottfredson, 1978), the job relevance of clinical training programs (Howe & Neimeyer, 1980), the work preferences of clinical psychologists (Peterson & Knudson, 1979), and even attitudes concerning Psy.D. training (Peterson, 1969), and the career experiences of Psy.D. graduates (Peterson, Eaton, Levine, & Snepp, 1982).

While a detailed review of these various surveys is beyond the scope of this chapter, overall, these studies indicate that there may be as many as 60,000 psychologists functioning in the United States, with perhaps up to 32,000 offering health services. Detailed analyses of these statistics indicate that about 83% of these psychologists hold doctorates, 71% are men, and approximately 84% are licensed or certified. It is estimated that collectively these psychologists provide over one-third of a million hours of service each week, and that the number of people who receive services from psychologists may be as many as three million, with almost half this total being rendered in private practice settings. The three most common services offered are individual psychotherapy, assessment/diagnosis, and consultation.

Regarding the geographic distribution of psychologists, Richards and Gottfredson (1978) showed that psychologists, like their other health-providing colleagues, tended to be concentrated in affluent urban states and in university towns, and that they are not distributed in a way that offers any advantage to those traditionally underserved populations such as the poor, Blacks, or rural citizens.

A further finding of the career activities of psychologists has shown that, despite the fact that most present day psychologists were trained in programs based on the scientist-professional model, the vast majority of them produce no publishable-quality research. The previously mentioned and often quoted observation that the modal number of publications of clinical psychologists is zero (Kelly, Goldberg, Fiske, & Kilkowski, 1978; Peterson, 1976b) appears a reflection both of the state of affairs in present day clinical psychology and an indictment of the consequences of the scientist-practitioner training paradigm. Relevant here also is the finding that psychologists who work in human service settings typically spend less than 5% of their time engaged in any form of research (Gottfredson & Dyer, 1978), although, of course, such individuals may be effective consumers of research information. Given this state of affairs, it is not surprising that Strupp (1976) would have reflected with such grave concern on what he called "the erosion of excellence" that has occurred in the more traditional research-oriented clinical doctoral programs, as these programs have attempted to produce both scientists and practitioners.

The facts of the preceding paragraph bring us back to matters discussed earlier when we offered an account of the issues that were addressed at the various training conferences. Virtually all of these conferences, especially those focusing on clinical psychology, heard the demand raised for more and better experiential training. Clinical trainees, for example, have suggested program changes to align clinical education more with the eventual service-related role that most clinical graduates will assume (Walker, 1977). Similarly, Garfield and Kurtz (1976) have reported that the most commonly proposed program improvement offered by Ph.D. clinical psychologists following a review of their own education was the availability of more clinical experience under the supervision of experienced clinicians. Additionally, in their study of the work preferences of clinical psychologists, Peterson and Knudson (1979) noted that clinical psychologists employed in universities typically showed a strong interest in research but only a limited interested in practice. Professionally employed psychologists, on the other hand, typically reported strong interests in practice but indifference or aversion toward research. They concluded:

> It seems doubtful that the majority of practitioners . . . were well served by the research-dominated psychology departments in which most of them were trained. (p. 181)

There is a balance implied by the proponents of Boulder model programming. But both research in clinical psychology, and clinical practice, have become so demanding and so highly specialized that it may be unrealistic to continue to sustain the view that the practicing psychologist could (or would) engage in the production of worthwhile research in his/her "spare" time. The conferees at Vail, it may be recalled, not only endorsed the professional education model, but also supported the scientist-professional training model. Given the reality of the current practitioner programming (including the observation that increasing numbers of the clinical Ph.D. programs which previously had been *scientist*-practitioner programs appear to be moving more into the *practitioner*-scientist mold), a case could well be made that the scientist-practitioner model which found favor among the Boulder conferees may not be the most desirable model for training either research clinicians or practice-oriented psychologists. The Boulder model is, by definition, a model involving compromise. Given that the American academic philosophy of the post-Second World War period was committed to structure and permitted only limited flexibility in doctoral education, the research-practitioner compromise appeared eminently reasonable. Today, however, the model may be attempting to accomplish too much, and may thereby be accomplishing neither of its goals particularly well. Strupp (1981) touched on this matter and the larger context when he stated:

> The crisis facing psychotherapy (and psychology) today, couched in the demand for better scientific evidence on the safety and efficacy of our services, is part of a larger issue. That issue relates to the profession's inability to articulate in terms understandable and acceptable to the public that we have the means and commitment to alleviate human suffering. It reflects a crisis of trust. Though clearly essential, research by itself cannot solve this problem. Somehow we must search our own souls to determine our identity; our collective professional commitments; and the philosophies, criteria, and contents of our training programs. (p. 218)

Marwit (1979) sought a perspective on the attractiveness of alternate (practitioner) programming from Ph.D. students within the University of Missouri-St. Louis scientist-professional program. He found that 58% aspired to a strictly applied clinical psychology practice, 54% said they would have chosen a quality professional program had one been available, and, of most interest, 67% said that they would opt for a professional school were they to have it to do over again. While Marwit's study involved a small and highly select sample, it does imply that there may be considerable numbers of currently enrolled scientist-practitioner students who may have preferred training within an explicitly professional training program. Furthermore, it may be that the extent of this preference for professionally-oriented training expressed by many students enrolled in the more traditional Boulder model programs may increase with exposure to the scientist-professional curriculum.

Noteworthy too, Peterson, Eaton, Levine, and Snepp (1982) have shown, following their survey of 184 graduates of various Psy.D. programs, that most of their subjects were engaged in providing direct professional services in professional settings, they were generally well satisfied with their careers, and they were significantly more satisfied with the graduate training than were clinical psychologists trained in traditional Ph.D. programs. Very few problems were encountered in obtaining licensure, and almost no unfavorable attitudes toward the degree were perceived among clients, employers, or colleagues. Certainly, given the foregoing, and the professional community's support for practitioner-oriented programming as evidenced by the proliferation of programs noted in Table 1, by the increased attention given to these programs by the APA Board of Professional Affairs, the Education and Training Board, and the Policy and Planning Board, and as illustrated in the most recent revision of the APA program accreditation guidelines (APA, 1979), it must be concluded that professional psychology, in all its forms, will become the dominant force in psychology in the years to come. Perhaps, in fact, the influence of the practitioner and the professional training model which has been evolving, have already provoked this state of affairs.

Inevitably, we can be only myopic observers of the events swirling around us, and so, to predict the future with assurance is always a highly suspect activity. It would appear likely, however, that the controversy over the most appropriate degree for practitioner versus research psychologists will be existent within psychology for at least the next decade or so. It also can be anticipated that, within professionally oriented programming, even further specialization will occur over the next decade. (In this regard, it is noteworthy that, in 1983, the American Board of Professional Psychology added neuropsychology to the sub-specialties within which diplomate status may be awarded.) The questions for the future are not so much related to whether professionally oriented training and service will continue to expand, but rather what will be the form and the direction of this expansion.

Surely, though, the greatest challenge facing the professional psychology movement over the next decade will be to ensure quality and efficacy, both in service delivery and in the education of professional psychologists. Accepting the premise that the best quality of service is provided by those who are best trained to provide such service, and accepting also the premise that those who educate professional psychologists know how best to accomplish the task, educators of practitioner psychologists have much work ahead of them. A point often ignored is that, in education, consumer satisfaction and consumer protection can, at least in the short run, be in conflict.

In the decade of the eighties, even those universities which provide a high quality of psychology programming are going to be influenced by the economic realities of a continued shrinkage of undergraduate and graduate enrollments. With these reductions, it is likely that concern over comsumer satisfaction will increase. This, in turn, may prove a threat to the quality of higher education. Cole (1981), for example, projected that:

> . . . in a few years graduate school will be easier to get into than has been the case in recent years. Instead of turning students away in droves, schools will be scrambling for students, at least for the best ones. (p. 511)

Those professional schools whose existence is particularly dependent on a large enrollment, of course, will be the most vulnerable to this process. Certainly, a cursory review of some of the program parameters offered in Table 1 illustrates, unfortunately, that a distressing number of these programs must be considered vulnerable to the concerns of quality assurance. If professional programs in psychology are to flourish, they must not be second rate nor be perceived as such when compared to other psychology doctoral programs. To the extent that, today, some of the professional psychology programs, especially those housed in free-standing schools, may be seen as inferior, the discipline as a whole will suffer. The remediation of this state of affairs must be seen as the most pressing concern facing contemporary professional psychology.

REFERENCES

Adler, P. T. (1972) Will the Ph.D. be the death of professional psychology? *Professional Psychology, 3,* 69-72.

Albee, G. W. (1970). The short, unhappy life of clinical psychology. *Psychology Today, 4,* 42-74.

Albee, G. W., & Loeffler, E. (1971). Role conflicts in psychology and their implications for a reevaluation of training models. *Canadian Psychologist, 4,* 465-481.

American Psychological Association, Committee on Training in Clinical Psychology. (1947). Recommended graduate training program in clinical psychology. *American Psychologist, 2,* 539-558.

American Psychological Association, Committee on Training in Clinical Psychology. (1948). Clinical training facilities. *American Psychologist, 3,* 317-318.

American Psychological Association, Committee on Training in Clinical Psychology. (1949). Doctoral training programs in clinical psychology. *American Psychologist, 4,* 331-341.

American Psychological Association, Division of Counseling and Guidance, Committee on Counselor Training. (1952). Recommended standards for training counseling psychologists at the doctorate level. (Northwestern Conference). *American Pscyhologist, 7,* 175-188.

American Psychological Association, Committee on the Scientific and Professional Aims of Psychology. (1965). Perliminary report. *American Psychologist, 20,* 95-100.

American Psychological Association, Committee on Scientific and Professional Aims of Psychology. (1967). The scientific and professional aims of psychology. *American Psychologist, 22,* 49-76.

American Psychological Association. (1977). *Standards for providers of psychological services.* (Rev. ed.) Washington, DC: Author.

American Psychological Association. (1979). *Criteria for accreditation of doctoral training programs and internships in professional psychology.* Washington, DC: Author

American Psychological Association. (1982). *Graduate study in psychology:* 1983-1984. Washington, DC: Author. (a).

American Psychological Association. (1982). APA-approved doctoral programs in clinical, counseling, and school psychology: 1982. *American Psychologist, 37*(12), 1374-1376. (b).

Bardon, J. I. (1981). Small group synthesis, Group C..*School Psychology Review, 10,* 297-306.

Belar, C. D. (1980). Training the clinical psychology student in behavioral medicine. *Professional Psychology, 11,* 620-627.

Berelson, B. (1960) *Graduate education in the United States.* New York: McGraw-Hill.

Boneau, A. (1974, September/October) Job market holding firm. *APA Monitor,* p. 18.

Boneau, A., & Cates, J. (1972, September/October). Report on employment status of new doctorates disappointing. *APA Monitor,* p. 16.

Bron, D. G. (1979). Where will they all get good jobs? *Division 25 Recorder, 14*(2), 1-7.

Busch, F. (1969). Present clinical training in its relationship to Chicago Conference on the professional preparation of clinical psychologists: A preliminary report. *Newsletter of the Corresponding Committee of Fifty,* Division 12, *6,* 3

Caddy, G. R., Rimm, D. C., Watson, N., & Johnson, J. H. (Eds.). (1982). Educating professional psychologists. *Proceedings of the Virginia Beach Conference on Education in Professional Psychology: And beyond. Rutgers Professional Psychology Review, Vol 1.* New Brunswick, NJ: Transaction Books.

Cates, J. M. (1973, September/October). Too many Ph.D.s, not enough jobs. *APA Monitor,* p. 23.

Cattell, J. M. (1937). Retrospect: Psychology as a profession. *Journal of Consulting and Clinical Psychology, 1,* 1-3.

Cole, D. L. (1981). Teaching tomorrow's psychology students. Who pays the piper? *American Psychologist, 36,* 506–513.

Cook, S., Bibace, R., Garfield, S., Kelly, G., & Wexler, M. (1965). Issues in the professional training of clinical psychologists. In C. N. Zimet & F. M. Throne, (Eds.). *Preconference materials: Conference on the Professional Preparation of Clinical Psychologists.* Washington, DC: American Psychological Association.

Crane, L. (1925–1926). A plea for the training of professional psychologists. *Journal of Abnormal and Social Psychology, 20,* 228–233.

Cuca, J. (1975, July). Job crunch hits scientists harder than professionals. *APA Monitor.* p. 10. (a).

Cuca, J. (1975, November). Survey shows deteriorating job market for new doctoral psychologists. *APA Monitor,* p. 11. (b).

Cutts, N. E. (1955) *School psychologists at mid-century* (Thayer Conference). Washington, DC: American Psychological Association.

DeLeon, P. H. (1979) The legislative outlooks for psychology: A health care profession. *American Psychology Bulletin, 1,* 187–192.

Diana v Board of Education, C-70-37 RFP (N.D.. Cal. June 18, 1973).

Dohrenwend, B. P., & Dohrenwend, B. S. (1974). Social and cultural influences on psychopathology. *Annual Review of Psychology, 25,* 417–452.

Dorken, H. (1977). The practicing psychologist: A growing force in private sector health care delivery. *Professional Psychology, 8,* 269–274.

Dorken, H., & Cummings, N. A. (1977, May). A school of psychology as innovation in professional education: The California School of Professional Psychology. *Professional Psychology,* 129–148.

Dorken, H., & Rodgers, D. A. (1976). Issues facing professional psychologists. In H. Dorken (Ed.), *The professional psychologist today.* San Francisco: Jossey-Bass.

English, H. B. (1938). Organization of the American Association of Applied Psychologists. *Journal of Consulting and Clinical Psychology, 2,* 7–16.

Fernberger, S. W. (1932). The American Psychological Association: A historical summary, 1892–1930. *Psychological Bulletin, 29,* 1–39.

Fichter, M. M., & Wittchen, H. (1980). Clinical psychology and psychotherapy: Survey of the present state of professionalization in 23 countries. *American Psychologist, 35,* 16–25.

Flexner, A. (1915). Is social work a profession? In *Proceedings of the National Conference of Charities and Corrections.* Baltimore, MD: Social Work.

Flexner, A. (1925). *Medical education: A comparative study.* New York: MacMillan.

Fox, R. E., Barclay, A. G., & Rodgers, D. A. (1982). The foundations of professional psychology. *American Psychologist, 37,* 306–312.

Freeman, M. (1979, January) Nick Cummings. *APA Monitor,* pp. 1, 6–7.

Freud, S. (1927). *The problem of lay analysis.* New York: Brentano's.

Fryer, D. (1946). The proposed American Association for Applied and Professional Psychologists. *American Psychologist, 1,* 3–6.

Garfield, S. L., & Kurtz, R. (1974). A survey of clinical psychologists: Characteristics, activities, and orientations. *The Clinical Psychologist, 28*(1), 7–10.

Garfield, S. L., & Kurtz, R. (1975). Clinical psychologists: A survey of selected attitudes and views. *The Clinical Psychologist, 28*(3), 4–7. (a).

Garfield, S. L., & Kurtz, R. (1975). Training and career satisfaction among clinical psychologists. *The Clinical Psychologist, 28*(2), 6–9. (b).

Garfield, S. L., & Kurtz, R. (1976). Clinical psychologists in the 1970s. *American Psychologist, 31*(1), 1–9

Gottfredson, G. D., & Dyer, S. E. (1978). Health service providers in psychology. *American Psychologist, 33,* 314–338.

Grisso, T., Sales, B. D., & Bayless, S. (1982). Law-related courses and programs in graduate psychology departments. *American Psychologist, 37,* 267–278.

Harris, J. W., Troutt, W. E., & Andrews, G. J. (1980). *The American doctorate in the context of new patterns of higher education.* The Council on Postsecondary Accreditation: Washington, DC

Hickson, D. J., & Thomas, M. W. (1969). Professionalism in Britain: A preliminary measurement. *Sociology, 3,* 37–53.

Hobson v Hansen, 269 F Supp. 401 (D. D.C. 1967) Affirmed sub nom. Smuck v Hobson, 408 F 2d 175 (D.C. Cir. 1969).

Hoch, E. L., Ross, A. O., & Winder, C. L. (Eds.). (1966). *Professional preparation of clinical psychologists: Proceedings of the Conference on the Professional Preparation of Clinical Psychologists meeting at the Center for Continuing Education, Chicago, Illinois, August 27-September 1, 1965.* Washington, DC: American Psychological Association.

Hodges, W. Small group synthesis, Group B. *School Psychology Review, 10,* 290–296.

Howe, H. E., Jr., & Neimeyer, R. A. (1980). Job relevance in clinical training: Is that all there is? *Professional Psychology, 13*(2) 305–313.

Iscoe, I. (1982). Toward a viable community health psychology. *American Psychologist, 37,* 961–965.

James, W. (1911). *In memories and studies.* New York: Longmans, Green, & Co.

Kelly, E. L. (1961). Clinical psychology–1960. Report of survey findings. *Newsletter: Division of Clinical Psychology of the American Psychological Association, 14*(1), 1–11.

Kelly, E. L., & Goldberg, L. R. (1959). Correlates of later performance and specialization in psychology: A follow-up study of the trainees assessed in the VA selection research project. *Psychological Monographs, 73,* (12, Whole No. 482).

Kelly, E. L., Goldberg, L. R., Fiske, D. W., & Kilkowski, J. M. (1978). Twenty-five years later. *American Psychologist, 33,* 746–755.

Kessler, S., McKenna, W., Russell, V., Stang, D. J., & Sweet, S. (1976). The job market in psychology: A survey of despair. *Personality and Social Psychology Bulletin, 2,* 22–26.

Korman, M. (Ed.). (1976). *Levels and patterns of professional training in psychology: Conference Proceedings, Vail, Colorado, July 25-30, 1973.* Washington, DC: American Psychological Association.

Lambert, N. (1981). School psychoiogy training for the decades ahead, or rivers, streams, and creeks–Currents and tributaries to the sea. *School Psychology Review, 10,* 194–205.

Larry P. v Riles, 343 F. Supp. 1306 (N.D. Cal. 1972) (preliminary injunction), affirmed, 502 F. 2d 963 (9th Cir. 1974) opinion issued No. C-71-2270 RFP (N.D. Cal. October 16, 1979).

Levy, L. H. (1962). The skew in clinical psychology. *American Psychologist, 17,* 244–249.

Liptzin, B. (1978). Supply, demand, and projected need for psychiatrists and other mental health manpower: An analytic paper. In D. M. Kole (Ed.), *Report of the ADAMHA manpower policy analysis task force, Vol. II.* Washington, DC: Alcohol, Drug Abuse, and Mental Health Administration.

Marwit, S. J. (1979). *School of professional psychology: Doctor of psychology (Psy.D.) degree.* Unpublished manuscript, University of Missouri, St. Louis.

Meehl, P. E. (1971). A scientific, scholarly, nonresearch doctorate for clinical practitioners: Arguments pro and con. In R. R. Holt (Ed.), *New horizons for psychotherapy: Autonomy as a profession.* New York: International Universities Press.

Mills, D. H., Wellner, A. M. & VandenBos, G. R. (1979). The National Register survey: The first comprehensive study of all licensed/certified psychologists. In C. A. Kiesler, N. A. Cummings, & G. R. VandenBos (Eds.), *Psychology and national health insurance: A sourcebook.* Washington, DC: American Psychological Association.

National Research Council. (1971). *Summary report 1970. Doctorate recipients from United States universities.* Washington, DC: National Academy Press.

National Research Council. (1974). *Summary report 1973. Doctorate recipients from United States universities.* Washington, DC: National Academy Press.

National Research Council. (1976). *Summary report 1975. Doctorate recipients from United States universities.* Washington, DC: National Academy Press.

National Research Council. (1981). *Summary report 1980. Doctorate recipients from United States universities.* Washington, DC: National Academy Press.

National Research Council. (1983). *Summary report 1982. Doctorate recipients from United States universities.* Washington, DC: National Academy Press.

Perry, N.A. (1979). Why clinical psychology does not need alternate training models. *American Psychologist, 34,* 603-611.

Peterson, D. R. (1969). Attitudes concerning the doctor of psychology program. *Professional Psychology, 1,* 44-47.

Peterson, D. R. (1976). Is psychology a profession? *American Psychologist, 31,* 572-581. (a).

Peterson, D. R. (1976). Need for the doctor of psychology degree in professional psychology. *American Psychologist, 31,* 792-798. (b).

Peterson, D. R. (1981). Overall synthesis of the Spring Hill Symposium on the future of psychology in the schools. *School Psychology Review, 10,* 307-314.

Peterson, D. R. (1982). Origins and development of the doctor of psychology concept. In G. R. Caddy, D. C. Rimm, N. Watson, & J. H. Johnson (Eds.), *Educating professional psychologists. Proceedings of the Virginia Beach Conference on Education in Professional Psychology: And Beyond.* New Brunswick, NJ: Transaction Books.

Peterson, D. R., Eaton, M. M., Levine, A. R., & Snepp, F. Q. (1982). Career experiences of doctors of psychology. *Professional Psychology, 13,* 268-277.

Peterson, D. R., & Knudson, R. M. (1979). Work preferences of clinical psychologists. *Professional Psychology, 10*(2), 175-181.

Polonsky, I., Fox, R. E., Wiens, A. N., Dixon, R. R., Freedman, M. B., & Shapiro, D. H. (1979). Psychology in action: Models, modes, and standards of professional training: An invited interaction. *American Psychologist, 34, 339-349.*

Pusar, A. (1976, May). A new development: A college of professional psychology. *SPAA Newsletter* (State Psychological Association Affairs, Division 31, American Psychological Association), *7,* 5-6

Raimy, V. (Ed.). (1950). *Training in clinical psychology.* (By the staff of the Conference on Graduate Education in Clinical Psychology held at Boulder, Colorado, in August of 1949). New York: Prentice Hall.

Reisman, J. M. (1966). *The development of clinical psychology.* New York: Appleton-Century-Crofts.

Richards, J. M. R., (1979). *The distribution of psychology graduate students in the United States.* Unpublished manuscript, Center for Social Organization of Schools, Johns Hopkins University.

Richards, J. M., Jr., & Gottfredson, G. D. (1978). Geographic distribution of U.S. psychologists. *American Psychologist, 33,* 1-9.

Rodgers, D. A. (1964). In favor of separation of academic and professional training. *American Psychologist, 19,* 675-680.

Rodgers, D. A. (1980). The status of psychology in hospitals: Technicians or professionals. *The Clinical Psychologist, 23,* 5-7.

Roe, A., Gustad, J. W., Moore, B. V., Ross, S., & Skodak, M. (Eds.). (1959). *Graduate education in psychology* (Miami Conference) Washington, DC: American Psychological Association.

Rosenzweig, M. R. (1982). Trends in development and status of psychology: An international perspective. *International Journal of Psychology, 17,* 117–140.

Rothenberg, P. J., & Matulef, N. J. (1969). Toward professional training: A special report from the National Council on Graduate Education in Psychology. *Professional Psychology, 1,* 32–37.

Sarason, S. B. (1981). An asocial psychology and a misdirected clinical psychology. *American Psychologist, 36,* 827–836.

Schaar, K. (1974, August). Jersey opens professional school. *APA Monitor,* pp. 1, 6.

Schneider, S. F. (1981). Where have all the students gone? Positions of psychologists trained in clinical/services programs. *American Psychologist, 36,* 1427–1449.

Shakow, D. (1976). What is clinical psychology? *American Psychologist, 31,* 553–560.

Shakow, D. (1978). Clinical psychology seen some 50 years later. *American Psychologist, 33,* 148–158.

Singer, J. E., & Krantz, D. S. (1982). Perspectives on the interface between psychology and public health. *American Psychologist, 37,* 955–960.

Stapp, J., Fulcher, R., Nelson, S. D., Pallak, M. S., & Wicherski, M. (1981). The employment of recent doctorate recipients in psychology. 1975 through 1978. *American Psychologist, 36,* (11), 1211–1254.

Stern, J. A. (1976). An "optimist" looks at employment opportunities for psychologists. In P. J. Woods (Eds.), *Career opportunities for psychologists: Expanding and emerging areas.* Washington, DC: American Psychological Association.

Stricker, G. (1975). On professional schools and professional degrees. *American Psychologist, 30*(11), 1062–1066.

Strother, C. R. (Ed.). (1956). *Psychology and mental health; A report of the Institute on Education and Training for Psychological Contributions to Mental Health, held at Stanford University in August, 1955.* Washington, DC: American Psychological Association.

Strupp, H. H. (1976). Clinical psychology, irrationalism, and the erosion of excellence. *American Psychologist, 31*(8), 561–571.

Strupp, H. H. (1981). Clinical research practice, and the crisis of confidence. *Journal of Consulting and Clinical Psychology, 49,* 216–219.

Sundberg, N., Lowe, R., & Wiens, A. (1979). The case against OGSPP. *Newsletter, Oregon Psychological Association, 25,* 2–3.

Syverson, P. D. (1983). *Summary report 1982. Doctorate recipients from United States universities.* Washington, DC: Office of Scientific and Engineering Personnel, National Academy Press.

Tanabe, G. (1982). The potential for public health psychology. *American Psychologist, 37,* 942–944.

Thorndike, R. L. (1955). The structure of preferences for psychological activities among psychologists. *American Psychologist, 10,* 205–207.

United States President's Commission on Mental Health. (1978). *Report to the President from the President's Commission on Mental Health.* Washington, DC: U.S. Government Printing Office.

VandenBos, G., Nelson, S., Stapp, J., Olmedo, E., Coates, D., & Batchelor, W. (1979). *Memorandum to M. Pallak, APA Executive Officer, re: APA input to NIMH regarding planning for mental health personnel development.* Unpublished report, American Psychological Association, September 27.

VandenBos, G. R., Stapp, J., & Kilburg, R. R. (1981). Health service providers in psychology. Results of the 1978 APA human resources survey. *American Psychologist, 36,* 1395–1418.

Walker, M. J. (1977). Graduate students' views regarding training models. *The Clinical Psychologist, 30,* 16–17.

Walsh, J. (1979). Professional psychologists seek to change roles and rules in the field. *Science, 203*, 338–340.

Watson, R. I. (1953). A brief history of clinical psychology. *Psychological Bulletin, 50*, 321–346.

Watson, N., Caddy, G. R., Johnson, J. H., & Rimm, D. C. (1981). Standards in the education of professional psychologists. The resolutions of the conference at Virginia Beach. *American Psychologist, 36*(5), 514–519.

Whitehead, A. N. (1929). *The aims of education.* New York: Macmillan.

Wolfle, D. (1946). The re-organized American Psychological Association. *American Psychologist, 1*, 3–6.

Wright, L. (1976). Psychology as a health profession. *The Clinical Psychologist, 29*, 16–19.

Ysseldyke, J. E. (1982). The Spring Hill symposium on the future of psychology in the schools. *American Psychologist, 37*, 547–552.

Ysseldyke, J. E., & Weinberg, R. A. (Eds). (1981). The future of psychology in the schools: Proceedings of the Spring Hill symposium. *School Psychology Review, 10*, 113–318. (Special issue).

Zimet, C. N., & Throne, F. M. (1965). *Pre-conference materials: Conference on the professional preparation of clinical psychologists.* Washington, DC: American Psychological Association.

Zimet, C. N., & Wellner, A. (1977). The council for the National Register of Health Service Providers in Psychology. *International Encyclopedia of Neurology, Psychiatry, Psychoanalysis, and Psychology, 5*, 329–332.

PART II

FUNCTIONS OF PROFESSIONAL PSYCHOLOGISTS

Chapter 2

Psychotherapy

by Amy Lamson

San Diego, California

When I was a graduate student learning about psychotherapy, I wanted to learn everything I could from the great masters of therapy and absorb what seemed to me their "magical" expertise. When I actually started seeing patients, I was extremely nervous about whether I would say the right thing at the right time. I even felt sorry for my patients for being sent to such an inexperienced therapist as myself. Even though it had been my dream since the age of 13 to be a therapist, I vowed to myself that, if I didn't help anyone in 5 years, I would switch to another field. To my great relief and delight, I found that I was helping people long before that deadline. During that time and since then, I've learned many things about the process of therapy which I would like to share with you.

First of all, psychotherapy is not one thing. For some patients, it is the understanding which they cannot obtain elsewhere, but without which they would have great difficulty carrying on their lives. For some patients, it is permission and/or encouragement to do something which they feel they have to do and they believe is right, but which they fear doing because of possible negative reactions of other people. For some patients, it is learning to accept their human weaknesses and to like themselves, nevertheless. For some patients, it is learning to become more sensitive to the needs and feelings of other people. For some patients, it is discovering what forces within them drive them to self-defeating behavior. For some patients, it is coming to terms with an overwhelming loss so they can go on with their lives. For some patients, it is getting a new perspective on a troubling situation so that it can be dealt with more easily. For some patients, it is exploring alternative ways of handling a problem and then deciding which is the most suitable. For some patients, it is learning to develop skills in relating to others. For some patients, it is developing goals in life and arriving at a course of action to reach these goals. With so many different agendas, it is obvious that the process of therapy varies from situation to situation. The important thing is to find out what the patient needs and then try to provide it. For example, if the patient needs a crisis intervention, it is important to help the patient resolve the crisis as quickly as possible. Then, if the patient wants to, he or she can work on other long-term problems. However, it would be inappropriate to impose a goal of idealized mental health on such patients and encourage them to continue in long-term treatment when they themselves do not see a need for such.

A second thing I learned about doing therapy is that, in any one situation, there is no one correct way to proceed. Of course, each school of therapy has something special to offer, and some methods of therapy are more suitable for certain types of problems. But, overall, it is astonishing how many different therapeutic approaches and styles can yield good results for the same kind of problem.

Thirdly, the different therapeutic approaches do not work as differently as one might imagine. In fact, research has shown that the most successful therapists from different schools of therapy have more in common with each other than with the less successful therapists from their own school of therapy. A strong interest in, and caring for, other people seem to be the most essential characteristics of a successful therapist.

Fourthly, the more relaxed and spontaneous I became in doing therapy, the better the results. My supervisors throughout my graduate training were strict Freudians. While I appreciated their depth of psychoanalytic understanding of my patients, I did not enjoy their frequent criticism that I was too active in therapy. I kept trying to restrain myself, but it never felt right. Then, in my first post-doctoral employment, I had a supervisor with a completely different approach. He kept telling me that I was doing fine. Occasionally he would indicate how he would have handled something differently from the way I did, but he never made me feel that what I did was actually wrong. With this type of support, I found myself freer and freer to employ whatever techniques came to my mind and seemed suitable for the situation. I knew I was going against much of my training and was doing some things that were quite unorthodox, but I felt, and my colleagues noticed, I was getting very good results. It was at this point that I reached the conclusion that psychoanalytic theory has a lot to offer in terms of understanding the psychodynamics of patients, but its treatment methods are too limited and too impractical for the vast majority of patients. I no longer worried about my unorthodoxy, and instead prided myself on my growing skill in devising techniques to fit different problems. I also noticed that doing therapy was so much easier that it almost seemed effortless. Furthermore, instead of being emotionally drained by each session, more often than not I found the sessions emotionally energizing. Sometimes I would make interventions so spontaneously, I wasn't fully aware of my rationale. However, afterwards I could justify the intervention in clinical terms and often I felt it worked better than anything I could have carefully planned. For several years during this period of time, I did not read much in the field of psychology and psychiatry. Instead I read novels and biographies, which were, of course, a rich source of insight into people and their reactions. I was enjoying the freedom to choose what I wanted to read, in contrast to the required reading in graduate school, as well as reacting against the pressures to conform to a specific clinical mold. Later on, I started attending psychological conferences and workshops, where I got wind of many new trends in the field, and I started reading again in the fields of psychology and psychiatry. It was at this point that I learned with great satisfaction that many of the useful techniques that I had discovered on my own were being promoted by several new schools of therapy.

I've shared this self-affirming experience because I think it offers a valuable lesson to beginning therapists. Things work out much better for us when we receive the encouragement and have the courage to be ourselves.

THE INGREDIENTS OF SUCCESSFUL THERAPY

Given a basic interest in and caring for people, and a basic knowledge of human psychology and therapeutic techniques, I believe the beginning therapist should focus his or her attention on trying to understand the patient, instead of focusing on particular techniques of treatment. Once the therapist is totally tuned in to the patient, solutions for the patient's problem will start flowing. In a mood of mental relaxation and emotional sharing, the right side of the brain, with its intuitive, creative solutions takes over. That is why the most effective therapy seems like the least work. Regardless of what school of therapy we have been trained in and what techniques we might employ, I believe our most successful therapy occurs when we are our natural selves and offer our humanness and our personal resources to our patients. It takes much more effort, and therapy is far less effective, if we are following a model and/or maintaining a pose.

By the same token, it is important to encourage patients to be themselves. I can think of countless examples of people restraining themselves to fulfill some notion of what they should be, only to have their best intentions backfire. One prime example is the person who, in an effort to always be agreeable, holds in all anger until it explodes into violence. Another example is the mother who can't admit to herself that she needs some time away from her children, because she believes a good mother would never feel that way, and then has difficulty controlling her temper with her children or develops neurotic fears for her children's safety. Of course there are cases where people are unrestrainedly acting out harmful impulses. These people need to get in touch with their underlying hurt and their wish to have better interpersonal relationships, which they are defending against by their acting out behavior. So regardless of whether a patient appears to be overly restrained or unrestrained, that patient needs to get in touch with his or her basic feelings. In this regard, one thing that I have found very helpful in doing therapy is to always keep in mind that there are two sides to a coin, and when a patient presents one side very strongly, it is often a defense against the opposite side. Of course, it is necessary to proceed cautiously in presenting this insight to the patient. By putting oneself in the patient's place and empathizing with the patient's feelings, a therapist will know when the patient can handle this insight.

Keeping in mind that there is no one right way to proceed with therapy that every beginning therapist should learn, and that a flexible approach depending on the situation is usually best, a description of how I generally proceed in therapy may provide you with some techniques that you can draw upon when you are doing therapy.[1]

THE FIRST SESSION

My first contact with a patient is by phone, when the patient calls for an appointment. I ask the patient how he or she was referred to me, and for a general statement of the problem, to be sure the referral is appropriate. For example, if a patient newly arrived in town with a history of manic-depressive illness is looking for a doctor to supervise his or her medication, I would refer him or her to a psychiatrist. If the referral is appropriate, I ask the patient if he or she has any questions. This gives the patient an opportunity to ask about the fee. If everything is in order, we set up an appointment and I give directions on how to get to my office.

At our first face-to-face contact, I notice how the patient is reacting to being in my office. If the patient looks comfortable, I start off by asking what prompted his or her seeking therapy at this time. If the patient looks uncomfortable, I ask how he or she feels about being there. This gives the patient the opportunity to air his or her fears, misgivings, and embarrassment about seeking therapy. If the patient still appears uncomfortable, I ask if he or she has ever known anyone who has gone for therapy, and what he or she generally thinks about someone seeking psychological help. If the patient says something to the effect that everyone he or she knows thinks only crazy people see a psychologist or psychiatrist, I agree that many people feel that way, but the truth is there is no direct correlation between the seriousness of one's problems and willingness to seek help. Many people with very serious problems never seek therapy because they would rather suffer than admit they could use help, while other people with much less serious problems would rather seek help in order to improve their lives, to resolve problems more quickly than they would otherwise, and to prevent bigger problems from developing. I also add that most people could benefit from therapy at some point in their lives. As soon as the patient seems more comfortable about entering therapy, I ask what brings him or her to therapy at this time.

If the patient is entering therapy under duress from the Court, parents, or a spouse, I acknowledge that he or she is probably not too happy about being there, and I also am not too happy to be working under these conditions, for I much prefer a willing client. However, I say I am willing to give it a try for a

---

[1] The specific ways I approach different diagnostic categories is described in my book, *Guide for the Beginning Therapist*, published by Human Sciences Press, 1978.

reasonable length of time to see if the therapy can be beneficial. Accordingly, we set up a contract for a trial period of therapy. By joining the patient in not liking the forced situation, the therapist breaks down a lot of the patient's initial resistance. The idea of a few months trial period of therapy is also very useful in marital therapy, where one partner is nearly ready to end the marriage. By establishing a short-term trial therapy, the dissatisfied partner has an oppressive sense of obligation lifted from his or her shoulder, so he or she can participate more freely in the therapy.

While the patient is explaining his or her immediate dilemma, I listen very attentively to pick up information about what is going on in his or her life, and also for any clues as to his or her characteristic ways of handling stress. I interrupt with questions whenever I need clarification or when I feel that the patient is going too far off on a tangent. I also sometimes interrupt the patient's statement of the problem with spontaneous comments denoting understanding or sympathy for his or her dilemma. When the patient has completed his or her statement of the problem, I ask for any previous incidents or problems of this nature and how he or she coped with them in the past.

During the first session I also get some general background information, if time allows. I ask where the patient was raised, who was in his or her family while growing up, and for a description of his or her childhood. If any particular problems are mentioned, I go into them in depth. Then I ask about his or her high school years, what kind of student he or she was academically, and socially. I then ask what he or she did after high school with regard to any further education and work. If he or she is married, I ask how the relationship developed and how the marriage is going. If he or she is not married, I ask about his or her dating experiences.

By the end of the first session I usually have a pretty good picture of how the patient's presenting complaint fits in with his or her life history, and I also have an idea of how to approach his or her problem. Of course, these skills develop with experience. In the last 5 to 10 minutes of the session, I give the patient some feedback on how I see his or her problem and what I think we need to do to overcome it. I explain that my opinions are tentative at this point because I do not know him or her well, and I might make revisions as therapy progresses. I also ask for his or her reactions to my formulations. When the time for the session is over, I indicate that we will have to continue our discussion at our next session and I set up another appointment.

SOME CASE EXAMPLES

In many ways, this first session is the most crucial one for the whole therapy. For one thing, if rapport is not established there will be no future sessions. For another thing, if the patient's initial resistance to the therapy is not significantly reduced, future sessions will be fruitless. In addition, the initial formulation is often the key to the rest of the therapy. I can think of four recent cases in which this was true.

Case I

In one case, the patient, a woman in her late 20s, had been unhappily married for nearly 10 years. She had never dated before meeting her husband and, when he proposed marriage, her mother told her she had better accept because she might never get another chance to marry. She knew she was making a mistake the day of the wedding, but she didn't have the heart to cancel it since all the arrangements had been made. The marriage continued for as long as it did because of pressure from her mother not to bring on herself the shame of a divorce. (Their religion frowned on divorce, but did not forbid it.) However, for the past few years her husband had lived on his military base instead of with her and only visited on Sunday to go to Church with her and her parents. She could not stand seeing her husband at these times, and fervently wished that he would stop making his weekly appearances. This patient also mentioned in our first meeting that she receives a lot of criticism from acquaintances for spending so much of her free time with her parents and never socializing with people her own age. She stated she enjoys her parents' company and she feared the therapist would tell her she shouldn't spend so much time with them. At the end of our first session, I told the patient that I thought her marriage was over and that it was only a question of when she would make it official so she could start a new life for herself. She responded to this statement with relief, and contacted a divorce lawyer before our next session. I also told the patient that I thought she was lucky to have such a close relationship with her parents because it is a great source of security. Moreover, her parents are very lucky that they have a daughter who enjoys their company so much; not many parents could say the same thing. Therefore, I didn't think she should give up her closeness to them. On the other hand, it would be nice for her to socialize with people close to her age in addition to socializing with her parents. She was very relieved upon hearing this, and our subsequent sessions focused almost entirely on her desire to overcome her awkwardness and shyness with people. In time, she started dating, and without any feeling of guilt she would cancel some of her standing "dates" with her parents, who incidentally did not seem to mind, in order to go out with a man she cared for. Obviously, if I had pointed out to her that she was too dependent on her parents as many other people had pointed out, she would have been very threatened and would have probably dropped out of therapy. However, as it was I established a therapeutic alliance by joining her dependency needs and suggesting that, in addition to fulfilling them, she could have some fun with people her age.

Case II

In another case, a young divorced woman had taken an overdose after an argument with her boyfriend during which he intimidated her about a lot of things she later realized were foolish. She was most upset that her normally good self-control had broken down to the point where she tried to take her own life. She had always prided herself on being strong and capable and carrying on against all odds. In fact, she described herself as the "backbone" of her family. Accordingly, her suicide attempt was very shameful to her. This incident was also frightening to her because she loved life and she never wanted to get to the point where she would actually end up taking her life. After hearing all this, I reframed the problem as follows. First, I explained to her the difference between a suicide gesture and attempt. Then I told her that, in my opinion, she did not really want to take her life. She was tired and worn-out from the arguing and she just wanted to get her boyfriend to leave her alone. In other words, her problem is not that she is suicidal, but that she is so gullible that she believed the falsehoods her boyfriend told her. Furthermore, in stressful situations she operates too much on emotion and does not use her head. This woman strongly agreed with this formulation and committed herself to working in therapy on these problems.

Case III

In another case, a young married woman had gone totally blind at the age of 15 and had recently learned that her blindness was not the result of an isolated illness, as originally supposed, but was part of a syndrome that affects numerous organs in the body. She came for therapy because of a great deal of anxiety about her physical condition and her fear of dying, although the doctors had assured her that in most cases her disease was not fatal and in her case everything seemed under control. She also complained of symptoms of dizziness which she thought might be due to nerves, but which she worried might be due to her disease. She sounded apologetic for being anxious, and, when I told her there was no need for her to be apologetic, she said psychologists whom she had previously seen told her she should stop worrying. I then spontaneously commented that I wondered how they would be in her situation, adding that I thought they too would be worried. After having been given this permission to worry, she then had the strength to argue the opposite point of view: "But I can't spend all my time worrying. I have to go on with my life." I agreed, and added that it would probably be impossible to spend every minute of her waking life worrying about her health. Besides, there were probably plenty of other aggravations that caught her attention. She laughed in agreement. Then I proposed that we focus on these and work on making her life as enjoyable as possible for as long as she has. Anyway, no one knows how long he or she has to live. Someone in perfect health could be killed in a car accident, and she in her imperfect health could live for many years and waste them by worrying when she was going to die. From then on, the therapy focused on her frustrations of feeling trapped in her home all the time and what she needed to do to develop a more fulfilling life for herself.

Case IV

In the case of an extremely rough-mannered man in his early 30s, with a history of violent explosions, I told him that, contrary to what other people might think, I thought his problem was he is too nice and rather naive. He was always so generous and kind to others, he would be disappointed when he did not get the same in return. That was why he kept blowing up. If he would not extend himself so far for others and would not have such high expectations of others, he'd have much less occasion to be angry. Throughout the therapy, I kept repeating he was one of the nicest people I knew, aside from his violence, and over a long period of time his aggressive ways markedly diminished. My receptionist, who used to be afraid of him when he entered the waiting room, started having friendly chats with him, and more and more he was able to handle frustrations in his life without resorting to violence.

Obviously, it is very important to zero in on what the patient needs and not superimpose your needs on the patient. I can think of one vivid example of that. A 19-year-old girl came to a community mental health clinic because she was very upset by her first sexual experience. She was not emotionally involved with her sexual partner, and did not even know him long. She had simply decided it was time that she lose her virginity. Instead of focusing on the important issue of why she felt the need to engage in sex under such circumstances and why she wasn't willing to wait until she was with someone she really cared for, the male clinical trainee who interviewed her asked her for the details of the sexual experience. Naturally, this only made her more upset and did not shed any light on the psychological issues underlying the behavior.

Sometimes, in the first session, I totally identify with the patient's upset and completely share the patient's anger towards whatever or whomever is bothering him or her. Sometimes I go so far as to express the patient's feelings even more strongly than the patient has expressed them. After a while, I calm down and I start reasoning out loud how the patient might have contributed to the development of the problem and what the patient can now do to overcome it. In these situations, the patients are remarkably receptive to what I have to say, even though I am saying some things that they ordinarily would view as criticisms of them. I believe they are so receptive because, once they have seen me share their feelings of outrage, they know I am their ally. I was not fully aware of this process until I saw the movie "Resurrection." After a car accident in which she nearly died, the main character became a healer wthout knowing the source of her power. In one stirring scene, she healed a women whose whole body was grossly contorted. The healer went into a sort of trance as she took on the patient's contortions, and in the process the patient was freed from them. Then the healer started wrestling with the contortions to free her own body from them. After many dramatic moments, she managed to do just that. While seeing this movie, it suddenly struck me that I often do something very similar in psychotherapy, and I wonder how many other therapists ever approach patients' problems in this manner.

THE PROCESS AFTER INTAKE

At the beginning of the second therapy session, I ask the patient how he or she felt after the first session, because I think it is important to bring to light any lingering negative reactions to therapy that the patient might have. If the patient expresses any, we explore these before going on to the presenting problem. At the beginning of the second and every subsequent session, I also ask how the week went for the patient. This gives the patient an opportunity to share some of the things going on in his or her life unrelated to his or her presenting problem, and it also gives him or her the opportunity to share any new developments related to his or her problem. Sometimes a whole session is devoted to these new developments, but most often our discussion returns to the point where we left off in the previous session.

I don't focus on the past unless the presenting complaint is a direct result of a past situation. However, frequently I weave back and forth between past and present to make connections between past experiences and present attitudes and behavior.

I also point out examples of the patient's self-defeating attitudes and behavior, and ask the patient to think of alternative ways he or she could have reacted to the same situations. If the patient can think of none, I present several for him or her to consider.

If the patient has a great deal of anxiety, I teach a relaxation exercise which can be practiced every day to keep anxiety levels down. If the patient is obsessive, I teach the behavioral technique of thought stopping whereby the obsessing is repeatedly interrupted with the inner word "stop" until the obsessing ceases.

In the course of therapy, if one method doesn't work, I'll try another. Never do I want to appear as the infallible expert. I want to do everything I can to help the patient improve his or her functioning, but I can't do it by myself. No matter how much psychological knowledge I have, there are many ways in which the patient knows himself or herself better than I ever will. That is why I need the patient's continual feedback. At times, I am the leader in the therapy, at times the patient is. But at all times we must work together. My belief that something will eventually work sustains me through the times when nothing seems to work.

Usually, I initially approach problems in a straightforward manner relying on reason. For example, if someone is engaging in behavior that risks future happiness, I point out the risks. When the patient is resistant to this direct approach, I tend to lapse into true stories that give a lesson on the subject at hand. These stories just pop into my head, and sometimes I am halfway through them before I fully realize how telling their point is. The stories are usually about people I know. Sometimes they are examples from my own life. If the patient continues to be resistant, I switch gears and approach the problem from the opposite side. In cases where a patient has a long history of people being opposed to him or her for a particular reason, I assume there is going to be a lot of resistance if I am seen as siding with the opposition. Accordingly, instead of approaching the problem in a straightforward manner, I immediately try to approach the problem from another direction. I now know that storytelling and paradoxical approaches are methods popularized by followers of Milton Erickson. Here are some examples of some paradoxical interventions which were pivotal to the whole therapy.

Case I

A young homosexual woman sought psychological help to attain her goal of undergoing a sex change operation. She indicated that she had felt like a boy for as long as she could remember, and she felt very inadequate because she did not have a penis. When she was 5, she had asked her mother why she didn't have one, and her mother had jokingly replied that it forgot to grow. From that time on, she was possessed with the hope that she would eventually have one. This patient also expressed the belief that, if she had had one, she would have kept her first female lover, with whom she was seriously involved, instead of losing her to a man. After some discussion, it also became evident that she wanted a penis as a protection against sexual assault by males. I recommended that this patient undergo psychological testing to assess her mental health. If she exhibited no significant disturbance and she still wanted the operation after 6 months of therapy, during which she would explore the pros and cons of the operation, I told her I would write a letter recommending the surgery. She tested quite normally and I gave her a copy of my report with the recommendation that she research the surgery as part of her therapy. She went to medical libraries and read many articles on the subject. Most of them were confusing to her, but she did surmise that most people who underwent the operation were satisfied with the results. She was anxious to see some photographs, which the articles did not show. I obtained a book for her with some photographs. She initially stated they looked okay to her, but she expected the surgical methods would improve in time and she would go for further surgery when that occurred. However, at our very next session she stated that she had decided it would really be better if she worked on accepting herself as she is instead of undergoing the surgery. She mentioned that a friend of hers had convinced her that she is much more socially acceptable as a boyish homosexual female than as a transsexual, something she had never previously considered. After some discussion, it became clear that, in the past, she had completely blocked out this type of input. From then on, her therapy dealt with general issues of self-esteem and her tendency to wish she was a boy whenever her sense of self-worth fell. I believe it was my acceptance and support of her wish to have a sex change which enabled her to more objectively explore the pros and cons of the operation so that she was able to reach the decision that it was not such a good idea for her after all.

Case II

A professional married man in his 20s sought therapy to overcome his habit of wearing female tights while riding his bike during his early morning exercise. He had been wearing dark tights for years, but the morning he phoned for an appointment he had put on sheer nylon tights. Many years before, he had gone in public wearing only sheer tights and had almost been arrested for indecent exposure. He was in a panic that he would keep wearing the sheer tights and eventually be arrested, thereby ruining his career and causing both himself and his wife great embarrassment. To ward off this immediate threat, I suggested that he keep imagining the sequence of his wearing the sheer tights in public and then being arrested with all its negative repercussions. He thought this was a good idea and agreed to try it. After a trial run of this fantasy with prompting from me, he reported that he was not afraid of being attacked by anyone in jail, as I had suggested. He stated he has such powerful legs that he is sure he could fight off any would-be attacker. He then related that he identifies very strongly with Spider Man, who has very powerful legs and he likes wearing tights in public to show off his powerful leg muscles. He did not have much confidence in his ability to attract women and it was his fondest dream that, while he was dressed in tights, a goodlooking woman would be attracted to him and treat him as if there was nothing unusual about the way he was dressed. Questioning about his history revealed that his fascination with tights began shortly after entering puberty, when he would use his mother's nylon tights as an auxiliary to masturbation. He also indicated that he had enjoyed a very close relationship with his mother until she had a nervous breakdown when he was 11. From then on, she was irrationally hostile towards him. He believed that she was and continued to be psychotic, although she had refused all psychiatric treatment. He ceased to have any more contact with her 2 years prior to his coming for treatment, because she threatened him with a gun after he urged her not to pick on his sister-in-law. At our second session, this patient reported that the fantasizing had actually increased his acting out, because the first part of the fantasy was so exciting to him. After some discussion, he revealed that, in contrast to the incident when he was almost arrested for indecent exposure, he was wearing shorts over his sheer tights. Upon hearing this, I spontaneously expressed great relief that he was not actually in danger of being arrested. I also questioned why he should give up this habit when it gives him so much pleasure and is not really harming anybody. Furthermore, I pointed out how this habit cleverly satisfies three totally different needs all at the same time. Firstly, for heterosexual men, wearing female clothes is a way of relaxing and escaping for awhile from the tensions of the male competitive world. Secondly, wearing the tights brought him back in time to a feeling of closeness with his mother Thirdly, by wearing the tights he could display what he considered his most attractive features and thereby build up his confidence to attract females. Somehow, this permission to continue the habit worked paradoxically, because for over a month he did not wear even dark tights during his morning bicycle ride. During this period of time, his twice weekly therapy sessions were devoted to an exploration of his anger towards his mother and his sexual frustration with his wife. Then, when he was going through a particularly stressful period of time at work, his habit of wearing dark tights suddenly returned. I reminded him that his habit is basically a harmless way for him to release tension. He insisted, nevertheless, that he wanted to overcome it. After analyzing his various reasons for wanting to quit the habit, he realized most did not hold up. For example, he feared social embarrassment, but at that early hour of the morning there were very few people around, and, if he ever saw someone he knew, he was confident that he could ride by so swiftly they wouldn't even know it was he. He also feared punishment from God. However, this was not the only way he had deviated from his fundamentalist upbringing. Finally, he concluded that the real reason he wanted to stop his habit was for his own self-esteem. I told him it all boiled down to a choice of either giving into the impulse for his pleasure or resisting the impulse for his self-esteem. Either way was fine with me. Besides, there was really nothing I could do about it. The impulse would probably be with him his whole life, sometimes more strongly than at other times. It was just a matter of what was more important to him, his pleasure or his self-esteem. If his self-esteem meant more to him, then he would control the habit. On the other hand, if he continued the habit, that meant his self-esteem was not as important to him as he thought. These comments had a lasting impact. From then on through the several months of continuing therapy and follow-up contact over a period of years, this patient reported no further recurrence of his habit.

Case III
In another case, this time of a teenage prostitute, a paradoxical intervention had a dramatic, but unfortunately only temporary impact. This girl, whom I saw at a rehabilitation center for delinquent girls, went on and on about how wonderful and exciting she found the life of a prostitute. She had always felt materially deprived as a child, and she revelled in the things she could now afford to buy. She also felt very glamorous going out with her pimp in his fancy car to fancy restaurants dressed in what she considered to be high style. When I suggested various pitfalls to her way of life, she immediately dismissed them as untrue or inconsequential. Finally, I said to her: "I've been trying to convince you to quit your way of life, but you keep telling me how great it is. If it's so great, why don't you try to convince me to become a prostitute?" The girl's reaction to this was amazing. Without missing a beat in the conversation, she launched into a detailed description of how she was terrorized, beaten, and almost killed by one of her tricks. Obviously, all she needed was some support for the positive aspects of being a prostitute for her to acknowledge the negative aspects. We continued

to talk throughout her 4-month detention. She and her mother agreed it would not work out for her to return home, so the plan was for her to go to a foster home. Just before she was placed in one, her natural father, whom she had not seen since she was a baby, contacted her mother and, upon hearing what had been going on with his daughter, offered her a home with himself and his second wife. The home was found to be suitable and the girl was placed there. It was like a fairy tale come true. However, a few months later I learned that this girl left her father's home after only a few weeks, because she felt he was too strict, and she was back on the streets.

Sometimes a breakthrough in therapy occurs when the patient is finally convinced that the therapist has a positive regard for the patient.

Case IV
In the case of a divorced female in her early thirties, the patient announced in the first session that she had the worst problem anyone could have. She had no friends. Within a short time, I understood why. She was extremely negative and seemed bent on defeating any and all attempts to be helpful to her. Not surprisingly, her progress in therapy was exceedingly slow. Then after a year and a half of therapy, there was a dramatic turning point. She announced that she had done something so disgusting that, upon hearing it, I would need the waste basket to throw up in and I would finally see what a terrible person she is. However, upon hearing this thing (which I could not deny was disgusting), I calmly asked her if she enjoyed it. She expressed great repugnance, whereupon I calmly stated that in that case she probably wouldn't do it again. She strongly agreed, whereupon I told her that she is obviously not hung up on that behavior and all it said about her was that she was more experimental than most people. It seems that this acceptance of her as an okay person, despite her unappealing behavior, had a dramatic effect, because from then on she started showing marked improvement in every area of her life.

With some patients who get stuck in a situation or position that is self-defeating, I find it helpful to separate their feelings from their thinking. For example, when someone feels extremely worthless, I might say that I know he or she feels that way, but I wonder if he or she really believes it. That way, the patient can gain more control over feelings that have been overwhelming.

Case V
In the case of a teenage boy who resented his parents' strictness, the boy entered therapy after an acting out incident that got him in trouble with the juvenile authorities. Much of the therapy was aimed at having the boy and his parents develop a better understanding of each other and arrive at some compromises. Improvements were noted, but there were still periods of time when the boy

would become intensely angry at his parents. In one session, he informed me that his mother was not going to let him go to a school dance which he had been looking forward to because she did not like all his behavior when they had out-of-town guests. I sympathized with him, because the dance meant a lot to him, and I offered to speak to his mother about the possibility of her substituting another punishment for this one. His mother said she had always been the easy parent and she was determined this time to follow through on the original punishment. Besides, she wanted the punishment to mean a lot to her son, because he had really embarrassed her in front of her guests when he was rude to her, although he had behaved nicely most of the time they were there. At this point, I turned to the boy and told him that I still sympathized with him for the punishment and felt it was severe. On the other hand, I reminded him that these are his parents and he might as well learn to get along better with them so he won't have to go through this kind of thing again. I told him that, if I were he, instead of brooding over the punishment, I would take a lesson from it and avoid doing anything in the future to bring on a similar punishment. From this point on, the mother reported a marked improvement in the boy's overall attitude. He was much more cooperative, he was no longer testing her rules, and he was accepting limitations on his freedom much more graciously. I believe it was the combination of sympathizing with his feelings about the situation and providing him with some constructive ideas on how to handle it that enabled him to make such positive changes.

When a patient gets stuck on a position in which he or she is being unreasonable, after a period of time I tend to depart from my usual supportive style and become rather confrontive.

Case VI
A married woman in her twenties bitterly resented the time and attention her husband gave his son from a former marriage whenever the boy visited in their home. However, it was obvious that, due to the boy's problems, her husband derived much more pleasure from her and their baby daughter. After hearing her complain about her stepson's visits over several sessions and my pointing out, to little avail, why she should not feel threatened, one day I said quite bluntly, "You've got to remember his son was there first in his life," and I repeated the statement for emphasis. Between sessions, I worried that perhaps I had been too harsh. However, at the next session the patient announced that, though she had been initially upset by what I said, it was the best thing for her to hear it. Somehow, she is no longer feeling upset by the situation and she can now accept her husband giving attention to his son. Evidently, being forced to face the reality of the situation enabled her to finally accept that which could not be changed.

TERMINATION

Before ending this chapter on therapy, it is appropriate for me to address the subject of termination. I know that this is widely considered a very delicate matter, but I have not found it to be much of a problem. After a period of time in which the patient has demonstrated decided improvement in his or her functioning, and feels he or she has achieved his or her goals in therapy, I have found the patient has less and less to bring up in the therapy hour. Then either the patient or I suggest reducing the frequency of the sessions. After a period of time, we phase out the sessions altogether, with the understanding that the patient can return for one or more sessions whenever the patient has a need to do so. I know that this method of termination does not confront the issues of separation and abandonment. However, I don't feel that is essential for every patient. Besides, if these are important issues to a particular patient, I would rather deal with them in the context of their significant past relationships. I am not primarily interested in working analytically on transference issues. I am much more interested in working from a commonsense point of view on the practical issues in my patients' lives. While recognizing the significance a therapist can have to a patient, I'd like to be viewed by patients as a bridge to other relationships and not as the central relationship on which to focus. With this approach, termination does not become a significant issue.

Naturally, matters are more complicated when circumstances force a premature termination. If the patient is at the beginning of therapy, but has already seen some benefits, I emphasize the value of therapy in general and what more he or she can gain from therapy, so that he or she will be positively disposed towards transferring to another therapist.

If the patient is in the middle of therapy and expresses a lot of regret about starting over with someone else, I point out the benefits of getting input from a second therapist with a somewhat different point of view. Switching therapists also gives the patient the opportunity to experience therapy with both a male and female therapist.

If the patient is nearing the end of therapy, I remind the patient of all the gains he or she had made in the course of therapy, with the assurance that these gains will not be lost just because the therapy has to abruptly end. I also explain the process of introjection, whereby people carry within themselves all the people who have had an impact on their lives. Then I suggest that, when the patient is having a problem, he or she can imagine my reactions and use them to help deal with the situation. Finally, I remind the patient that since he or she has learned how helpful therapy can be, he or she will know enough to seek this help when needed in the future.

One of the hardest things for me to deal with personally is when a patient terminates before any real progress has been made. At these times, I go over in my mind what went on in therapy and I try to think of what I could have done differently to motivate the patient to continue treatment long enough to be helped.

CONCLUSION

In conclusion, my advice to beginning therapists is to read as much as you can on psychological development, theories of personality, psychopathology, and techniques of psychotherapy. Then, when you are with a patient, focus all your attention on the patient with the intent of understanding what is going on inside the patient and in the patient's life. At the same time, consider what needs to be done to improve the patient's situation. If the first approach doesn't work, keep trying different approaches until something does work. Finally, it is my recommendation that you have the courage to be yourself with your patients while encouraging them to be true to themselves.

Chapter 3

Clinical Assessment

Richard H. Dana

University of Arkansas

Clinical assessment refers to both a process and its instrumentation. Historically the assessment process was applied to the diagnosis of mental illness. Currently, 90% of professional time is allocated to clinical services for approximately seven million of the 35 million persons who suffer from anxiety, depression, alcohol addiction, functional psychoses, and brain syndromes of the aged (Fox, 1982). Assessment of the major personal problems—"bad" habits and ineffective life styles—which affect all persons at some time in their lives has been virtually ignored by practitioners.

Gordon Allport (1937) described 52 methods, clustered in 14 main varieties of data, for studying personality and available for clinical assessment. Included were studies of cultural setting, physical/social/personal records, expressive movements, ratings, standardized tests, statistical analysis, miniature life situations, laboratory experiments, prediction, depth analysis including interviews, ideal types, and synthetic methods. Clinical psychologists have only infrequently used many of these data sources, and some of their labels are now familiar.

After an historical introduction, four data sources (instrumentation) will be described: interview, observation, objective tests, projective techniques. Each of these data sources may be processed informally and subjectively using judgment, or formally, either by functional analysis of behavior or by statistical analysis. Psychoanalytic and phenomenological theory consider assessment data to be signs which are indicants of underlying dynamics, traits, or characteristics of personality. Social-learning assessors view data as samples of behavior which are to be generalized directly without appreciable inference to other similar behaviors in the client's repertoire. Other assessors with psychometric orientations consider data to be correlates, and use data in terms of their statistical relationships to external criteria and/or other data. Data, regardless of source or manner of processing, is used for classification (clinical diagnosis of psychopathology), personality description (both literal/behavioral and conceptual dynamic), and outcome prediction (kind of intervention, prognosis, etc.).

CLINICAL DIAGNOSIS

Once upon a time, assessors practiced magic. Our professional forefathers described a modus operandi for generating hypotheses from a chosen instrument, or test battery, which often included an intelligence test and one or more projective techniques—Rorschach, Thematic Apperception Test (TAT), Sentence Completion Test (SCT), Draw-A-Person (DAP), and Bender-Gestalt (BG). Test batteries were used because of a desire to have data from different levels of personality, although there has never been clear evidence of incremental validity as a result of additional sources of data. These hypotheses were woven together using logic, acumen, and experiential wisdom to compose descriptive reports that led to clinical diagnoses. While Rorschach examples abound, TAT reports from different assessors who describe one patient provide a less frequent documentation of clinical skills (e.g., Schneidman, 1951).

This clinical approach to data processing has been described using a four-step hierarchal model: data (I), abstraction (II), conceptualization (III), and clinical diagnosis (IV). Quasi-reliable assessment data (I) are transformed into adjecteval descriptors (II) without benefit of operational validity, and further attenuated to become reports (III) which have limited predictive validity for treatment procedures and prognosis. Finally, an ultimate abstraction provided a clinical diagnosis (IV). In spite of singular artistry and profound conceptual skills, this process had diminished reliability with each step in the inferential process. Because it was intuitive and subjective, the communication of clinical assessment skill to students was difficult. In addition, substantive research on the adequacy of report content for personality conceptualization, clinical diagnosis, or treatment planning was simply not forthcoming. This deficit occurred because many psychoanalytic assessment practitioners eschew empirical research, and few extant methodologies were relevant either to clinical processing of data or to applications of projective techniques. Nonetheless, projective techniques have continued to be among the most frequently used instruments for clinical diagnosis (Wade, Baker, Morton, & Baker, 1978).

The use of these instruments was further complicated because diagnosis was not a reliable process; expert diagnosticians of all professional persuasions differed remarkably on all but the most gross classifications. The functions of psychiatric classification—consensus among experts and an extention of knowledge from the act of classification—did not provide a scientific taxonomy of mental illness. The 1980 American Psychiatric Association Diagnostic and Statistical Manual (DSM-III) has attempted to increase reliability by detailing the criteria necessary for each diagnosis, and should substantially improve assessor agreement on diagnoses.

This era of magic (circa 1940–1960) had costly side-effects for clinical psychologists. Assessment was a low status specialization, because it was not integrated into a service delivery system. Psychological reports were one basis for inferring treatment of choice, but the goodness-of-fit between diagnosis and

treatment was haphazard and the probabilities of successful application of particular treatments could not be predicted. As a result, assessors were isolated
from the professional mainstream of service providers. Their instruments had
been developed outside of the context of legitimate service delivery systems
and were ancillary procedures to be integrated into a treatment plan by someone else, usually a psychiatrist.

By 1960, Boulder model programs emphasizing the unique scientist-practitioner training model were graduating clinical psychologists who were increasingly sophisticated in psychometrics. Learning theory was being applied in a
behavioral idiom. Research findings became a mandatory basis for responsible professional practice. Assessment data was demonstrated to be mechanically or
statistically manipulable (nomothesis) in order to provide valid probability statements for decision-making. Outcome statements, improvement of existing procedures, and test as well as nontest procedures were viewed within a framework
of utility. The use of communal common sense, judgment, and creative inferential skill to understand a unique person (idiography) was being questioned.
The idiographic-nomothetic controversy pitted clinician against statistician, clinical skill against formula, and for many decisions the tally of research studies
favored the actuary. However, this false dichotomy was not resolvable by research but only amenable to reconciliaton. For some decisions in some situat-
tions, especially those involving infrequent events, there is no substitute for the
human head.

Increasing psychometric sophistication led to research with objective tests,
especially the Minnesota Multiphasic Personality Inventory (MMPI), in order to
provide an empirical basis for practice. The hierarchal model was truncated.
Data from objective tests were compared with empirical knowledge from an ac-
cumulation of research studies and a decision/prediction was forthcoming. In
this model, there was no way to know why a decision was useful, and behavior
was assumed to be simple and consistent.

Two issues suggest the complexity of this equation. First, personality traits
may have temporary or stable/chronic expression. Second, the trait may have
origins within the person (dispositional), or be more specific to the context in
which it occurs (situational). It has been empirically determined that descriptors
of temporary and stable expressions have approximately equal representation
(40%) in the language, while social roles, relationships, and affects account for
the remainder. Similarly, proponents of the interactionist view have repeatedly
demonstrated that, although person (dispositional) and setting (situational)
sources of variance are considerable, it is the interaction of person X setting
that contributes the greater portion of variance. We have replicated research
demonstrations that stable/dispositional sources of traits can be differentiated
from temporary/situational sources of personality conditions or states, particularly for anxiety (Spielberger, Gorsuch, & Lushene, 1970). The perception of
locus may be either within the person in the form of underlying, internal traits,
or a by-product of circumstances and life situations. Moreover, attribution

theory informs us that assessors consistently attribute acts to stable, personal dispositions, while persons see their own behaviors as situationally determined (Jones & Nisbett, 1971). Perhaps this occurs because of the person-blaming stance of many assessors, a professional contribution to stability and conservation.

With the advent of behavioral medicine, medical patients were added to the historic assessment population of psychiatric patients. These medical patients had specific physical problems which were exacerbated by anxiety, life stress, beliefs in the efficacy of physical medicine, tolerance for pain, and the extent to which they felt in control of their own destinies. All of these variables became suitable candidates for new assessment procedures. In addition, the contribution of life style to physical illness, and assessment for illness proneness and hence prevention, became of concern.

Finally, the emergent area of clinical health psychology refers to the maintenance of individual mental and physical health. Assessment, particularly in the form of self-assessment, contributes to prevention of distress or dysfunction. Individual styles of coping with life stress are examined for efficacy, preference, and goodness-of-fit. Prevention of dysfunction occurs through increased self-awareness and application of problem-solving technology to the events in daily life. A self-managed life is the goal and assessment procedures contribute information that is systematically related to unique personal situations.

As this brief history has suggested, clinical assessment is beset by paradoxes. First, we rely heavily on antique instruments which were devised in an era of psychometric naivete but were subsequently frozen into usage by practitioners. Some of the consequences are visible in the role of clinical assessment in a service delivery system. Broad gauge instruments (i.e., description of general personality characteristics) are used for discrete decision (i.e., diagnostic statements or therapeutic interventions). Clinical assessment and clinical assessors are often not taken seriously by other professionals as peers, because their findings are considered to by ancillary and technician-derived services. Second, there is the paradox of clinical psychologists who have been trained to use more focused and psychometrically adequate instruments but who have access primarily to this heritage of broad spectrum tests which antedate their own more sophisticated training. If these psychologists choose to be assessment specialists, they must use instruments that are not generally recognized by referral source persons and consumers alike, or they must employ traditional instruments with an altered service delivery paradigm. This altered paradigm refers to the use of feedback to both consumers and referral source persons that is accomplished in such a manner as to transform ancillary services into professional consultations.

The material that follows is organized to consider briefly the major sources of assessment of data, interview, observation, and tests. Within each data source, traditional and novel/sophisticated examples will be presented, for psychiatric and medical patients as well as for well functioning persons who are not patients.

This review is a systematic potpourri that seeks to blend an assessment rationale with examples of applications or instruments.

Interviewing

Historically, interviewing has been the basic assessment stance. Regardless of theoretical origin, a demonstration to the assessee of caring, confidence, and clearly used skills is required. These skills are coupled with clinician self-awareness to provide a context for rapport and trust. We presume that assessment as well as psychotherapy is "for better or for worse"; clients may be damaged or enabled by our assessment interactions with them.

The basis for an assessment interview is a set of implicit or explicit guidelines that reflect the purpose of the interview and the theoretical orientation. For example, a neutral orientation (Sundberg, Tyler, & Taplin, 1973) includes identifying data, reason for interview, present situation, family, early memories, development, health, education, work, recreation, sexual development, marital data, self-description, and turning points in life. A psychoanalytic orientation would elicit additional information on early experience, personality dynamics and motives, ego functions, and ego identity. A social-learning orientation would be focused on an analysis of antecedent and consequent conditions for both aversive and prosocial behaviors. The data would be directly relevant to the tactics of future behavior change.

It has been conventional to consider interview stages that include a beginning (making contact, establishing rapport, clarifying purposes, suggesting what is expected of client, and reducing anxiety), a middle which focuses on content and purpose of interview (intake, problem-identification, crisis alleviation, orientation, or termination in particular clinical settings), and a closing phase (signaling an imminent conclusion, support and reassurance, plan for final minutes, recap of session, anticipated future events as outcome of interview).

Assessment interviews mirror their theoretical frames-of-references, preferences for informal or formal processing of data, and data usage as sign, sample, or correlate. Examplar interview procedures for psychiatric illness, physical illness, and psychological health will be described.

The Structured Clinical Interview (Burdock & Hardesty, 1969) exemplifies the format of a test within an interview. This schedule contains 179 yes/no items and can be administered in 20–30 minutes. There are 10 nonoverlapping subsets of items: anger-hostility, conceptual dysfunction, fear-worry, incongruous behavior, incongruous ideation, lethargy-depression, perceptual dysfunction, physical complaints, self-depreciation, and sexual problems. In addition to a gross severity score, there are profiles available for diffrent diagnostic groups, before and after treatment. Reliable diagnosis in terms of frequency and kind of aversive behaviors can be provided with this interview format. This kind of format has been developed because interviews are often deficient in reliability or validity and are susceptible to distortion either by the interviewer or by situation-specificity as a result of the process and interaction. Interviews may also be dependent upon assessee willingness to be interviewed and to be self-revealing.

One interviewing approach of Rogerian origin has been used by a variety of health professionals, including physicians and nurses who usually have not been specifically trained in interviewing but who need to relate effectively with medical patients (Bernstein & Dana, 1970). Interviewers are trained to distinguish among evaluative, hostile, reassuring, probing, and understanding responses. For assessment of current status, the understanding response is presented as the most facilitative. Understanding includes acceptance and reflection of feeling, nonverbal behavior and silence.

Many assessors have used interviews to examine psychological health or wellness, either cross-sectionally or longitudinally in selected groups or individuals. We are all familiar with Erik Erikson's psychohistorical study of Gandhi, which depended in part on interviews with informants and upon examination of archival sources. Usually, however, the informants have been the exceptional persons themselves. Maslow interviewed a handful of anonymous persons to provide examples of living self-actualizers. Others—Daniel Levinson, Robert White, George Valliant—have used interview formats that are semi-structured, detailed, and have content that suggest their theoretical origins. These interview formats have been used together with the gamut of assessment devices—objective tests, projective techniques, ratings, and autobiographical material.

Observation

Assessment by observation has been described as a "technical smorgasbord" (Bernstein & Nietzel, 1980), although it may be the oldest assessment strategy. Shakespeare had his personages use a sign approach when they inferred nonobservable personality characteristics from physical appearance, but there has been movement in professional observation from a sign to a sample strategy. The observation process begins with selection of behaviors to be observed. Sometimes, no selection occurs, and behavior is observed naturalistically as it occurs. The observer/assessor may be a participant or detached from the activity. As a participant, the assessor can potentially affect the behaviors to be observed. As an observer, there may be adaptation effects before the presence of an observer is accepted without disruption. Whenever selection does occur, control is being exercised so that the observer is prepared to observe; what to look for (selection) and how to look (record) are predetermined. The setting may be either natural or contrived. Recording may be by memory, or preferably by verbatim recording in situ (using audio or video assistance). Obviously, the goal is accurate and complete representation. Encoding is provided by format or system that permits data to be used as sign or sample.

Clinical assessment of distressed behavior may be accomplished by observation in hospitals, schools, and at home. There are many systems for immediate observation of hospitalized psychiatric patients. Descriptions of psychopathological behavior are provided by a profile of dimensions generated from items that have been previously rated by ward personnel. It is feasible to monitor hospital behavior as observed at different times by different persons and to relate these behaviors to specific treatments.

There are also many controlled observational systems that have a standard stimulus or situation. A tape recording and occasionally a staged naturalistic event (phone calls, conversation with a stranger) may be used to elicit responses which are subsequently rated. Such systems provide narrow-band observation for use with specific behaviors such as assertiveness or social skills. Anxiety may be assessed in relationship to specific situations/objects using Behavioral Avoidance Tests. Such tests measure the amount of fear on a variety of parameters relevant to subsequent fear-reduction techniques. Performance measures of many consummatory behaviors—eating, drinking, smoking—and physiological activities—heart rate, brain waves, muscle tension—may be used to establish base rates or to provide details of the response process that are subsequently related to self-control activities of the client.

Observations of school behavior typically have used a priori categories with time-sampling focused on one child or on a small group of children. However, it is also feasible to obtain several hours of complete behavior recording on a particular child called a behavior glossary. The behavior glossary is subsequently used to develop child-specific behavior categories which are used to gather baseline data on frequency of prosocial and aversive behaviors. Behavioral recording systems have also been devised for application in the home. In these systems the behavior of all family members is recorded simultaneously in a standard setting often at supper time. These data are then used to construct a problem-checklist to specify treatment of children and other family members.

These systems all share common features. They are systematic and apply control to the behavior itself and/or in the recording process. Observers must be trained to ensure reliability of recording, or coding, and reliability checks are often built in to the observational procedure. Attention to validity is another hallmark of observational systems. Finally, representativeness of observed behavior, or ecological validity, is a critical issue.

Objective Tests

Objective personality tests consist of collection of statements, or items that the assessee responds to in a forced-choice manner. These items may be generated by rational processes, consensual human judgment or wisdom, by empirical method that provides differences between groups that possess or do not possess the quality/behavior/trait to be measured, or by statistical procedure to obtain the measures (factors). Scores can be represented in standard score format, so that the mean and standard deviation are agreed upon, and individuals can be compared to the same test or across tests. Norms are developed to specify the characteristics of persons for whom the test is to be used. Since persons may obtain consistent rank orders on scales, reliability is documentable. Validation provides evidence obtained from systematic procedure that specified characteristics are indeed being measured (construct validity) or that predictions can be made on the basis of the score/test with high probability (predictive validity).

MMPI. The MMPI was designed to provide psychiatric diagnosis of the major clinical syndromes during the 1940s. The clinical scales were Hypochondriasis, Depression, Conversion Hysteria, Psychopathic Deviate, Paranoia, Psychasthenia, Schizophrenia, and Hypomania. Social Introversion and Masculinity–femininity were added at a later date to make a total of ten scales embedded in a pool of 550 items. Four validity scales permitted estimates of bias/distortion and provided weighted corrections for five clinical scales. Over the years, hundreds of special scales were constructed. Such scales required that one group saturated on a particular characteristic be compared with a control group which did not possess that characteristic. Selected special scales are often used in addition to the clinical scales.

The validity and clinical scales are presented on a profile in which 50 is the mean score, with 30 and 70 representing two standard deviations in either direction. High scores are those above 70 and statistically deviant and presumably pathological. Since high scores were not invariably associated with a particular diagnostic category, scale numbers replaced scale names. Interpretation was initially accomplished by inspection of the profile using intuition and accumulated clinical experience with other MMPI profiles. In addition, rationally derived subscale scores were used. However, more sophisticated analysis was data based and used high point codes for comparison with research literature.

Two recent textbooks clearly describe this research foundation for application and interpretation (Graham, 1977; Greene, 1980). Potential users of the MMPI should also be aware of the variety of computerized scoring and interpretation that are currently available (Buros, 1978). At least six short-forms of the MMPI have been constructed to represent the long-form in cost-effective terms by choice of a small number of items and appropriate validation of scale scores, ratios, and diagnostic content obtained on this basis. Since these short-forms have clear deficiencies as well as legitimate clinical usages in many settings, assessors are advised to read the standard text on short-forms (Faschingbauer & Newmark, 1978).

Millon Tests. A new generation of objective tests is represented by three Millon instruments. The Millon Clinical Multiaxial Inventory consists of 175 items arranged in 20 scales that measure syndromes derived from theory and relevant to the DSM-III (Millon, 1982). Basic Personality patterns, or premorbid status, and current psychopathology are differentiated by inclusion of eight Axis III basic personality patterns and nine Axis I clinical symptoms plus three personality disorders. Correction scales for random/confused responding and attitudes of denial/complaint are included. Multiple validation strategies were used, in addition to cross-validation. Similar construction/validation procedures were followed for the Millon Behavioral Health Inventory, used with patients who are physically ill or behavioral medicine and rehabilitation recipients, as well as for the Millon Adolescent Personality Inventory, used with high school students. While these instruments are relatively new, they represent contemporary objective measurement approaches that combine brevity, sophisticated construction/validation methodologies, and relevance to current diagnostic nomenclature.

Neuropsychology. Clinical neuropsychologist assessors use objective tests and other measures for the diagnosis of brain damage and to illuminate brain-behavior relationships. Typically, a variety of separate function sensitive to brain impairment are measured, including verbal/perceptual/cognitive/visuopractice skills and memory. These functions are measured in concert with an individual intelligence test (WAIS), an achievement test (Peabody Individual Achievement Test, Wide Range Achievement Test), and an objective personality test (MMPI). Each assessor develops a battery (often 6–8 hours duration) from many available tests, and tailors assessment to specific referral questions. The Halstead-Reitan battery subtests, the Bender-Gestalt, the Benton Visual Retention Test, the Luria-Nebraska, the Wechsler Memory Scale, and the Graham Kendall MFD provide many of the components for neuropsychological test batteries (Lezak, 1976). Prediction of functional recovery, compensation, response to rehabilitation, and psychological adjustment are referral issues that stem from assessment for diagnosis of brain damage and brain-behavior relationships.

16 PF. This test was designed to have separate scales for different aspects/ factors of personality structure in a normal population. There are five forms with a maximum of 187 multiple-choice items. Raw scores for 16 scales are translated into sten scores, or standard scores with a mean of 5.5., a sigma of two, and a range from one to ten. These scales measure warmth (Factor A), intelligence (B), ego strength (C), dominance (E), impulsivity (F), group conformity (G), boldness (H), emotional sensitivity (I), suspiciousness (L), imagination (M), shrewdness (N), guilt proneness (O), rebelliousness, (Q1), self-sufficiency (Q2), anxiety binding (Q3), free floating anxiety and tension (Q4). Second order factor scores are derived which reflect basic tendencies that underlie two or more scales: Extraversion-introversion (Factor I), anxiety (II), tough poise (III), independence (IV), and sociopathy (V). In addition, corrections are applied for faking bad, faking good (motivational distortion), and for infrequent or rarely omitted answers (Random Scale). Interpretation provides descriptive information and extreme scores are within two sigmas of the population mean. Computerized scoring and interpretation are available. For further information, see Karson and O'Dell (1976).

Measures of Psychological Health.   There are many single instruments that purport to measure psychological health or wellness. For example, ego strength may be equated with wellness and measured by an MMPI scale, a TAT ego sufficiency scale, or Rorschach scores. A variety of psychological health measures are independent of frequently used techniques, but these indices have little to recommend them because they represent narrow definitions and have not been extensively validated. The Q-sort, or set of statements to be sorted by assessees or observers in a forced normal distribution, received early use by Carl Rogers to examine the process of client-centered psychotherapy. A Q-sort was combined with Loevinger's ego development theory to explore personality change over time in normal persons (Block, 1971) and this research exemplifies appropriate use of a relevant measure of psychological health.

However, it is anticipated that future developments will include batteries of carefully selected instruments for specific measuring purposes that can be administered, or self-administered with economy. Examples include a popular and perennial Course-in-Oneself developed for West Virginia University college students by Phil Comer, and self-assessment courses for community persons (Dana & Fitzgerald, 1976), and undergraduates who are interested in human service occupations (Dana, 1980). Components of a wellness test battery currently being developed for practitioners by the author include world view as illumined by values, locus of control, and locus of responsibility. There are also brief measures of physical health, psychological well being, coping, and crisis resolution techniques, as well as questions pertaining to attention to self including use of alcohol, tobacco, junk food, sleep and dietary habits, exercise, sexual satisfaction, etc.

Projective Techniques

The word "test" includes objective tests and projective techniques. Projective techniques are usually not tests in any strict psychometric sense, and have been aptly criticized for failure as psychometric instruments. However, there is much confusion over this matter. If projective techniques are merely samples of behavior, then our attempts to legitimitize them by reliability and validation studies may only further confound the dilemma. Samples of behavior need to be representative for a particular assessee, and generalizable to other behavior settings. Nonetheless, we do know that these samples of behavior may be assessor-specific to some unknown extent, a by-product of very human and often unverbalized parameters of interaction. If the constraints exercised over the behavior are provided by assessor and/or technique in a haphazard manner, generalization is not feasible and we encourage an idiosyncratic art form called projective assessment. As a result, there has been continual pressure to transform projective techniques into tests, either by persistent research on particular instruments or by deliberate design of new instruments that are more adequate psychometrically.

Criteria for identification of projective techniques have been suggested (Lindzey, 1961). Projective techniques employ relatively ambiguous stimuli whose specific meaning are generally not known by assessees. They elicit fantasy material that reveals unconscious levels of personality. A broad range of responses are possible, with no right or wrong answers. A large amount of complex data are generated that measure many different aspects of personality. Interpretation yields an integrated portrait of personality.

Rorschach. Hermann Rorschach acted as a scientist by creating a large sample of inkblots, subjecting his scores to a variety of validation procedures, and recognizing the need for norms. Those Rorschachers who subsequently popularized the instrument were interested in applications within a psychoanalytic framework. And Rorschach's publisher decided which inkblots and how many inkblots were to be used by assessors! Moreover, different editions of the same blots had printing variations that astound clinical assessors who search (in vain) for a standard set of stimuli. As a result, each would-be Rorschach practitioner must figuratively reinvent the wheel, a difficult and lonely preoccupation in a professional world searching for cost-effective instrumentation.

The Rorschach procedure consists of 10 inkblots administered in fixed order with relatively consistent directions to tell what blots look like. The responses are recorded verbatim and coded by scoring systems that purport to reflect the substance of the response process as contained in response locations, determinants, and content. An inquiry procedure provides an additional opportunity to elicit sufficient information for reliable scoring.

It is assumed that the major perceived dimensions or determinants of the blots—movement, shading, form, achromatic, and chromatic color—have immutable meanings both separately and in their combinations and permutations, at least for persons within the White, middle-class culture. These meanings ostensibly determine what the technique measures, and stipulate the report content. The intuitive/theoretical content of Rorschach reports does accord with empirical demonstrations of the report content for college students and schizophrenic patients. For example, college students include interpersonal relationships, disruptive internal process, rigidity-flexibility, intellectual control, achievement, creative integration, introversion, affectional needs, self-concept, authority responsiveness, etc. (Dana, Bonge, & Stauffacher, 1981).

Rorschach scores are often reported in psychogram format, together with some derived combinations and ratios that are used in conjunction with clinical inferences from response content, goodness-of-fit between response and stimulus-areas, symbolism, etc. Either the scores themselves, the clinical inferences, or both data sources are used within the hierarchal model to provide a conceptualization of the assessee that may lead to a clinical diagnosis and choice of intervention. Figure 1 is a flow chart for Rorschach interpretation that contains sequential steps, process activities, and assessor attitudes. Assessors have special feelings reserved for the Rorschach and a remarkable treasury of clinical experience with it.

John Exner (1974) developed a comprehensive system based upon his own re-

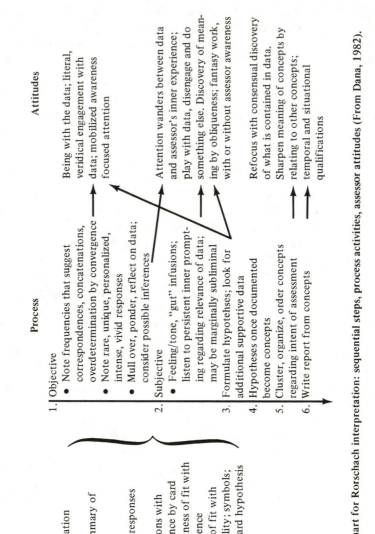

FIGURE 1.   Flow chart for Rorschach interpretation: sequential steps, process activities, assessor attitudes (From Dana, 1982).

search and a compilation of five previous Rorschach systematizers. Since Exner also teaches his system in workshops and has been thereby responsible for a significant fraction of training, his book will impress traditional assessors simply by having packaged the history of Rorschach usage. More recently, another book illustrates the impact of an altered paradigm—a human science approach—upon research, training, and practice with projective techniques, particularly the Rorschach (Dana, 1982). The Rorschach, however, is losing much of its charisma as an open sesame to personality. It occupies considerably less of the entire assessment spectrum than it once did, although there are legitimate domains for Rorschach practice, notably for the study of human growth and relationships (Dana, 1975). The future of clinical assessment is well serviced by putting all projective techniques into perspective, something that Allport accomplished long ago and Sundberg has done more recently (1977).

Holtzman Inkblot Test (HIT).   The HIT, a substitute for the Rorschach, appeared more than 30 years ago (Holtzman, Thorpe, Swartz, & Herron, 1961). This inkblot test contained 49 cards, two practice cards, two parallel forms, and required one response per card followed by a systematic inquiry. There were 22 scoring variables, a blend of traditional and novel categories. When a textbook appeared that summarized the empirical literature on the HIT into a basis for interpretation, it appeared that the Rorschach had been transformed into a respectable psychometric test (Hill, 1972). However, there were few "takers" among assessors, who soon settled back into their comfortable routines with the Rorschach.

SERVICE DELIVERY

The contextualization of assessment within service delivery is undergoing a transformation. At one time, assessment was an ancillary evaluation in which a set of procedures were administered to a client with nominal preparation, and little information about the instruments themselves or the purposes of testing. Informed consent, in the sense of clear understanding regarding the process and outcome of assessment, did not occur. Feedback was provided orally or in writing to the referral source person only.

Currently, feedback on assessment findings is more-or-less routinely provided to the client, and often happens in the presence of and with participation by the referral source person (Table 1). Feedback thus becomes part of an ongoing clinical process, germane to service delivery rather than ancillary to it. In addition, other practitioners—pediatricians, psychiatrists, and surgeons, among other medical specialists—have the opportunity to evaluate assessor competence during an interaction with a client focused on a current service issue. Finally, what the assessor gains from providing feedback in a face-to-face professional encounter may be instrumental to the development of competence.

Table 1.   A Comparison of Traditional and New Formats for Assessment
           Practice*

Steps	Old	New
1	Assessor receives referral (written/oral) from referral source person	Assessor confers with referral source person to define problem and assessor stance during feedback
2	Client is informed by referral source person that assessment is necessary	Assessment procedures and rationale for consultation are discussed with client. Specific emphasis on roles of all participants and potential usages of findings
3	Assessor sees client, administers tests	Assessor sees client, describes procedures, administers tests
4	Assessor provides referral source person with written report	Assessor describes and discusses findings with client and referral source person simultaneously
5		Assessor provides copies of written report to referral source person and to client
6		Assessor and referral source person maintain communication in order to provide feedback for assessor on subsequent utilization of assessment findings

*From Dana (1982).

Psychological assessment reports often have a "flavor" to them that may either be "on target" or "slightly off center," a distillation of a viewpoint that is an admixture of data and personal values/beliefs of the assessor. I am not referring to eisegesis (Dana, 1966), the personalized and distorting infiltration into reports of assessor personality characteristics and/or problems, but simply to a more subtle, more pervasive, and more human infusion. For example, an assessee recently examined the seven reports and separate concepts contained therein generated from her Rorschach by graduate student assessors and myself. She commented articulately on the harshness of one report, the inclusion of pathologizing labels in another, the sex role stereotypy in another, and the difference between reports prepared by male and female assessors.

As assessors, we need the feedback from assessees not only to provide evidence for adequacy of data usage but to make us more aware of our power to diminish or augment their humanity. Assessment reports should be sufficiently concrete in order to provide behavioral examples that describe the experience/ health status of a unique person in recognizable terms. It is difficult to be unambiguous in description, because of the everyday language used in reports. Unambiguous description also makes the assessor vulnerable to error. Potential error can be obscured by generality, Barnum statements, and the caution provided by data-oriented rather than person-oriented statements. We can learn as a result of error whenever reports are written clearly in behavioral idiom and the opportunity for feedback is routinely available.

ETHICS

While there is a chapter on ethics in this book, Principle 8 (Assessment Techniques) of the 1981 APA code will be elaborated in two areas here. Scientific probity, or general honesty, requires that a psychometric test not be used with persons for whom the test has not been standardized. However, this restriction is continuously violated. There are cultural differences and resultant learning styles and functional beliefs/behaviors that make for distortion on objective tests. Caricature, discrimination, and pathologization are unwilling outcomes of using standardized, objective tests inappropriately. For further documentation of this problem and potential remediation, see Dana (1983) and Sundberg and Gonzales (1981). Even when instruments are standardized for minority persons, we should be cognizant of the middle-class values and culture that has produced our assessment devices. Ralph Nader's assault on college board and professional school entrance examinations is a harbinger of greater controls to be exercised by consumers over all objective tests.

The specific relevance of the test, or purpose for use, also must be clearly in focus as a matter of fairness. Personality tests used for evaluation of job applicants may be inappropriate. Finally, assessors need to be aware of the limitations in construction and validation of the instruments they employ. Application of the standard error of measurement and the reliability of differences to tests with profiles of scores (e.g., WAIS, MMPI), especially when not included in the test manual, is mandatory and will result in greater caution during interpretation.

A second ethical issue pertains to respect for the individual as exemplified in informed consent for assessment and feedback. As psychologists, we have been consistent in fulfilling the literal intent and ignoring the spirit of this matter. Informed consent implies genuine understanding of the purposes for assessment, limitations of procedures, and possible outcomes of assessment. Similarly, feedback reflects a professional obligation to provide services with tangible products that may be evaluated for consensual practices, clinical skill, professional judgment, etc. We need to treat our assessees with dignity and respect as an integral component of our human services.

CLINICAL ASSESSMENT FOR THE FUTURE

Up to this point, the chapter has been descriptive, a partial laundry list. If we can believe a pool of experts on the future of psychotherapy (Prochaska & Norcross, 1982), there will be much less individual treatment and change technologies will be more similar to self-change processes in vivo. This suggests that the assessment domain now requires conceptualization based on awareness of a probable future in which informed consumers will require information from us concerning the potential options for management of their own lives. As assessors, we are faced with the dilemma of how to best use what we know to improve the quality of living for many persons. We require a perspective that assigns relative value and priority to specific technologies and then provides formal learning structures to student assessors.

One perspective that makes sense at this time focuses on opportunities for assessment practice using our available technology (Table 2). We can begin with the life changes, or milestones, that embody crisis, health, dysfunction, and recovery. We can juxtapose human development with specific prototypical and accidental or unanticipated stressors, and look at each individual's status within the life cycle. The past history of stressors creates expectations for the likelihood of coming to terms with present stressors. Stress must be perceived as stress, and be intense and timely for negative impact. As we discover variables that moderate between stress and subsequent health/illness, we augment our knowledge of the personal equation that transforms experience into physical/psychological effects.

Antonovksy (1979) has provided a salutogenic model of health, a perdurable confidence that inner and outer environments are predictable and precurse "good" outcomes for life experiences. The ingredients for a model of clinical psychological health presented here (Table 2) acknowledge some of Antonovksy's specific resistance resources.

Each person has a lexicon of resistance resources which may be poorly or relatively well chosen and balanced for effectiveness. Also included among these resources are the beliefs the person has about the self and the universe, especially with regard to the availability of the personal power to change one's own life. Similarly, the size and constituency of the social support system contributes to resources. Energy level and physical health are also critical ingredients. We are just beginning to learn about life style response dispositions, those consistent behaviors that keep many persons shortcircuited by apparent happenstance that is only understood dimly and in retrospect. Ego identity, of course, directly relates to the sense of coherence that is the heartland of salutogenesis. Intelligence and knowledge provide more opportunities for problem-solving. Commitment denotes the dedication and perserverance required for follow through in spite of stressors. Religion/philosophy/art endow experience with meaning which provides additional motivation for coherent experience. Finally, a preventive health orientation suggests conscious, deliberate planfulness-awareness in advance of the interactions of life stages, stressors, moderator variables, and resistance resources as they impinge upon subsequent behaviors and the more generalized and abstract personal outcomes.

A variety of behavioral resolutions are products of stress mediation by use of resistance resources. Decision-making translates to problem-solving; stress

Table 2.   Specific Opportunities for Assessment Using Existing Instruments
Within a Clinical Psychological Health Framework

Life Stage	Stress	Stress Moderation	Resistance Resources	Behavioral Resolution	Personal Outcome
1, 2, 3, etc.	Protypical stressors	Perception of stress	Coping skill repertoire	Decision-making	Compe-tence
	Inadvertent stressors	Magnitude of stress	Energy level	Stress reduction	Growth
		Timing of stress	Social supports	Eliminate "bad habits"	Physical health
			Beliefs in self/world	Better interpersonal relations	Sense of coherence
			Life style response pre-dispositions	Veridical thinking re self	
			Intelligence/ knowledge	More satisfactory sexuality	
			Ego strength		
			Commitment		
			Religion/ philosophy/ art		
			Preventive orientation		

reduction equates with an adequate coping skill repertoire; "bad habits" include eschewing smoking, overeating, alcohol/drug abuse; better interpersonal
relations may require effective social skills; veridical thought about oneself enhances self-concept; and more satisfactory sexuality rests upon information,
technique, and loving practice. Personal outcomes are those generalized conditions that enhance quality of life. Competence, growth, physical health, and
sense of coherence are examples.

This model points toward the immediate future of clinical assessment for a
clinical health psychology. We possess all of the instrumentation to fill in this
model with specific measures for data collection. By accomplishment of this research task, we will learn something about the generalization of resource use
across settings and persons. It is feasible to envision an individual psychogram
of resistance resources with qualifications for settings/persons. As a result,
prescriptive remediation by the assessee can occur. The assessee as consumer
of these assessment services will be an equal partner in prevention of dysfunction and maintenance of psychological health.

Presentation of this model here does not impugn our history of preoccupation with a few measures of psychiatric illness. This model represents one statement concerning the current threshold of assessment technology. Students still need to incorporate psychometric basics as well as clinical fantasy to compose a blend of empirical thought with the creative disposition to make applications for new populations within an altered vision of human psychological functioning.

SUMMARY

1. The history of clinical assessment provides a context for dilemmas faced by contemporary assessors. We have moved from a few global techniques to a wide variety of specific measures, from single sources to multiple sources of data, from clinical diagnosis by label to diagnosis by description, and toward a clear distinction between legitimate uses of inferential (sign) and descriptive (sample) approaches.
2. Interview, observation, objective tests, and projective techniques were described by exemplar instruments for use with psychiatric patients, medical patients, and the non-pathological general population.
3. Recognition of an altered service delivery format incorporates the assessee as consumer of services with an explicitly shared role in the assessment process. This format also emphasizes the ethical constraints upon assessors to have sufficient psychometric knowledge and human integrity to use assessment devices with fairness, recogntion of appropriate norms, and adequate understanding of culturally-different assessees.
4. A preliminary model for contemporary assessment domains was presented that includes clinical psychological health as well as psychiatric dysfunction. While the dovetailing of specific assessment instruments with components of this proposed model is beyond the scope of this chapter, such instrumentation already exists.

REFERENCES

Allport, G. W. (1937). *Personality: A psychological interpretation.* New York: Holt.
Antonovsky, A. (1979). *Health, stress, and coping.* San Francisco: Jossey-Bass.
Bernstein, D. A., & Nietzel, M. T. (1980). *Introduction to clinical psychology.* New York: McGraw-Hill
Bernstein, L., & Dana, R. H. (1970). *Interviewing and the health professions.* New York: Appleton-Century-Crofts.
Block, J. (1971). *Lives through time.* Berkeley: Bancroft Books.
Burdock, E. I., & Hardesty, A. S. (1979). *SCI Structured Clinical Interview.* New York: Springer Publishing Co.
Buros, O. K. (1978). *The eighth mental measurements yearbook.* Highland Park, NJ: Gryphon Press.
Dana, R. H. (1966). Eisegesis and assessment. *Journal of Projective Techniques & Personality Assessment, 30,* 215–222.

Dana, R. H. (1975). Ruminations on teaching projective assessment: An ideology, specific usages, teaching practices. *Journal of Personality Assessment, 39,* 563–572.

Dana, R. H. (1980). *Clinical psychology training and self-assessment for program selection and professional activities.* Lexington, MA: Ginn.

Dana, R. H. (1982). *A human science model for personality assessment with projective techniques.* Springfield, IL: C. C. Thomas.

Dana, R. H. (1983). Personality assessment: Practice and teaching for the next decade. *Journal of Personality Assessment, 48,* 46–57.

Dana, R. H., Bonge, D., & Stauffacher, R. (1981). Personality dimensions in Rorschach reports: An empirical synthesis. *Perceptual and Motor Skills, 2,* 711–715.

Dana, R. H., & Fitzgerald, J. (1976). Educational self-assessment, A course-in-oneself. *College Student Journal, 10,* 317–323.

Exner, J. E. (1974). *The Rorschach: A comprehensive system.* New York: Wiley.

Faschingbauer, T. R., & Newmark, C. S. (1978). *Short forms of the MMPI.* New York: Lexington Books.

Fox, R. E. (1982). The need for a reorientation of clinical psychology. *American Psychologist, 37,* 1051–1057.

Graham, J. R. (1977). *The MMPI: A practical guide.* New York: Oxford University Press.

Greene, R. L. (1980). *The MMPI: An interpretive manual.* New York: Grune & Stratton.

Hill, E. F. (1972). *The Holtzman Inkblot Technique.* San Francisco: Jossey-Bass.

Holtzman, W. H., Thorpe, J. S., Swartz, J. D., & Herron, E. W. (1961). *Inkblot perception and personality: Holtzman inkblot technique.* Austin: University of Texas Press.

Jones, E. E., & Nisbett, R. E. (1971). *The actor and observer: DIvergent perceptions of the causes of behavior.* New York: General Learning Press.

Karson, S., & O'Dell, J. W. (1976). *A guide to the clinical use of the 16PF.* Champaign, IL: Institute for Personality and Ability Testing.

Lezak, M. D. (1970). *Neuropsychological assessment.* New York: Oxford University Press.

Lindzey, G. (1961). *Projective techniques and cross-cultural research.* New York: Appleton-Century-Crofts.

Millon, T. (1982). *Millon Clinical Multiaxial Inventory.* Minneapolis: Interpretive Scoring Systems.

Prochaska, J.O., & Norcross, J. C. (1982). The future of psychotherapy: A Delphi poll. *Professional Psychology, 13*(5), 620–627.

Shneidman, E. S. (1951). *Thematic test analysis.* New York: Grune & Stratton.

Spielberger, C. D., Gorsuch, R. L., & Lushene, R. (1970). *The State-Trait Anxiety Inventory Manual.* Palo Alto, CA: Consulting Psychologists Press.

Sundberg, N. D. (1977). *Assessment of persons.* Englewood Cliffs, NJ: Prentice-Hall.

Sundberg, N. D., & Gonzales, L. R. (1981). Cross-cultural and cross-ethnic assessment: Overview and issues. In P. McReynolds (Ed.), *Advances in psychological assessment.* Vol. 6. San Francisco: Jossey-Bass.

Sundberg, N. D., Tyler, L. E., & Taplin, J. R. (1973). *Clinical psychology: Expanding horizons.* Englewood Cliffs, NJ: Prentice-Hall.

Wade, T. C., Baker, T. B., Morton, T. L., & Baker, L. J. (1978). The status of psychological testing in clinical psychology. Relationships between test use and professional activities and orientations. *Journal of Personality Assessment, 42,* 3–10.

Chapter 4

Supervision

Anthony J. DeVito

Fordham University

INTRODUCTION

The highest level of professional activity attained by a clinical or counseling psychologist is probably that of supervision of less experienced psychologists or psychology graduate students. Supervision is the process whereby one professional (the supervisor) helps, works with, or trains a less experienced person (the supervisee) to become a better practitioner. The supervisor must not only be experienced, but should also have sound theoretical and practical knowledge of the field. A psychologist supervising psychologists-in-training should minimally have state licensure. Legal problems might otherwise arise. Supervision is usually regarded as therapeutic skill training and is therefore differentiated from personal therapy.

Learning to be a Supervisor

Amazingly little formal training in the process of supervision has been incorporated into graduate instruction in clinical psychology (cf. Bartlett, Goodyear, & Bradley, 1983). The increasing emphasis now placed on continuing education will probably include more abundant opportunities for training in supervision.

While supervisors almost never receive explicit training in supervision, most are exposed to a variety of supervisors and supervisory styles in the course of their clinical training and presumably pattern themselves after their own supervisors. We can often see our supervisors' influence on our own supervisory style, just as we can see the influence supervisors have exerted on our therapeutic style. Occasionally, we, as supervisors, may avoid a practice used by a supervisor because we, as supervisees, did not find it useful. Other, more formal, methods involving both theoretical training and exercises similar to those used by Truax and Carkhuff (1967) are emerging. While the Truax and Carkhuff procedures were geared to training *therapists*, the more recently developed procedures (e.g., Loganbill, Hardy, & Delworth, 1982) are intended to train *supervisors*. A video tape of statements made by a supervisee is played, and the supervisor-in-training responds to the supervisees statements. This mode of training is most conducive to working with groups of supervisors-in-training. The aim is to provide accurate feedback to the supervisor-in-training regarding the genuineness, empathy, and nonpossessive warmth of responses to the supervisee's statement.

Functions of the Supervisor

There are similarities and differences between supervision and psychotherapy. Many of the characteristics one values in a good therapist are similar to the characteristics of a good supervisor. Yet most would agree the supervisor should not function as a therapist to the supervisee. The supervisory focus is the interaction between the supervisee and the client. If the supervisor feels that the supervisee requires therapy, the supervisor may make that recommendation rather than provide psychotherapy within supervision.

In training settings, legal responsibility for the treatment of the client rests with the supervisor. Therefore, monitoring the care and welfare of the client is the most basic function of the supervisor. If, for example, the supervisee wishes to terminate prematurely or socialize with the client, the supervisor may decide to intervene directively in the therapy. The supervisee may learn something from a supervisor who does nothing more than monitor the client welfare because, presumably, the supervisee will learn what to do if similar situations occur in the future. However, supervision which does not include or progress to something more than monitoring the client's welfare is limited, and the supervisee will have difficulty functioning autonomously, especially in situations not encountered during supervision. Taken to its extreme, this type of supervision may become little more than therapy delivered by the supervisor, with the supervisee acting as surrogate.

The essence of supervisory function involves the growth and development of the supervisee. Loganbill, Hardy, and Delworth (1982) have conceptualized supervision as the supervisee's progression through three distinct stages. According to their conception, the supervisor enhances growth within these stages and promotes transition from one stage to the next. The interventions used by the supervisor could include: establishing an atmosphere conducive to growth; expressing warmth, liking, and respect; tying together a number of events; intervening directly; and acting as a catalyst. Aspects of the model developed by Loganbill et al. will be discussed later, with attention given to developmental issues that the supervisee confronts, and interventions that the supervisor may use in promoting transition and growth of the supervisee. In the view of this writer, it is essential that the supervisor try to establish a supportive atmosphere, one in which the anxieties of the new therapist can be kept to a minimum, one in which learning can take place, one in which mistakes are viewed as part of the learning experience.

The third function of the supervisor is the evaluation of the supervisee. The supervisee is entitled to accurate feedback regarding strengths and weaknesses, so that strengths can be used to advantage and the weaknesses improved upon.

If the supervision is within a training program, it is customary for a written evaluation to be forwarded to the academic department. The evaluation can help to integrate the placement experience with the other aspects of the training program. The contribution the supervisee has made is recognized; the supervisor gains satisfaction in the knowledge that the feedback will be useful in the overall training of the student; and the academic department is better able to program what is best for this individual student. While not often done, a collective study of all supervisory evaluations within a department is recommended to reveal need for change in training and curriculum.

A further refinement of the evaluative function of the supervisor is also possible—but carried out too infrequently—within a training program. It is common for a student to have four or more supervisors in the last few years of training. All supervisors for a supervisee could meet, perhaps once each semester, to discuss their experience with a supervisee and to determine the supervisee's strengths and weaknesses. If there is consensus on areas requiring improvement, then all supervisors could be aware of problem areas and work with the supervisee to develop in these areas. When the next meeting of that student's supervisors takes place, improvement can be noted and new issues reflecting the higher level of functioning can be identified by the supervisors.

FORMATS OF SUPERVISION

We have discussed some general issues regarding supervisory training and functions of supervisors. We will now consider some commonly used formats of supervision. These are techniques or tools that can be useful in doing supervision. Supervisors will each favor certain formats and commonly use more than one format, even within the same supervisory session. Additional formats may be found in Hart (1982) and Hess (1980).

Self-report
Self-report of the supervisee is probably the most common manner in which the supervisor learns about what has taken place in the psychotherapy session. The self-report need not be limited to what the client and supervisee said, but may also extend to the description of emotions of the client and trainee, and impressions and interpretation of what went on during the session. One form of self-report is the process note or process summary, typically written soon after the session has taken place. It is sometimes presented to a case conference where supervisor and colleagues may make a variety of interpretations and comment on what is going on between therapist and client.

Like all of the formats we will discuss, self-report has its strengths and weaknesses. It allows the supervisee the opportunity to reflect on the major points of the session and to grapple with the material, reworking it so it is coherent and makes sense from a theoretical point of view. Based on the self-report of the supervisee, the supervisor should be able to get a good idea of what went on in the therapy sessions. The supervisee's observations, distillations, and affect as the self-report is given can communicate a lot more than the content of the session. Thus, the self-report is a medium through which the supervisee and supervisor interact.

A major drawback of self-report is its potential for inaccuracy. One type of inaccuracy occurs when the supervisee intentionally distorts what has taken place. During my own internship training, I recall a fellow intern sharing with me the fact that the process notes he presented during case conferences were often fabricated in places, usually times he had made therapeutic mistakes. He justified this practice by saying that, according to his theoretical orientation and training perspective, his perceptions, impressions, and fantasies of what went on were at least as important as the reality. He also said that it was a genuine learning experience to essentially relive the session, giving a more appropriate response than the one given initially. I was not convinced of that rationale then, just as I am not now convinced. Referring again to the importance of a supportive relationship, I am struck by the lack of supportiveness that existed as I reflect on the setting; perhaps if the situation had been different, he would have felt more comfortable giving an accurate self-report.

Fortunately, the incidence of *intentional* distortion is probably rare in a supportive one-to-one supervisory situation. There are, nevertheless, distortions introduced. One supervisee may be self-effacing and another grandiose about psychotherapeutic efficacy. Naturally, the view of self will shade the manner and content of what is reported to the supervisor. Probably the most common manner in which distortion is introduced in self-report is due to misperception or to faulty judgment regarding the importance of what has been perceived. I can recall the first case of thought disorder I encountered in my own training, which I misperceived as exceptional intelligence in the client. I thought my inability to follow the client was due to her own extraordinary intelligence. Not having previous experience, I was unable to convey the true flavor of the case to my supervisors.

A typical example of distortion would be the following: The client may be 20 minutes late for several consecutive sessions, but, as the client offers a plausible excuse each time, the supervisee abandons any further working hypothesis regarding lateness. The supervisee does not share the client's tardiness with the supervisor. Some of the other supervisory formats discussed below should assist in more accurately conveying to the supervisor what went on during the therapy session.

Audio and video tape
Audio and video tapes are very useful in the conduct of psychotherapy supervision, because the supervisor need not rely on the memory and selective perception of the supervisee. However, taping represents a considerable intrusion into

the dyadic relationship of client and therapist. Discussions in supervisory and therapy sessions prior to and during taping should truly reflect the magnitude of the intrusion. Some care and thought should go into the explanation given to the supervisee and the client. Since the supervisee will usually present the idea to the client and secure the client's permission, the client's compliance is more likely if the supervisee believes taping will be useful. The client is usually told the reasons for the taping, including the fact that a more experienced person will listen to the tape. The client may want assurances regarding the safeguards to confidentiality, and is entitled to these. Some clients (e.g., the more narcissistic types) may be very receptive to taping. It's probably better *not* to record sessions of certain types of clients, (e.g., those with paranoid ideation). Since taping may require preparatory discussion with the client, one usually selects clients one expects to see for several sessions.

In my own experience as a therapist, clients have rarely objected to being recorded. It's important to convey to clients that the taping should ultimately result in better treatment, thereby benefiting them. Those objecting have typically been paranoid or had some hesitation for legal reasons (e.g., drug use, spouse beating). In the latter case, their statements could be incriminating if the tape fell into the wrong hands. When resistance is slight, complaince can often be secured by telling the client he or she is free to turn off the tape recorder if there is something he or she would prefer to discuss without being taped.

What clients sometimes imagine about the tapes is also instructive. Here's an example from personal experience: I taped a client from early in the treatment using a single tape and recording over it each week. After the treatment was underway, the client made no mention of the taping until more than a year had gone by. Then he announced that he wanted to listen to all the tapes to see how he had changed over the past year. He apparently thought that I had a tape for each of the 75 sessions that had taken place. Being somewhat narcissistic, he was disappointed to learn that the only tape was the one being used to record the current session.

As a supervisor, having supervisees tape their sessions has usually gone smoothly. There are anxieties and insecurities that must be discussed. The way in which the supervisee should approach the client should also be discussed. As with clients, more narcissistic supervisees seem to take best to taping. The anxiety of taping usually disappears within a few sessions.

There are, of course, some notable and instructive exceptions. Supervisee "resistance" to taping usually takes form in the production of inaudible tapes. In a humorous vein, I have given supervisees instructions on how to produce inaudible or nonexistent tapes: forget to bring the recorder, forget to bring the tape, sit on the microphone, mumble a lot, don't plug it in, etc. Even with instruction, it's interesting that certain supervisees consistently produce good quality recordings and others seem to have mastered, with equal facility, the ability to produce an inaudible recording!

Audio vs. video recording. Several years ago, I initiated a discussion of taping with a supervisee. The general tenor of her response was, "Why bother to use audiotape, given how little is captured on audio and how misleading audio can be?" While this response may have been indicative of her preference not to have her sessions heard, she did have a point. That point is probably best exemplified in connection with presidential debates: The majority of those hearing the Carter/Reagan debate on radio thought that Carter "won," whereas Reagan was the generally recognized winner among those viewing the debate on TV. Video tapes, then, permit the supervisor and therapist to view much of the nonverbal communication (facial expression, body language, gesticulation) which are absent from audio alone. While videotaping is superior in that it conveys the verbal as well as nonverbal aspects of the therapeutic interaction, there are some disadvantages to using video: it is more expensive; it is less portable; the equipment is more complicated to operate; it represents a greater intrusion, especially if a third person does the recording; when the session is held in a small room, it's sometimes difficult to include both therapist and client on the screen, even with a wide angle lens. Despite these disadvantages, it's probably wise for supervisors and supervisees to get experience with both types of recordings. While research has not demonstrated the superiority of either audio or videotape, preferences are commonly expressed. There is a tendency for beginning supervisees to prefer audiotape and experienced supervisees to prefer videotape (Yenawine & Arbuckle, 1971).

How to use audio or video tape. After the issues involving taping have been discussed and one has begun taping, then what? It is usually worthwhile for the supervisee to listen to or view the tape prior to supervision. Anxiety is alleviated because, upon listening, one is pleasantly surprised to learn that the tape usually did not turn out so badly as one had imaged. One approach may be to have the supervisee select important segments, problematic segments, or especially good segments to play during supervision. The supervision is more helpful if the supervisor also listens to the tape before the session, although this practice is admittedly infrequent. Probably the most common way supervision is conducted is to play back some parts of the tape, usually the first few minutes, and discuss the segment or segments. Rarely are more than about 5 minutes of session ever heard using this method within a supervisory session. While there is undoubtedly plenty of "grist for the mill" even in those few minutes, it is usually more satisfying if both hear the entire session prior to supervision.

Coaching

A technique that has been used with increasing frequency during recent years involves direct intervention by the supervisor with the supervisee while the session is in progress. Typically, the supervisor observes the session while it is taking place on closed-circuit television or through a one-way mirror. From time to time, therapeutic interventions are suggested by the supervisor via earphone, by telephone, or by speaking directly to the supervisee. While this novel technique has potential, it may also result in confusion and intrusion.

Co-therapy
One commonly used teaching or supervisory technique is the conduct of treatment with the supervisor and supervisee acting as partners in treatment. This supervisor–supervisee pairing is often used in group or family work where theoretical considerations might also recommend the use of co-therapists. While this arrangement may have many advantages such as the opportunities for modeling of therapeutic skills, the following powerful disadvantages must be taken into account: In my view, co-therapists should think of themselves as equal, should be viewed that way by the client or clients, and should complement each other. While the power relationship between co-therapists is about equally balanced, the nature of the supervisory relationship is not one of equal power. Therefore, there would appear to be much opportunity for role conflict and confusions when supervisor and supervisee are co-therapists. Having been a party to this supervisory format on a number of occasions as both supervisor and supervisee, I found it difficult for the co-therapists to be spontaneous, to be open, and to share leadership in the session and responsibility for the treatment.

Before embarking on this type of supervision, certain questions must be satisfactorily answered: How will the co-therapist relationship be portrayed to the client? When there is conflict or disagreement regarding the therapy during the co-therapy session, how will this be dealt with? Outside of treatment and in supervision, how will the same disagreements be resolved? The answer to each of these questions would seem to follow from the location of power in co-therapist and supervisory relationships.

Hart (1982) also distinguishes another form the co-therapy format may take. Supervision can be combined with co-therapy when two supervisees are co-therapists who are jointly supervised. This format lacks the pitfall of the previous format—there is no inherent hierarchical relationship between the co-therapists. As with any co-therapy relationship in which the co-therapists are equal, opportunity exists for mutual support. Part of the supervision here will deal with the tendency of the co-therapists to compete with each other for the affection, regard, and attention of the client (or clients) as well as the supervisor. One of the other challenges of this supervisory format is dealing with the relationship between co-therapists within the co-therapy, within the co-supervision, in their personal relationship.

Role playing
One of the most useful supervisory techniques, role playing, can readily be combined with self-report and/or use of audio-video recording. Role-playing, modeling, and simulation have certain aspects in common and are considered

synonymous for our purposes. Supervisor and supervisee may alternate in role playing therapist and client. Typically, the supervisor might ask the supervisee to role play the client. This gives the supervisor a feel for what the client is like, admittedly overlaid with the therapist's perception of the client. Then the supervisor might role play the therapist, with the supervisee assuming the role of the client. This provides an opportunity for the supervisor to model the intervention that could be used. When the supervisee is ready, the supervisee can role play the therapist and the supervisor role plays the client. This allows the supervisee to practice new therapeutic skills before using them with the client.

It's important that the therapist be comfortable with the way he or she is doing therapy, and role playing allows the supervisee to experiment and become comfortable with different styles before using them as a therapist. The supervisor might also wish to give feedback to the supervisee regarding how he or she might be coming across to the "client."

In training programs, role-playing, modeling, and simulation techniques may be used long before any therapy is performed by a trainee. In a very real sense, therapy "experience" is gained through these simulation techniques. Therefore, when it comes time to do therapy with a real client, the therapist is not entirely lacking in experience. Prior simulation experience reduces anxiety in the beginning clinician, improves the quality of service to the client, and addresses ethical concerns regarding prior training and experience before actual use with clients.

Simulation techniques have been used in a variety of training programs, most notably by Truax and Carkhuff (1967) in the training of the essential therapeutic ingredients of genuineness, empathy, and nonpossessive warmth. Trainees listen to therapy tapes in groups. After a client statement is made, the tape is stopped and the trainee is expected to respond to what the client has said. The trainer and group of trainees discuss the responses to the tape, and help the trainee to display the essential therapeutic ingredients by commenting on content and other aspects of the response.

In the Kent State Program (Akamatsu, 1980), a didactic presentation is followed by a videotaped modeling sequence of appropriate therapist behavior; the trainees then role play the therapeutic situation in triads. The larger group then meets to discuss general issues involving the treatment strategy and role playing. Microcounseling (Ivey, Normington, Miller, Merrill, & Haase, 1968) is a method of skill training (similar to Traux and Carkhuff) which relies heavily on modeling by the supervisor.

Vertical Supervision

Vertical supervision is a rather interesting format described and discussed by Glenwick and Stevens (1980). While the typical supervisory format has two hierarchical levels (supervisor and supervisee), vertical supervision has at least three levels. The person at the top of the hierarchy has responsibility for all those below. In a possible scenairo, one finds an experienced professional supervising an advanced peer (e.g., graduate student) who, in turn, supervises a junior peer (also a graduate student). This format has a great advantage which distinguishes it from the other formats: it directly teaches supervision. The person(s) in the middle of the hierarchy is (are) being taught to supervise those lower in the hierarchy by their own supervisors. As the therapists at the lower level gain additional training, competency, and experience, they, too, progress to peer supervisors. Vertical supervision has certain disadvantages. From my own experience as a supervisor in the middle rung of the three-tier hierarchy, I sensed a certain disappointment in my supervisees when I described the vertical arrangement to them. The supervisee at the lowest rung may feel he or she is receiving inferior or "surrogate" supervision. An insecure intermediate supervisor may find himself or herself continually striving to assert his or her competence. The main obstacle to using vertical supervision generally involves professional ethics: State regulations usually specify that psychological treatment must be provided by someone who is licensed or by persons receiving supervision from a licensed psychologist.

SUPERVISION FROM VARYING THEORETICAL PERSPECTIVES

Different psychotherapeutic orientations take different apporaches to psychotherapy supervision, and emphasize different aspects of what occurs in supervision. The psychoanalytic, client-centered, and behavioral approaches to supervision will be discussed. The rational-emotive approach is not discussed here, but good summaries of this orientation may be found in Wessler and Ellis (1980, 1983). There is probably something to be learned from each orientation. Most practitioners are eclectic (Garfield & Kurtz, 1977) and the integration of various theoretical perspectives and techniques in counseling and supervision is a valid approach (Loganbill & Hardy, 1983).

Psychoanalysis

A few of the basic concepts as applied to supervision will be discussed here. Extended discussion may be found in Moldawsky (1980), Doehrmann (1976), and Fleming and Benedek (1966). According to the psychoanalytic viewpoint, supervision is a teaching-learning process "similar to the psychoanalytic process requiring diagnosis, interpretation, and the working through of resistance by both student and teacher" (Wolberg, 1977, p. 949).

The psychoanalytic supervisor displays an analytical attitude toward the supervisee, just as the supervisee is expected to do toward the patient (client). This analytic attitude consists of listening with interest, empathy, and respect. Just as a working alliance is formed in psychoanalytic psychotherapy, a learning alliance is formed in psychoanalytic supervision. The aim of a working alliance is to get at the roots of the patient's conflicts by allowing transference to take place. Countertransference arises in the therapist. While it is fitting for the supervisor to point out countertransference, it is not appropriate for the supervisor to help the supervisee work through or get at the roots of the countertransference. Were he or she to do so, the supervisor would be engaging in psychotherapy rather than supervision. Instead, it is recommended that the supervisee work out the countertransferential issues in personal therapy or in his or her own psychoanalysis. Which brings us to another hallmark of psychoanalytic supervision—personal therapy or psychoanalysis of the supervisee is often a requirement. Most analytic training programs and analytic institutes either strongly encourage or require that the trainees (candidates) themselves be in psychoanalysis.

Anxiety is a central concept in Freudian theory and the supervisee can expect to feel anxious when conflict arises within. The supervisor and supervisee join in their alliance to uncover what is causing the anxiety (e.g., countertransferential issues). Another caveat is that the supervisor must also work with the supervisee to avoid having the supervisee "lead" the patient to do what serves the fantasies of the supervisee. For example, a sub-assertive supervisee may subtly encourage aggressive acting out in the patient.

Parallel process is the term used to indicate that the supervisee—supervisor behavioral interaction in supervision reflects the patient—supervisee behavioral interaction in treatment. According to Doehrmann (1976), parallel process also works in the reverse direction: the problems in the supervisory relationship can also become manifest in (be reflected in) the therapeutic relationship. One of the first supervisory experiences I had was that of co-supervisor of a group of third-year graduate students in clinical psychology. What we tried to do in that group was work with certain analytic concepts like transference and resistance. We tried to draw parallels between the therapeutic interaction and the supervisory interaction. When the case presentation had aspects of resistance, we often were able to draw parallels to supervisees' resistance. The effects of termination experienced by the clients on the therapy had similar effects upon the trainees, who were also terminating their graduate careers. Sometimes even the mood of the group would reflect that of the client whose case was being presented. In that it was easy to share communalities and draw parallels among the client interactions of the 10 group members, we truly had parallel process going on. This supervisory group was reputed to be an extremely beneficial and enjoyable part of graduate training.

Client-Centered Therapy

Interestingly, Rogers (1975) wrote some of the earliest work on supervision. Good expositions of the client-centered approach to supervision may be found in Rice (1980) and Patterson (1983). We will first review some aspects of the client-centered approach, and then discuss supervision. Underlying the client-centered approach is the view of the person as basically good and worthwhile because he or she exists. There are two major theoretical emphases: a theory of process and a theory of relationship (Rogers, 1957, 1975). The theory of process refers to the client's self-exploration. It's the therapist's job to facilitate this process in the client by focusing on the client's process and by responding and commenting so as to allow the client to further his or her own self-exploration, to follow the path he or she has begun to follow. The client's process of self-exploration is furthered by the types of remarks the therapist makes and by the style of the therapist. According to Rogers (1975), earlier emphasis on the theory of process had a major pitfall, however. There was a tendency to emphasize technique, to say the right thing at the time, like a machine. To avoid this misconception of what client-centered therapy is all about, Rogers began stressing his theory of relationship. While the relationship between therapist and client is necessarily limited, it is nevertheless a *real* (genuine) relationship. Having this type of relationship should result in personal growth. In addition to having a real relationship with the client, the client-centered therapist strives to display the therapeutic ingredients of *unconditional positive regard* and *congruence*. Unconditional positive regard is simply an affirmation of the person's inherent value, the basis of the Rogerian view of the person mentioned previously. Congruence refers to the ability of the therapist to be consistent in what he or she feels, does, and says to the client.

The client-centered approach attempts to engender or increase the therapeutic ingredient in the supervisee by encouraging listening to clients, taping of sessions, and responding to the client. Therapist and supervisor listen to the tapes for the client's self-exploration, noting when it was facilitated or impeded by the therapist's remarks. The supervisor gives feedback regarding the moment-to-moment process.

Because the client-centered approach views the person as innately good, there is the belief that the client will imporve if left to his or her own devices. Therefore, when no progress is being made, there is a tendency for the therapist to blame him or herself for the lack of progress. To counteract this intropunitiveness, Rice (1980) suggests that the supervisor assume a neutral or impunitive stance, "letting the tape speak for itself."

While it is acknowledged that supervision is more of a didactic process than therapy, the supervisor demonstrates unconditional positive regard and congruence toward the supervisee. Yet Rice (1980) notes there are times when the supervisor must appraise the supervisee or suggest termination from a training program, realities that should be discussed openly with the student. Rice advises that evaluation of the supervisee be kept to a minimum.

The group training programs like those by Truax and Carkhuff (1967) and Ivey et al. (1968) are strongly associated with the client-centered approach, and often a good way for the novice to learn the client-centered approach.

Behavior Therapy

While every orientation would acknowledge that there is a learning component involved in supervision, behavior therapy highlights the fact that supervision aims to help the supervisee learn to do therapy. Paralleling the aim of behavioral therapy, the aim of behavioral supervision may be stated as follows: To modify certain responses in the supervisee by systematically applying certain behavioral principles (Levine & Tilker, 1974; Lloyd & Whitehead, 1976).

The salient characteristics of behavioral supervision are well explicated by Linehan (1980). The procedures used by a behavioral supervisor might include "response rehearsal, systematic feedback, reinforcement, shaping of responses and even relaxation or systematic desensitization" (Linehan, 1980, p. 151). The goals or focus of supervision are "modification or strengthening of specified behavioral patterns which the trainee engages in" (p. 152), with little emphasis on personal growth in the trainee. There is a strong emphasis on experimental methodology which, according to Yates (1970), is one of the features distinguishing behavioral treatment from other approaches. There is also a strong emphasis on the idiographic approach: "What works with this particular client?" The supervisor then helps the supervisee become more empirical in working with the client. The supervisor must use an effective procedure with a *particular* trainee working with a *particular* client; therefore, the supervisor assumes an idiographic, empirical approach to the supervisee. Whenever conflict results between supervisor and supervisee over the approach, Linehan suggests resolving the conflict by collecting data to determine which approach is most effective.

The behavioral approach to supervision does not emphasize the importance of the relationship that develops between supervisor and supervisee, but Ullman and Krasner (1965) suggest that there is no reason why behavioral supervision should be devoid of personal warmth. As training of behavior therapists is viewed as learning or skill training, the behavioral orientation places less of an emphasis on supervision. The skills could be learned about as well, and perhaps more efficiently, in the classroom, in a seminar, or from a book.

The approach to evaluation of the supervisee is usually limited to an evaluation of the skills of the supervisee. This evaluation is accomplished by examining the behavioral change in the client. If the client's behavior is not modified, it means that the treatment procedure used by the supervisee was not correct. The interested reader may consult Hosford and Barmann's (1983) excellent summary of the social learning approach to supervision.

A MODEL OF SUPERVISION

One of the most novel, interesting, and useful models of supervision is that of Loganbill et al. (1982), who posit what is basically a developmental model. The model is useful, regardless of the theoretical orientations. This work was alluded to previously in discussing the functions of the supervisor. According to this model, there are certain issues that repeatedly arise in supervision. In confronting each issue, the supervisee passes through the three distinct stages, called Stagnation, Confusion, and Integration.

Developmental Issues

The following eight developmental issues of Loganbill et al. are adaptations of Arthur Chickering's (1969) vectors of development.

1. *Competence* is the ability to use and master techniques and skills. This is probably the most basic issue in that, unless there is a certain level of competence, the supervisee may not be afforded the opportunity to engage in any psychotherapeutic or counseling endeavor. The competence of the trainee is one of the first things the supervisor will wish to assess as the supervisory relationship is established.

2. *Emotional awareness* is the ability to be aware of one's feelings and to know oneself. The supervisee should be able to recognize, accept, and use his or her feelings in the therapeutic situation.

3. *Autonomy* is the genuine feeling that one is independent and can make one's own choices and decisions. When one begins working as a therapist, it is quite common to feel that what one is doing simply reflects every course in counseling and psychotherapy ever taken, and that one is merely parrotting one's supervisor. Supervisees, even beginning supervisees, must deal with this issue. There are two rather obvious ways in which autonomy can create problems: the supervisee may wish to assume more autonomy than is appropriate for the level of training, or the supervisee may wish the supervisors to make all choices and decisions.

4. *Identity* usually refers to a sense of wholeness or oneness with respect to one's theoretical orientation as a psychologist. An eclectic identity need not be a source of concern so long as there is a sense of synthesis and wholeness.

5. *Respect for individual differences* refers to tolerance and acceptance of others and the ability to be nonjudgmental. This issue has similarities to Rogers' unconditional positive regard and Chickering's idea of freeing interpersonal relationships.

6. *Purpose and direction* refers to setting goals and appropriateness of those goals. The therapist necessarily takes into account the characteristics of the client and the client's situation. This issue may be contrasted with the previous issue, because maladaptive behaviors (which both client and counselor should view negatively) are referred to here, whereas "respect for individual differences" refers to an abiding respect in the basic human qualities (adaptive) of the client.

7. *Personal motivation* refers to the reasons why the beginning counselor chose to enter the field. Loganbill et al. discuss six general areas of motivation: intimacy, power, financial, personal growth, intellectual, and altruism. Each of these motivations can be healthy or unhealthy. For example, an intellectual motivation to do counseling because of a fascination with psychological process and finding out about people, or to gain knowledge of the field is quite healthy: less healthy would be motives which disregard the human aspects of counseling but which assess, categorize, and look dispassionately at the client in a depersonalizing fashion.

8. *Professional ethics* are standards or values espoused by a field and to which members of that group are expected to adhere. Supervisees must internalize the values that society, in its laws, and relevant professional associations, have set out. The supervisor can be instrumental in explaining and discussing professional issues to the supervisee.

According to this model, the individual moves along three stages (Stagnation, Confusion, and Integration) with respect to each of the supervisory issues discussed above. Let's take issues of personal motivation as an example: unhealthy motivation may not be recognized in the Stagnation stage; in the Confusion stage, the supervisee recognizes the motivation, but may become frightened or ashamed in reaction to the recognition of motives; in the Integration stage, the supervisee is aware of motivations and uses them constructively. If there are unhealthy motivations in the last stage (Integration), they are conscious and monitored.

Enhancing Growth and Promoting Transition

Within the conceptualization of this model, the supervisor's function is to enhance growth within stages and promote transition to the highest stage—Integration. Various interventions may be used by the supervisor to enhance growth and promote transition. Loganbill et al. discuss five types of interventions: facilitative, confrontive, conceptual, prescriptive, and catalytic.

Facilitative interventions should give the supervisee a sense of personal security, trust, or unconditional positive regard, and reduce anxiety so that he or she may develop of his or her own accord.

Confrontive interventions highlight discrepancies such as those between what the supervisee says and does, between feelings and behavior, or between supervisees interpretation and what the supervisor perceives. The idea is that, once the supervisor has pointed out the discrepancy, a state of dissonance will ensue in the supervisee and the supervisee will be motivated to bring about a situation of consonance.

Conceptual interventions allow the supervisor to offer a conceptual or theoretical framework, theories, and principles to the supervisee. Sometimes the conceptual issues are offered by the supervisor and the supervisee acts in accordance with these principles; at other times, the supervisee's conduct may exemplify a principle and the supervisor can in a sense "hang" a theory on what the supervisee has done. Conceptual interventions are especially useful in moving from the Confusion stage to the Integration stage. Conceptual interventions permit the supervisee to have some theoretical or conceptual basis for the therapy rather than to conduct it in a vacuum. The internalization of concepts and theory is learning which the therapist takes with him or her in the treatment of the next client.

Prescriptive interventions consist of telling the supervisee what to do. They would include setting up a treatment plan and telling the supervisee to eliminate behaviors, e.g., hugging the client. While prescriptive interventions are generally geared to maintenance of the client welfare, they often are counterproductive to the natural growth of the trainee.

Catalytic interventions promote change and movement. By questioning, probing, exploring, and raising issues in select areas, the supervisor can be a catalyst. Through catalytic interventions, the supervisor can make the counselor aware of client improvement and may encourage the counselor to experiment with a variety of therapeutic roles.

LEGAL AND ETHICAL ISSUES

Previously, we talked about professional ethics as an issue with which the supervisee must deal. There are also ethical and legal issues of which the supervisor must be cognizant. Excellent discussions of the legal and ethical issues in clinical supervision may be found in Cormier and Bernard (1982) and Slovenko (1980).

The supervisor has ethical and legal responsibilities to both client and supervisee. According to American Psychological Association ethical standards (1981), supervisors accord informed choice and confidentiality to their supervisees. They avoid exploiting the trust and dependency of their supervisee, and avoid dual relationships which might impair their professional judgment or increase the risk of exploitation.

Supervisees have a right to know about training objectives, procedures, expectations, goals, and criteria for evaluation. The right to periodic feedback and evaluation is especially important if the feedback to the supervisee is negative. One implication of confidentiality of the trainee is that the supervisor should tell the trainee the extent to which aspects of supervision will be discussed within the training program or within the clinical/counseling facility.

Dual relationships place the supervisee in a position of diminished consent. The supervisor will want to avoid entering into any sort of a dual relationship with the supervisee, because the supervisor's own role is diminished, because the client's welfare may suffer, and because it may cloud the supervisor's objectivity. One type of dual relationship involves sexual contact, and the special nature of the supervisory relationship seems to make the supervisory relationship susceptible. Sexual activity between psychologist and supervisee are considered unethical according to American Psychological Association (1981) standards.

A more common type of dual relationship involves the personal counseling of the supervisee. American Personnel and Guidance Association (APGA, 1981) and Association for Counselor Education and Supervision (ACES, 1973) ethical standards support the position that personal counseling of a trainee should be conducted by someone other than a supervisor, especially if the supervisor is also a faculty member. As mentioned previously, if the need for therapy is apparent, it is appropriate to make a referral.

The legal responsibilities of the supervisor to the client are quite weighty, and should give pause to anyone supervising. Suits against supervisors are much more commonly brought by clients than by supervisees. W̶ standards state that the client should be informed that the supervised, it is not my experience that this information is ty̶p̶ clients unless they specifically ask. The superivsor may wish to meet ̶w̶ client, because there have been times when supervisors have been faulted for not actually making contact with clients (cf. Slovenko, 1980). Of course, the supervisor, too, is bound to preserve the confidentiality of the client.

The ethical issue having the most far-reaching implications is the doctrine of vicarious liability, whereby the supervisors are ultimately legally responsible for the actions of their supervisees and the welfare of their supervisees' clients. This doctrine of vicarious responsibility is far reaching; according to it, the supervisor might be held responsible for premature termination, negligent referrals, or a supervisee having sex with the client. The supervisor assumes responsibility much as if the client were under his or her own care. According to Slovenko (1980), there would be little justification in assigning partly-trained students to clients unless the locus of clinical responsibility rests squarely on the shoulders of the supervisor.

The supervisor can protect him or herself by being familiar with every case of every supervisee and by having documentation (notes) to that effect (cf. Cormier & Bernard, 1982). If a counselor is not able to deal adequately with a particular case, more supervision may be required or referral of the client to a different counselor may be indicated. If the trainee is not competent, the supervisor may not agree to be responsible. It is important for a facility to be knowledgable about the limitations of the trainees sent by academic departments, just as it is important for the agency to be able to accept or reject trainees sent by academic departments. Professional liability insurance covering both supervisor and supervisee is advisable.

SUMMARY AND CONCLUSIONS

To supervise is a privilege and a responsibility which represents one of the highest levels of functioning in clinical and counseling psychology. The supervisor's primary function is promotion of professional growth and development in the supervisee, while simultaneously guarding the welfare of the client and adhering to a code of professional ethics. Supervision within the Behavioral, Psychoanalytic, and Client-centered approaches was discussed to enable the reader to decide on which approach or combination of approaches he or she wishes to incorporate. Despite controversy regarding the superiority of eclecticism or theoretical purity, the Loganbill et al.'s model of supervision is applicable regardless of theoretical orientation. Supervisor and supervisees will have to deal with issues involving the supervisee's competence, emotional awareness, purpose and direction, etc. Working with and through these issues is the essence of supervision. Establishment of a warm, supportive atmosphere by the supervisor is essential. The formats one chooses are largely dependent on one's personal preferences—what one has been exposed to, what seemed to work best in one's own experience as a trainee or supervisor.

REFERENCES

Akamatsu, T. J. (1980). The use of role-play and simulation techniques in the training of psychotherapy. In A. K. Hess (Ed.), *Psychotherapy supervision: Theory, research, and practice.* New York: John Wiley & Sons.

American Personnel and Guidance Association. (1981). *Ethical standards.* Falls Church, VA: APGA.

Association for Counselor Education and Supervision. (1973) *Standards for the preparation of counselors and other personnel services specialists.* Washington, DC: APGA.

American Psychological Association. (1981). Ethical principles of psychologists. *American Psychologist, 36,* 633–638.

Bartlett, W. E., Goodyear, R. K., & Bradley, F. O. (1983). Guest Editors' Introduction. *The Counseling Psychologist, 11*(1), 1.

Chickering, A. W. (1969). *Education and identity.* San Francisco: Jossey-Bass.

Cormier, L. S., & Bernard, J. M. (1982). Ethical and legal responsibilities of clinical supervisors. *The Personnel and Guidance Journal, 60,*486–490.

Doehrmann, M. J. G. (1976). Parallel processes in supervision and psychotherapy. *Bulletin of the Menninger Clinic,* 40(1).

Fleming, J., & Benedek, T. (1966). *Psychoanalytic supervision.* New York: Grune and Stratton.

Garfield, S. L., & Kurtz, R. A study of eclectic views. (1977). *Journal of Consulting and Clinical Psychology, 45,* 78–83.

Glenwick, D. S., & Stevens, E. (1980). Vertical supervision. In A. K. Hess (Ed.), *Psychotherapy supervision: theory, research, and practice.* New York: John Wiley & Sons.

Hart, G. M. (1982). *The process of clinical supervision.* Baltimore: University Park Press.

Hess, A. K. (Ed.). (1980). *Psychotherapy supervision: theory, research, and practice.* New York: John Wiley & Sons.

Hosford, R. E., & Barmann, B. (1983). A social learning approach to counselor supervision. *The Counseling Psychologist, 11*(1), 51–58.

Ivey, A. E., Normington, C. J., Miller, D. C., Merrill, W. H., & Haase, R. F. (1968). Microcounseling and attending behavior: An approach to prepracticum counselor training. *Journal of Counseling Psychology, 15,* (Monogr. Suppl. 5).

Levine, F. M., Tilker, H. A. (1974, Summer). A behavioral modification approach to supervision of psychotherapy. *Psychotherapy: Theory, Research and Practice, 11*(2), 182–188.

Linehan, M. M. (1980). Supervision of behavior therapy. In A. K. Hess (Ed.) *Psychotherapy supervision: theory, research, and practice.* New York: John Wiley & Sons.

Lloyd, M. E., & Whitehead, J. S. (1976). Development and evaluation of behaviorally taught practica. In S. Yen and R. W. McIntire (Eds.), *Teaching behavior modification.* Kalamazoo, MI: Behaviordelia.

Loganbill, C., Hardy, E., & Delworth, U. (1982). Supervision: a conceptual model. *The Counseling Psychologist, 10*(1), 3–42.

Loganbill, C., & Hardy, E. (1983). In defense of eclecticism. *The Counseling Psychologist, 11*(1), 79.

Moldawsky, S. (1980). Psychoanalytic Psychotherapy supervision. In A. K. Hess (Ed.). *Psychotherapy supervision: theory, research, and practice.* New York: John Wiley & Sons.

Patterson, C. H., (1983). A client-centered approach to supervision. *The Counseling Psychologist, 11* (1), 21–25.

Rice, L. N. (1980). A client-centered approach to the supervision of psychotherapy. In A. K. Hess (Ed.), *Psychotherapy supervision: theory, research, and practice.* New York: John Wiley & Sons.

Rogers, C. R. (1957). Training individuals to engage in the therapeutic process. In C. R. Strothers (Ed.), *Psychology and mental health.* Washington, DC: American Psychological Association.

Rogers, C. R. (1975). Empathic: An unappreciated way of being. *The Counseling Psychologist, 5,* 2–9.

Slovenko, R. (1980). Legal issues in psychotherapy supervision. In A. K. Hess (Ed.), *Psychotherapy supervision: theory, research, and practice.* New York: John Wiley & Sons.

Truax, C. B., & Carkhuff, R. R. (1967). *Toward effective counseling and psychotherapy: Training and practice.* Chicago: Aldine.

Ullman, L. P., & Krasner, L. (Eds.). (1965). *Case studies in behavior modification.* New York: Holt, Rinehart and Winston.

Wessler, R. L., & Ellis, A. (1980). Supervision in rationale-emotive therapy. In A. K. Hess (Ed.), *Psychotherapy supervision: theory, research, and practice.* New York: John Wiley and Sons.

Wessler, R. L., & Ellis, A. (1983). Supervision in counseling rationale-emotive therapy. *The Counseling Psychologist, 11*(1), 43–49.

Wolberg, L. R. (1977). *The technique of psychotherapy, Part 2.* New York: Grune and Stratton.

Yates, A. J. (1970). *Behavior therapy.* New York: Wiley.

Yenawine, G., & Arbuckle, D. S. (1971). Study of the use of videotape and audiotape as techniques in counselor education. *Journal of Counseling Psychology, 18,* 1–6.

Chapter 5

Consultation

Judith L. Alpert
Jody Boghossian Spencer
New York University

INTRODUCTION

The field of psychological consultation is diverse. Psychological consultants offer diverse services to a variety of consultee organizations. However, despite the diversity, the stages in consultation are stable.

The primary focus of this chapter concerns the stages of consultation. These will be explored through a consideration of four excerpts from student consultants cases. Most of these cases focus on schools. In addition, at the beginning of the chapter there will be a brief consideration of the history of consultation, definition of consultation, consultation models, and internal versus external consultation.

History of Consultation Practice

Psychological consultation developed in response to mental health practitioners' increasing dissatisfaction with the traditional clinical approaches of psychodiagnosis and psychotherapy. This disenchantment began at the end of W.W. II, when the numbers of people in need of psychological services became too numerous. At this time, mental health practitioners realized that means other than the traditional and individual clinical approaches were needed to meet the enormous demands for psychological services. The traditional emphasis on individual clients was perceived as an unaffordable luxury. There was a need for mental health professionals to move from the medical and psychiatric settings to the community in order to share their training.

Gerald Caplan was one of the first mental health practitioners to make such a pioneering effort. In the early fifties, he and the late Erich Lindemann, both psychiatrists, established contact with the Wellesley Public Schools in order to do research on classroom screening of disturbed children. While in classrooms, they were interrupted by questions from teachers. Quite by accident, then, they realized that teachers were eager to talk with them and that they could enhance a teacher's understanding of child problems by means of discussion. This realization led to one of the first systematic provisions of consultation services.

A second major influence on psychological consultation is Seymour Sarason, a clinical psychologist. Sarason was dissatisfied with the limited and restrictive nature of traditional medical and psychiatric settings, feeling that these facilities provided few of the preventative and early identification services which communities needed. In response, Sarason developed the Psycho-Educational Clinic at Yale University. This clinic's function was one of exploring new means of providing community mental health services. Early on, Sarason and his staff recognized the potentialities of the school setting for preventive mental health work. The clinic staff began to talk with teachers and administrators about understanding and coping with difficult children. Sarason, like Caplan, tried to alter the teacher's perception of a problem in order to make the teacher better able to support a student. However, while Caplan focused on the teacher's unconscious negative activity, Sarason focused on problems inherent in the teacher's role and setting. These two approaches, one psychodynamic and the other social psychological, provided the foundation for contemporary psychological consultation.

In the years since these earliest attempts at providing indirect mental health services, the field of psychological consultation has grown. Presently, consultants provide numerous indirect services to a variety of social service and other organizations.

Definition of Consultation

Mental health consultation is the process in which the mental health professional assists another, called the consultee, regarding clients for whom the latter has responsibility. In school, the clients are students, whereas the consultees are teachers, administrators, aides, or other school staff.

Mental health consultation involves indirect activity around particular individuals. The consultant hears about and sometimes observes a client. Then he or she works with staff to find some way of dealing with the client. Mental health consultation is treatment oriented in that it involves treatment, although indirectly, to clients who are having problems. It also is prevention oriented in that, it is assumed, the consultee's increased learning will result in changes in attitude and behavior that will prevent future problems. Although it is possible that through such meetings organizational change may result, the mental health consultant's primary goal is not to alter the system. Rather, the consultant attempts to work within it and to help consultees more effectively toward meeting client's mental health needs.

Client-centered case consultation and consultee-centered case consultation differ with respect to focus. In client-centered consultation, the focus is on assessing the client's difficulty. The goal here is to help the consultee find a way to most effectively deal with the handling of a client. It involves giving the consultee information to enable problem resolution. In consultee-centered consultation, the focus is on understanding why a consultee is having difficulty dealing with a client and how he/she may be contributing to the problem. The distinction between client-centered and consultee-centered case consultation breaks down in practice. Usually, cases require both types of consultation, although a consultee may not experience the shift in consultation focus.

Models of Consultation
As the field of mental health consultation has developed, so too have methods and models of consultation. Most prominent among the consultation models are the mental health, behavioral, and organizational approaches. The consultation models differ in theoretical orientation, goals, and methods. As a result, they provide the consultant with options from which to choose how to best meet the needs of a consultee organization. A very brief description of each of these consultative models follows. For a much more in-depth review, see Caplan (1970), Gallessich (1982), and Meyers, Alpert, and Fleisher (1983).

The behavioral model has roots in social learning theory, and is the most case specific of the models. It focuses primarily on an investigation of a client's behaviors and the antecedent and consequent conditions for behavior. The goal of behavioral consultation concerns extinguishing or reducing the frequency of undesirable behaviors in order that they can be replaced with more desirable and appropriate ones.

In contrast to behavioral consultation, the goal of mental health consultation, which has roots in personality theory and concerns the consultee, is to extend and enhance a consultee's knowledge and skills base so the consultee cannot only handle the present difficulties but also prevent or effectively prepare for such difficulties in the future.

Finally, the focus of the organizational model involves improving the functioning of the consultee organization. Consequently, this type of consultation involves various aspects of the system or the entire system. Efforts may be made, for example, to improve the consultee organization's decision-making strategies or communication patterns so that the organization can begin to operate more effectively and responsively.

In sum, the type of service which each of these models advocates differ, and these differences provide the consultant with options for consultative activity.

Internal versus External Consultation
Consultants differ not only in the particular emphasis they give their indirect service but also in the type of employment relationship they establish with the consultee organization. At one extreme, a consultant may be hired as an internal or in-house consultant, and be employed by the consultee organization on a full-time and on-going basis. At the other extreme, a consultant may be hired on a part-time basis, and be available to offer services for only a short duration. Of course, there are other combinations of consulting schedules which mediate

these two extremes. However, the extremes indicate the range of internality—externality to the consultee system. These variations carry with them distinct and different advantages and disadvantages.

The first distinction—that of system knowledge—seems to place the internal consultant at an advantage. The internal consultant typically is much more knowledgeable about the organization than an external consultant, an outsider, would be. As a result, the internal consultant more likely has a greater understanding of the context and background of problems, and is more aware of the system resources. On the other hand, an internal consultant may be more susceptible to the lack of objectivity which often accompanies status as a full fledged member of the consultee system. Therefore, in this regard, an external consultant may have an advantage and may be more able to see the system as it is.

A second distinction focuses on degree of the consultant's vested interests. Here the internal consultant, probably at a disadvantage, has an investment in system maintenance rather than system change or, alternatively, an investment in system change that is consistent with self interest. As an outsider, an external consultant may be less personally invested in the consultee organization and, as such, may be more willing to help affect system change. Changing a system involves some risk, and an internal consultant may be less willing to take risks that involve the system upon which he/she depends.

A third distinction concerns the consultant's degree of accountability to the system. Typically, the internal consultant feels more accountable and responsibile to the system. As a result, the internal consultant may be more cautious than the external counterpart. The internal consultant may avoid risky interventions, and only be willing to focus attention on projects with a high probability of success. Although this can often be disadvantageous, it also can be advantageous in that changes which are not forced too quickly onto the consultee system may have the potential for longer-lasting success. The external consultant, on the other hand, bears the burdens of responsibility and accountability less directly, and, consequently, may be more willing to take risks. Sometimes this is appropriate and advantageous. However, when the external consultant's eagerness to affect change is mixed with a denial of any direct responsibility for it, this may leave the consultee organization feeling like the victim of a hit-and-run accident.

The fourth and final distinction focuses on the consultant's legitimacy. The internal consultant's greater availability to the system and longer association with it may facilitate the consultant's credibility and legitimacy. However, in some cases, stability and familiarity may be detrimental , as familiarity may make consultees feel less comfortable and more vulnerable about the prospects of problem sharing. On the other hand, both the anonymity and the glamour of the outside expert can be very appealing, and can result in the external consultant being awarded attention and expertise not given to the more familiar internal consultant.

Stages of Consultation

Any consultative process, no matter what the model nor who the consultant, is comprised of a series of stages. While these stages do not necessarily follow in a neat invariant order, and instead often overlap and interact, they act as the core of any consultative practice. As a result, the issues and concerns which they raise must be addressed by all consultants, regardless of their expertise or experience.

The first and perhaps most difficult stage in the consulting process is that of entry into the consultee system. Entry sets the tone for the development of the consulting relationships which will follow. Entry may be by invitation from the system, or it may be by initiation from the consultant. In either case, the entry phase demands that the consultant dedicate time to assessing and understanding the values and dynamics of the consultee system, so that an initial contract of mutual acceptability can be negotiated and consulting relationships can be initiated.

The second stage of the consultative process is diagnosis. The stage involves exploring the nature of a consultee's presenting problem and investigating the factors influencing it. The intervention stage overlaps and may cycle simultaneously with the diagnostic stage. This stage focuses both on solving the consultee's immediate problem and on fostering consultee growth. Finally, there is the stage of evaluation. Although this stage is often neglected, it can be as important as the entry stage. It is concerned with assessing the degree to which the goals of the consultant's intervention have been achieved, and acts as a gauge against which future consultative attempts can be measured. This stage often signals the termination of the consultative relationship. As a result, the consultant must be conscious of its timing, its gradual approach, and the careful altering of the consultee as this phase draws near.

In the following sections of this paper, case study material, modified from the actual experiences of several student-consultants, will be presented. This material highlights some of the issues associated with the stages. Rather than providing the reader with an exhaustive review of the issues associated with each stage, the following consideration should throw light on the complexities of the consultation process. For the reader interested in a more in-depth analysis of consultation, the following references are recommended: Alpert (1982); Alpert and Meyers (1983); Caplan (1970); Gallessich (1982); Meyers, Parsons, and Martin (1979); and Sarason, Levine, Goldenberg, Cherlin, & Bennett (1966).

ENTRY

Case Study

Initially, Liza Hodges was enthusiastic about her consultation course field placement. The Fieldstone School had a reputation as an innovative private high school which tailored its offerings to the needs of its students.

The reports Liza received from previous student-consultants at the school supported this reputation. Liza was delighted by the prospect of spending one day a week as the Fieldstone psychological consultant-in-training. "I saw this as a chance to really roundout my experience. I had lots of previous school-based experiences, and had even functioned as a learning disabilities consultant for several years. However, all these experiences were in very traditional public school settings. I welcomed the chance to become involved in a setting which seemed to be receptive to innovation and change."

Liza's on-site supervisor was Fieldstone's new school psychologist, and, in the weeks prior to Fieldstone's September opening, Liza established contact with her. It was Liza's opinion that these initial meetings with Fieldstone's new school psychologist had gone fairly smoothly. "She seemed to understand that my role was to be one of providing indirect rather than direct service, and said that she would do what she could to facilitate my entry in this capacity. However, she seem relieved that I was not a novice consultant and that Fieldstone's teachers were not novice consultees, because, as the new school psychologist, these initial weeks of school were going to be hectic ones for her."

Liza's introduction to the Fieldstone School and its faculty and staff took place at the initial faculty meeting of the school year. Liza's impressions of that meeting were vivid. "In reality, the assembling of the Fieldstone staff for that first faculty meeting was more like the reuniting of a large, closely knit family than a group of professional colleagues. I was immediately struck with how comfortable most of the staff seemed to feel about airing their own professional and personal opinions." In addition, Liza was impressed with how freely the faculty both supported and challenged each other.

However, it was also Liza's impression that this close knit family style seemed to be fostered and even encouraged by the indirect leadership style of Fieldstone's principal. During the first faculty meeting, Ms. Woods, or Helen as she was called by staff and students, seated herself in the midst of her faculty rather than in front, and deferred the actual running of the meeting to other members of her staff. However, as the meeting ensued, Liza became aware that, despite the principal's indirect style, "Helen managed to keep a pretty tight rein on the meeting's essentials. This she did by allowing her opinion to be known at timely junctures in the meeting's proceedings."

Liza felt that the Fieldstone faculty had been warmly receptive to her brief introduction as a student-consultant. "This faculty had had previous experience with student-consultants. As a result, they understood that my placement at Fieldstone would not be dedicated to the traditional testing and evaluating of students, but instead would involve enhancing students' school experiences indirectly, through collaborative work with them."

Liza spent her first several days at Fieldstone becoming familiar with the school, its staff, and its students. She visited classrooms, drank coffee in the cafeteria which the faculty shared with the student body, and became a fixture in the main office, where teachers, for lack of a teachers' lounge, tended to congregate.

On the second day, Liza ran into Helen, Fieldstone's principal. Helen greeted Liza warmly and invited her into her office. Liza described the principal as interested in how she was finding the school. Liza responded enthusiastically and expressed her eagerness to start offering her services. It was Liza's opinion that "Helen immediately latched onto my eagerness by mentioning a problem that she was having with the new English teacher." The principal explained that she felt this new teacher was not meeting the needs of his ninth grade students, and lamented that, although she offered him suggestions, she felt he viewed her as intrusive.

It was Liza's impression that the principal's concern was sincere and that her classroom advice was sound and specific. Around this issue, Liza enthusiastically agreed. "Helen was so eager for my input that I sensed she wanted me to go right up to this teacher's class to observe." However, Liza explained that she was more comfortable establishing a friendly contact first outside of this teacher's classroom and then asking permission to come and observe. It was Liza's opinion that she would function more effectively if she had the chance to meet the teacher on neutral territory first. Liza described this approach as acceptable to Helen.

Liza's first meeting with the teacher, David, occurred by chance in the school cafeteria. Liza was struck by how willingly this teacher discussed his disillusionment around teaching. "Daivd divulged the difficulties he was having with his ninth grade class, and, when I offered my services, he accepted. Before I knew it, I had gained entry to his classroom."

Liza's observations of David's ninth grade class confirmed that he was having trouble. "The class was rowdy and David had difficulty keeping them on task." Liza made appointments with both David and Helen to discuss her observations and offer suggestions. David, however, remained unaware of Liza's initial discussion with the principal and the continuing conferences between Liza and Helen.

In the weeks that followed, the pattern remained the same. Liza observed and conferred with David and then discussed material from the observation and meeting with the principal. Liza admitted she began to feel uncomfortable about the arrangement. "David and I were establishing a good collaborative relationship and he was beginning to turn his ninth grade class around." However, the progress was slow and Helen soon became impatient with what she assessed as a hopeless situation. Helen complained that she continued to receive negative reports from David's ninth grade students, and threatened that if things did not change quickly she would be "forced to take desperate action."

Liza began to realize that she had erred by agreeing to act as the principal's agent, and was uncertain how she could rectify the situation.

Discussion: Entry Issues and Concerns
Entry into any organizational system as a consultant may be the most difficult and the most important phase in the consultative process. As a result, it cannot and should not be rushed. The way a consultant handles entry sets the emotional

tone and provides the contractual foundation for all the consultative relationships which follow. The case study above illustrates poor entry with respect to making preliminary contacts with the consultee organization, negotiating a contract with the consultee system, understanding the culture of the consultee organization, negotiating sanctions throughout the system's hierarchy, and establishing individual consultee contracts, as will be described more fully below.

Making Preliminary Contacts with the Consultee Organization

Entry may be conceptualized as a stage of substages. The first substage involves establishing initial contact with the consultee organization, and this initial contact can take many forms. In the case above, initial contact consisted of a preliminary meeting with the on-site supervisor, the school psychologist, and a general introduction at the first faculty meeting of the year. While these initial contacts are appropriate, and attendance at faculty and staff meetings is an effective means by which to become familiar with an organization, these contacts alone are insufficient. Any initial contacts with the consultee organization should also include a personal contact with the organization's chief administrator(s), which, in this case, is the school's principal. It does not matter how or at what level the consultant came into the consultee organization. Such direct contact remains critical. The consultant here assumed that, because her graduate program had been in contact with the principal and had discussed placement arrangements with her, she could postpone her own direct contact with the principal. Thus the consultant erred by not establishing contact with the principal initially and by not defining how she would and would not work.

Negotiating a Contract with the Consultee System

The first contractual agreement which the consultant negotiates is with the consultee organization as a whole. This contract need not be a formal legally worded document. In fact, usually it is a verbal agreement which places some general parameters on the consultant's role in the consultee organization. Novice consultants are often confused about the nature of this general contract. They wonder how they can contract for what they will or will not do without understanding the system and how they fit into it. However, the initial contract need not be very specific, and may, in fact, say more about what the consultant will not do than what the consultant will do. This contract is important. From the very beginning, it is the consultant's responsibility to provide the consultee organization with information on the range and limitations of the services which the consultant is willing to provide. Most important, the consultant needs to clarify that the relationship between a consultant and a consultee is confidential, and evaluation is not a task which the consultant will assume.

The consultant in the case above rushed into the process of consulting without having placed contractual boundaries on the types of activities in which she would and would not engage. Her rapid entry was motivated by her belief that the prior experience of both the consultant and the organization were generaliz-able to this current consulting situation. Not so. It is essential to bear in mind that, despite the prior experiences of both consultant and consultee system, the matching of a consultant to a consultee system presents a unique set of circum-stances which require exploration and negotiation.

It is also important to distinguish this general system contract from the con-tracts which the consultant will eventually negotiate with the individual consul-tees. Both types of contracts are vital, and neither can take the place or encom-pass the other. These individual contracts will be discussed in greater detail later.

Understanding the Culture of the Consultee Organization

Every consultee organization has its distinct culture. Novice consultants think they understand schools simply by virtue of their own attendance at one or two. However, this is not the case. Rather, each school, like all consultee organiza-tions, has its own distinct norms and values, unique communication patterns, and formal and informal power structures. In fact, case study research has illu-strated that schools which service the same community and are within the same school district can differ significantly around organizational variables (Alpert, 1982).

A consultant must learn the norms and values of the consultee organization's culture. The consultant in the above case assumed that the principal had observed the teacher and had based her assessment of the teacher's poor performance on direct classroom observations. This proved not to be the case. The consultant realized that the principal's evaluation was based on student reports only after the consultant had become involved with the teacher. The consultant intervened before the school culture or the nature of the presenting problem were under-stood. Regarding the latter, the consultant may have approached the problem by exploring with the principal how she understood the teacher's difficulty, and by helping the principal to deal directly with the teacher. Instead, the consultant acted before understanding the culture of the school with its accompanying norms, values, and patterns of communication, and the nature of the problem presented.

It takes time to learn about an organization's norms, as such aspects of an organizations structure often do not make themselves obvious. An entering consultant should allocate several weeks to learning about the consultee organi-zation's social system. There are a number of means to do this. The consultant can and should visit with as many staff members as possible, attend organiza-tional meetings, and walk the halls and "hang out" in central gathering places.

Such advice often worries novice consultants. They are concerned that, while they are involved in this cultural investigation, they will appear lazy or profes-sionally worthless. Thus, both novice consultants and consultees need to be ed-ucated about why the initial weeks are spent this way.

Negotiating Sanctions Throughout the System's Hierarchy

While the entering consultant is becoming familiar with the organizational culture, the consultees learn about the consultant. Initially, the consultant should expect staff members' reactions to involve skepticism and even paranoia. Staff members will be uncertain of the consultant's attitudes and behaviors, and will be wary of the changes that consultant involvement may require. This kind of resistance on the part of staff members is natural and healthy. The consultant has, in fact, unbalanced their social system by entering it.

The consultant can deal with the staff's initial concerns by making personal contact with as many staff members as possible. During these personal contacts, the consultant should clarify his or her activities and intentions. Through such clarification, the consultant begins to negotiate sanctions for consultative activities. In the case presented here, the consultant did not give the school staff time to learn about her and to allay their concerns about her presence. The negative effects of premature consultative activity would probably become evident over time.

Establishing Individual Consultee Contracts

The establishing of contracts with individual consultees is usually the final step in the entry process. These individual contracts are the basis for consultant–consultee relationships. Typically these contracts are verbal, and focus on the particular concerns experienced by a consultee or group of consultees. In addition, these contracts center on how the two parties can work together most effectively, and indicate that the consultation relationship is voluntary, nonevaluative, and renegotiable.

In the case above, the consultant failed to negotiate a contract. It is clear, for example, that the consultant and the principal had different expectations about the amount of time that would be needed in order to effect improvement in this ninth grade classroom. Because the consultant had not been explicit about the complex and often time-consuming nature of the consulting process, the consultant was not aware that the principal's expectations were unrealistic and that instantaneous and magical results were anticipated. In addition, the consultant launched into a consultative relationship with the principal involving the ninth grade teacher without that teacher's understanding of the nature of the consultant's relationship with the principal. The exact nature of the relationships should be clarified within the contract.

DIAGNOSIS

Case Study

A young foster care caseworker expressed interest in discussing a case which she said was causing her "some real headaches." The caseworker, Susan, began by lamenting that she spent more time worrying about this case than any other. She explained: The case involved an 11-year-old boy named James, who had been voluntarily placed in foster care several months before by his biological mother. "James' mother just determined that his behavior was too disruptive for her to handle, and so dropped him in our laps." In fact, Susan stated that Mrs. Packer's complaints about James were vehement. However, what Susan had not been prepared for was that this 11-year-old charge would turn out to be remarkably undisruptive. In fact, James had been doing so well that, several weeks prior, Susan rewarded him by arranging for him to start going home on weekends. "I was pleased, James was thrilled, and I thought his mother was enthusiastic. But I guess I thought wrong, for that was when my headaches began." Susan explained that James had not even made it through an entire weekend before Mrs. Packer's complaints and criticisms began again.

Susan stated that she was in a quandary over what had incited the mother's wrath in the past and continued to do so. She then added that all she could identify was the mother's expectations. "Mrs. Packer seems to be constantly comparing James to others and finding that he doesn't measure up. He can't do anything right as far as she is concerned. The poor kid—all he needs is a little love. But this is a mother who cannot give love, only criticism. This is a woman who really needs some kind of counseling."

The anger in Susan's tone was apparent. However, why was Susan so angry at this mother for her particular style of child rejection? Wasn't child rejection what foster care was to some extent about? Why did Mrs. Packer's form of rejection seem so much harsher, almost intolerable, to Susan? As Susan continued to talk, the consultant, Anna, began to piece the case together. For one, Mrs. Packer was not typical of the biological mothers that the case worker had experienced. The mother had, according to Susan, a very good job, a beautiful and spacious apartment, and a very comfortable life style. As Susan herself had concluded, "This woman has everything she needs to be a good parent." In Susan's estimation, Mrs. Packer's only difficulty was that she did not know how to parent properly.

Anna thought Susan's diagnosis of the problem was simplistic. She wondered how she might help Susan to comprehend how complicated this case might be, while remaining sympathetic to Susan's position. Anna began by acknowledging Susan's frustration. Yes, it certainly seemed from Susan's description that Mrs. Packer had a strange fantasy about the role that foster care might play in her child's life. Mrs. Packer seemed to be hoping that foster care was going to magically change James into "Mr. Perfect." Anna tried to help Susan to explore where this fantasy might have come from. Anna wondered whether James's father had been actively involved in his child rearing. Susan explained the father had abandoned Mrs. Packer and James when James was 2 years old. At this point, Anna brought Susan back to some of the case material which she had already shared. Hadn't Susan related that Mrs. Packer said that James "had been a problem ever since he could walk?" Didn't this time coincide with the departure of James' father? Anna expressed some sympathy for this mother's possible plight and suggested that her inability to cope with a less-than-perfect child might be based on having been rejected while holding both the baby and the bath water. Anna's next comment was a personal one, a simple "I think that's how I might have felt." Susan's response was to visibly soften her reaction towards Mrs. Packer and to admit that perhaps things weren't quite as easy for her as they first seemed.

Several days later, Anna and Susan met again to continue their discussion of the Packer case. Susan remained concerned about the situation, but expressed this concern in a calm professional manner, with no hint that her intense emotional involvement continued. As a result, Anna had the impression that she and Susan could begin to make headway. They reviewed what Susan knew of the Packers's past history. The story Susan presented suggested that this most recent surrogate care arrangement was not the first which James had encountered. In prior years, he had been in several residential schools and one boarding arrangement. Anna wondered what had been the reason for the many shifts in James's care. Were there reports from any of these schools or boarding homes on file at the agency? Susan responded that there were not, because James's case was so recent, these reports had not been received yet. However, Susan questioned what differences this past information could possibly have on James's present situation. There was frustration in Susan's questioning, but Anna chose to attribute it to a lack of objective understanding on Susan's part. As a result, Anna explained that perhaps these sources might shed further light on the nature of this family's difficulties. Susan nodded as if in understanding.

Anna and Susan's next session, which took place at the Packer home, involved both Mrs. Packer and James. There were several reasons for this session. First, Anna hoped it would provide both Anna and Susan some details of the case history; second, Anna hoped it would allow her to observe Mrs. Packer and her son, and provide a better understanding of how to assist Susan with the case.

The Packer home was as lovely as Susan had described. However, it became clear that Susan had distorted some aspects of the case. First, although Mrs. Packer was a mother with high expectations, her expectations for her son's conduct were not unreasonable. Second, although James might have the potential to be as sweet as Susan had described, it was clear to Anna, that, within his mother's presence, he was unmanageable.

In James's absence, Anna and Susan questioned Mrs. Packer about previous child care arrangements. Mrs. Packer's explanation indicated she was a single parent in desperate need of support. Mrs. Packer described her job and James as incredibly demanding, and described the surrogate care arrangements as her efforts to escape the pressure cooker. She attributed the many changes in these care arrangements as unavoidable. "James was forever stirring up one mess or another and being asked to leave." While it was clear to Anna that the Packers' situation was problematic, she did not see either this mother or her son as villains. Anna assumed that Susan would empathize also.

However, Susan could not. In fact, Susan could barely contain her rage "Now do you believe what I told you about that woman? Incredible, isn't it?"

Discussion: Diagnostic Issues and Concerns

The second stage of the consultative process, the diagnostic phase, brings with it a host of new complexities for the consultant to consider. The task of this stage requires examination of the context of a problem and investigation of the forces affecting it. However, as the case demonstrates, this is a task which is difficult.

The case illustrates the complexity of the diagnostic stage. For example, the consultant in the case needed to be concerned with acquiring an understanding of her consultee's clients. She had to gather information about James, his mother, and the nature of their relationship. In addition, the consultant needed to examine the relationships of the consultee with her clients. How did this consultee interact with James and his mother? Were there any aspects of this interaction which were especially problematic? Also, the consultant needed to address her consultee's coping abilities and difficulties. Were the problems experienced by the consultee case-specific, or were they symptomatic of difficulties experienced previously? Finally, the consultant needed to continually examine the nature of the relationship which she herself was having with her consultee. If the relationship was to be collaborative, she had to work to make it collaborative.

Clearly, the consultant made many errors in timing and judgment, as the case illustrates. The consultant assumed that the problem rested within the client, and, consequently, acted before considering details relevant to the case and to the consultee. Further, she misdiagnosed the extent of the consultee's difficulty, and wrongly assumed that the consultee was willing and able to alter perceptions. Finally, she misjudged her relationship with her consultee. The diagnostic complexity presented here is typical. Thus, the diagnostic process requires skill, sensitivity, and flexibility on the part of consultants.

Receiving the Consultation Request

The diagnostic phase of consultation begins when a consultant receives a request for consultation, or a referral from a consultee. Desire for help is only one of many motivating forces behind the referral request. An administrator's urgings that staff utilize the services of the consultant may motivate some consultation requests; staff members' desires to show off their performance and prove that they are not in need of consulting assistance are other motivators. Therefore, the consultant's first task is to assess the motivation behind a consultee's request for consultation. Once it has been established that the consultee is truly in need of help and has come for it voluntarily, the consultant and the consultee can together consider the case. In the case presented here, the consultant glossed over this diagnostic step. As a result, it remains unclear whether the caseworker did, in fact, want help on this case, or merely wanted the consultant to confirm her negative client assessment.

Diagnostic Process: Collaborative or Noncollaborative

The advantages of a collaborative diagnostic process are numerous. A diagnostic process which involves both the consultant and the consultee collaboratively minimizes the potential for misdiagnosis, reduces the possibility of consultee resistance, and promotes the sharing of expertise which can result in the growth of the consultee's assessment and problem solving skills. However, there are circumstances when a collaborative approach to problem solving is neither warranted nor advisable. More specifically, while assessments of a client's problems and a consultee's need for knowledge or skills training may be collaborative, assessments of a consultee's need for emotional or psychological support should not be. The consultant should enter into these assessments independently, and provide the consultee with the proper support without making her diagnosis known.

Scanning the Problem

It is important that the consultant and the consultee do not leap too quickly to conclusions about the nature of the presenting problem. Building a general scanning procedure into the diagnostic process is helpful in this regard. General problem scanning may, of course, only substantiate the consultant's or the consultee's original premonitions about the presenting problem. It also may, however, point to a deeper and more serious problem than was immediately apparent.

The consultant here plunged into a diagnosis and neglected to scan the entire context of the presenting problem. As a result, she assessed the consultee's emotional involvement in the case as less serious and less complicated than it was.

Consultee's Involvement in the Problem

Often, an initial scanning of the presenting problem indicates that the consultee's difficulties in handling a case have as much to do with his or her own functioning as with the client's. Caplan (1970) describes four different reasons for consultee difficulties, and they include: lack of knowledge, lack of skill, lack of self-confidence, and lack of professional objectivity. Ascertaining that a consultee's difficulties are due either to a lack of knowledge, lack of skill, or lack of self-confidence can be a fairly straightforward process. In fact, in many cases, if the consultant has been successful in establishing good rapport with a consultee, the consultee will be direct in admitting to these lackings.

Detecting the presence of a lack of professional objectivity is more difficult. In these cases, the consultee's work difficulties stem from an emotional involvement which does not allow the consultee to maintain the professional distance necessary to work effectively. According to Caplan, there are several reasons for this emotional involvement. A consultee may overidentify with the plight of a particular client, and, as a result, exaggerate and distort the circumstances which the client confronts. A consultee may transfer or project expectations and judgments from his or her own experience onto a client's life situation. Further, a consultee may lose objectivity when confronted with incidents of aggressive or sexual behavior. Finally, in the case of theme interference, a consultee may repeatedly displace past but as yet unresolved personal conflicts onto present work situations.

How does a consultant determine that a consultee is, in fact, suffering from a lack of objectivity? The consultant attends to a consultee's affective reactions while describing the case in question. The consultant focuses on whether the consultee appears intensely involved, unusually fascinated by case details, and appears confused and distorts some case material, stereotypes some key individuals, and predicts gloom, doom, and catastrophe.

If any of the above are present, undue emotional involvement and a lack of objectivity on the consultee's part are indicated. However, the consultant must further specify the type of emotional involvement with which his or her consultee is coping. Is it a case of simple identification or transference? Or is the consultee's emotional involvement of a more enduring nature and suggestive of theme interference? Caplan recommends that the consultant assume that a theme is present until it can be otherwise proven, since some of the simpler forms of emotional involvement contain identifying patterns similar to those found in cases of theme interference.

In the case described above, the consultant did not assume that a theme was present until she could prove otherwise. Instead, she immediately judged her consultee's form of emotional involvement to be of a case specific rather than an enduring nature. This resulted in a misdiagnosis.

Readiness for Change

Once the consultant has had an opportunity to scan the context of the consultee's presenting problem and assess the nature of the consultee's involvement, he or she should have an understanding of what needs to be changed. It also must be determined whether there is a readiness for the types of changes indicated. For example, the consultant above felt strongly that her consultee needed to be more objective with the case. If his or her consultee does not exhibit the readiness necessary to make such changes, these changes cannot and should not be forced. Instead, efforts should be exerted to effect changes in other ways.

INTERVENTION

Case Study

As Carrie, the student-consultant, understood it, William was a 7-year-old second grader who had managed to gain a considerable degree of behavioral and academic notoriety in his short school career at this Staten Island public school. "Thirty children and William is just too much to handle," explained the school social worker who initially presented Carrie with the case for referral. "He doesn't listen, never follows directions, and consistently bothers other children. He should be evaluated and placed in a smaller classroom setting where he can be guaranteed more individual attention."

As far as the social worker was concerned, William's testing "should have taken place last year," and would have if William's mother had not been "so dead set against it." The social worker labelled the mother's resistance as unreasonable. She then expressed the hope that, as a new person with a new perspective, Carrie might be able to help them to convince William's mother that testing and special placement were in her son's best interests. Carrie explained that, while she would be willing to talk to William's mother and his second grade teacher, she could not help convince anyone of anything until she had a firmer grasp of William's school problems herself. Carrie added that this would probably require that she not only interview the persons most familiar with William's school situation, but also observe that this approach made sense, and stated that she would convey Carrie's plans to the principal.

Carrie's initial interview with William's mother verified that she disagreed with the assessment of William presented by the school social worker. She attributed many of William's ongoing difficulties to a personality clash which had developed with William's first grade teacher. However, William's mother stated that she would consent to a formal evaluation if Carrie's informal assessment suggested that it was absolutely necessary.

The reports which Carrie received from William's second grade teacher contained both positive and negative information. On the positive side, the teacher reported that she liked William. However, the teacher admitted to being concerned about William's non-work-oriented behavior.

Carrie's next step was to observe William's classroom behavior. These observations made it quite clear to Carrie that William was not as consistent a problem as school personnel had led her to believe. Rather, it was Carrie's opinion that William's behavior seemed to fluctuate. "When William was given positive support and continual guidance, his behavior was very acceptable. However, when he was left to his own devices, his behavior rapidly deteriorated," Carrie assessed. Fortunately, it was Carrie's impression that the second grade teacher with primary responsibility for William had a teaching style with an extremely positive and structured theme. "Even her reprimands took on a gentle and very structured form." Carrie assessed that, when this teacher was at her most positive and most structured best, her impact on William was enormous. This behavior, Carrie added, was in marked contrast to that which William demonstrated while in the charge of a visiting English teacher with a very different teaching style.

These observations convinced Carrie that any formal evaluation and smaller class placement should be postponed. Instead, it was her assessment that William's present classroom teacher had made great strides towards improving William's classroom behavior, and that this present tact should be continued. Thus, in the final days of her classroom visit, Carrie began to reinforce this teacher's efforts and to stress what a difference these efforts seemed to have made not only in William's behavior but in the behavior of the entire class. As William's second grade teacher seemed both pleased and motivated by this positive feedback, Carrie made more direct offerings of help and support. She suggested that they experiment with strategies which might further refine the already successful efforts on behalf of William. William's teacher was interested in working with Carrie, and they met several times. Further, the teacher began implementing some of the ideas which she and Carrie had discussed.

In a sense, it was an already established and initiated plan for classroom intervention which Carrie presented to the social worker and the principal. Their response was of surprise and frustrated resistance. After what Carrie labelled "a great deal of persuading and convincing on my part," they finally though reluctantly agreed "to let Carrie give it a try."

In the next several weeks, Carrie focused her total attention on William's classroom and classroom teacher. Carrie helped the teacher to monitor her reinforcements of William, explaining that this would insure that William experienced small and frequent doses of success. Carrie also alerted this teacher to the types of reinforcement she should provide William, suggesting that he should not be reinforced merely for managing to keep still and silent. Rather, Carrie advised that he should be rewarded for getting his work done while remaining still and silent. William's teacher seemed interested and responsive.

However, this was not the case for the rest of the faculty and staff. Suddenly, it seemed that William and William's deviance had become Carrie's responsibility in full. The onus was on her to make certain that William's deportment was impeccable, and, when it was not, she was accountable. William's English teacher took to tabulating daily counts of William's ill deeds, and before long it became a favored school pastime.

Sensing that the tide was against her, Carrie took cover by becoming even more involved in William's second grade classroom and with William's classroom teacher. However, William's classroom teacher was also under storm and began to wearily complain that the amount of effort she was expending was not worth the little return she was receiving. The project was dropped in Carrie's lap. Three weeks later, William was evaluated and a special classroom placement was arranged.

Discussion: Intervention Issues and Concerns

The intervention and the diagnostic phases of the consultative process are interwoven. The diagnostic phase does not come to an immediate halt at the commencement of a consultant's intervention. Rather, the two stages often cycle together, with each reinforcing and enhancing the other.

Our case study acts as an illustration of what can occur when a consultant fails to recognize the interaction and the overlap of these two stages. However, this abbreviated case study also elucidates issues and concerns more specifically focused on the intervention stage of the consultative process. First, this case makes clear that there are many ways of intervening around an issue. Our consultant did not necessarily need to focus her intervention attentions on William's classroom and classroom teacher. In fact, her approach might have been better received if it had encompassed more of the school staff. Second, the case makes it apparent that an intervention at one level of an organization will involve changes at several levels. Keeping William in the classroom, rather than farming him out to a special placement, had an effect not only on William's classroom teacher but also on the rest of the faculty and staff. Third, the case helps to emphasize that an intervention cannot take place without administrative support. Our consultant obtained the principal's approval but not his enthusiastic and involved support. As a result, when her project began to disintegrate, he was not committed to its revival. Finally, it strongly suggests that any intervention process will be slow and difficult, and that resistance to it will be inevitable.

How to Intervene
The first step of any intervention is determining the best means for intervening. This determination should focus not only on what is best for the consultee and the client, but also on what is most feasible given the resources and constraints presented by the consultee organization.

Intervention strategies generally fall into three global categories: the empirical-rational, the normative-re-educative, and the power coercive (Bennis, Benee, Chin, & Corey, 1976). The first of these intervention strategies, the empirical-rational, is based on the assumption that the consultee lacks the knowledge necessary to understand and solve the confronting problem. This strategy suggests that, if the consultee is provided with the proper information, functioning will improve. Basic to the normative-re-educative is the belief that, in order for individuals to make any real commitment to change, this commitment must be emotionally based. This strategy assumes that the consultant's role should not only be one of knowledge broker, but also of values clarifier and change facilitator. The third and final intervention strategy, the power-coercive, is based on the premise that change can only be guaranteed when force is applied, and suggests that the consultant focus her attention on aiding consultees to employ such force.

Intervention strategies also vary with regard to their target or level of focus. They can be directed at the client, at the consultee, or at the organization as a whole. There are many advantages to directing intervention efforts towards those at higher levels of the organizational hierarchy, if it is at all possible. In addition, if time allows, there are premiums to be gained from simultaneously directing intervention efforts towards several fronts. For example, our consultant might have been more successful if she focused some of her intervention efforts on other faculty members as well as William's classroom teacher.

Our consultant overlooked many components important in determining how to intervene. She focused directly on her teacher consultee and her student, and neglected the role which organizational resources and constraints play in intervention. As a result, she was soon confronted by organizational setbacks.

Intervention Ownership

Although it is clear that a consultant will play a role in any intervention, the actual ownership of any intervention attempts must belong to the consultee and the consultee organization. Problems will be solved more effectively, and will stay solved far longer, if the consultee and the consultee organization see their role in the process as vital. Our case consultant neglected this. She became responsible for William's behavior.

Administrative Support

Administrative support for intervention is essential. Administrators should be involved in the intervention planning process in order to assure their support. Our consultant "sprang" her intervention plans on the school's principal, and ignored the principal's initial commitment to having William specially placed. It is no wonder then that his support for this intervention strategy was given grudgingly, and his assistance was unavailable when it began to flounder.

Coping with Initial Organizational Resistance

An initial resistance to change on the part of an organization is normal and healthy. When resistance is experienced, the consultant should not retreat as our case consultant did. Rather, it is advised that the consultant deal with resistance and consider it an integral part of the process of intervening.

Ripple Effect

Similarly, it is essential to realize that an intervention at one level within an organization has implications for all organizational levels. Change cannot be introduced onto one level of a system without influencing and to some extent changing other organizational levels as well. Our consultant focused all of her efforts at the classroom level. However, the influences of her intervention spread far further. What she failed to realize was that, although William's second grade teacher was primarily in charge of his care, she was not the only staff person who came in contact with William and would be influenced by his continued presence.

Commitment Level

The intervention process may be a long and unexpectedly arduous one for all those involved. As a result, the consultant may at some point be put in the position of determining how she can sustain interest and keep those involved working together and working effectively. This may be especially true in the case of interventions which require members from different levels of the hierarchy to stay in contact and communication with one another. One suggestion is not to wait until maintaining commitment acutally becomes a problem, but to begin every intervention with the knowledge that periodic feedback and reinforcement must be integral ingredients in the intervention process.

Change is Difficult

Finally, it is important to realize that the already-difficult process of change can be further complicated by the presence of chance factors. As a result, despite the vast skill and effort of the consultant, interventions sometimes do not proceed as planned.

EVALUATION

Case Study

As Will began to settle into the elementary school where he was to act as student-consultant, he was repeatedly struck with the realization that teaching was a profession which bred isolation. Independent classroom quarters and intricately overlapping schedules left these elementary school teachers little room for even the briefest of contacts with one another. As a result, their sharing of problems was cursory. They exchanged minor teaching concerns as they passed one another in the school corridors or lunch line. However, they rarely, if ever, had or made the time to share problems of a more involved or pressing nature. In fact, even when a problem was one of mutual interest or involvement, collaborative efforts were minimal. As Will saw it, the dearth of such collaborative problem solving efforts prohibited this elementary school from effectively employing its own resources in resolving school and child problems. Thus, Will took it upon himself as the school's consultant to attempt to provide teachers and other school staff members with both time and the forum during which to develop such collaborative problem solving efforts.

Will's first step was to bring this idea to the school principal. The principal was initially resistant. He expressed concerns about how such a group activity could possibly be squeezed into an already hectic school schedule. However, he promised to consider it and get back to Will within the week.

After 2 weeks, Will approached the principal with a reminder. The principal apologized before announcing that arranging time for such a group was an impossibility for the lower grade teachers. However, he hinted that the rest of the staff might be available on Wednesday afternoons for several hours. He suggested that Will attend the next faculty meeting to see what kind of interest he could arouse, and added that, if there was enough interest and the group was initiated, he would be interested in sitting in. Will encouraged him to do so.

Will's presentation to the faculty was only able to gather the interest of four upper grade teachers, the school social worker, and the learning disabilities specialist. The rest of the faculty expressed no interest in volunteering the little free time they had, and no pressure was exerted to help change their minds.

Will characterized the first meetings of this group as "chockful of mistrust, suspicion, and uncomfortable silence." In fact, he later admitted that "I often wondered during those initial group sessions whether we would ever get beyond that discomfort," for, although all group members had volunteered their participation, there was much that obstructed the process of collaborative problem solving. Most significantly, although group rules and norms provided all members with co-equal status, group members came from school positions that did not. For example, as far as the teachers in the group were concerned, the principal did not immediately join their ranks simply by virtue of sharing group membership with them. He remained their principal and their evaluator. They legitimately questioned whether their sharing of problems and feelings within this group setting would make them more vulnerable to his out-of-group review. This threat, and others of like kind, only dissipated after many discussions, according to Will.

Once some degree of trust had been established, the group began to collectively consider the problems of specific children. This action provoked the eruption of a different type of group dilemma. This was a faculty group which was very grounded in school procedures and unaccustomed to either collaboration or innovation. As a result, as soon as the group began to confront child problems, there was much discussion of the prohibitions which traditional school procedures presented. For example, when it was obvious that a certain child's disruptive behavior warranted a visit to the child's home, there was much debate over whether it was appropriate procedure for the child's classroom teacher to make the home visit, since visits of this sort typically fell under the jurisdiction of the school social worker.

Gradually, the group's stringent procedural definitions began to erode. As they did, the group's views of child problems became enhanced and their solutions to them became more creative and collaborative. However, this growth also presented the group with a new range of problems. For one, the actions of this collaborative group were beginning to provoke a surge of reactions from members of the school community not involved in the group's decision making processes. It seemed that, while viewing problems from a different perspective and engaging in alternative actions was advocated and applauded by fellow group members, it was beginning to be disparaged and seen as a threat by those on the outside. The principal began to get less-than-enthusiastic feedback from parents and supervisory school personnel. In group, he openly shared his concerns about having to "shut the effort down."

It was at this point in the group's process that the group itself began to demand an evaluation of itself. Members wanted to have some reading of whether their efforts were worth all the adverse publicity that they were beginning to attract. Had some of their problem solving made a difference? The group began to count the number of child cases which they felt they had in fact influenced. They were few—much fewer than the group had realized. Will's attempts to dissuade the group from this product-oriented assessment of their worth was ignored. Dismayed by the onslaught of public criticism and the dearth of countable positive results, the group voted to disband.

Discussion: Evaluation Issues and Concerns

The last stage of the consultation process is that of evaluation and termination. This stage is often ignored because the evaluation of consultation is complex. It is frequently difficult to determine what to evaluate, how to evaluate it, and who should be the evaluator. Yet the importance of gathering some measure of both the positive and negative outcomes of a consultant's efforts is unquestionable. It can provide both consultant and consultee with a sense of the consequences of their intervention attempts, and can act as a gauge against which plans for future interventions can be measured.

Our case study provides an example of what can occur when the evaluative process is not built into the framework of consultation. Our case consultant proceeded with his group intervention plans with clear objectives. He wanted to facilitate the improvement of communication among an unusually uncommunicative faculty group. However, he gave little consideration to how either he or the group would assess the attainment of group objectives and the factors which facilitated or impeded the attainment. Thus, when outside pressures confronted the group and an impromptu evaluation was demanded by group members, the evaluation attempt was disorganized and focused on the group's prod-ucts rather than their well-developed process.

Evaluative Process

Ideally, the evaluative process should be considered at the inception of the intervention stage. Beginning evaluative considerations at this time helps to assure that the evaluation will be an integral part of the consultative process and not a disjointed and hastily thrown together activity. In addition, early evaluative planning can help to clarify interventon goals and enrich intervention methods by promoting the use of evaluative feedback and review. Perhaps, if our consultant had incorporated evaluative planning into his intervention scheme, he would have been more cognizant of the fact that his goals and the goals of the group were not similarly directed.

Who Should Evaluate

Any evaluative planning should involve consultants and consultees collaboratively. As with all the other stages of the consultative process, an evaluation is better formulated and less threatening if it is devised jointly. Deciding who should actually do the evaluation should also be collaborative. Of course, this collaborative decision is highly dependent on how and what the consultee and the consultant choose to evaluate. It may be that it is most appropriate for either the consultant or the consultee to carry out the entire evaluation or for them each to be responsible for different parts. These decision can only be made after the whats and the hows of the evaluative process have been addressed.

How to Evaluate
All consultative evaluation need not be quantitative and data-based. In fact, in many cases, informal and more qualitative measures are better suited to the nature of the consultative process. Process reports, interviews, and attitude scales may serve to assess consultee and consultant feelings about the intervention process. Client observations and assessments may provide consultees and consultants with data on the intervention products.

What to Evaluate
The evaluative options are wide. However, they typically fall into two broad categories: product and process. Product evaluations are generally concerned with determining the degree to which the consultative intervention goals were attained. Process evaluations are focused on pinpointing those factors which contributed to both negative and positive outcomes of the intervention. It is not unusual, as our case study indicates, for one of these types of evaluations to be emphasized at the expense of the other. Both types are important and can be illustrative of growth. Data from process evaluation may be used to enable a more positive product evaluation at a later point.

Termination Issues
Termination is often difficult and may trigger complicated feelings on the part of consultant and consultee. A consultant may have worked with a consultee for some time, established a fruitful relationship, and become deeply involved in the consultee's professional development. As a result, the resolution of the case may signify loss for both the consultant and the consultee, and must be carefully considered. The following guidelines may help provide a framework. First, it is essential that the timing and planning for termination be a joint decision. Second, it is crucial that the resolution of the relationship be a gradual one in which the consultant will be available if needed.

CONCLUSION

The practice and the process of consultation is accompanied by complexities, as the case material presented here and discussion of the material indicates. The first and perhaps most difficult stage in the consulting process is entry. Entry sets the tone for the development of the consulting relationships which will follow. This stage demands that the consultant dedicate time to assessing and understanding the values and dynamics of the consultee system, so that initial contracts of mutual acceptability can be negotiated and consulting relationships can be initiated.

The second stage of the consultative process is diagnosis. The task of this stage is one of exploring the nature of the consultee's presenting problem and investigating the factors influencing it, so that a process of correction or alleviation can be developed. During this stage, the consultant should be careful to explore all facets of the consultee's presenting problem so that a much deeper and more complex problem is not mistaken for a superficial one. This stage requires both sensitivity and flexibility on the consultant's part.

The intervention stage often overlaps with the diagnostic one. This stage focuses both on solving the consultee's immediate problem and on fostering consultee growth, in order that the next round of problems can be handled more effectively and independently by the consultee. This stage can be of long duration. Consequently, it is essential that the consultee and the consultee organization be committed to its completion.

Finally, there is the stage of evaluation. Although this stage is often neglected, it can be as important as the entry stage and necessitates planning. It is important to establish, in advance, what will be evaluated, how it will be evaluated, and who will actually do the evaluating. In addition, this stage often signals the termination of the consultative relationship and may trigger complicated feelings on the part of both the consultant and consultee. As a result, the consultant must be conscious of its timing and its gradual approach.

REFERENCES

Alpert, J. L. (Ed.). (1982). *Psychological consultation in educational settings.* San Francisco: Jossey-Bass.

Alpert, J. L., & Meyers, J. (Eds.). (1983). *Training in consultation: Mental health, behavioral, and organizational perspectives.* Springfield, IL: Charles C. Thomas.

Bennis, W. G., Benne, K. D., Chin, R., & Corey, K. E. (1976). *The planning of change.* New York: Holt.

Caplan, G. (1970). *The theory and practice of mental health consultation.* New York: Basic Books.

Gallessich, J. (1982). *The profession and practice of consultation.* San Francisco: Jossey-Bass.

Meyers, J., Alpert, J. L., & Fleisher, B. D. (1983). Models of consultation. In J. L. Alpert & J. Meyers (Eds.), *Training in consultation: Mental health, behavioral, and organizational perspectives.* Springfield, IL: Charles C. Thomas.

Meyers, J., Parsons, R. D., & Martin, R. (1979). *Mental health consultation in the schools.* San Francisco: Jossey-Bass.

Sarason, S. B., Levine, M., Goldenberg, I., Cherlin, D. L., & Bennett, E. M. (1966). *Psychology in community settings: Clinical, vocational, educational, social aspects.* New York: Wiley.

Chapter 6

Forensic Practice

Glenn R. Caddy
Nova University

Elizabeth E. Loftus
University of Washington

INTRODUCTION

The past 10 years have borne witness to an ever growing number of psychologists becoming active in the interaction between the practice of pyschology and law. Whereas during the early 1970s book titles reflected almost exclusively the involvement of psychiatry in the legal system, increasingly today we see texts relating the law and psychology (Cohen & Mariano, 1982; Finkel, 1980; Robinson, 1980; Schwitzgebel & Schwitzgebel, 1980; Van Hoose & Kottler, 1977).

There is little question but that forensic practice is time consuming, stressful, and often less than accomodating. It is even somewhat risky because of the ever present likelihood of subsequent litigation and negative publicity which go hand in hand with involvement in the legal system. Nevertheless, for many psychologists forensic work is intellectually stimulating and otherwise rewarding. Moreover, given the extent to which the legal system has pervaded virtually every aspect of clinical practice, it has become increasingly difficult for the practicing psychologist to avoid at least occasional involvement in forensic matters. In fact, even some of our more reclusive academically-based psychology colleagues are today being called upon by attorneys to offer their particular expertise in the pursuit of justice.

Given the range of possible involvements of psychologists in the legal system, it is more difficult to contemplate the limits of forensic practice than its focus. Certainly, while psychiatrists continue to be the primary expert witnesses in cases involving the evaluation of mental illness (which bear upon legal decisions of criminal responsibility, civil commitment, competency to stand trial, testamentary capacity, and the like), clinical psychologists now routinely also are providing these services. Similarly, in cases involving child abuse, neglect, custody and visitation, and in matters of divorce, annulment, and domestic relations generally, the clinical psychologist is now playing a substantial role, as both the court and counsel come to appreciate the contributions available from the discipline. Psychologists also are being sought to offer their expertise in actions in tort (such as cases of negligence, malpractice, and the consequences of accidents), in consultation regarding therapeutic abortion and surgery, in social security disability evaluations and their appeals, in reports regarding parole, in the forecasting of dangerousness, in evaluations for sentence modification, and even in jury selection. Moreover, psychologists now are offering testimony on specific issues such as the veracity of eyewitness testimony, on the adequacy of warning labels and the meaning of particular words, on the public's likely perception of relevant events, and on a myriad of matters in which data concerning human reactions prove relevant (see the debate between McCloskey and Egeth, 1983 a, b; and Loftus, 1983 a, b).

ETHICS AND STANDARDS IN FORENSIC PRACTICE

Irrespective of the nature of a particular case, and irrespective also of whether involvement in the case has been initiated by an attorney or whether the psychologist has been appointed by the court, the psychologist contemplating his/her participation in a legal case inevitably must confront the fact that the ethics and professional issues of psychology are very different from those of law. Of course, when the court appoints the psychologist, for example, as occurs in a number of child custody matters, the psychologist is asked to serve within a framework in which the potential for a confounding of interest is reduced. In such cases, the best interests of the child are the only matters of significance, and the court and the child can be regarded as the client. In the vast majority of cases, though, the principle of responsibility in clinical practice can be sorely tested by exposure to the adversarial forces within the legal system.

Psychologists "make every effort to protect the welfare of those who seek their services" ... yet, simultaneously, "they show concern for the best interests of ... society" (Preamble, APA, 1981). Psychologists "avoid relationships that may limit their objectivity or create a conflict of interest" (Principle 1 (b), APA, 1981). They "are alert to personal, social, organizational, financial, or political situations, and pressures that might lead to misuse of their influence (Principle 1, (f), APA, 1981). And "when a psychologist agrees to provide services to a client at the request of a third party, the psychologist assumes the responsibility of clarifying the nature of the relationships to all parties concerned" (Principle 6 (b), APA, 1981). Further, "psychologists know and take into account the traditions and practices of other professional groups with whom they work, and cooperate fully with such groups" (Principle 7 (b), APA, 1981). All of these realms of ethical concern, and others too, routinely are tested in forensic work, where the somewhat conservative scientist/psychologist is obliged to interface with the legal professional, whose primary duty (and oftentimes perceived sole duty) is to represent zealously his/her client's best interests within the bounds of the law.

With the initial contact from an attorney, for example, the psychologist has the responsibiity to determine just who the client really is. Certainly, the issue is more complicated than simply who is paying the fee. Further, at least occasionally in the course of providing forensic consultation, it becomes apparent that the mental health interests of the client may not be well served by the strategies of his/her attorney; or even worse, it becomes clear that the actions of the attorney are contributing to a substantial escalation of the client's difficulties. Under such circumstances, occasionally the client may ask the psychologist what to do to reduce the conflict. In such instances, questions both of conflict of interest and of professional relationships become particularly relevant and are often not easily resolved. Which is the correct choice when the best interests of the client and the best interests of the society appear antithetical? How difficult is it to maintain complete objectivity regarding the client of a particular attorney, when you have just been paid a $2,000 retainer for about a dozen hours of work? And is it more difficult still when that same attorney is in a position to forward to you a great deal of business? Is it possible to offer effective testimony which is clearly at odds with the testimony of another mental health professional, when the agenda of an opposing attorney is to minimize your credibility, and yet your responsibility is to avoid presenting the opposing professional as lacking competence? Consider, too, the potential conflict that comes when the psychologist is required to give testimony which may be damaging to the client's case and any therapeutic relationship which has been established. Finally, consider the problems when an attorney calls requesting both evaluative and treatment services for a person of very limited financial means, say, in a personal injury case, where the prospect of a large financial settlement is considerable, the attorney is taking the case on a contingency basis, and he/she asks the psychologist also to serve the client on a contingency basis.[1]

Conceptual, philosophical, and ideological considerations relating the nature of psychological processes and the legal system must be integrated with ethical considerations if one is to attempt a thorough-going understanding of forensic practice. This integration, too, gives pause for concern. The Harvard law professor, Arthur Miller, while examing the basis of the adversarial system, once commented as follows:

> The adversary system, in sum is based on two premises: first, that the lawyers are competent in the matters dealt with, and second, that the

---

[1] As a general rule, we would regard the taking of a case on a contingency basis by a psychologist as poor practice (though not necessarily unethical), for one's credibility as an expert witness inevitably will be seriously questioned and perhaps compromised when it is established that the supposedly neutral psychologist/expert could be shown to have a vested interest in the outcome of the case.

system can provide enough of the right type of data to make viable decisions. Neither idea is valid. (1968, p. 40)

Noteworthy also is the argument of D. L. Bazelon, who, from his perspective as judge of the U. S. Court of Appeals for the District of Columbia Circuit, called psychiatry (and presumably psychology), the "ultimate wizardry."

> My experience has shown that in no case is it more difficult to elicit productive and reliable expert testimony than in cases that call on the knowledge and practice of psychiatry . . . they (psychiatrists) try to limit their testimony to conclusary statements couched in psychiatric terminology. Thereafter, they take shelter in a defensive resistance to questions about facts that are or ought to be in their possession. They thus refuse to submit their opinions to the scrutiny that the adversary process demands. (1974, p. 18)

There can be little question that there is a lack of congruence between the world as seen by laymen, the world of the law, and the world as seen by experts within the various mental health disciplines. A great part of the debate between mental health professionals and attorneys regarding the legal definition of insanity, for example, and its use within the mental health field, has its source in this incongruity. Weinstein (1966) sees this incongruity as a function of the difference in the frames of reference between the two fields. Whereas psychology and psychiatry have a frame of reference in which assessment leads to differential treatment, at law, assessment is associated with judgment which is tied to issues both of punishment and deterrence, and even innocence typically is established only after great emotional stress and financial expense.

Incongruity also exists between these two disciplines in the way that their respective practitioners evaluate the facts of the case. The court really does not appear interested in the truth, the whole truth, and nothing but the truth. Indeed, the court is not especially curious about much of what a witness may be capable of telling about a case. As Slovenko (1975) asserts, the life of the judicial process is composed of artifacts . . . facts skewed by a script. The facts of the case are merely samples of the whole truth, and they are what the law considers to be important. They are not necessarily facts which a mental health professional would view as the essential facts (the dynamics and the explanations of the actions) in the case. In fact, given the complexity of the various rules of procedure and of evidence in the adversary system, (such as, for example, the hearsay exclusionary rule), there is a definite tendency for many psychologists and other mental health professionals involved in forensic work to view the courtroom battles as accomplishing little more than the obstruction of justice.

Clearly there are numerous powerful and complex forces which affect the psychologist in forensic practice. Problems of conceptual integration, relevance of perspective, responsibility, ethical issues, and standards of practice all must be closely and continuously scrutinized to ensure competence and integrity in the practice of forensic psychology. Several illustrations showing certain aspects of these most difficult and complex interactions may prove helpful.

Take, for example, the instance in which a psychologist is required to give testimony which may be damaging to the case of a particular client . . . and, simultaneously to an ongoing therapeutic relationship with that client. Certainly, the client has a right to know the questions which his/her counsel will ask at the trial and to be knowledgeable of the psychologist's responses. Further, however, the client and the attorney must be fully appraised of the psychologist's view of the case, including any reservations about the client, which may, in turn, preclude unqualified support of the client. This is essential, because in competent cross examination some less than positive aspects about the client often will be elicited. And in deciding to have the psychologist testify, both the client and the attorney need to know the strengths and the shortcomings of the testimony for the case. Certainly, by requesting professional testimony both the attorney and his/her client waive much of the privilege and support which characterizes the pretrial consultive relationship. On the stand, the psychologist has the responsibility to be objective and to serve the court and his/her profession rather than the attorney or the client. The point here is, of course, that, when a clinician is engaged in every day clinical practice, this role requires honesty in the patient–therapist relationship, but not honesty delivered in such a way as to injure the patient. In the courtroom, however, the psychologist-witness cannot assert control over the scene, and so, quite routinely, the requirement of forthrightness produces a paradigmatic difficulty for the psychologist functioning outside of the more traditional therapeutic role.

Consider an example illustrating the possible difficulties involved in resolving the interpreted best interests of the client because of the differences in orientation between legal and psychological professionals. It is common today for people receiving mental health services simultaneously to be receiving care from other health professionals. Commonly, too, these various professionals render their specialized services in a health care network which is established through collaborative contacts which coordinate the delivery of care to the patient. Similarly, in the interface between the legal and mental health professions, a collaborative process designed to serve the overall best interests of the patient/client generally also is established. Generally, but not always. Again, the fundamental problem is that the strategies and concepts of the legal orientation, especially given the adversarial process, quite commonly conflict with the strategies of resolution which the mental health professional may regard as preferable. Recently, the first author was consulted by a man who had undergone a particularly protracted and destructive divorce. During the legal wrangling, the former wife had kidnapped and secreted their three children for a period of nearly 9 months, until she was located, arrested, and the permanent custody of the children transferred from herself to the father. At the time of the consultation request, which occurred independent of advice from legal counsel, the father was facing the prospects of further litigation from his former spouse who was threatening to appeal the custody decision. The client's purpose in seeking psychological consultation was not to confront any potential legal challenge. Rather, he wished to have conducted an evaluation of the emotional functioning of his children, so that he could determine how best to help them, especially as far as their relationship with their mother was concerned. Having completed the evaluation of the children, it became obvious that at least some evaluation of the mother would be necessary. Further, as an overall strategy aimed at resolution emerged, it seemed that only by attempting to defuse the emotions of both parents with regard to one another could the best interests of the children be served. In such situations, of course, it is common for the attorney of the former wife not to wish his/her client to see the ex-husband's psychologist, who is presumed to be biased against her, and if consulted, would have a first hand perspective that could be used against her best interests. In this case, however, it was not possible even to approach the children's mother and request her cooperation. Despite recommendations along such lines by the author, both to the father and his attorney, and despite a quite favorable response to these recommendations from the father, the prospect of such a resolution was lost when the father's attorney commanded him not to jeopardize his case by risking that the clinician may be swayed by the guile of the former wife. Given the conflict of these various options, and the fact that the author was unwilling to pressure the client to accept the mental health approach, the man chose not to risk the legal status quo. The consequence, of course, was that the destructive fires which may be fueled by the adversary process continued, as did their impact on the well-being of the children.

There is, of course, no inherent reason why the joint client of an attorney and a psychologist should not be afforded the opportunity to make informed decisions regarding the direction of the consultations being provided. Nevertheless, often this does not occur. And because of the orientation differences of the two professions, the professionals themselves occasionally experience difficulties working jointly to meet the respective best interests of their clients.

THE FORMAT OF FORENSIC PRACTICE

While the tasks of the forensic psychologist will differ depending upon the nature of the case and the specific role he/she is being asked to take, nevertheless, the following format offers a guideline for the delivery of forensic services.

Most frequently, a forensic consultation begins with an inquiry from an attorney whose agenda is to determine if the psychologist has the needed expertise in a particular case. At the outset, and even prior to an interview, the psychologist may be well served to seek some general information about the case in order to determine if he/she has the expertise required to address the consult being sought. At this point, also, it is typically good practice to advise the attorney of one's forensic fee schedule (this matter will be further discussed subsequently), and to ensure that the attorney is aware that psychological services will be provided only if the consultation can be provided within a context in which objectivity is foremost. The clear specification of both the fee and the commitment to objectivity is particularly desirable at the beginning of a forensic consultation. The psychologist who does not deal with these matters from the outset risks undertaking work for which payment may be especially difficult to obtain, or risks, at least occasionally, entering a consultation in which a specific outcome is being sought with payment being offered on the assumption of that outcome.

Assuming that the consultation proceeds, the psychologist typically takes on the role of a technical assistant and/or agent in support of the attorney managing the case. In this role, the psychologist searches for the facts which he/she considers relevant, reports these accurately to the attorney together with a clear statement of the limits of the available data, educates the attorney about the relevance of these facts from a behavioral science perspective, and provides information that would be relevant to his/her own examination on the stand as well as the cross examination of other witnesses.

Straightforward as this role and these tasks may seem, inevitably there is a great deal of work involved in any competent forensic consulation. Even in those consultations which may be viewed as commonplace, it is advisable (and sometimes essential) for the consultant to conduct a level of evaluation that otherwise may not be considered essential, in order to minimize the vulnerability of the evaluation and the subsequent testimony to attack. Certainly, too, it is advisable that the records created during a forensic consultation be developed from a conservative perspective and be both selective and comprehensive, for these records are just as liable to receive critical and robust examination as is the witness. Moreover, whenever a forensic consultation is offered, it is essential that the psychologist review the research literature related to the topic of the consultation, for the use of speculation based on general professional knowledge or the presentation of a non-demonstrably-convincing perspective can be devastating to the credibility of an expert when he/she is subjected to sophisticated cross examination.

Occasionally, of course, a consultation will be requested in which the psychologist is asked to offer an opinion on a topic on which either no directly relevant studies are available or where the literature is otherwise inadequate. In such instances, if resources permit, the psychologist may conduct a special purpose study. An example of such a study is offered by Haward (1981). This study arose out of a case of gross indecency. Following complaints of indecent behavior supposedly occuring in a public men's room, two policemen were assigned to watch the lavatory. The police stationed themselves in a broom closet, and peered through a zinc gauze screen into the room. After several days of watching, the officers observed two men acting "in a manner regarded as improper." Despite denial by both men, arrests were made. In the development of the case for the defense, the defense counsel hired Haward to testify on the probability that the two policemen may have been mistaken. In preparing for his testimony, Haward took photographs of the site, using actors who were placed in positions described in the police reports and under lighting conditions similar to those existing during the supposed crimes. Haward then showed these photographs to subjects under various expectancy sets, including the expectation that they would see an offense being committed. The finding, of course, was that even the most innocent of acts would be interpreted as indecent when the viewer held the expectation that a crime would be witnessed. The data from this study were used as a basis for invalidating the police evidence, and an acquittal was obtained.

Whatever the specific nature of the consultation, the consensus, it seems, is that the psychologist hired by an attorney is bound to serve his/her counsel until such time as he/she becomes an expert witness. If the case develops to that point, and counsel decides to have the psychologist testify, the psychologist then becomes professionally obligated to change his/her role from that of a consultant to that of a servant of the court.

PROVIDING TESTIMONY

The basic goal of any testimony is to provide useful and relevant information which the court may consider. A lay witness may testify only to events which he/she has first hand knowledge; opinions and inferences are not admissable. In contrast, the opinions of the specially trained and experienced expert witness are accepted as evidence (Cook, 1964). In a criminal case (see for example, Washington vs. United States, 1967), the expert may be expected to describe and explain "how the development, adaptations, and functions of the defendent's behavioral processes may have influenced his conduct." Merely stating a conclusion, such as a diagnosis, is not sufficient. Almost invariably, the court will wish to understand and evaluate the evidence in determining the facts at issue. Thus, a major facet of the role of the psychologist on the stand is to educate as simultaneously he/she provides an interpretation of the pertinent material. Of course, as Schwitzgebel and Schwitzgebel (1980) remark, the use of the expert witness also serves as "a convenient social ritual that permits the court to distribute the burden of making extremely difficult decisions with inadequate or irreconcilably contradictory evidence" (p. 245).

There can be little question but that a determination of the presence and absence of behavioral, occupational, or other psychological impairment can be of vital relevance in many court actions. However, it is erroneous for the psychologist to assume, because he/she possesses data and interpretations deemed relevant to a case, that such information will be eagerly received into evidence. Many judges, attorneys, and juries are ill-equipped to comprehend testimony presented by expert witnesses. Moreover, many expert witnesses who otherwise may be particularly competent often demonstrate the capacity to contribute to their own ineffectiveness in court by failing to communicate their intended message or by otherwise harming their credibility (see for example, Anchor & Sieveking, 1981; Morse, 1978; Ziskin, 1970). There is little question but that, under the stress and scrutiny of a deposition or a trial, expert witnesses do not always function effectively. There are however, a number of common-sense strategies which go hand in hand with competence and responsibility, and which can greatly facilitate the delivery of effective testimony.

One of the first tasks in introducing expert testimony is to have the court accept the testimony by qualifying the witness as an expert. Inevitably, rules of evidence notwithstanding, the trial judge has wide discretionary powers as to who will be qualified. In qualifying a witness, the court generally takes into account both the academic credentials and the experience of the witness, with the matter of specific experience being weighed quite seriously. The authors are aware of one case, for example, in which a psychologist with years of experience was prevented from offering testimony regarding sentence mitigation in the case of a 20-year-old multiple drug offender because of his lack of direct clinical experience with such individuals. (See the classic case People vs. Hawthorne, 1940). The point here is that a psychologist can serve the best interests of a client in court only when he/she can be shown to be expert on the matters in question.

Long before the qualifying of the expert, however, there is much work to be done by the forensic psychologist as he/she sets the stage for the delivery of the testimony. The psychologist must be intimately familiar with the topic of the case and the related literature, and he/she must understand the general legal context. The psychologist's actions must maximize the prospects of objectivity, and the methods used must be comprehensive and appropriate to the conclusions being developed. For example, if testing is to be administered, such testing ideally should be administered only by the psychologist offering the testimony, for an expert witness may be required to prove the source of his/her answers, and should be able to counteract suggestions from the opposing counsel that the answers or the test results were obtained under conditions that could in any way call into question their validity.

As the date of the testimony draws near, a detailed planning session should be scheduled between the psychologist and the attorney so that the entire action can be orchestrated to maximize the effectiveness of the testimony. During this conference, it behooves the case and all concerned if both the legal and psychological professionals can take pointers from one another as they jointly explore issues such as the meaning of terms and the most comprehensive way of communicating this meaning, the accuracy and appropriateness of any assessment methods employed, the existence of alternative methodologies to address the matters at hand, the recommendations indicated by the findings, the certainty of the conclusions reached, and the possibility of developing alternative interpretations or conclusions which might be tenable, given the same data. During such a meeting, the attorney also is offered an excellent opportunity to clarify the concept of reasonable psychological probability (Conrad, 1964) and other legal terms that are likely to be introduced during the trial, and to discuss and role play the most effective methods of presenting testimony. The experienced and astute attorney also will use this conference to explore with the psychologist those areas of weakness in the testimony, and will plan strategies for recovering or repairing the testimony after damaging cross examination. During such discussions, it is particularly important for the psychologist to specify clearly the limits and the weaknesses in the testimony, for. under perceptive and pointed cross examination, even expert testimony may be modified. Planning for such an event may actually strengthen the testimony rather than weaken it. (Such a strengthening also may occur when the expert reveals limitations in his/her support for the client.) Ultimately, the interests of the client are best served by the expert presenting him/herself as reasonable and flexible, and thereby a credible witness.

When actually providing testimony various guidelines have been suggested (see for example, Anchor & Sieveking, 1981). The essence of providing competent expert testimony involves adopting an approach which is relaxed and indicative of assurance and confidence. The expert witness who seeks to assist the court by offering a fairminded and comprehensive view of the issues, who avoids defensive, arrogant, or aggressive styles of communicating, who presents as confident in explaining his/her theoretical framework, the methods employed, and the conclusions based on these methodologies, who projects a degree of flexibility and an awareness both of the limits of his/her role in the case and the data he/she is able to offer, is a witness who will best serve the interests of the court and of the case for which he/she is providing testimony.

FORENSIC FEE SETTING

There are some special features of forensic practice as far as fee setting and the methodology of collections are concerned which warrant particular attention. Earlier in this chapter, it was recommended that fees be discussed from the outset with the attorney seeking the consultation. Given the very uncertain nature of forensic work, from a time involvement point of view, and the fact that considerable noncontact time may be required for report preparation and for documentary review, it may be unrealistic for the psychologist to provide the attorney or his/her client with an specific quotations for the cost of the entire consultation. Rather, the psychologist should specify his/her hourly rate(s) for forensic work, and should offer an estimate of the likely number of hours involved in conducting certain specific procedures.

Forensic fees commonly are higher than the usual and customary fee charged for other consulting psychology services. There are a number of reasons for this differential loading. Firstly, with the increased recognition of the value of psychologists to the legal profession, and the still relatively small numbers of experienced psychologists who engage in forensic work, the laws of supply and demand permit the forensic specialist to set a fee that commonly will be 25% or more above that charged for, say, routine clinical services. Secondly, as has been noted previously, forensic work can be particularly stressful and demanding. Thus, the fee schedule for forensic consultation is set to reflect this fact. In this regard also, it is common for the fee schedule of the psychologist to be higher for depositional testimony or for court appearances than when other forensic services are being rendered. Finally, many clients involved in the legal system are subjected to such financial strain that even the most financially responsible of them are unable to pay the entire cost of all the services they require at the time these services are rendered. Thus, it is not uncommon for the forensic psychologist to carry some of the balance associated with a consultation for at least a while after the service has been provided, and such procedures routinely result in higher costs in almost any business enterprise.

With few exceptions, (for example, when the court appoints a psychologist or when the attorney specifically agrees to cover the psychologist's services), even though a forensic consultation may have been arranged between a psychologist and an attorney, the party responsible for the psychologist's fee is the joint client or his/her family. There can be little question but that, relative to psychologists, attorneys have developed the methodology associated with the collection of fees to the point of an art form. The taking of quite substantial retainers is commonplace in the legal profession and, of course, often necessary. The failure to make payment against a debt also tends to be handled far more definitively by attorneys than by psychologists. It does not take the novitiate forensic psychologist long, however, especially if he/she is acting for the defense in criminal cases, before the value of the attorney's art form becomes apparent. It is often particularly difficult, for example, to obtain payment from a defendant who has just been sentenced to a 15-year jail term. And certainly, whether or not the psychologist protects part or all of his/her fee with a retainer, in the vast numbers of instances one can be confident that the attorney with whom the psychologist is acting has most definitely protected his/her fee. Of course, if the psychologist is acting for the defense in a personal injury case which is being covered by a liability insurance carrier, then the prospects of being paid in full at the completion of the case are excellent, irrespective of the outcome.

There are a number of guidelines which the psychologist involved in forensic practice is well served to consider as far as fees are concerned. Firstly, the psychologist should beware of those attorneys who begin their request for psychological assistance by seeking to haggle over the reasonable and customary fee. There is little question but that such a procedure is reflective of a failure on the part of the attorney to respect fully the professionalism and the worth of the psychologist. (Of course, this caution does not extend to the attorney, who will acknowledge one's hourly rate forthrightly, but will advise the psychologist that his/her client's funds are limited and, therefore, that some limitations on the scope of the consultation may be necessary). Secondly, the psychologist should avoid contributing to the view that psychologists do not make strenuous demands for payment, similar to those of their legal counterparts. There can be little question but that many psychologists, even some in full-time private practice, experience difficulty separating their role as members of a helping profession from their role as people of business. While concern for others and generosity are qualities to be admired, they are also qualities which are manipulated, especially by many of those clients involved in the criminal justice system. Avoiding such manipulation can be achieved best by the psychologist placing the same type of general payment demands on the client as those placed by the attorney. Thirdly, if the psychologist is being asked to consult on a case which an attorney has taken on a contingency basis, the major fee related issue is whether the psychologist's fee will be paid at the time of the service or whether this fee, too, will be charged on a contingency basis. If the latter situation applies, the psychologist is well served to discuss the case with the attorney and attempt to gain a perspective on the likely strength of the case before committing him/herself to render the consultation. Thereafter, if the consultation proceeds, it is good practice to have both the client and the attorney sign a letter of protection. This letter represents an approval by the client and an agreement by the attorney that, in the event of a money verdict in favor of the client, the attorney will pay directly to the psychologist all fees and costs associated with the consultation before disbursement to the client. Fourthly, and this recommendation really relates to all practice but is especially important in the litigiously oriented environment of forensic practice, the psychologist should detail in writing, and have the client sign before a witness, an acknowledgement that he/she understands the psychologist's fee structure and policies and that he/she agrees to abide by these policies. (Included in these fee related policies should be the specification of what constitutes billable versus nonbillable time, the obligation of the client regarding cancelled or late appointments, insurance recovery matters, the application if any, of carrying charges billed against overdue accounts, and the policy regarding collections to recover unpaid balances.) By considering the aforementioned guidelines, and implementing fee-related policies based on them, the psychologist involved in forensic practice increases his/her ability to deal effectively and equitably with clients and with attorneys, to ensure the integrity of his/her fee and to maximize the projection of a positive businesslike and professional image, both of him/herself and the practice of psychology.

A final fee-related issue worthy of mention relates to the common practice of attorneys requesting information on fees during the course of testimony of an expert witness. Occasionally, at least, counsel for the opposing side will couch a series of questions about fees and the expert's previous service on behalf of an attorney in terms that easily may be construed to imply, not only that the testimony was biased, but that it had been bought. "Well, Doctor, tell me . . . how many times in the past year have you provided testimony for counsel here? . . . I see . . . and how much are you being paid for providing your testimony today, Doctor? . . . " It is the customary procedure for those skilled in the art of providing testimony to answer the first question in a matter-of-fact manner, and to answer the second by specifying your hourly rate and by adding that it is your time and not your testimony on which the fee is charged.

CASE EXAMPLES

Evaluating the Reliability of Eyewitness Testimony

Notwithstanding the arguments of McCloskey and Egeth (1983), it has been articulated quite convincingly in the literature that expert psychological testimony can contribute a number of important perspectives regarding the entire matter of eyewitness identification. Lindsay, Wells, and Rumpel (1981), Loftus (1979), Loftus and Monahan (1980), and Wells, Lindsay, and Tousigant (1980), for example, have noted that jurors experience considerable difficulty in discriminating between accurate and inaccurate eyewitnesses. Accordingly, these authors have expressed the view that expert psychological testimony addressing memory and perception factors known to influence witness accuracy can improve the discriminating ability of jurors vis-a-vis eyewitness testimony, in part by cautioning them against undue reliance on factors which may be irrelevant. Further, it has been pointed out (Ellison and Buckhout, 1981; Lindsay et al., 1981; Loftus, 1974, 1979; Wall, 1965; Wells et al., 1980) that jurors are, in general, too willing to believe eyewitness testimony. Given such a tendency, it is believed that expert psychological testimony presenting the research which demonstrates the unreliability of eyewitness testimony could increase juror skepticism about eyewitness testimony and thereby produce a more realistic level of evaluation of such testimony. A brief examination of a case employing expert testimony to call into question eyewitness testimony may prove instructive.

About 5:30 p.m. on April 1, 1981, two young gay men were out hustling for tricks on Polk Street in San Francisco when a car stopped nearby, the driver—a man in his forties—motioned to one of the men to get in, the young man did so, and the car moved out into the traffic. There was nothing particularly remarkable about this incident, for Polk Street was well known as a place where prostitution was easily solicited. Three days later, however, the young man's body was found in a wooded area some 70 miles south of San Francisco. The medical examiner's report revealed that the young victim had died as a result of a band or cord of some type which was tightened about the neck, causing asphyxiation and death.

Five weeks later, the victim's friend was shown a six-person photographic line-up and he picked out a 47-year-old man, D. C. The witness quite quickly picked D. C. from the photographs and became nauseated almost immediately thereafter. The quick selection of the photograph, together with the witness' strong emotional reaction convinced the police that they had detected the killer. D. C. was arrested and tried for murder.

During his trial in the fall of 1981, D. C.'s counsel introduced the expert testimony of a psychologist who addressed both the general problems of reliability of eyewitness reporting and the specific factors in this case that could have influenced the accuracy of perception and memory. It was established, for example, that during the late afternoon of April 1, the principal witness had been using marijuana and cocaine, both of which, of course, have an influence on memory and perception. Further, just before viewing the photographs, the witness reported that he had seen a photograph of D. C. lying on a desk in the police station. Surely, such a coincidental observation could have influenced the witness' photographic selection. Additionally, some 5 weeks intervened between April 1 and the date of the photographic viewing. This period, as well as being reasonably long, was filled with stress for the witness because of continuing and repeated police questioning. These were some of the factors about which expert psychological testimony was given.

In the end, the jury in this case deadlocked. As with any case, it is difficult to know the precise reasoning behind the inability of the jury to reach a verdict, or to appreciate the particular impact of the expert testimony given. One can only speculate, based upon interviews with jurors in other cases, and on empirical studies with simulated jurors, that the expert testimony caused a greater scrutiny of the eyewitness aspects of the case than otherwise may have occurred. In turn, such an influence may have led to the particular outcome noted.

A second case involving an evaluation of eyewitness testimony illustrates the fact that, in the life of the expert witness, at least frequently, things do not go as planned.

The *Los Angeles Times* ran the following headline on December 15, 1980: "Robbers kill 3, wound 6 at restaurant." The text went on to report that: "Two shotgun-packing thugs herded two customers and nine employees into a small back room of a Los Angeles restaurant early Sunday, robbed them and then with no apparent reason, opened fire, killing three and wounding six." The incident became known as the "Bob's Big Boy Massacre," named after the restaurant in which the tragedy occurred.

One of us (E. L.) first became involved in the case after the counsel defending one of the alleged assailants sought her services to address the questions of the veracity of the eyewitness testimony in the case. After generally reviewing the incident with the attorney, E. L. agreed to assist the defense. It was readily apparent that there were numerous psychological factors in this case about which expert testimony regarding eyewitness perceptions and memory could be offered. Moreover, there were factors operating in this case that could affect eyewitness accounts, about which the public in general, and jurors in particular, might be unaware. For example, we know that, when people view particularly violent events, two kinds of memory impairment can occur. First, retrograde amnesia, or the forgetting of information that occurred prior to the onset of the violence, may occur. There is also the possibility of anterograde amnesia, or the forgetting of information that occurred following the violent incident (see Clifford and Hollin, 1981; Clifford and Scott, 1978; Loftus and Burns, 1982). The retrograde phenomena would appear especially important in this case, for the effect is, in some respects, counterintuitive. Many people, for example, believe that if there is a period of relative calm prior to the eruption of violence, the perception and memory of this period would be unaffected by the violence. In fact, the effects demonstrated in retrograde amnesia indicate that memories acquired prior to the violence are affected in a negative way.

E. L.'s preliminary analysis of the important psychological factors in this case were communicated to the attorney in a report dated April, 1982. This report was developed after a lengthy review of the police reports, witness statements, preliminary hearing testimony, photographs used in eliciting identification . . . in fact, anything that related to the eyewitness aspects of the case. It took into account, in particular, the extreme violence to which these witnesses had been exposed.

The development of the expert testimony was quite straightforward. The attorney and the expert simply spent time together organizing the presentation, deciding what should be included and in what order it should be offered. The plan was to discuss first the nature of human memory and the mental processes involved in making an eyewitness identification, and then to discuss the factors that are known to influence accuracy, and especially to highlight those factors present in the Bob's Big Boy case.

The following morning, the testimony was presented to the judge, out of the presence of the jury. It is common for the judge to make the initial determination of whether or not to permit expert testimony. If a positive decision is made, the jury then hears the testimony and is free to weigh it as seems appropriate. Usually the offering of the expert testimony to the judge, along with the cross examination, takes only an hour or two, but things did not go as planned. This was a high-publicity death penalty case, and the expert found herself on the stand for 2 days.

A major thrust of the cross examination concerned the external validity of the research being cited. The prosecution sought to elicit, with some success, the many differences between the experimental studies and the particular case at bar. As such, the prosecutor was engaging in the common and legitimate maneuver of questioning the generalizability and relevance of research findings with respect to a particular case. (See also Ellis, 1980; Konecni & Ebbeson, 1979).[2]

---

[2] Generally, the best way to handle the charge that generalization from the laboratory to real life is illegitimate and invalid is to acknowledge the problems but also to present some of the solutions to and strengths of the generalizability argument. In the case of eyewitness testimony research, for example, several investigators have convinced subjects that

The prosecution in the Bob's Big Boy case also challenged the assertion that jurors need expert testimony regarding the veracity of eyewitness testimony.[3] The prosecution challenged the conclusions based upon existing research, and wondered whether other experts might not reach different conclusions.

In the end, the judge decided not to allow the jury to hear the testimony. His opinion was expressed as follows: "There may come a day, there may come a time, when experimental psychology will be sufficiently developed to offer something to us, . . . but this is not that day, nor that time."

Analyzing Misconceptions about Human Behavior

While the research area involving the veracity of eyewitness testimony offers some important perspectives on the role of the expert in pointing out misconceptions about human behavior, a further and specific case example addressing this area and the importance of expert psychological testimony would appear instructive. An ideal case for this illustration is Ibn-Tamas vs. United States (1979).

Beverly Ibn-Tamas, a registered nurse living in Washington, D. C., was accused of killing her physician husband. The marriage was marred by recurring violent episodes. On at least two occasions during her pregnancy, the husband punched Beverly in the head and face. On February 28, 1976, after attempting to repel his violent attacks, she shot him with a .38 caliber revolver.

During the trial which followed, Ibn-Tamas attempted to introduce the testimony of a psychologist on the subject of battered women. Specifically, the purpose of this testimony was to describe the phenomenon of wife battering,

---

they were witnessing real crimes (Sanders & Warnick, 1981: Ruback, Wilson, Mills & Greenberg, 1982). Further, when a range of research studies tends to converge in support of a particular finding, reliability of the conclusions across related research settings is an indication of the likelihood that the results will generalize to the setting in question. Additionally, not uncommonly there is a well developed scientific theory for the phenomenon in the research from which we wish to generalize. Irrespective of the procedure used however, clearly, the expert must be particularly well prepared to handle the testimony and the cross examination.

[3] It was once quite common to hear an objection to the introduction of expert testimony on the grounds that such testimony invades the province of the jury. It is the job of the jury, according to this argument, to decide whether a particular witness was in a position to see, hear and remember what is being claimed in court. The expert testimony would only usurp this function. Since the adoption in 1975 of the Federal Rules of Evidence, which are quite liberal regarding the use of expert testimony, this objection is heard less and less. It is now more common to hear an objection to expert testimony in this area on the grounds that the subject matter is not beyond the knowledge and experience of a juror and therefore, it is not a proper subject matter for expert testimony. This objection, in the eyewitness area, has sparked a series of survey-type studies designed to assess what is commonly known by individuals regarding eyewitness ability. At least seven such studies have now been conducted (see Loftus, 1983a). In general, these studies point uniformly to the conclusion that there are many areas in which lay individuals do not understand how a particular psychological factor influences perception and recollection.

and the psychological literature on this subject. The defense claimed the testimony to be relevant, for it would help the jury to evaluate the credibility of the defendent's contention that she had perceived herself to be in such imminent danger from her husband that she shot him in self-defense. The expert, in this instance, was neither called to, nor intended to, express an opinion on the ultimate question of whether the defendant actually believed she was in danger when she shot her husband. The expert's role was merely to supply background information to help the jury make that crucial determination.

The trial court refused to admit the testimony, an action that troubled the appellate court. In taking up this case, an appellate court argued that the testimony of the psychology expert could have supplied an interpretation of the facts that differed from the ordinary lay perception. For example, the prosecution had implied to the jury that the logical reaction of a woman who was truly frightened by her husband and was regularly brutalized by him would have been to call the police or to leave. In contrast, the expert testimony would have explained why the mentality and behavior of such women is often at variance with this ordinary lay perception of how someone would be likely to react in a chronic and very violent spouse abuse situation.

Providing Testimony in Family Law

Psychologists have been employed perhaps more in the area of family law than in any other forensic area. Nevertheless, the psychologists' relative familiarity with the special problems created when people choose to have the law address matters of family dynamics and domestic relations does not make consultation in this area all that much less difficult. The essential problem, of course, is that the forensic psychological evaluation of matters such as child custody, visitation, parental duty, and the like is conducted within an adversarial context which virtually always makes the evaluation difficult and so causes the conclusions drawn to be somewhat tenuous. Moreover, while psychologists may be qualified and competent to determine the nature and scope of psychopathology in a willing (and sometimes even unwilling) participant, in many instances in family law the people involved are neither bad nor sick, and the prevailing best interests of the child doctrine is in most instances rather poorly defined. In an effort to make this concept more clear, one state, Michigan, had adopted a set of guidelines upon which court decisions regarding child custody matters should be made. The Michigan legislature requires an examination of each of the following: (a) The love and other emotional ties existing between the competing parties and the child; (b) the capacity and disposition of the competing parties to give the child love, affection, and guidance, and to the continuation of education and raising of the child in his/her religion, or creed, if any; (c) the capacity and disposition of the competing parties to provide the child with food, clothing, medical care, and other material needs; (d) the length of time the child has lived in a stable, satisfactory environment, and the desirability of maintaining continuity; (e) the permanence, as a family unit, of the existing or proposed custodial home; (f) the moral fitness of the competing parties; (g) the mental and physical health of the competing parties; (h) the home, school, and community records of the child; (i) the reasonable preference of the child, if the court deems the child to be of sufficient age to express a preference; and (j) any other factor considered by the court to be relevant in a particular case. (Referenced from Watson, 1973).

With the aforestated guidelines offering both somewhat of a perspective and a caveat to psychologists engaging in family related forensic services, the following case examples are offered for consideration. (See also Goldstein, Freud, & Solnit, 1973; Sadoff & Billick, 1981; Schetky & Benedek, 1980).

In 1977, a couple, whom we will call Lane and Brenda McLane, divorced in Florida. Primary custody of their only child, a 5-year-old son, was awarded to the mother. The father was granted reasonable visitation, although the exact times of the visitation were not stipulated. Later that year, Mr. McLane remarried. Over the next 6 months thereafter, the father experienced some minor problems in obtaining access to his son for the purposes of visitation. In reaction to these difficulties, in early 1979 he filed a petition for modification of child custody, which, when heard, resulted in the specification of exact visitation times, including specific hours on weekends, an even-odd year holiday system, a system wherein both the mother and father would see their son around his birthday, and a 2-week visitation for the father during the summer.

Two years thereafter, the father filed a second petition for modification of child custody. In this petition, Mr. McLane alleged that his former wife and her boyfriend were not taking adequate care of the child. The petitioner was seeking a transfer of custody, with the hope that, if he did not receive primary custody, he would at least receive a further increase in visitation. At this point, the petitioner's counsel sought the services of the first author in order to determine if a transfer of custody would be in the best interests of the child.

The psychological consultation involved a total of 3 hours of consulation with the petitioner's attorney (including 1½ hours of pre-trial planning, and ½ hour of briefing regarding preparation of the attorney to take the deposition of an opposing expert witness). Five hours were spent comprehensively testing the child, an additional three 1-hour appointments also were involved in interviewing/confirming over a 6-week period the stability, functioning, attitudes, and desires of the child. A further 14 hours were spent interviewing and testing the father and his new wife. Finally, a total of 3 hours were billed for time involved in court testimony.[4]

---

[4]Clearly, the total of 28 hours involved in this case resulted in a substantial cost to the client (even excluding, of course, his legal expenses). In order to be relatively clear and comprehensive on all matters involved, however, (i.e., in order to be expert on the specific matters before the court), such a level of involvement commonly is required to do justice to the case at hand.

In this case, the comprehensive presentation and interpretation offered to the court by the author proved particularly valuable, for the opposing psychiatric testimony was presented in a written summary statement which appeared less credible, especially because the opposing expert was not present to defend the rigor of his methods or to provide assurance regarding the legitimacy of his conclusions.

A brief summary of the critical points of the psychological testimony is as follows: The child's profile was one of a relatively mature and responsible 10-year-old with an I.Q. of 110 and a pattern of consistently good work at school. Unfulfilled dependency needs, however, and somewhat distorted views of the maternal figure were noted in the child's projections (as measured by the Children's Apperception Test and the Blacky Test). The boy had not yet developed a strong male identification, and he appeared attached to his mother in an exceedingly protective way ("I have to take care of mother. She might get married again, but she would be really lonely if I stayed with my dad."). Assessment of the father and his second wife revealed a number of traditionally positive traits which were subsequently stressed in court. The father, in particular, evidenced a strong work ethic, a dedication to others, a rational solution orientation to problems and a balance between encouragement and firm discipline. Presented together, these data suggested at least that the interests of the boy could be best served by either increasing the father's access to his son, or by transferring the custody of the boy to his dad.

The opposing attorney in this case employed a number of tactics not uncommonly employed against expert witnesses. Upon beginning the cross examination, the attorney questioned the expert's education, work history, other credentials, and relevance of his work experience to the case at bar. Unable to discredit the testimony by this approach, he asked to see the psychologist's notes and attempted to find discrepancies both in the notes and by asking the witness to recount some minor details of the evaluation in order to provoke possible inconsistencies between the notes and the statements of the witness. The best protection against these latter strategies is to: (a) always make comprehensive and understandable notes and bring them to the trial, and (b) always ask to see the record, and answer with it in front of you, rather than getting caught up in an unnecessary game of memory. A final tactic used by the opposing attorney in this case involved objecting to the rendering of any opinion by the expert, as not all parties (i.e., the mother) had been examined. Here, the expert witness can do no more than candidly explain that the validity of an opinion would be greater if all parties had been examined, but this is not a necessity for rendering an opinion within some degree of probability. It was significant also in this case that the expert was able to point out that he had attempted to examine all parties, and that he even had made an appointment to see the mother, but that she had chosen not to keep the appointment.

Despite the various and rather stressful tactics of the opposing attorney, the psychological testimony would appear to have been rather successful in this case. While a transfer of custody was not achieved, a significant increase in the father's visitation was ordered.

Before leaving the domestic relations area, it should be noted that, while most commonly the disputes in family law are between competing parents, there are also many disputes between one or both parents and the youth or family service agencies of a particular jurisdiction, or between the child and the juvenile justice system. In such actions, the county or state agency may be accusing the parents of child abuse or neglect or the child may have been found in legal violation. In either case, the court is interested in the professional assistance of a psychologist or other mental health or child care specialist in order to determine that action which the court will deem to be in the best interests of the child.

Providing Services in Tort Action

A tort is defined as a noncriminal wrong, and in tort action, it is the psychological consequences of personal injury which occupy the bulk of present forensic psychological services. The expert may be called upon, for example, to evaluate and perhaps render treatment services to an individual who has charged another with negligence as a result of an accident. The other major psychological services in the area of tort involves social security disability or disability evaluations for insurance pruposes. Worker's Compensation also often requires a similar consultation. In worker's compensation cases, however, a pre-existing agreement between the employee and the employer already exists. This agreement provides for the injured party to receive essentially immediate payment for time lost at work and for medical expenses, in exchange for not filing a lawsuit against the employer. (Such an agreement, of course, in no way precludes the worker from filing other suits for negligence against, for example, the manufacturer of a piece of equipment that may have contributed to the accident.)

Many labels have been applied to the psychological conditions which follow trauma, but there are essentially three ways of accounting for a person's psychological condition following an injury: (a) an essentially healthy and psychologically well integrated individual may become psychologically disordered as a result of the stress or other aspects associated with the injury, a condition that has been called *post-traumatic neuroses*; (b) an individual psychologically predisposed to emotional disorder experiences a triggering of that pre-disposition as a result of an injury, and thereafter perpetuates his/her difficulties by mechanisms over which he/she appears to have little control, but which impede emotional recovery . . . the so-called *compensatory neuroses*; and (c) the individual deliberately sets out to manipulate the situation to his/her own ends, or *malingers*. (See, for example, Keiser, 1968; Sadoff, 1973; Trimble, 1981).

Given the above three possibilities, and the fact that pre-post accident evaluative material is virtually never available, it is crucial in such tort cases for the psychological consultant to obtain as comprehensive a perspective as possible on the client's pre-injury history and functioning, and to monitor the adjustment of the person during as long a period as possible following the accident. The obtaining of records to confirm or deny clinical impressions and preliminary diagnoses, and the integration of the psychological findings with those of other experts, are all particularly critical aspects of case success in this difficult and often multi-disciplinary area of forensic practice.

In the Fall of 1980, a 25-year-old, attractive, but overweight woman, Fern A., consulted the first author at the recommendation of her attorney. Fern was clearly in a state of agitated depression. Episodic crying and some generally hysterical features characterized the first and several subsequent sessions. Her distress was so severe, in fact, that she was referred to a psychiatrist colleague who placed her on a regimen of Tofranil (100 mg). During the history taking, Fern revealed that she was an unemployed medical assistant, that she had worked in several capacities in physicians' offices since she graduated from technical training at age 20, and that she had not been able to get a job in her field since she had been fired 6 months previously. It also became obvious that Fern was experiencing significant impulse control difficulties as far as anger was concerned, and that she was having problems in social interactions both with friends and family, and that she was particularly sensitive and defensive in dealing with men. Following interviews both with Fern, her mother and her father, and following a request for records, the impression that developed regarding Fern revealed the complex picture of a young, rather strong-willed, but nonassertive woman of rather average scholastic achievement who, up until January 1978, had been coping moderately well psychologically. It was obvious, though, that Fern was at least somewhat predisposed to emotional difficulties. Of significance during the history taking was the fact that Fern was found to be quite a flirt during her latter teen years. Nevertheless, she was a girl who was very timid regarding sexual intimacy. She had only a small num-ber of close emotional contacts with young men, and she had sexual relations with only one male, and on only a very limited number of occasions. In fact, Fern revealed that at age 12 years she had been sexually fondled by the father of a young friend of hers, and that, following this quite traumatic incident, she had come to distrust men and believe that they "were only after one thing." Additionally, partly because Fern viewed herself as an "ideal mother to be" and because she was the only child of parents who had raised her to believe that she would bring them grandchildren, Fern had come to place a high priority on her future role as a loving mother of three or four children.

In January, 1978, Fern began to experience excruciating pain in her lower abdomen. Within a week she had had an appendectomy, but the pelvic inflam-matory condition persisted. A quite severe bladder infection was then diagnosed and antibiotics were prescribed. The bladder condition improved, but still the pain persisted. At about this time, Fern's primary physician was reported to have accused her of having a very low tolerance for pain. Exploratory surgery some 4 weeks later, again by the same surgeon, failed to find the etiological basis of Fern's pain. After this second surgical procedure, Fern's surgeon made a series of comments both to Fern and to her mother which hurt and further angered Fern. While she was waking from the operation, Fern interpreted her surgeon to be inferring that she must be a rather loose woman or else she would not have been experiencing the difficulties she was having to deal with. It was Fern's reaction to these comments which led her to seek consultation aside from her then present surgeon.

After a further period of nearly 8 months of continuous pain, and following a series of consultations at a local university teaching hospital, a third surgical examination revealed that severely abessed ovaries were the basis of Fern's discomfort. Now experiencing even greater pain, Fern accepted the advice of her new surgeons and underwent both an ovariectomy and a hysterectomy.

After Fern's recovery from the final surgery, she and her mother consulted a personal injury attorney who, with consultation from a series of medical experts, concluded that appropriate diagnostic and therapeutic intervention in the earliest stages of Fern's medical difficulties could have resulted in a successful outcome rather than the outcome which ultimately became inevitable.

During the early stages of the psychological consultation with Fern, a comprehensive intellectual and personality evaluation was conducted which permitted a degree of quantification of Fern's level of anxiety and depression, defined clearly the identity and sexuality conflicts she was experiencing, and added further depth and clarity to the question of the separation of her presurgical state from her current level of functioning. The validity of Fern's MMPI profile, the consistency of her overall functioning as variously evaluated using different measures, and the subtleties and intensities of her current psychopathology, all pointed to the fact that malingering was not a factor in this case. (Of course, such a statement does not imply the absence of secondary gain mechanisms which in fact were operating quite blatantly in this case.)

A program of therapy was instituted which lasted throughout the 11 months preceeding the trial and terminated quite successfully 6 months thereafter. Therapy in this case involved an array of generally cognitively oriented techniques designed to improve Fern's self concept and alleviate the depressive episodes she was experiencing. Specific procedures were utilized to desensitize Fern to her feelings about her unattractiveness (due to her multiple surgical scars and her inability to bear children), and to reduce the anticipatory anxiety which she was experiencing about the trial. Therapy also was directed at aiding her in her opposite-sex interactions, introducing assertive training and anger control procedures, helping her take personal responsibility for controlling her emotions, undertaking some family therapy to bring about improvement in her strained relationships with her mother, etc. The value, of course, of the forensic consultant also providing treatment services is that he/she is in a position to have a far more comprehensive view of the extent of the difficulties being experienced by the client, and also to appreciate most completely the degree to which these problems are resistant to therapeutic alleviation.[5]

The petitioner in this case was seeking damages of $1 million; the case involved several medical experts on both sides, including a psychiatrist for the defense. The trial lasted a total of 5 days (after various delays and several offers to settle). The psychologist was on the stand for a total of 5 hours, including nearly 2 hours of cross examination.

During the testimony, Fern's emotional status was presented, from the time of the first interview and the formal testing through to the time of the trial. The jury was presented also with the background psychological functioning which was predicted to be operating prior to her surgeries, and the concept and mechanisms of compensatory neuroses and the predisposing factors existing in this case were presented. Then, an expose of the various triggering events was offered, and these events integrated, to illustrate their specific impacts on Fern's emotional functioning. Finally, a set of prognostic interpretations was presented.

During the cross examination, the opposing counsel attempted many strategies to discredit the testimony. He ranged, for example, from suggestions that the petitioner was competently using pity to manipulate the entire situation, including the psychologist, to asserting that presumably the emotional disorder which was the essence of the psychological testimony must have been a pre-existing condition and as such, was not relevant to the present proceedings.

In the end, the weight of evidence both medical and psychological convinced the jury of both the medical negligence of the defendant and the extent of the direct psychological consequences occasioned by this negligence. A quite sizable amount was awarded in settlement of the case.

We will now turn to offer a final case example of the role of the psychologist functioning in a forensic capacity, this time in a criminal case.

Testimony Regarding Dispostion in a Criminal Case
Since the Durham decision (*United States vs. Durham,* 1954), there has been an increasing significance given to psychiatric and psychological testimony. In Durham, Judge Bazelon stated his opinion that the expert should tell the court

---

[5] There are always those, however, who would assert that when the expert extends his/her relationship beyond that of the evaluator to that of a therapist a level of bias is introduced. It is the view of the present authors that providing therapeutic services may aid even further in establishing clearly the extent of an incident-related impairment, and that it is possible for the psychologist in such a situation to offer this clarity to the court without compromising his/her professionalism or integrity.

whatever he/she can about the defendent in order to provide as comprehensive an understanding of his/her functioning as possible.[6]

Clearly, to be capable of doing his/her job competently, the mental health professional involved in criminal cases must go well beyond the familiar diagnostic and therapeutic role. He/she must have a broad general knowledge of the law and the legal system, must understand the nature of prison life and its effects on various individuals, must appreciate the resources of the probation and other court related services, and he/she must have a specific and detailed knowledge of the treatment facilities available to the court in the state in which the case is being tried.

Mark G. was referred to the first author by his attorney in order to evaluate his mental/emotional functioning as a prelude to the possibility of making an appeal to the court for a rehabilitation-oriented disposition following Mark's guilty plea. At the time of the evaluation, Mark was incarcerated in a local county jail and was facing a total of 20 years in prison for violating probation, possession of cocaine, and grand theft. A total of 18 hours was involved in interviewing Mark's parents (1½ hours), his girlfriend (½ hour), his probation officer (½ hour), in conducting a comprehensive evaluation of Mark (6½ hours), in consulting with a psychiatrist also brought into the case by the defense (1 hour), in consulting with and seeking support from the court based Alternatives to Street Crime Program (½ hour), in reviewing his previous records (1 hour), in consulting with the attorney (2½ hours), in preparing a formal report (1 hour), and in providing testimony (3 hours).

Mark was described by his parents as having emotional and behavioral problems from a very early age. By age 5, for example, Mark was taking money from his parents and creating disturbances in school and in public generally. It was reported by the parents, and it was reiterated by Mark, that the boy frequently played one parent against the other. His mother would take the role of the strict parent: the father, who proved entirely incapable of disciplining Mark or the other son, would smooth over the problems Mark created. In essence,

---

[6]Following the Durham case, a number of other jurisdictions also have expanded the rules of evidence for psychiatric/psychological testimony. Thus, today issues including heat of passion, diminished responsibility, and diagnostic considerations other than psychosis influencing the ability to form specific intent are given serious considerations by courts throughout the country. Today also, psychological experts are being employed by courts and by attorneys in criminal cases ranging across alcoholic and drug abuse, armed robbery, arson, burglary, homicide, sexual offenses . . . the entire spectrum of criminal offenses. Not only are mental health professionals being asked to offer the perspective of their discipline to the courts regarding the nature of the accused and his/her state of mind at the time of the crime; increasingly, they are becoming involved in recommending to the court that course of action which would offer the defendent the most suitable prospects for habilitation or rehabilitation.

Mark's parents unwittingly reinforced in both their sons the capacity to manipulate, and in Mark's case they contributed to his failure to develop any real sense of self worth or responsibility.

Mark's school history was particularly poor. He reported that he early developed a sense of his inability to succeed; his records showed that he could not read beyond a fourth grade level, and that he regularly failed to attend class by the age of 9. In fact, his behavior in class was so disruptive, and his parents so determined that he should not be held back, that each year Mark was passed to the next grade and each year he became more academically incompetent.

Mark's drug usage began in middle school, and, by his own acknowledgement, by age 13 his main goal at school was to stay high on marijuana, thus being the center of considerable peer attention. By high school, Mark had switched from marijuana to the extensive use of quaaludes and other drugs, this habit being supported largely by stealing money or manipulating it away from his parents. Mark withdrew from school in the tenth grade.

Mark was addicted to mood altering street-derived drugs by his late teens. Given this drug habit, and his pattern of constant petty theft in the neighborhood, Mark eventually was arrested and placed into a juvenile drug rehabilitation facility. This pattern repeated itself on several occasions, and each time Mark's father would arrange to save his son at the son's expense. After the arrest prior to the present one, for example, Mark spent only 20 days in a rehabilitation center before his father arranged for a family friend and physician to coordinate Mark's removal from the treatment facility, based on exaggerated claims that interactions between Mark's asthma and his allergies created a serious health hazzard for Mark at the facility. At the time of Mark's present arrest, therefore, despite even multiple involvements in the criminal justice system, Mark had received no appropriate treatment to help reverse his now seriously ingrained psychopathology.

The results of the comprehensive testing which Mark underwent showed a full scale I.Q. of 84, and a rather flat WAIS-R profile. Quoting from the report provided to the court:

> Mark's responses on the intellectual and other testing were typically rapidly given with little or no time given to evaluating his responses. The MMPI profile is of questionable validity, but reflects a cry for help with a number of the scales being above the 70T point. Projective responses by Mark are reflective of a young man who is defensive, resistant toward perceived authority, with poor self image and esteem, and very limited insight into his current situation. His thinking is barely adequate even when situations are presented in a concrete manner. As situations become more abstract, or likely when drugs interfere with his functioning, Mark's ability to utilize effective judgment becomes extremely reduced. He sees himself as wanting to be happy but has no idea how to achieve this goal. He also feels particularly inadequate, insecure and is afraid of his future.

When these results were presented to the attorney at a joint conference with the defense psychiatrist, there were some moderate disagreements regarding certain diagnostic and other implications between the two experts. The psychologist interpreted the client as relatively limited in his intellectual appreciation of his actions, and impelled largely by those forces in his personality that have been indicated previously. The psychiatrist, on the other hand, asserted that he viewed Mark as brain damaged, likely from a pneumonia which he had undergone during his second year. Thus, according to the psychiatrist, Mark was particularly vulnerable to the effects of drugs. The young man was, in his opinion, insane at the time of his most recent arrest because, under the influence of drugs, he was incapable of cognitively discriminating that what he was doing was wrong or illegal (M'Naghten Rules, 1843). Further, according to the psychiatrist expert, Mark was suffering from a mental illness at the time of the act such that he lacked substantial capacity either to appreciate the criminality of his behavior or to conform his conduct to the requirements of the law (*The American Law Institute Model Penal Code,* 1962).[7]

In the context of the agenda of the attorney, the discrepancy between the two experts required some reconciliation, if possible. Thus, following a discussion between the two experts, the psychiatric expert agreed that he would accept the evidence from the psychological testing and not unduly press his initial view that the defendant was likely to be so influenced by his drug usage that at the time of his commission of the crime he was, in all medical probability, insane.

During the trial, the psychological testimony proved to be crucial to the success of the case. The defendant had pleaded guilty, thereby giving up essentially all of his rights to appeal, and the prosecutor was pressing the court for a 20-year prison sentence. After the swearing and the acceptance of the psychologist as an expert, testimony was given that lasted 2½ hours. The testimony began with a review of each of the tests administered, and a test by test analysis. A technique used to great benefit in this case involved blowing up both the MMPI profile and the WAIS-R profile onto a 60 x 42 inch cardboard display to facilitate their presentation to the judge. In fact, having the data presented this way, the judge asked numerous questions about the implications of a number of the subtest scores, and the incompetence of Mark's parents, and vice versa. It was argued that the course of Mark's behavior problems and his involvement with drugs could be predicted, even expected, given what the psychological literature has to tell us about such individuals. A final point stressed by the psychologist during the history presentation focused on the fact that, despite this being Mark's

[7]In the ALI Code the primarily cognitive view expressed under M'Naghten is replaced with the more comprehensive present view of individual psychology, combining the functions of cognitive, volition and conation. There have been a number of attempts to modify the insanity rules, but it is primarily the M'Naghten Rule and the ALI Penal Code that are used throughout the United States (see Quen, 1978).

fourth arrest, and perhaps his twentieth offense, Mark's orientation towards short-term solutions, his father's need to constantly save Mark, and the court's lack of follow through when previously inadequate treatment services had been offered led Mark to receive no meaningful habilitative services from the legal process, despite his almost constant involvement in that process.

Thereafter, the recommendations for habilitation were given. In brief, it was recommended that Mark be ordered to undergo treatment for at least 1 year in duration in a forensic drug facility, that his progress in this facility be monitored for the court by the Treatment Alternatives to Street Crime Program, and that, following such treatment, Mark be engaged in relatively long-term individual and family therapy programming.

The prosecutor, who was presented prior to the trial as being out for blood in this instance, began his cross examination by acknowledging that the testimony had quite markedly influenced him and, in fact, he restricted his questioning to two brief areas. His first question dealt with the MMPI, and he wished the expert to advise the court of the likely profile of a sociopath. Clearly, the presentation was seeking to elicit from the witness a profile not unlike that of the defendant. This line of questioning permitted the expert to further point out the lack of congruence between the defendant and the so-called sociopathic personality. The prosecutor's second line of questioning focused on an opinion expressed by the expert that imprisonment as an adult for more than 9 months would be against the best interests of habilitation in this case. Repeatedly, the prosecutor stressed to the court the need to punish the defendant in order to deter other would-be criminals. He also sought the concurrence of the psychologist as he asserted, given the early release program, that 5 years of imprisonment would likely be the maximum Mark would actually serve, and that such a time in prison would not disrupt Mark's habilitation but would serve the best interests of the society by illustrating the court's commitment to punish offenders.

The psychological testimony was so effective in this case that the defense attorney attempted to limit quite substantially the subsequent psychiatric testimony, for counsel did not wish to have any confounding or possible disagreement between the two defense experts used against the best interests of his client. In the end, the court ordered Mark to serve 6 months in the county stockade (and to be treated as a youthful offender), to be followed by at least 1 year in a restricted drug treatment program, with subsequent out-patient individual and family therapy to be provided throughout a subsequent probationary period, or until such time as the clinician providing such services would certify that Mark has been successfully treated.

A FINAL WORD OF CAUTION

Ziskin (1975), himself a clinical psychologist and an attorney, remarks in a text written primarily for attorneys that, when he was offering psychological testimony:

I became increasingly concerned with the deference that was accorded to me by lawyers and judges who consistently treated me as though *they totally believed* that *I really knew* what I was talking about. I knew how shaky the grounds on which my conclusions rested and could not understand how lawyers could be so naive as not to be aware of this? (p. vii)

Ziskin's comments are especially relevant at a time in which psychology is becoming ever more involved in the practice of law, for, as this process continues, we can expect to see attorneys becoming far more sophisticated in appreciating both the merits and the limitations of the contributions available from the behavioral sciences. Moreover, just as today we see in forensic medicine attorneys seeking the consultation of physicians to aid them in damaging or overcoming the testimony of other medical experts, so too we can expect that, with increasing frequency, psychologists will be asked not only to offer forensic testimony but also to prepare the attorney to deal with other expert psychological testimony. With a careful consideration of many of the issues posed in this chapter, there is every reason to believe that both the psychologist expert and the legal process will benefit from the interaction provided by forensic practice.

REFERENCES

American Psychological Association. (1981). *Ethical principles of psychologists,* Washington, D. C.: Author.

Allen, R. C., Ferster, E. Z., & Rubin, J. G. (1975). *Readings in law and psychiatry.* Baltimore, MD: Johns Hopkins University Press.

American Law Institute Model Penal Code. Section 4.01, Official draft, Philadelphia: May 4, 1962, p. 66.

Anchor, K. N., & Sieveking, N. A. (1981). Constructive utilization of psychological testimony in the courtroom. *Trial, 17,* 46–49; 69.

Bazelon, D. L. (1974, June). Psychiatrists and the adversary process. *Scientific American,* p. 18.

Clifford, B. R., & Hollin, C. R. (1981). Effects of the type of incident and the number of perpetrators on eyewitness testimony. *Journal of Applied Psychology, 66,* 364–370.

Clifford, B. R., & Scott, J. (1978). Individual and situational factors in eyewitness testimony. *Journal of Applied Psychology, 63,* 352–359.

Cohen, R. J., & Marino, W. E. (1982). *Legal guide book in mental health.* New York: Free Press.

Conrad, E. C. (1964, October). The expert and legal certainty. *Journal of Forensic Services, 9,* 445, 449.

Cook, C. M. (1964, October). The role and rights of the expert witness. *Journal of Forensic Sciences,* 456, 459.

Ellis, H. (1980). Psychology and the law. *Science, 208,* 712–713.

Ellison, K. W., & Buckhout, R. (1981). *Psychology and criminal justice.* New York: Harper & Row.

Finkel, N. J. (1980). *Therapy and ethics: The courtship of law and psychology.* New York: Grune and Stratton.

Goldstein, J., Freud, A., & Solnit, A. J. (1973). *Beyond the best interests of the child.* New York: Free Press.

Haward, L. (1981). *Forensic psychology.* London: Batsford.

Ibn-Tamas vs. United States. District of Columbia Court of Appeals, 12614. 1979.

Keiser, L. (1968). *The traumatic neurosis.* Philadelphia: Lippincott.

Konecni, V. J., & Ebbeson, E. B. (1979). External validity of research in legal psychology. *Law and Human Behavior, 3,* 39–70.

Lindsay, R. C. L., Wells, G. L., & Rumpel, C. M. (1981). Can people detect eyewitness identification accuracy within and across situations. *Journal of Applied Psychology, 66,* 79–89.

Loftus, E. F. (1974). Reconstructing memory: The incredible eyewitness. *Psychology Today, 8,* 116–119.

Lotfus, E. F. (1979). *Eyewitness testimony.* Cambridge, MA: Harvard University Press.

Loftus, E. F. (1983). Silence is not golden. *American Psychologist, 38,* 564–572. (a)

Lotfus, E. F. (1983). Whose shadow is crooked. *American Psychologist, 38,* 576–577 (b).

Loftus, E. F., & Burns, T. E. (1982). Mental shock can produce retrograde amnesia. *Memory and Cognition, 10,* 318–323.

Loftus, E. F., & Monahan, J. (1980). Trial by data: Psychological research as legal evidence. *American Psychologist, 35,* 270–283.

McCloskey, M., & Egeth, H. E. (1983). Eyewitness identification. What can a psychologist tell a jury? *American Psychologist, 38,* 550–563. (a)

McCloskey, M., & Egeth, H. E. (1983). A time to speak, or a time to keep silent? *American Psychologist, 38,* 573–575 (b).

Miller, A. S. (1968). Drawing in indictment 51. *Saturday Review, 30,* 40.

Morse, S. J. (1978). Law and mental health professionals: The limits of expertise. *Professional Psychology, 9,* 389–399.

M'Naghten Rules 10 Clark and Finney 200, 8 English Reporter 718 House of Lords, 1843.

People vs. Hawthorne, 291 N. W. 205 (Michigan, 1940).

Quen, J. M. (1978). A history of the Anglo American legal psychiatry of violence and responsibility. In Sadoff (Ed.), *Violence and responsibility: The individual, the family and society.* New York: S. P. Medical and Scientific Books.

Robinson, D. N. (1980). *Psychology and law. Can justice survive the social sciences?* New York: Oxford University Press.

Ruback, R. B., Wilson, C. E., Mills, M. K., & Greenberg, M. S. (1982). *Eyewitness identification by theft victims.* Unpublished manuscript, University of Pittsburgh.

Sadoff, R. L. (1973). Traumatic psychosis. In L. R. Frumer & M. K. Minzer (Eds.). *Personal injury annual.* New York: Matthew Bender.

Sadoff, R. L. (1982). *Legal issues in the care of psychiatric patients: A guide for the mental health professional.* New York: Springer.

Sadoff, R.L., & Billick, S. (1981). The legal rights and difficulties of children in separation and divorce. In I. R. Stuart & L. E. Abt (Eds.), *Children of separation and divorce: Management and treatment.* New York: Van Nostrand Reinhold.

Sanders, G. S., & Warnick, D. H. (1981). Truth and consequences: The effect of responsibility on eyewitness behavior. *Basic and Applied Social Psychology,* 69–79.

Schetky, D. H., & Benedek, E. P. (1980). *Child psychiatry and the law.* New York: Brunner/ Mazel.

Schwitzgebel, L., & Schwitzbegel, R. K. (1980). *Law and psychological practice.* New York: John Wiley & Sons.

Slovenko, R. (1975). Preface. In L. Sadoff. *Forensic Psychiatry. A practical guide for lawyers and psychiatrists.* Springfield, IL: Charles C. Thomas.

Trimble, M. R. (1981). *Post-traumatic neurosis.* New York: John Wiley.

United States vs. Durham, 214 F, 2d 862, (D. C. Cir., 1954).

Van Hoose, W. H., & Kottler, J. A. (1977). *Ethical and legal issues in counseling and psychotherapy.* San Francisco: Jossey–Bass.

Wall, P. M. (1965). *Eyewitness identification in criminal cases.* Springfield, IL: Charles C. Thomas.

Washington vs. United States, 390 F 2d 444,457, (D.C. in Cir.), 1967.

Watson, A. S. (1973). Contested divorces and children: A challenge for the forensic psychiatrist. In C. Wecht (Ed.), *Legal medical annual, 1973.* New York: Appleton-Century-Crofts.

Weinstein, J. B. (1966). Some difficulties in devising rules for determining truth in judicial trials. *Columbia Law Review, 66,* 223.

Wells, G. L., Lindsay, R. C. L., & Tousigant, J. P. (1980). Effects of expert psychological advice on human performance in judging the validity of eyewitness testimony. *Law and Human Behavior, 4,* 275–285.

Ziskin, J. (1970). *Coping with psychiatric and psychological testimony.* Beverly Hills, CA: Law and Psychological Press.

Ziskin, J. (1975). *Coping with psychiatric and psychological testimony.* (2nd ed.) Beverly Hills, CA: Law and Psychology Press.

WORK SETTINGS OF PROFESSIONAL PSYCHOLOGISTS

Chapter 7

Private Practice

Georgiana Shick Tryon
Fordham University

Most graduate students in clinical psychology look forward to a full-time or part-time private practice. The number of psychologists entering private practice has grown considerably over the past decade. A 1981 survey of 479 members and fellows of Division 12 (Clinical) of the American Psychological Association (APA) found 31% of these clinicians were engaged in full-time private practice and an additional 61% were engaged in part-time practice (Norcross & Prochaska, 1982) Approximately a decade earlier, only 23% of a sample of Division 12 members had full-time practices and 47% had part-time practices (Garfield & Kurtz, 1974).

There are a number of possible reasons for this dramatic increase in the number of private practitioners. There has been a rapid growth in the number of graduate programs in clinical psychology and in the number of students graduating from these programs (Caddy, 1981). The number of jobs in academia is not keeping pace with the number of clinical graduates, and positions in public hospitals and clinics often depend on governmental aid, which varies with the priorities of the administration in power. Private practice offers the clinician a chance to make more money than he/she would in the public sector. The private practitioner is also his/her "own boss."

Graduate students generally receive little information regarding private practice. Faculty members may have their own private practices, but often they do not present their independent practice experiences to students in any organized fashion. Few graduate programs offer practicum placements in private practice (Lowe & Ritzler, 1980).

Until recently, little was known about the private practice experience other than what was communicated in anecdotal accounts (e.g., Tamkin, 1976; Taylor, 1978; Weinrach, 1980). This changed in 1981, when two surveys of independent practitioners were conducted. Norcross and Prochaska (1983) surveyed 210 full-time private practitioners, while I (Tryon, 1983a, 1983b, 1983c, 1983d, 1983e) surveyed 165 full-time private practitioners. Much of the information regarding full-time private practice presented in this chapter comes from these surveys.

This chapter is designed to inform the reader regarding the private practice experience. It addresses the following topics: qualifications of independent practitioners, beginning and maintaining the practice, services offered and patients seen, fees and incomes, theoretical orientations, jobs in addition to private practice, organizational memberships, research and publications, satisfactions and dissatisfactions, differences between male and female full-time private practitioners, and the future of private practice. It is hoped that the information will be useful to the student, the beginning practitioner, and even the established practitioner. There are a number of books regarding the establishment of private practice which the reader may also wish to consult (Browning, 1982; Cookerly & McClaren, 1982; Hendrickson, Janney, & Fraze, 1978; Lewin, 1978).

QUALIFICATIONS OF INDEPENDENT PRACTITIONERS

Almost all private practitioners in psychology have a doctoral degree. The doctorate is generally a requirement for state certification or licensure. After receiving the doctorate, most practitioners obtain state certification or licensure. Certification generally restricts the use of the title "psychologist," while licensure generally restricts certain practices. Often, all types of psychologists (e.g., clinicians, counselors, developmental specialists, experimentalists) can be certified; so having this credential does not indicate specialty. Licensure or certification is important for practitioners wishing to receive third-party payments, and is required of practitioners wishing to be included in the *National Register*. Contact your state licensing agency for information regarding qualifications and the nature of the license or certificate. Most states require a doctoral degree and 2 years of supervised experience for licensure/certification.

The *National Register of Health Service Providers in Psychology* was established in 1975 to identify psychologists who are health service providers from among the larger group of psychologists who are licensed or certified. The *Register* is useful to insurance companies providing third-party payments and also serves as a referral listing. I have both received and provided referrals from the *Register*.

National Register listing is voluntary. Practitioners wishing to join must have a doctoral degree from a regionally accredited university, state certification/licensure, and 2 years (one postdoctoral) supervised experience, with 1 year being at an organized health service training program. For further information, write the Council for the National Register of Health Service Providers in Psychology, 1200 Seventeenth Street, N.W., Washington, D.C. 20036.

The highest credential of competence a professional psychologist can receive is American Board of Professional Psychology (ABPP) diplomate status, which is granted in four fields: clinical, counseling, school, and industrial psychology. ABPP diplomates do not have to take state examinations for certification/

licensure and are highly respected practitioners within their fields. Fifteen percent (*n* = 24) of my sample of 165 full-time private practitioners were ABPP diplomates in clinical psychology, and two respondents were diplomate candidates. The ABPP diploma is the only credential depending primarily upon an examination of the candidate's skills. The ABPP candidate must submit a work sample to the board of diplomates and pass an oral examination conducted by the same board. The work sample consists of transcriptions and audio tapes regarding some aspect of the candidate's professional practice of psychology. Contact ABPP at 2100 E. Broadway, Suite 313, Columbia, MO 65201-6082 for further information.

To summarize, the professional psychologist beginning an independent practice should have a doctorate and be certified/licensed in his/her state. Membership in the *National Register* and ABPP diplomate status are additional credentials well worth obtaining.

Continuing Education

Some states require continuing education for renewal or maintenance of licensure/certification (Albee & Kessler, 1977) to ensure the continuing competence of professional psychologists. The *APA Monitor* provides a calendar of continuing education offerings and approved continuing education sponsors. Full-time private practitioners regularly attend continuing education workshops and seminars. Besides offering an educational experience, these workshops provide the independent practitioner with the opportunity to interact with others who have similar interests.

A substantial minority (42%) of respondents to my questionnaire regarding full-time private practice had completed or were completing a program of postdoctoral study in psychotherapy. Such programs offer the practitioner an opportunity to receive additional supervised training in a specialized area.

BEGINNING AND MAINTAINING THE PRACTICE

Before beginning private practice, the psychologist should make certain he/she is legally qualified to start a practice in his/her state. Consideration needs to be given to the projected size of the practice, types of patients who will be seen, and services to be offered. The therapist's office should be located in an easily accessible area. Some private practitioners have offices in their homes, others rent offices, and still others own their offices or the buildings in which they are located.

Office supplies need to be purchased, and the therapist should set up a record keeping system. Professional liability insurance should be obtained, as well as additional liability insurance in case someone should sustain an injury on the practitioner's property.

Beginning the Practice

There are many ways to begin a private practice. Traditionally, most practitioners seeking to do private work have simply made this fact known to co-workers and the students and clients they serve at their regular full-time jobs. In this manner, it is not too difficult to establish a small part-time practice. Some practitioners then expand their practices and eventually quit or drastically reduce the hours spent at their full-time jobs. About half the full-time private practitioners in my sample started their practices in this manner.

Other practitioners start their practices while having part-time jobs. This pattern was most prevalent among suburban practitioners and women in my sample.

Some private practitioners begin their practices without having a job. These individuals must carefully plan their practices to ensure survival. The needs of the community where the practice is located should be assessed, and the practitioner must set clearly defined marketing and service goals. Over 20% of my sample started their practices in this manner.

Group practices are becoming increasingly prevalent, and were particularly popular among practitioners in my sample who had received their degrees relatively recently. Some new practitioners join established group practices rather than attempt to set up practices on their own. A group practice provides its members with colleagues. Solo practitioners often feel isolated. In a recent presidential address to APA Division 12 members, Bonnie Strickland (1983) saw an end to the solo private practitioner in the future. The wave of the future appears to be group practices which contract with companies and organizations to provide care (Samuels, 1983a).

Marketing Services

Independent practitioners, particularly those in full-time practice, must market their services to establish, expand, and maintain their practices. The books cited in the introduction of this chapter contain numerous marketing suggestions. Many practitioners offer workshops for key community groups or referral sources, making sure to provide handouts with the practitioner's name, address, and phone number prominently displayed. Some practitioners volunteer consultation time to a particular group or agency to demonstrate how useful their services can be. Other practitioners speak about psychological problems on radio or television. Most practitioners establish direct, personal contact with referral sources.

The full-time private practitioners in my sample were asked to list their most effective marketing techniques. The most frequently mentioned technique was to do good professional work. Evidently satisfied patients spread the word about their therapists' effectiveness, and this results in more patients seeking the therapists' services. The next five most frequently mentioned techniques were giving speeches, displaying professional behavior toward referral sources, advertising, having contact with physicians, and giving workshops.

Referral Sources

The 165 full-time private practitioners in my sample indicated the percentage of referrals they received from a variety of sources. The best referral source was other patients, which was mentioned by 147 practitioners and accounted for an average of 30% of each practitioner's referrals. The next best referral source was physicians, other than psychiatrists, followed by self-referrals, psychologists, and psychiatrists.

SERVICES OFFERED AND PATIENTS SEEN BY PRIVATE PRACTITIONERS

The individual private practitioner does not generally offer all types of services to all kinds of people. Practitioners vary in the extent to which they offer individual, group, and family therapy. Individual practitioners work well with some types of patients and less well with others. Based on his/her training and experience, the beginning practitioner should consider what types of services to offer and to whom.

Services

The 210 full-time private practitioners surveyed by Norcross and Prochaska (1983) spent almost 70% of their professional time engaged in psychotherapy. The most frequently offered therapy modality was individual therapy (provided by almost 100% of the sample). Over 80% of the practitioners offered marital therapy, over 55% offered family therapy, and over 40% offered group therapy. Individual therapy, however, consumed the bulk (67%) of professional time, followed by marital (15%), family (8%), and group (6%) therapy. In addition to doing psychotherapy, over 70% of the practitioners engaged in diagnostic work, which consumed about 11% of their professional time.

Patients

Not all practitioners work well or have training with all types of patients. In my sample of full-time private practitioners, 98% saw adult patients, 82% saw adolescents, 63% saw children, and 43% saw elderly patients.

Most of these practitioners (63%) further restricted the types of patients they saw by diagnosis. Within the age range of patients they would normally see, 32% of the sample would not see psychotics, 14% of the sample would not see suicidal patients, and 41% of the sample would not take patients with other disorders (generally alcohol/drug abusers or sociopathic/acting out disorders).

Women were more likely than men to restrict the type of patients they saw. Although no questions about therapists' family lives and responsibilities were asked, a number of women reported restricting their practices because of family consideration. For example, one woman practitioner said she would not see "alcohol and drug abusers who are not making an effort to stop; violent or homicidal clients. As a solo practitioner with small children, I am not equipped to handle frequent 24-hour emergencies for treatment."

There were times when some full-time practitioners' economic situation made it necessary for them to take patients they would not ordinarily see. Thirty percent of my sample said they had done so. At least two practitioners regretted this experience. As one put it, "It was not the best decision; it often took years to get out of untoward situations." Another said, "Once my narcissism led me to see a patient I shouldn't have seen, but I referred the patient to someone else after a *brief* period of treatment."

Because they generally have practices to supplement their incomes, part-time practitioners can afford to be even more selective of the types of patients they see. There has been no survey of the diagnostic categories of patients seen by part-time practitioners, but my own experience seems to be somewhat typical. I see patients who usually do not require much professional time outside of therapy hour. Because I have a full-time job, I have only a limited amount of time to give private patients.

Referrals to Other Practitioners

Most practitioners need to occasionally refer patients to other mental health professionals, and private practitioners are no exception. Most (85%) of the 165 full-time private practitioners I surveyed indicated they sometimes or often referred patients to other practitioners. Fifteen percent of the sample said this was a rare occurrence, and none of the respondents said they never referred patients to others.

A total of 144 of the 165 practitioners listed the reasons for their referrals. Many of the most frequently mentioned reasons for referral (e.g., patient needs specialized treatment, medication, hospitalization) were related to therapists' lack of expertise with patients' problems. Other reasons (e.g., lack of interest in patient's problem, patient's inability to afford fee) related to the attractiveness of patients to the therapists. Private practitioners have greater freedom to choose their patients as compared to practitioners in public agencies. Because they are their own bosses, independent practitioners can be more selective of the types of patients they see and the times at which they see them than agency practitioners.

Legal and Ethical Issues

The individual about to begin a practice should carefully assess his/her own competence with particular types of treatments and patients. The practitioner should be familiar with the *Ethical Principles of Psychologists* (American Psychological Association, 1981a; a free copy can be obtained by writing APA at the previously mentioned address). Practitioners should pay particular attention to Ethical Principles 1 through 8. Principle 2 (Competence) directly states that psychologists should offer services in accord with their training and experience.

In 1977, the APA Council of Representatives adopted a set of generic *Standards for Providers of Psychological Services* to provide a means of self-regulation to serve the needs of users, providers, and third-party purchases of professional psychological services. Subsequently, *Specialty Guidelines* for providers of clinical (American Psychological Association, 1981b), counseling (American Psychological Association, 1981c), and industrial/organizational (American Psychological Association, 1981d) services were issued. The *Specialty Guidelines*, along with *Guidelines for Therapy with Women* (American Psychological Association, 1978), may be obtained directly from APA. The reader is encouraged to consult the chapters of this volume regarding ethical and legal issues for further information regarding ethical and legal standards.

FEES AND INCOMES

The prospect of making a substantial amount of money is one of the attractions of private practice. A glance at APA's annual salary survey (APA, 1982) shows that independent practitioners have higher average incomes than other psychologists.

Fees

Before opening his/her practice, the psychologist needs to establish fees for service. Practitioners generally have separate fees for individuals, groups, and families, plus rates for psychological testing. Fee setting should not be done arbitrarily. Most practitioners charge fees comparable to those of other practitioners in their area. This value can be determined by contacting other practitioners in your area. Fees vary from region to region.

The practitioner also needs to decide how flexible to be regarding fees. Most (78%) of the 165 full-time private practitioners in my study reported occasionally or frequently adjusting their fees to accommodate patients who could not afford their regular rates. Many said that the patient's ability to pay was an important factor in the decision to lower rates. Most practitioners set a fee and then occasionally accept less if they have to in order to see a particular patient. However, there is generally a limit below which the practitioner will refer the patient elsewhere.

Fees charged can relate to expenses. For example, a practitioner with an office in his/her home could charge less than a practitioner who rents an office and employs a secretary. New practitioners may wish to set aside several low-fee hours to promote their services. Some practitioners promote service by offering patients a free initial consultation.

Income

Private practitioners make a good income, but each practitioner has expenses. There may be a sizeable difference between gross and net incomes; in my sample, this difference was $20,000 on average.

About half of the private practitioners I surveyed reported that their practice income fluctuated somewhat. No-shows, cancellations, and terminations reduce income, as do unpaid bills. Unpaid bills plague most every practitioner, and some employ bill collectors. In my practice, I try to keep the amount owed me to a minimum by insisting on payment from individuals at the beginning of each session.

THEORETICAL ORIENTATIONS

Private practitioners subscribe to a number of theoretical orientations. The most frequently listed orientation of the 210 full-time independent practitioners surveyed by Norcross and Prochaska was eclecticism, selected by 31% of the sample. A psychodynamic perspective was next (14%), followed by psycho-analysis (11%), cognitive (8%), and behavioral (6%). Adlerian, existential, gestalt, humanistic, Rogerian, systems, and Sullivanian orientations were each endorsed by less than 5% of the sample.

The majority (56%) of the 165 full-time independent practitioners in my sample were eclectic in orientation; however, in contrast to Norcross and Pro-chaska, I counted all practitioners who checked more than one orientation as eclectic. Another 20% were psychoanalytic, 8% were behavioral, and 15% were other orientations (primarily systems and humanistic).

Relationship of Orientation to Practice

The practitioners surveyed by Norcross and Prochaska indicated that their theoretical orientations profoundly influenced their practices. A practitioner's orientation affects the services offered and the patients seen. For example, in my sample significantly more behaviorists and eclectically-oriented practi-tioners than statistically expected, and fewer psychoanalysts than expected, re-ported seeing adolescent patients (χ^2 (4) = 11.97 $p<.02$). More behaviorists and eclecticaly-oriented practitioners than statistically expected, and fewer psycho-analysts than statistically expected, reported seeing suicidal patients (χ^2 (4) = 15.77, $p<.003$).

Theoretical orientation was also related to receiving supervision, with more psychoanalytically oriented practitioners than statistically expected, and fewer eclectic and behavior therapists than statistically expected, receiving supervision on their cases (χ^2 (4) = 12.00, $p<.02$). Not surprisingly, there was a relationship between orientation and area of the country in which the practitioner was lo-cated. Psychoanalysis was more popular among Easterners than Westerners, while newer orientations (e.g., systems) were more popular among Westerners than Easterners.

Satisfaction with Orientation

Norcross and Prochaska asked their sample to rate level of satisfaction with their theoretical orientation on a 6-point scale where 1 was "very dissatisfied" and

6 was "very satisfied." The mean response was a rating of 4.8, indicating that these full-time private practitioners were satisfied with their orientations. Thirty-five percent were "very satisfied" and 86% responded in the satisfied range.

JOBS IN ADDITION TO PRIVATE PRACTICE

Independent practitioners often are involved with other jobs in addition to their practices. For many, private practice represents a limited, part-time activity. About 46% of doctoral-level human service providers in psychology spend 10 or fewer hours per week doing private work, and two-thirds spend 20 or fewer hours per week providing private fee-for-service care (VandenBos, Stapp, & Kilburg, 1981). Private practice fees supplement the paychecks of university professors, hospital staff members, and community health workers.

A substantial minority of full-time independent practitioners have other jobs (part-time teaching, supervision, and consultation) in addiition to their practices. Private practitioners generally do not seek outside employment for financial reasons. As one practitioner said, "Some consulting arrangements pay rather poorly." Another said, "No paid job can do as well as private practice." The practitioners in my sample rated opportunity to interact with colleagues, variety of work, learning experience, opportunity to supervise, and opportunity to teach as important factors in their decision to seek outside employment. A teaching or consulting job provides variety for the practitioner, and an opportunity to "get out of the office."

ORGANIZATIONAL MEMBERSHIPS

There are numerous organizations private practitioners may join. To begin with, it is a good idea for all psychologists to join APA to be informed of important happenings in the field. Each member receives free subscriptions to *American Psychologist* and the *Monitor*. Low-cost professional liability insurance is also available to APA members.

There are a number of APA Divisions which may interest the private practitioner. In particular, Divisions 42 (Psychologists in Independent Practice), 29 (Psychotherapy), and 12 (Clinical) provide important information regarding practice and legislation. Other divisions (e.g., 25—Division for the Experimental Analysis of Behavior; 39—Division of Psychoanalysis) offer useful information regarding therapeutic specialties. The full-time private practitioners in my sample indicated APA membership was somewhat important to them (mean rating = 2.55 on a 6-point scale where 1 was the positive and 6 the negative polarity).

State psychological associations are sometimes highly influential regarding legislation affecting psychologists. The private practitioner wishing to have input into his/her profession on a statewide level should join. However, some practitioners may not agree with the philosophy of their particular state association. State dues are sometimes very high. The full-time independent practitioners in my sample viewed membership in state psychological associations as somewhat important.

Some communities have local psychological associations which, in addition to dealing with issues of interests to psychologists on a local level, may serve as support groups for independent practitioners. However, many local associations don't seem to be doing this. Often, local associations are controlled by the special interests of a few psychologists. The practitioners in my sample did not view local psychological association memberships as positively as they did memberships in APA or state associations.

There are also regional psychological associations which hold annual conventions. These associations are generally more attractive to the academic or research psychologist than to the independent practitioner.

There are other professional organizations which may be of interest to therapists in general (e.g., American Academy of Psychotherapy, American Orthopsychiatric Association) or to therapists subscribing to particular orientations (e.g., Association for the Advancement of Behavior Therapy). Most associations have their own newsletters and/or journals which keep members up to date regarding issues of particular interest. Professional organizations generally hold annual conventions which provide the independent practitioner with learning experiences and an opportunity for collegial interaction. Respondents to my questionnaire did not rate attendance at national and state conventions as important. Perhaps, full-time private practitioners benefit more from the specialized workshops they attend then they do from the larger conventions. Large conventions are often time consuming and expensive. It has been my experience that full-time private practitioners enjoy conventions once they get there. Solo private practice can be a lonely experience, and it is often a tonic to interact with colleagues, some of whom one has not seen for years, at a convention.

RESEARCH AND PUBLICATIONS

Most psychologists do not conduct research or publish. Even in universities where jobs often depend on professional publications, research productivity lags behind expectations.

There are few incentives to conduct research in independent practice. The research process is costly. Hours spent collecting data, in the library, and writing are hours not spent in practice. Typing and other expenses also detract from the process. The practitioner's job is not dependent on publications, and after long hours spent with patients, the prospect of doing still more work is not attractive.

Yet publications do offer the practitioner an opportunity to become known to other practitioners and to the public. Also, research on real live patients communicates more relevant information about pathology and psychotherapy than does analogue research using university students. As one full-time private practitioner put it, "Most so-called professional journals are slightly less than useless and will continue (to be) so until 'researchers' find an experimental population other than college students."

Results from Norcross and Prochaska's study indicate that, despite a lack of incentives to do so, 210 full-time private practitioners published significantly more articles (mean = 5.5) and presented significantly more papers (mean = 6.5) than did 72 psychotherapists in institutional settings (mean for articles = 3.3, mean for papers = 3.4). Eighty-six percent of the 165 full-time independent practitioners I surveyed found at least one professional journal useful to them in their practices. The practitioners mentioned well over 100 different professional journals, with each practitioner listing an average of 3.

Thus, private practitioners publish and read journals more often than might be expected. Both of these activities are to be encouraged. Professional psychology cannot progress without input from its practitioners.

SATISFACTIONS AND DISSATISFACTIONS

There are pros and cons to every occupation, and private practice is no exception. This section focuses on the extent to which full-time independent practitioners are satisfied with their training and their practices.

Training

As was noted in the introduction, most graduate schools do not provide placements at, or coursework, concerning private practice. As a result, psychologists do much of their learning about independent practice outside of formal educational settings. The popularity of the books regarding the establishment of practices cited at the beginning of this chapter, and the publication of a journal exclusively devoted to private practice issues *(Psychotherapy in Private Practice)*, indicate that there is an eager group of consumers who want to know as much as possible about the independent practice of psychology.

Norcross and Prochaska asked their sample of 210 practitioners to indicate level of satisfaction with their graduate training on a 6-point scale where 6 was the positive polarity. Respondents gave an average rating of 4.1 indicating slight satisfaction with training. Seventy-four percent of the sample gave ratings in the satisfied range (4–6), while 26% had some dissatisfaction with training.

The 165 practitioners in my sample were more neutral regarding their educational experience. Rather than asking private practitioners how satisfied they were with their graduate training, I asked how well they felt this training had prepared them for their practices. On a 6-point scale where 1 was the positive polarity, respondents gave an average rating of 3.3. Sixty percent of the sample rated it in the useful range, while the remaining 40% rated their graduate training as not that useful.

Respondents were asked to explain their ratings in writing. Only 31% wrote entirely favorable comments. The following represents typical statements: "We had good teachers and helpful and reasonable mentors. My training was rigorous. We put in *long* hours of hard work. We were encouraged to find our own way with this rigorous training and to pursue our own theoretical orientation." "(My training) taught me to use myself as teacher, guide, and therapeutic agent."

Another 17% indicated mixed feelings about the usefulness of their graduate training. Most were satisfied with the clinical training but felt there should have been more emphasis on the business and ethical aspects of private practice. Here are some typical comments: "Training was super as far as practice—not at all helpful as far as the private part of it—a lot of unlearning had to be done." "Excellent clinical training, *but* there was literally no focus on the mechanics of private practice."

Finally, 52% wrote unfavorable comments. Here are some examples: "The clinical supervision was generally poor and unsophisticated and advice regarding the practical aspects of private practice was absent altogether." "It did not prepare me for psychotherapy, which is my practice essentially." "No real time spent on important ethical issues in a private setting or on matters related to practice management, cooperation with other disciplines, etc."

It seems that, in future, graduate schools should pay more attention to training regarding private practice. This training should be particularly directed toward the practical aspects of operating an independent practice. The books listed at the beginning of this chapter, as well as articles by Cantor (1983) and Samuels (1983b) provide helpful suggestions regarding the business aspects of private practice.

Practice

Many psychologists considering private practice view it as an ideal job where one is truly one's own boss and the financial rewards are plentiful. Indeed, most independent practitioners find their jobs highly rewarding, but there are negatives associated with private practice as well.

Norcross and Prochaska asked the 210 full-time private practitioners they surveyed to rate their career satisfaction on a 6-point scale where 6 was the positive polarity. The mean satisfaction rating was 5.3, indicating that the average practitioner was quite satisfied with his/her career. A whopping 93% of the practitioners gave ratings indicating satisfaction (4-6). The modal rating was a 6.

Norcross and Prochaska further asked practitioners what careers they would choose if they had their lives to live over again. Seventy percent of the respondents chose the independent practice of psychology. Many others would have pursued psychiatry. The authors indicated that answers to this item generally yield an overly pessimistic estimate of career satisfaction; yet a great majority chose to stick with the careers they currently had.

I asked full-time independent practitioners to list what pleased them most about their practices. Professional independence was the most frequently reported satisfaction, followed by success, high income, flexible hours, variety, challenge of the work, and enjoyment of the work. Here are some typical responses: "The independence and freedom I have in scheduling my time. The freedom from agency rules and regulations and the politics associated with agency employment." "The excitement and challenge of the work, the complexity of understanding other people." "Independence, satisfaction of feeling that I truly help people and in a small way make the world a little better, financial rewards, no red tape to deal with."

The most frequently listed displeasures were isolation, time pressures, problems in the therapeutic relationship, economic uncertainty, personal depletion, business aspects, caseload uncertainty, and lack of fringe benefits. Here are some typical comments: "Long hours that are frequently necessary, sense of isolation, and difficulty scheduling contact wtih colleagues." "Never know where your next dollar is coming from." "Vacations difficult to schedule sometimes because of clients' needs. No sick or vacation pay; difficulty budgeting because of varying income; insurance, disability policies, etc. are very expensive." "It's hard, relentless, involves super responsibility and requires constant vigilance regarding patient care." "Paperwork and third-party payments." "That it's piecework—no work, no money—and having to drum up business. I deal with the loneliness by being in a peer supervision group once a week."

As the reader can discern from the comments, independent practice can be very rewarding but there are pressures involved. The practitioner must live with a certain amount of economic uncertainty, and there is a great temptation to overwork. The hectic pace required can lead to professional burnout, and, not surprisingly, a few of the respondents used this term to describe themselves.

DIFFERENCES BETWEEN MALES AND FEMALES

When I began to study private practitioners, I did not expect to find many differences between male and female practitioners. After all, private practice is an independent business not subject to discriminatory hiring policies, and there is evidence indicating that both male and female patients are more satisfied with female therapists (Betz & Shullman, 1979; Hill, 1975; Jones & Zoppel, 1982). Therefore, private practice was expected to be a "great equalizer," with women doing just as well as men in terms of income and patient hours. But a number of sex differences were found indicating that women in full-time private practice had more limited practices than men.

Women had significantly fewer practice hours per week than did men (31 versus 36), and consequently made significantly lower gross and net incomes than men. Women reported significantly fewer marketing techniques than men, were significantly more likely than men to refer patients to other practitioners, and were significantly more likely than men not to see certain types of patients.

The reasons for this are not clear, but it may be that these women had more family and household responsibilities than the men. However, no questions concerning domestic responsibilities were asked. Women started their practices while having part-time jobs significantly more often than expected. Perhaps they held part-time rather than full-time jobs because of domestic responsibilities. Women were significantly more likely than men to have offices in their homes, perhaps indicating a preference to be at home. Research on dual-career couples indicates that women bear the majority of domestic responsibilities in these marriages (Tryon & Tryon, 1982). Professional women tend to marry professional men, and, if the women in my sample were married, there is a good chance they were involved in dual-career marriages.

For whatever reasons, women's private practices were smaller than those of men. The size of independent practices can be regulated, and, thus, it is probably one of the more desirable jobs for anyone (women or man) who has other duties to attend to.

THE FUTURE OF PRIVATE PRACTICE

The independent practice of psychology seems to be a growing business. The numbers of both full-time and part-time practitioners increase with each passing year. Individual practices are growing; 69% of the 165 full-time private practitioners I surveyed indicated their practices had grown during the past 5 years. One wonders how much growth is possible. Perhaps there will be areas of the country that become saturated with private practitioners.

There will always be a great need for psychotherapeutic services, but the finances necessary to satisfy the need may not always be available. Much of the continued growth of independent practices will depend on the ability or willingness of third-party agencies to provide payment to psychologist practitioners. Third-party funding for psychotherapy has been declining in recent years (Baker, 1983).

The future should bring increased attempts to regulate private practice to ensure quality care. Currently, each APA-affiliated state psychological association has a Professional Standards Review Committee as a peer review mechanism by which consumers may have questionable claims or practices investigated. The Civilian Health and Medical Program for the Uniformed Services (CHAMPUS) also has a Peer Review Project. Peer review will become more prevalent in the future.

In his 1983 article, Robert Baker wrote about five ominous trends regarding the future of private practice: First, the population of the U.S. is not growing. There will be fewer young people, the customary consumers of psychotherapy, around in the 1980s and 1990s than there were in the 1960s. Second, people are seeking answers to questions about themselves from sources other than psychotherapy (i.e., religion, drugs, politics). Third, people will not continue to pay for psychotherapy when its efficacy has not been demonstrated. Fourth, third-party funding for psychotherapy has declined. Fifth, during economic downturns, psychotherapy will become a luxury that few can afford. We will then be faced with problems of manpower oversupply. The future of the private practice of psychotherapy may not be as bright as its past.

As indicated above, the trend toward group practices will probably continue. These group practices will offer more varied services than can be offered by any one individual.

Insurance companies and other third-party payment agencies will increasingly dictate the nature of independent practice. Therapy in private practice will be briefer than it was in the past, because insurance companies will no longer pay for virtually limitless numbers of sessions. Third-party payers may even obtain the right to choose the individual service providers for their clients (Frankel, 1983).

There will continue to be debate about and changes in licensure/certification laws. "Sunset" legislation will ensure some of this process.

Graduate education will change to accommodate the needs of the future private practitioners. Training in the practical and ethical aspects of private practice may become more prevalent. Internships in private practice settings may increase.

Finally, support groups for solo practitioners may become more prevalent. Private practice can sometimes be a lonely business, leading to professional burnout. Such groups would provide the practitioner with a much-needed service.

SUMMARY

The following is a summary of the points made in this chapter:

1. Independent practitioners generally have a doctoral degree in psychology and are licensed/certified to practice in their respective states. Listing in the *National Register* and ABPP diplomate status are highly desirable, as are attendance at continuing education workshops and postdoctoral training.
2. Independent practitioners begin their practices in a variety of ways. Care needs to be given to marketing the practice. The best referral sources are satisfied patients.
3. Private practitioners provide a variety of services to a variety of patients. Practitioners should offer services in accord with their training and experiences, making referrals to other practitioners when appropriate.
4. Fees charged by private practitioners vary from region to region. Independent practitioners generally make more money than other psychologists, but their incomes are decreased by expenses and patients who do not pay their bills.
5. Private practitioners have a variety of theoretical orientations. Each practice is influenced by the orientation of the practitioner.

6. Some full-time private practitioners have jobs in addition to their practice, to provide them with colleagues and a varied experience.
7. There are a number of professional organizations private practitioners may join.
8. It is costly for independent practitioners to conduct research, yet research about real clinical cases has the potential to greatly add to our knowledge of psychotherapy.
9. Private practitioners are generally satisfied with their careers, but not as satisfied with their graduate educations. Isolation and financial uncertainty are sources of dissatisfaction for the private practitioner.
10. Women full-time private practitioners tend to have similar practices than do men.
11. Private practices will thrive in the future if there is money to pay for services. Peer review will become more prevalent, the number of group practices will increase, licensure/certification laws will continue to be reviewed, graduate coursework should increasingly address the private practice experience, and support groups for solo practitioners should become more prevalent.

REFERENCES

Albee, G. W., & Kessler, M. (1977). Evaluating individual deliverers: Private practice and professional standards review organizations. *Professional Psychology, 8,* 502–515.

American Psychological Association. (1977). Standards for providers of psychological services. *American Psychologist, 32,* 495–505.

American Psychological Association. (1978). Guidelines for therapy with women. *American Psychologist. 33,* 1122–1123.

American Psychological Association. (1981). Ethical principles of psychologists. *American Psychologist, 36,* 633–638. (a)

American Psychological Association. (1981). Specialty guidelines for the delivery of services by clinical psychologists. *American Psychologist, 36,* 640–651. (b)

American Psychological Association. (1981). Specialty guidelines for the delivery of services by counseling psychologists. *American Psychologist, 36,* 652–663. (c)

American Psychological Association. (1981). Specialty guidelines for the delivery of services by industrial/organizational psychologists. *American Psychologist, 36,* 664–669. (d)

American Psychological Association. (1982). *Salaries in psychology–1982.* Washington, DC: Author.

Baker, R. L. (1983). Supply side economics in private psychotherapy practice: Some ominous and encouraging trends. *Psychotherapy in Private Practice, 1,* 71–81.

Betz, N. E., & Shullman, S. L. (1979). Factors relating to client return rate following intake. *Journal of Counseling Psychology, 26,* 542–545.

Browning, C. H. (1982). *Private practice handbook: The tools, tactics, & techniques for successful practice development* (2nd ed.). Los Alamitos, CA: Duncliff's.

Caddy, G. R. (1981). The development and current status of professional psychology. *Professional Psychology, 12,* 377–384.

Cantor, D. W. (1983). Independent practice: Minding your own business. *Psychotherapy in Private Practice, 1,* 19–24.

Cookerly, J. R., & McClaren, K. (1982). *How to increase your private practice power.* Fort Worth, TX: The Center for Counseling and Developmental Services, Inc.

Frankel, S. (1983). Preferred providers, platitudes and panic: Standard of practice and the insurance industry. *The Independent Practitioner, 3*(1), 9–10.

Garfield, S. L., & Kurtz, R. (1974). A survey of clinical psychologists: Characteristics, activities and orientations. *The Clinical Psychologist, 28*(1), 7–10.

Hendrickson, D. E., Janney, S. P., & Fraze, J. E. (1978). *How to establish your own private practice.* Muncie, IN: Contemporary Press.

Hill, C. E. (1975). Sex of client and sex and experience level of counselor. *Journal of Counseling Psychology, 22,* 6–11.

Jones, E. E., & Zoppel, C. L. (1982). Impact of client and therapist gender on psychotherapy process and outcome. *Journal of Consulting and Clinical Psychology, 50,* 259–272.

Lewin, M. H. (1978). *Establishing and maintaining a successful professional practice.* Rochester, NY: Professional Development Institute.

Lowe, J. D., & Ritzler, B. A. (1980). Private practice practica and graduate training in clinical psychology: A survey of APA-approved programs. *Professional Psychology, 11,* 925–929.

Norcross, J. C., & Prochaska, J. O. (1982). A national survey of clinical psychologists: Affiliations and orientations. *The Clinical Psychologist, 38*(3), 1, 4–6.

Norcross, J. C., & Prochaska, J. O. (1983). Psychotherapists in independent practice: Some findings and issues. *Professional Psychology: Research and Practice, 14,* 869–881.

Samuels, R. M. In K. Herman (Chair) (1983). *Building, maintaining, and marketing a professional practice in the 1980's.* Symposium presented at the meeting of the American Psychological Association, Anaheim, CA. (a)

Samuels, R. M. (1983). What a man has learned about the business of psychology and will now share with women. *Psychotherapy in Private Practice, 1,* 31–37. (b)

Strickland, B. R. (1983, August). *Over the Boulder(s) and through the Vail: Toward new directions.* Paper presented at the meeting of the American Psychological Association. Anaheim, CA.

Tamkin, A. S. (1976). Adaptability: A paramount asset for private practice. *Professional Psychology, 7,* 661–663.

Taylor, R. E. (1978). Demythologizing private practice. *Professional Psychology, 9,* 68–70.

Tryon, G. S. (1983). Full-time private practice in the United States: The results of a national survey. *Professional Psychology: Research and Practice, 14,* 685–696. (a)

Tryon, G. S. (1983). How full-time private practitioners market their services: A national survey. *Psychotherapy in Private Practice, 1,* 91–100. (b)

Tryon, G. S. (1983). The pleasures and displeasures of full-time private practice. *The Clinical Psychologist, 36,* 45–48. (c)

Tryon, G. S. (1983). Professional publications of most use to full-time private practitioners. *Professional Psychology: Research and Practice, 14,* 549–553. (d)

Tryon, G. S. (1983). Why full-time private practitioners refer patients to other professionals. *Psychotherapy in Private Practice, 1,* 81–83. (e)

Tryon, G. S., & Tryon, W. W. (1982). Issues in the lives of dual-career couples. *Clinical Psychology Review, 2,* 49–65.

VandenBos, G. R., Stapp, J., & Kilburg, R. R. (1981). Health service providers in psychology: Results of the 1978 APA Human Resources Survey. *American Psychologist, 36,* 1359–1418.

Weinrach, S. G. (1980). Part-time private practice for the reluctant entrepreneur. *The Counseling Psychologist, 9*(1), 87–89.

Chapter 8

Community Mental Health Centers

Wade H. Silverman

Emory University

Since the decade of the 1960s, the professional practice of psychology has broadened dramatically to meet the mental health needs of new populations in an ever-more-diverse variety of settings. An early impetus for the growth of mental health service was President Kennedy's support for community mental health centers. Legislation enacted during the Johnson administration greatly augmented manpower development and deployment in the mental health arena. The Community Mental Health Centers Act of 1963 and Amendments in 1965 provided federal monies for building construction, staffing, and mandated services. In addition, those centers which emphasized commitment to underserved populations received special status in funding.

The purpose of this chapter is to examine the role of the psychologist in the Community Mental Health Center (CMHC). We will begin by outlining the purpose and settings of contemporary CMHCs, and how they differ from other public health services and private practice. Next we will examine CMHC programming and staffing. We will elaborate on the functions of mental health professionals, with special attention to the skills required to perform particular roles. This will be used as the foundation for the last two sections, which explore psychologist's work within CMHCs in relation to current trends and future directions in community service.

WHAT IS A COMMUNITY MENTAL HEALTH CENTER

At the most basic level of description, a CMHC is a system of services designed to meet the mental health needs of a geographic population. By "system" we mean an array of programs integrated first to address a multiplicity of mental health problems and their degrees of severity, and second to insure continuity of care. Whether the system is housed under one roof, in several clustered buildings, or scattered at various sites, the significance of serving a specific geographic population highlights the importance of mental health planning. In other words, the rationale for a particular program is based on the needs of *current and potential* consumers rather than solely on actual users, walk-ins, and referrals.

While the components of any CMHC are unique to its community and staff, there is an identified ideology common to its development. Often referred to as the community mental health movement, this ideology is typified by nine characteristics (Bloom, 1973): (a) working in the community rather than in institutions, (b) focusing on the total community rather than on individual clients, (c) emphasizing prevention and early intervention, (d) preferring indirect rather than direct services, (e) using innovative intervention strategies to serve the largest number of people in the shortest possible time, (f) planning rationally with objective evidence, (g) deploying manpower creatively, (h) operating under community control, and (i) identifying stress producers rather than psychopathology.

The Importance of Service Orientation

One way to categorizing CMHCs is by orientation toward direct or indirect service (see Silverman, 1981a). A controversy of community development vs. direct service reached its zenith in the early 1970s, and still is a relatively major issue among planners and practitioners. The direct service approach posits that the purpose of a CMHC is to offer the same kind and quality of service as is available in the private sector. Advocates are particularly sensitive to the issue of CMHCs' offering second class service to an underserved population, so that their goal has been quality care for the general public. On the other hand, the community development approach assumes that not only are traditional forms of service delivery irrelevant to the vast majority of service recipients, but that they do not address such major causative factors as poverty, racism, sexism, and stress. The goal of community developers is to improve the quality of life of all community residents by changing their institutions and by increasing their decision making power.

The Impact of Setting

Another way of categorizing CMHCs is in terms of setting. Each CMHC can be placed on an urban-suburban-rural continuum. We know that these settings vary markedly on many variables, including population density, accessibility to service, types of social problems, and availability of personnel. In a recent study by the author, several other variables distinguished urban and suburban centers from rural ones, including years of experience of staff, the primary function of the agency, median family income, size of the population, percent of minority residents, and percent of state funding (Silverman, in press).

What do these findings imply? Personnel issues are of major importance at rural CMHCs, because it is usually much more difficult to recruit individuals, particularly more experienced professionals, for specialized roles. Also, rural

CHMCs cannot afford to specialize. They must see their mandate as encompassing more marginal areas, such as substance abuse and developmental disabilities, as well as traditional mental health problems. Rural populations tend to be poorer but more homogenous than their urban and suburban counterparts. Minority mental health issues are usually nonexistent. Since the population of the catchment area is smaller and more scattered in rural areas, there are fewer waiting lists and casefinding becomes more important. Finally, rural CMHCs tend to be much more dependent on state resources than urban/surburban ones. Because alternative financial resources are simply not as available, much closer working relationships between state officials and local administrators are expected.

Another aspect of setting is whether the CMHC is hospital-based or free-standing. A hospital-based center is established when an initial federal grant is awarded to a sponsoring hospital, medical center, or medical school. In most cases, there is sharing of a common physical plant, so that the entire center is on or adjacent to hospital grounds. Also, both the hospital and CMHC tend to be under the same governing authority. In contrast, a free-standing CMHC is usually begun by grass-roots citizen organizations in order to bring mental health service to their community (see Chiarmonte, 1981). This center is typically located in a neighborhood building, and is either governed or advised by boards of local residents.

There are advantages and disadvantages to both hospital-based and free-standing centers. Staff at the hospital-based CMHC enjoys ready access to hospital facilities and personnel for support, referral, and back-up; easier recruiting, because of prestige; and the satisfying accoutrements of professional life, colleagues, books, and scholarly pursuits (Huffine & Craig, 1973). In contrast, there are many drawbacks for hospital-based programs. The most difficult problem is the inherent conflict between the mandate of a hospital and that of a CMHC. A hospital accepts patients based on physician referral networks and traffic patterning, while the CMHC operates according to geographic boundaries and the assessment of consumers needs. This difference leads to competition for resources, disagreements over targets for intervention, and rivalry in treatment units. (Fiester, Silverman, & Beech, 1975). Since the CMHC and the hospital are under the same governance, and since the hospital always has more power and prestige, the CMHC loses most battles it must wage to assert its priorities. A hospital-based program is oriented more to treatment than community development, and is more conservative in that treatment.

A free-standing CMHC is more fully integrated into its neighborhood setting: It has better and more frequent interactions with other agencies; flexible policies and procedures leave more time for staff to deliver services; governance tends to be more democratic; and the team approach is preferred over rigid professional roles. However, the free-standing CMHC has a much more unstable work environment than its hospital-based counterpart, due in part to an unreliable funding base, more conflict among staff, administrators, and boards, and decidedly more face-to-face experience with extreme and complex psychosocial difficulties. Staff burnout is a major concern. For the freedom of more indirect service, citizen participation, and independence in programming, the free-standing CMHC pays the price of more financial instability, less professional colleagueship, and greater work stress.

CMHCs, OTHER PUBLIC SERVICES, AND PRIVATE PRACTICE

One of the most exciting changes brought about by the community mental health movement that continues to differentiate CMHC work from other sectors is the opportunity to function in diverse settings with new populations. The private practitioner is supported almost exclusively by fee-for-service. By virtue of his/her funding base, clients, the individual patient, and third-party payors, the service population is usually upper-middle class. The private practitioner must work in an environment which is conducive to attracting this type of person and to maintaining close contact with a referral source, typically a physician or lawyer. The private practice office is usually in or near major office complexes or shopping areas in a downtown location or large suburb. The private practitioner is immobile in that clients come to the office. Home visits are financially impractical, as are co-therapy arrangements. The types of interventions a practitioner can perform are limited, since he/she is dependent upon those problems which show up at the door. The private practitioner has little time, space, or energy to devote to alternative interventions. Finally, continuing education, professional colleagueship, liaison work, continuity of care, and availability are achieved at his/her direct expense.

Mental health work in the CMHC and other public service agencies is different in several ways. First, public service agencies, particularly state-sponsored ones, have concentrated on the "sickest and poorest." While these are populations of extreme need, there are critics who contend that emphasis on tertiary care is not cost-effective and does not reduce either the incidence or prevalence of mental disorders. A proportionally greater amount of staff time and support service has been assigned to treating chronic schizophrenics. As in the private sector, this reduces the number of services a practitioner can offer as well as the variety of problems he/she may encounter.

A second difference between CMHCs and other public service agencies is the locus of treatment. Whereas it is not unusual for CMHCs to have mobile treatment units, on-site professionals placed at other institutions, flexible scheduling, and home visits, these accomodations are rare at other agencies. They tend to be too costly because they require special work rules, liability coverage, and transportation contingencies.

A third important factor, more subtle yet just as significant which differentiates CMHCs from other public agencies, is the political factor. Whereas most CMHCs are directly linked either to a governing board or hospital authority, public agencies are accountable to state and local governments. The link between mental health issues and the funding authority is much more direct for CMHCs than other public agencies. The latter must not only compete with social service agencies, but they may have to penetrate through several levels of bureaucracy for their needs to be addressed. In an interesting study of the impact of training for change with mental health supervisiors (Silverman, 1981b), we found that trainees from private agencies were more likely than those from public agencies to report that their training had greater usefulness and made more impact on job activities, their agency, and attainment of personal goals. Indeed, trainees from public agencies indicated that their organizations were more interested in politics rather than in service.

As one can readily see by now, there are many considerations, both positive and negative, in deciding on whether one will work at a CMHC, another public service agency, or in private practice. The CMHC offers the greatest variety of tasks, clients, and work sites. The opportunity to work as a team with other professionals and learn from each other is always present. However, job security at a CMHC is tenuous. Rarely does a civil service ranking or professional union exist to protect the employee. While private practice offers the greatest monetary reward, it is only as secure as the referral network. Not only is it isolating, but there are none of the fringe benefits of vacation time, sick days, or continuing education. Public service work offers the most security, but at the price of sameness on the job and limited freedom to pursue special professional interests.

A SYSTEMATIC LOOK AT CMHC OPERATIONS

What Does Comprehensiveness in Programming Mean?
Since the passage of the Community Mental Health Centers Act in 1964, the trend has been toward greater comprehensiveness in programming. The 1965 Amendments called for five basic services; emergency, inpatient, outpatient, partial hospitalization, and consultation and education. Succeeding amendments have added supplemental services of diagnosis, rehabilitation, pre-care and after-care, mental health training, research and evaluation, services to the elderly and to rape victims, and alcohol and drug treatment.

Debates emerged in the early 1970s concerning the usefulness of the goal of comprehensiveness. Many professionals were deeply worried that CMHCs were trying to accomplish too much too soon with too little training. Others were committed to the notion that mental health must develop alternative strategies for a multi-ethnic, multi-racial society. These latter professionals contended that major sub-populations had never received accessible, available, and appropriate mental health care.

Today, comprehensiveness is no longer at issue. CMHCs stretch their dollars to include as many relevant services as they can afford. To promote comprehensiveness, the National Institute of Mental Health (NIMH) has sent review teams to assist CMHCs on service delivery issues. It has also given funds under the auspices of its Continuing Education Branch, and now under its State Manpower Development Program, to offer training and technical assistance to centers.

The JCAH Matrix as a Guide to CMHC Operations

What does a contemporary, comprehensive CMHC offer? To whom? And in what setting? The most descriptive and thorough classification has been devised by the Accreditation Program for Psychiatric Facilities (AP/PF) of the Joint Commission on Accreditation of Hospitals (JCAH). One unit under the AP/PF, the Community Mental Health Program Branch, has been accrediting CMHCs on a voluntary basis since 1975. In order to describe the full array of potential services they survey, the AP/PF constructed a service activities matrix (see Table 1).

The *columns* are age/disability groups: The four age groups are children, adolescents, adults, and the elderly; the three types of disabilities are emotional disorders, mental retardation/developmental disabilities, and substance abuse. The *rows* consist of eight different functions, with the specific services for each function listed underneath.

Definitions for the 42 identified services may be obtained by consulting JCAH's *Principles for Accreditation of Community Mental Health Services Programs Manual* (1979).

Inspection of the matrix reveals that many types of interventions are not psychotherapeutic. Also note the variety of environments in which the interventions can take place, e.g., on the job, at school, at home, in a hospital. The manual also distinguishes three types of environments—protective, supportive, and natural. A protective environment is one that safeguards an individual's well-being, two examples being inpatient hospital units and jails. A supportive environment promotes the client's interests, participation, and responsibilities— a CMHC outpatient department or a private practitioner's office. The natural service environment is one which is in conformity with the ordinary course of community life, such as school, workplace, or home.

Now consider the enormity of the training of mental health professionals to perform all these 42 functions with four age groups and three groupings in protective, supportive, and natural environments. Surely, it is an impossible undertaking for any graduate program! Yet service work is but one area in which mental health professionals work. The JCAH identifies four others: administration, citizen participation, research and evaluation, and staff development.

Administration entails planning, management, and control, the purpose being to organize, frame, and facilitate service delivery. Citizen participation increases the CMHCs sensitivity to community need and consumer activity in all areas of operation, while research and evaluation attempts to discover new knowledge about service activities and determine the effectiveness and efficiency of current methods of operation. Staff development enhances the skills and productivity of all staff at a CMHC, primarily through career development and education and training.

TABLE 1. Service Activities Matrix

	Children			Adolescents			Adults			Elderly		
	Emot.	MR-DD	Sub. Abuse	Emot.	MR-DD	Sub. Abuse	Emot.	MR-DD	Sub. Abuse	Emot.	MR-DD	Sub. Abuse
Identification												
Case Finding												
Screening												
Crisis Stabilization												
Crisis Care												
Crisis Support												
Temporary Residence												
Crisis Intervention												
Temporary Sponsorship												
Growth Services												
Remotivational Care												
Social Training												
Task and Skill Training												
Vocational Training												
Sheltered Training												
Consumer Education												
Transitional Living												
Verbal Therapies												
On-Site Training												
On-Site Visit												
On-the-Job Training												

TABLE 1. Service Activities Matrix (continued)

	Children			Adolescents			Adults			Elderly		
	Emot.	MR-DD	Sub. Abuse	Emot.	MR-DD	Sub. Abuse	Emot.	MR-DD	Sub. Abuse	Emot.	MR-DD	Sub. Abuse
Transitional Sponsorship												
Sustenance Services												
Sustaining Care												
Socialization:												
Sheltered Work												
Verbal Therapies												
Indefinite Residence												
On-Site Visit												
Subsidized Work												
Indefinite Sponsorship												
Case Management												
Assessment												
Planning												
Linking												
Monitoring												
Advocacy												
Prevention Services												
Public Information												

TABLE 1. Service Activities Matrix (continued)

	Children			Adolescents			Adults			Elderly		
	Emot.	MR-DD	Sub Abuse	Emot.	MR-DD	Sub Abuse	Emot.	MR-DD	Sub Abuse	Emot.	MR-DD	Sub Abuse
Public Education												
Public Consultation												
Somatic Intervention												
Ecological Change												
General Health												
Primary Care												
Secondary Care												
Tertiary Care												
Ancillary Services												
Dietary												
Pharmacy												

MANPOWER AT CMHCs

A major contribution of the community mental health movement has been a redistribution of manpower resources. Roles and tasks have been defined by skills and talent rather than by discipline. While specific tasks (prescribing and dispensing medication) may be controlled through licensing or accreditating rules, most activities at CMHCs are not defined by profession or discipline. It was in the trenches of the overwhelming service loads of the late 1960s and early 1970s that we learned that many direct service jobs were carried out as successfully by paraprofessionals as by professionals.

Job Levels at the CMHC

One way of viewing the role functions of CMHC manpower systematically is through levels within the organization. At the highest level is the administrator. Typically, he/she is a mental health professional, with at least 5 years of experience. In a recent state-wide study of CMHCs, we found that about half of the administrators were social workers, and a third psychologists. Almost 75% held Master's degrees, and about 20% were M.D.s or Ph.D.s While we did not obtain job description duties, we did inquire about areas in which administrators perceived that they needed further training. Leadership skills, clinical service training, and planning and evaluating were the most frequently mentioned. In terms of content, administrators wanted to learn more about supplemental services, accountability, and accreditation (Silverman, 1984).

Supervisors and program chiefs are at the next level. In smaller agencies, the supervisor and chief administrator are one and the same person. Interestingly, in another state-wide survey, the percentage of supervisors who are psychologists was 50%, compared to the third cited above who were administrators. Another 45% were social workers. Only 18% held Doctorates, while 80% had received Master's degrees. Average years of experience was 4. What does the supervisor do on the job? About 45% of the time was in direct service, 24% in administration and support, 22% in supervising, and 7% in training (Silverman, 1982a).

Since supervisors are located in the service structure at the intersection of the front-line worker and top management, they must possess both clinical and administrative talents. They perceive themselves as experienced psychotherapists, but in need of more administrative skills. More specifically, they would benefit from training in planning, monitoring performance, understanding work motivation, and working with job stress.

Front-line workers are the backbone of the CMHC. Not only do they provide the myriad of available services, but they work at all hours on a no-decline basis. As a JCAH surveyor, I have observed that there is no typical front-line worker. They are true generalists in terms of educational background, level of sophistication, and work abilities. There is no evidence to suggest that years of training, discipline, or therapeutic orientation are related to successful outcomes at CMHCs.

Whereas clinical staff are involved in direct service, the CMHC relies on support staff to perform the basic services to open the doors of the agency. A typical job title for support staff includes administrative assistant, office manager, secretary, receptionist, and clerk. At many centers, they are the first contacts for clients. While these jobs are seldom occupied by psychologists, it is essential for the smooth operation of any CMHC to know the responsibilities and the needs of the individuals at this level. We found that the typical support worker has a high school diploma and spends about a quarter of his/her time in business communication and a quarter in accounting. Budgeting occupied about 12% of work hours, supervising about 14%, and record keeping about 10%. Of the two major categories of support staff, one group, lower-level management personnel, tend to perform the administrative and financial tasks of accounting, budgeting, and financing. Their training interests are in grant writing, methods of finance, and budgets. The second group, secretaries and clerks, maintain business communication and record-keeping. They want to learn more about client contact and effective letter writing (Silverman, 1982b).

Citizen participation in the form of advisory and governing boards allows residents to represent their community and to monitor the center's performance. Psychologists may be involved in citizen participation as board members, technical assistants to boards, or as information gatherers.

Job Functions at the CMHC

Another way of analyzing work tasks at a CMHC is to view them in clusters of services. Services performed by psychologists at CMHCs include all the traditional ones of individual, group, family, and crisis intervention, plus those activities which require planning for target populations. We will use the eight service functions listed in Table 1 for our discussion, with the exception of general health and auxiliary functions which are not performed by mental health workers. Following the brief description of the functions, we will explore how much psychologists participate in each.

Identification

The purpose of the two activities under identification, case finding and screening, is to seek persons with problems who are either unidentified or currently not under treatment. Schools and churches can be contacted, and the public media used. The aim is to spread service to fill unmet needs. Screening assesses the client's problems and the interventions necessary to solve them, while assessment includes interviews, testing, medical or vocational consults, and a psychiatric examination. The goal is to determine if the client needs service and where in the system he/she should be placed to ensure a successful outcome.

Crisis Stabilization

Utilized to reduce acute emotional disabilities, crisis stablilization is most commonly seen in the form of crisis support or emergency service (ES). ES at a CMHC offers the broadest range of treatment to the community. As Rines (1981) points out, it is usually the first and often the only one used by clients. Its major purpose is to keep the chronically mentally ill out of the inpatients unit, through community agency linkages and crisis intervention. Among the forms ES may take are working with general hospital emergency rooms, assisting police and fire departments, and giving specialized counseling to victims of assault and rape.

Although ES is available on a 24-hour, 7-day basis, typically only the day cases are seen at the CMHC. In the evening and weekends, an answering service pages an on-call worker. Most emergencies can be alleviated by telephone, with an appointment scheduled for the regular shift. In the minority of cases, direct contact is necessary. ES may take place in a hospital emergency room, a satellite office, or even in the client's home. When the crisis cannot be stabilized, hospitalization may be required, but rarely does this course exceed 3 weeks. Interestingly, there is no correlation between diagnostic category and length of hospitalization (Val, 1981). The crisis may also be handled by placement in a temporary residence or by the sponsorship of a surrogate family.

Growth Services

Growth services are those activities which enhance personal functioning. Not only are all of the traditional psychotherapeutics growth services, but so also are the competency building interventions of life skills training, vocational training, social skills training, educational instruction, and transitional living. Mental health workers, teachers, job counselors, and lay citizens may all participate in these activities.

Case Management

Case management assures continuity of care by linking and coordinating the client to those parts of the service system he/she requires. There is heated debate whether the case manager should be the most skilled clinician or the least formally trained worker. The job is complex but vital, as the case manager advocates for the client in the system, interacts with the client's family and friends, and brings together other agencies which could be of benefit.

Prevention Services

Primary prevention reduces the incidence or the number of first occurrences of mental disabilities. Zolik (1981) differentiates two types: person-oriented and social-system-oriented approaches. The person-oriented approach is, as its name suggests, directed at high risk individuals and groups in order to reduce the incidence of specific kinds of disorders such as mental retardation, or lead poisoning. Working in this field does not necessarily entail psychotherapy.

Staff might perform genetic or nutritional counseling, conduct prenatal classes, design and implement screening procedures, or organize support groups.

Other person-oriented preventative programs are milestone programs and competency development programs. Milestone programs are geared to transitions in the normal lifespan—birth, marriage, retirement—each of which has its own set of stressors. Competency programs attempt to expand psychosocial coping and cognitive behaviors through mental health education seminars, life skills workshops, and parent-effectiveness groups.

The second type of prevention approach is oriented to the social system. Interventions under this category focus on societal rather than individual problems or concerns, such as unemployment, racism, sexism, and agism. Advocates of the community development ideology are primarily concerned with responding to these more global and complex issues. Through program consultation, community organization, and environmental design, the change agent or social engineer works at enhancing the social order and the well-being of its citizens.

Administration

We have described previously the basic goals of mental health administration and the background of the typical administrator. The workload is enormous. Developing plans, delineating budgets, overseeing quality control, managing information, and conducting public relations are but a few of his/her responsibilities. Typically, the administrator works at the pleasure of the governing board, which, more than likely, means without a contract.

A frequently voiced criticism of the community mental health movement was that professionals made bad administrators. Not only was the clinician's role very different than that of a manager, but our graduate and medical schools did not familiarize future clinicians with organizational charts, line item budgets, or policy manuals. During the 1970s, a high turnover rate at the executive director level was due partly to professionals' disenchantment with the position and partly to termination of inadequately trained directors.

Citizen Participation

Much lip service has been paid to the goal of citizen participation and community control of CMHCs. However, it was not until passage of the 1975 CMHC amendments that NIMH formally required CMHCs to have advisory or governing boards.

The CMHC related to citizen groups most frequently through its consultation and education unit. Mental health professionals have worked tirelessly in mobilizing community support and in forming coalitions for lobbying political leaders. Not only have these efforts been successful at the local and state levels, but the various CMHC statutes have been some of the most consistently favored pieces of social legislation in Congress.

Community planning is another critical function performed by citizens with the assistance of CMHC staff. Some of the planning is done directly by advisory and governing boards to decide upon program priorities and fiscal matters.

Citizen participation in the form of boards has long been a controversial issue in community mental health. Although most professionals would advocate grass-roots participation at CMHCs, boards have been soundly criticized as being unrepresentative of their communities, tokens for the administration, or poorly organized. In a city-wide study of advisory boards (Silverman, 1979), we found that many of these criticisms simply were not accurate. Board members and professionals tended to have a positive and productive relationship. The CMHC director attended most of the board meetings, an action which was perceived by board members as contributing to their own importance in decision-making ability, freedom of expression, and interest. Board members most frequently worked with administrators on personnel matters, evaluation, and improvement of administrative operations.

Research and Evaluation

The most rapidly growing functional area in community mental health is research and evaluation (R&E). With the trend toward a tighter fist in dispensing public monies to human services, there has been a dramatic rise in personnel and technology-devoted accountability. NIMH officially sanctioned R&E activities in the 1975 CMHC amendments. The lion's share of these resources is applied to evaluation rather than research. The latter is considered a luxury by most CMHCs, best carried out by academic institutions. Also, research was debunked by the community in the late 1960s and early 1970s for invasion of privacy and for not contributing to the welfare of neighborhoods. In addition, research with human subjects entails ethical and design issues which most CMHCs simply do not want to take on.

So evaluation has become the prime activity of most R&E departments. In determining the effectiveness and efficiency of CMHC operations, this department establishes objective standards, collects data to assess performance, evaluates these data in relation to standards, and reports the results to the system. Depending upon the size of the CMHC, the R&E director may employ a computerized management information systems (MIS) or simply tabulate data by hand. Results are used to assist the planning process at *all* levels of the organization.

Staff Development

If we were to survey priority topics in community mental health, staff development would certainly be at the bottom of the list. One can easily argue that improving employee's competencies is as important as any activity performed at a center. Yet staff development is often perceived by administrators as a reward rather than as an integral part of each job. It is usually the first to feel the cost-cutting ax.

The staff development director should either be part of the personnel department or work closely with it. Ideally, the director should comfortably wear the hats of educator, administrator, and negotiator. His/her first task is to design and implement training which will improve the center's functioning. This is accomplished by monitoring all center undertakings and deciding which program, staff, or functional area needs the most help. Curricula are then put together to solve the problem. The results of such a study might be, for instance, middle-level management learning zero-based budgeting, board members being able to recruit more effectively, or day hospital staff performing bioenergetics with clients.

The second major task of the staff development director is to promote mobility in the organization. Each employee is given the opportunity to qualify for either another job at the same level (lateral move) or a more responsible position (vertical move). To accomplish this, the CMHC must have a career gird which depicts steps at each level. Then each designs an individualized plan outlining personal career needs. The staff development office reviews these plans and attempts to link the employee to training resources. The director sometimes negotiates with universities, business colleges, industries, and professional organizations to obtain training not available at the CMHC.

CURRENT TRENDS OF PSYCHOLOGY AT CMHCs

By now many readers have begun to compare their own educational experience in the clinical/community field with those activities described in the last section. An identical comparison has been made systematically by Zolik and his colleagues. The initial study (Zolik, Sirbu, & Hopkinson, 1976) surveyed 305 graduate students from 103 clinical/community doctoral programs. Amost 75% of the respondents indicated that there was no specific community psychology or community mental health (CP/CMH) sequence at their school. Only 21% indicated that CP/CMH was available as a major area of specialization. The topics covered by the majority of programs were primary prevention, program evaluation, crisis intervention, and ethics of community intervention and research. The topics least covered were social indicators, planning, development, management of non-mental-health services, city and regional planning, and management information systems. Finally, 62% of respondents considered their training in CP/CMH to be inadequate.

In an interesting followup, Zolik, Soucy, and Bogat, (1982) surveyed psychology doctoral programs with a CP/CMH component. About 200 schools were represented by almost 1,000 respondents. It was similarly found that respondents regarded more traditional activities as higher priority. Thus, the four highest-rated topics were substance abuse, crisis intervention, early screening, and identification and primary prevention. The lowest rated topics were normative stresses, city and regional planning, epidemiology, management information systems, research on quality of life, and social indicators.

In another recent study by Zolik, Bogat, and Jason (1980) directors of training at each of the 589 CMHCs were surveyed. Amost 80% returned the survey. About half of the CMHCs offered practicum training to graduate students and 30% offered internships. The typical intern devoted 7.5 hours per week in diagnostic and 18 hours in psychotherapeutic activities. About 7 hours were spent in consultation. The five areas of greatest involvement were adult outpatient, adolescent outpatient, child outpatient, crisis intervention, and case consultation. The areas of least involvement were management information systems advocacy and social action, epidemiology, pre-natal programs, and social indicators. Also, about half of the 850 psychologists who supervised these interns work exclusively in supervising traditional clinical activities. Only 15% supervised nontraditional areas exclusively such as consultation or community organization.

Data from the three studies by Zolik and his colleagues confirm my observation that the psychologist's role at CMHCs continues to be traditional and limited. Our strongest functional area is services. Most of us have received complete in-depth training in screening and growth therapies. Unlike our psychiatric colleagues, many of us have not had the intensive background in protective environments and crisis stabilization. Because primary prevention may be the service in which we make our unique contribution in the future, it will be discussed in greater detail in the next section. Suffice it to say that there has been a growing awareness and interest at the graduate level in preparing future practitioners for CP/CMH as the number of job opportunities expands.

Administration is the area in which psychologists are the least prepared for the mental health professions. Whereas many schools of social work offer mental health administration tracks, and medical schools grant allied degrees in public health administration, psychology tends to ignore the significance of management skills except as applied to industry. This is most unfortunate, for the practice of professional psychology, whether in the public or private sphere, will increasingly include planning and control of personnel and resources.

Psychology has made a modest contribution to citizen participation through consultation and education services. While we have a lackluster history as advocates for citizen boards, we have worked with community people through our mental health education programs and our research on support groups. It was surprising that citizen participation was a low priority area among graduate students, a finding I feel reflects a continuing conservatism toward mental health service delivery.

Research and evaluation has been almost the exclusive domain of the psychologist, particularly the Master's level professional. Our empirical background at the graduate level has led to strong showing in this area. However, the Zolik surveys appear to suggest that we are missing some key ingredients as in the case of knowledge about management information systems. How can a CMHC plan its programs rationally without epidemiological and social indicators? In being more than a program evaluator, the R&E professional must also have knowledge of fiscal accountability, planning, computer technology, and policy information.

I feel that the trend in staff development is that of a steady downslide. Although NIMH's State Manpower development Branch encourages skills development and deployment, most public agencies, particularly CMHCs, are *not* interested. Most agencies simply do not appreciate the notion that investment in personnel is an investment in the future of the agency. Most administrators continue to view staff development as a "perk" for good work rather than as an integral part of the growth and maturation of the agency. Psychology's role in this area has been abysmal, particularly in light of our knowledge about learning, group dynamics, job assessment, and program evaluation.

FUTURE DIRECTIONS

CMHCs will continue to be the most popular setting for public mental health services. The innovations brought about by the concept of a "system of service responding to a multiplicity of needs" is not only cost-effective but more responsive to the population. A large segment of the public has not only availed itself of mental health care but is also more involved in its planning and advocation. There is no doubt that the funding pattern for CMHCs has changed. As part of President Reagan's philosophy of New Federalism, responsibility for mental health is being returned to the states. Consequently, CMHCs must depend much more on their geographic constituency for support, so that a new grassroots movement has already begun to save CMHCs throughout the country. While there have been rumblings that community mental health is dead and that many CMHCs have been shut down, most have survived and have built more solid funding bases as a result of local commitments. Federal dollars will, however, continue to flow in prevention. The President's Commission on Mental Health (PCMH, 1978) spotlighted prevention as one of eight priorities for federal action. Recently, APA distributed a memo to its members which described opportunities for funding in prevention through federal dollars (Kraut & Duffy, 1982).

How can psychology contribute to prevention in the context of CMHCs? A revealing finding by Zolik and his colleagues in a 1976 study was that training in consultation, education, and prevention was greater at CMHCs than at other facilities. Thus, CMHCs will continue to be the testing ground for primary prevention and graduate schools will have to adopt a more flexible stance. Person-oriented approaches of case consultation and mental health consultation are emphasized currently; training will incorporate social system-oriented skills and content. While today the neglected topics are program consultation, social system analysis, advocacy, and epidemiology (Zolik, 1983) psychologists of the future will routinely have supervision in change agentry, program consultation, and system diagnosis.

Another major trend in mental health services is accountability. Practitioners in both the private and public sectors are under pressure from government and third party payors to carry out quality assurance and cost-effectiveness procedures. Funding sources want to know what they are getting for their mental health dollars. There is a growing body of literature concerned with methodolgy, tools, and equipment for assessing cost effectiveness. A variety of formats have been established for professional review of quality assurance, including peer review, utilization review, hazardous procedures review, and length of stay review. The educational background of the psychologist is uniquely compatible with this trend. Not only are we reared on empiricism, but we also learn measurement, experimental design, and program evaluation. If graduate schools can add cost-accounting and cost-benefit analysis to curricula, many opportunities for new psychologists will open up in the public sector, notably in the R&E departments of CMHCs.

A final trend that we should discuss is the growing field of Health Psychology. How does this affect community mental health? Many centers are a decade old and have saturated their geographic areas in terms of secondary prevention. The populations that they have not worked with are those currently experiencing stress not yet classified as emotional disorders. These are "normal" people who could improve their quality of life so that they can avoid psychological casualty at some future date. Some of these at risk people are problem drinkers, isolated housewives, overtaxed executives, police officers, firemen, and air traffic controllers. Many of the interventions can be considered primary prevention and are otherwise labelled employee assistance programs, well clinics, or stress management. They are exciting ventures because they work with new populations without the concept of psychopathology in natural settings. Also, psychologists can use techniques other than testing and psychotherapy and still be considered practitioners. CMHCs find that these programs are a boon, because they are a source of independent dollars to support primary prevention while increasing the visibility of the center in the community.

REFERENCES

Bloom, F. L. (1973). *Community mental health, a historical and critical analysis.* Morristown, NJ: General Learning Press.

Chiarmonte, F. (1981). The constant battle: The politics of advisory boards. In Silverman, W. H. (Ed.), *Community mental health: A sourcebook for professionals and advisory board members.* New York: Praeger.

Fiester, A. R., Silverman, W. H., & Beech, R. P. (1975). Problems involved in delivering emergency services in a hospital based community mental health center. *Journal of Community Psychology, 3,* 188–192.

Huffine, C. L., & Craig, T. J. (1973). Catchment and community. *Archives of General Psychiatry, 28,* 483–488.

Joint Commission on Accreditation of Hospitals. (1979). *Principles for accreditation of community mental health service programs.* Chicago, IL: Author.

Kraut, A. G., & Duffy, S. W. (1982, August). *New NIMH support for prevention activities.* Memo from American Psychological Association.

President's Commission on Mental Health. (1978). *Report to the President from the President's Commission on Mental Health.* (Vols. 1–4). Washington, DC: Government Printing Office.

Rines, W. B. (1981). Emergency service in a community mental health center. In Silverman, W. H. (Ed.), *Community mental health: A sourcebook for professionals and advisory board members.* New York: Praeger.

Silverman, W. H. (1979). Some aspects of advisory board functioning in a large urban area. *Journal of Social Service Research, 2,* 323–334.

Silverman, W. H. (1981). Accountability. In Silverman, W. H. (Ed.), *Community mental health: A sourcebook for professionals and advisory board members.* New York: Praeger. (a)

Silverman, W. H. (1981). Self-designed continuing education for supervisors in community mental health. *Journal of Community Psychology, 9,* 347–354. (b)

Silverman, W. H. (1982). A statewide assessment of training needs of community mental health supervisors. *Journal of Psychiatric Treatment and Evaluation, 4,* 51–55. (a)

Silverman, W. H. (1982). Supporting support staff: A training needs assessment. *Journal of Psychiatric Treatment and Evaluation, 4,* 371–376. (b)

Silverman, W. H. (1984). A statewide assessment of training needs of mental health administrators. *Journal of Psychiatric Treatment and Evaluation, 11,* 55–58.

Val, E. R. (1981). Adult service delivery. In Silverman, W. H. (Ed.), *Community mental health: A sourcebook for professionals and advisory board members.* New York: Praeger.

Zolik, E. S. (1981). Primary prevention. In Silverman, W. H. (Ed.). *Community mental health: A sourcebook for professionals and advisory board members.* New York: Praeger.

Zolik, E. S. (1983). Training for preventive psychology in community and academic settings. In Felner, R., Jason, L., Moritsugu, J., & Farber, S. (Eds.), *Preventive psychology: The theory, research, and practice.* New York: Pergamon.

Zolik, E. S., Bogat, G. A., & Jason, L. A. (1983). Training of interns and practicum students at community mental health centers. *American Journal of Community Psychology, 6,* 673–686.

Zolik, E. S., Sirbu, W., & Hopkinson, D. (1976). Perspectives of clinical students in training in community mental health and community psychology. *American Journal of Community Psychology, 4,* 339–349.

Zolik, E. S., Soucy, G., & Bogat, G. A. (1982). *Perceived importance of areas in community psychology/community mental health.* Paper presented at the meeting of the American Psychological Association, Washington, DC.

Chapter 9

School Psychology

Charles A. Maher

Rutgers University

Robert J. Illback

Ft. Knox Dependent Schools

Providing psychological services in public and private schools has evolved considerably since the turn of the century. During the 1900s, psychologists in schools functioned as psychometrists, i.e., as testers of the mental ability of children as reflected in IQ scores. During the 1930s and 1940s, psychologists began to broaden their roles and functions in school settings, beyond mental testing, to include personality assessment and some one-to-one counseling of pupils. During the 1940s and 1950s, the practice of psychology in schools took on features that set it apart from clinical psychology and psychometry. That time period saw the term "school psychologist" increasingly used to describe a particular kind of school-based practitioner. For instance, Symonds described this new breed of practitioner as follows: "The school psychologist is a psychologist in a school—that is, one who brings to bear on the problems of the school and its administrators, teachers, and pupils the technical skills and insight which the science of psychology can provide" (Gray, 1963, p. 37).

Since the 1950s and up to the present time, school psychology has expanded in many directions. It has been recognized as a major professional speciality alongside clinical, counseling, and industrial/organizational psychology. Graduate education in school psychology has proliferated at both the doctoral and nondoctoral levels. School psychologists have continued to broaden their roles and functions, thereby providing an increasing range of psychological services to individuals, groups, and organizations.

In terms of professional practice, it is useful to view school psychology from a systems perspective. From this vantage point, school psychology can be distinguished as a system comprised of a set of interrelated services. These services are provided by school psychologists in order to develop and improve the performance of individuals, groups, and entire school organizations (e.g., schools, school districts). School psychological services, therefore, take the form of various programs and activities including psychoeducational assessment of individual pupils, individual and group counseling, parent education, teacher and administrator consultation, and educational program evaluation. In providing school psychological services at individual, group, and organizational levels, the practitioner employs a generic problem solving process. This process includes the elements of (a) clarifying the problem or need of the client, i.e., an individual, group, or organization; (b) designing a program that is intended to alleviate the problem or prevent one from developing; (c) implementing the program or intervention; and (d) evaluating the extent to which program outcomes were realized. Information derived from empirical research, program evaluation, and professional experience assists the practitioner in deciding what level of school psychology service to offer, and to what particular client that service is best targeted.

It is the purpose of this chapter to provide an overview of the practice of school psychology. In the chapter, the kinds of services provided by psychologists in the schools are described, and directions for school psychology practice are considered.

INDIVIDUAL LEVEL PRACTICE

It is at the individual level of practice that most school psychologists who are employed in public schools spend their professional time. School psychology service at this level also is the most well developed in terms of methods, procedures, and intervention programs. The targets or clients of service at this level are a variety of individuals: a normal and exceptional pupil, a parent or guardian, a regular and special education teacher, or a school administrator. Individual level psychological service takes the form of many programs and activities. Most frequently provided ones include (a) psychoeducational assessment of individual children to determine the child's eligibility to receive special education; (b) one-to-one pupil counseling to help the student develop a better self-image; (c) meeting with a parent to provide recommendations about improving their child's home study skills; (d) consulting with a classroom teacher to offer suggestions about how to improve a child's classroom behavior; and (e) reviewing the progress made by a pupil toward the goals and objectives of a special education program to decide how the child's individualized program can be revised.

Individual Assessment

School psychologists conduct individual assessments to facilitate decision making in a number of areas, including diagnosis and classification, educational placement, instructional planning, and progress toward educational goals. A variety of assessment techniques and strategies are used in data gathering, ranging from traditional, norm-referenced tests of cognitive functioning, to innovative and more informal measures (Salvia & Ysseldyke, 1981).

Cognitive/intellectual assessment. There are as many different types of intelligence tests as there are theories. Although there are similarities, each test measures somewhat different skills, utilizing a range of stimulus materials. A partial list of behaviors sampled by these tests, as compiled by Salvia and Ysseldyke (1981) includes: discrimination, generalization, motor behavior, general information, vocabulary, induction, comprehension, sequencing, detail recognition, analogies, abstract reasoning, memory, and pattern completion. Most of the intelligence tests used by school psychologist employ one or more of these tasks.

Undoubtedly the most widely used instrument is the Wechsler Intelligence Scale for Children-Revised (WISC-R) and its companion versions, the Wechsler Preschool and Primary Scale of Intelligence (WPPSI) and the Wechsler Adult Intelligence Scale-Revised (WAIS-R). Each test is divided up into at least ten subscales measuring a range of cognitive skills. For the most part, the scales have been found to have excellent reliability and validity characteristics, and research on these tests has accumulated over the past few decades to yield a rich data base and tradition.

While the Stanford Binet preceded the development of the Wechsler tests, its popularity has waned of late. It employs an age scale which samples responses to a broad range of developmental tasks, yielding a global intelligence quotient (IQ). The test norms and standardization have become outdated, however, and recent studies have pointed to some fundamental inadequacies in the test. Moreover, many practitioners find the test more difficult to interpret, because only a global IQ score is derived.

The McCarthy Scale of Children's Abilities is designed to assess 2- to 8-year-old children's cognitive functions. The scale yields scores in five general domains: verbal, perceptual–performance, quantitative, memory, and motor. It also yields a general cognitive index (GCI). Due to both its psychometric characteristics and its educational relevance, this test has become quite popular for use with pre-school and young school age children.

Another relative newcomer to the school psychology scene is the Woodcock-Johnson Psychoeducational Battery. This is actually, a combined battery of cognitive, achievement, and interest tests, which allows for direct data comparisons and instructional profiling. The scale has excellent psychometric characteristics and is likely to be widely used in the future. Another prominent diagnostic approach is the System of Multicultural Pluralistic Assessment (SOMPA). This battery grew out of the debate about discriminatory assessment and placement practices (primarily in California). The SOMPA purports to control for racial/cultural differences through the use of group-specific norms and a flexible integration of medical, social system, and "pluralistic" models of the child's behavior. The end product is assumed to be a more fair and valid diagnosis, as well as an estimate of the child's learning potential. Research has not yet validated the test for these purposes, and, while often used, the SOMPA has not become standard practice, as was originally expected by some. Finally, the Kaufman

Assessment Battery for Children (K-ABC) is a recently developed approach to cognitive assessment that may be demonstrated as useful for school psychologists. The K-ABC is based on Luria's theory of neuropsychological functioning. As such, it is based in sound psychological theory and may have considerable practical value for educational decision making purposes.

Perceptual assessment. Assessing children's auditory and visual perceptual processes grew out of theories of learning which emphasize the brain's efficiency and effectiveness in processing information. Especially in the field of learning disabilities, these theories have held great sway. Their basic assumption is that children with learning problems may have lesions or other definable neurological dysfunctions which limit their ability to accurately perceive sounds and/or symbols (decoding), or which cause them to be unable to integrate information (association), or which inhibit their use of information in responding (encoding). Originally, tests were developed to discriminate between clearly brain-injured and "normal" populations. However, these and similar measures are not frequently used to assess a broad range of children with learning difficulties. Perceptual testing has come under criticism of late because many question the neurologically-based perceptual deficit hypothesis which underlies the practice. Also, the measures are often unreliable, and recent validation studies have shown no clear relationship between academic performance and perceptual functioning; many poor readers perceive well, while many good readers obtain low scores. The perceptual testing approach does not appear to mirror the complexity of learning disabilities, either from a neuropsychological or an ecological perspective (Salvia & Ysseldyke, 1981).

The Bender Visual Motor Gestalt Test (BVMGT) is frequently administered by school psychologists. It requires the child to reproduce nine figures, and yields a developmental age score and a neurological soft sign indicator score (some practitioners also use it for personality assessment). The BVMGT has a rich tradition, but the research on it is mixed (Coles, 1978). Another perceptual test, the Frostig Developmental Test of Visual Perception, purports to measure five perceptual skills: eye–hand coordination, figure–ground perception, form constancy, position in space, and spatial relations. The Frostig yields a perceptual quotient. The test has come under considerable criticism for its reliability and validity characteristics. Research has not borne out the claims for the test as originally construed. A final perceptual test which has often been used is the Illinois Test of Psycholinguistic Abilities (ITPA). Based on an information processing model of learning, the ITPA attempts to measure specific decoding, associational, and encoding processes, in the hope of isolating specific learning dysfunctions. Unfortunately, research has not borne out the efficacy of either the model or the measurement approach.

Personality and behavioral assessment. School psychologists are oftentimes called to appraise a child's emotional and behavioral status. This information not only enables the school to make decisions about classification and placement (e.g., placement in a program for emotionally disturbed children), but it also should contribute to a better understanding of the child's mental health needs and help teachers plan programs of instruction.

There is a strong clinical tradition in the area of personality assessment. Projective tests such as the Rorschach method (Rorschach, 1951) and the Thematic Apperception Test (Murray, 1943) are widely used by clinicians in work with adults and adolescents, but these tests are of limited utility in work with children. School psychologists are prone to use other devices, such as the BVMGT (Bender, 1983), the Children's Apperception Test (Bellak & Bellak, 1965), the Draw-A-Person (Urban, 1963), the House-Tree-Person (Buck & Jolles, 1966), and the Piers—Harris Children's Self-Concept Scale (Piers & Harris, 1969).

However, there has been a clear decline in projective/personality assessment as psychology has moved away from psychodynamic/psychoanalytic models of behavior. In its place, behavioral assessment has emerged as an important set of methods. In behavioral assessment, the emphasis is on determining the frequency, intensity, and duration of problem behaviors and relating these to antecedent and consequent conditions (Kratchowill, 1982). This is seen by many practitioners as more relevant educationally in that specific and evaluable treatment plans are more likely to result. Behavioral assessment methods may include the use of rating scales (parent, teacher, peer ratings), self-report measures, systematic observation, and sociometry, among others.

Accompanying the trend toward measurement of specific problem behaviors is the recognition that problems may arise out of specific contexts. Thus, school psychologists have begun to focus some of their attention on situational and ecological variables such as classroom climate, teacher behavior, curricular variables, and home and family status.

Academic assessment. In many states, school psychologists perform both psychological and the educational assessment functions. In educational assessment, the goals revolve around determining the child's current performance levels in a variety of academic areas, ascertaining specific areas of deficiency, and making recommendations for remedial intervention. Naturally, educational assessment requires sophisticated understanding of educational tests, as well as thorough knowledge of curricular and instructional approaches. Some school psychologists are better prepared than others for this function. However, it seems likely that facility with instructional design concepts and applications will be a primary need for the future, and school psychology training programs will increasingly incorporate these functions into their curricula.

Educational and psychoeducational tests are being published at an ever-increasing pace, and space does not permit a full explication of their breadth and depth. Suffice it to say that both norm-referenced and criterion-referenced devices are available in nearly every domain of academic functioning, including reading, writing, spelling, language, and mathematics.

Individual Intervention

School psychologists have increasingly become involved with the planning, implementation and evaluation of intervention programs for children. They have done so in two ways: working directly with the child, and helping others who work with the child.

Direct interventions. School psychologists often are trained in counseling techniques with children. This reflects the strong influences of clinical and counseling psychology on the field. As is true in clinical and counseling psychology, a broad and diverse range of theoretical approaches and specific methods are seen. For example, some school psychologists are dynamically-oriented, and utilize evocative techniques such as free association and reflection in their counseling. Others rely on more behaviorally-oriented therapy in which specific problem behaviors are modified. Problems inherent in conducting therapy with children have also resulted in the use of innovative approaches, such as play therapy, psychodrama, short-term family therapy, and affective education. Vocational counseling is another area of recent interest to school psychologists.

However, concerns have been raised in the school psychology literature about the appropriateness of direct intervention services. Some question whether school psychologists are adequately trained to carry out therapeutic activities with children. Also, there has been dispute over the appropriateness of providing such services in school settings, as opposed to mental health clinics and other community agencies. Finally, given the magnitude of child problems seen in schools, practitioners have wondered whether this is the most efficient manner in which to expend the school psychologist's resources.

Consultation. An alternative to direct intervention is psychological consultation. Here, the intervention focus changes, as the school psychologist is not likely to work directly with the child. Rather, the psychologist works with those who are experiencing difficulties with a particular child (e.g., parents, teachers). This help may take a variety of forms. For example, it may be that the teacher does not have certain skills which are necessary to achieve success with the child, such as behavior management skills. In this instance, specific training (or retraining) can occur through consultation. On the other hand, it may be that the teacher misperceives the child's problems and is unable to generate alternative methods of instruction. As consultant, the school psychologist can be helpful in "reframing" the problem, which may result in more appropriate educational strategies.

Over the past 10–15 years, there has been an increasing emphasis on consultation as an alternative to more circumscribed roles, such as testing and special education "gatekeeper." For one, it is presumed that meaningful problem solving is more likely to occur through consultation than through testing (which may result in a placement change, but little else). Also, as the teacher gains greater skills in problem solving, it is assumed that they will generalize these skills to their work with other children, resulting in more effective teaching and less referrals for testing and placement.

As interest in consultation roles has increased, so has the literature in this area, both in terms of theory and research. There are numerous models for the practice of consultation, and, as is the case in counseling and psychotherapy approaches (which these closely parallel), these models are often difficult to distinguish from one another. One frequently relied on model is termed "behavioral consultation" (Bergan, 1977). In this approach, the consultant emphasizes the clear specification of problem behaviors, delineates antecedent and consequent conditions which develop and maintain the behaviors, helps the consultee modify these contingencies to foster more appropriate behaviors, and evaluates behavior change by continuous monitoring. In contrast, the "mental health consultation" model is likely to focus more on process variables, both in the consultant–consultee relationship and in the consultee-child relationship (Caplan, 1970). Many other consultation models exist, and it seems clear that no one approach is appropriate for all problems (as is true for psychotherapy). Also, there is much commonality between these approaches, as they are practiced. While no single approach has been shown to be exclusively effective, the research on consultation as a problem-solving process is quite promising (Medway, 1979).

However, there are some potential problems with regard to consultation. For one, not all school psychologists are well-trained in this area. Also, some do not seem to view this approach as central, and are content to perform more circumscribed functions (e.g., testing). Finally, many school organizations do not perceive consultation as a critical role, and may not sanction this as a legitimate and necessary activity. Nonetheless, many believe that school psychologists will have to modify and expand their roles to include consultation services, or risk being relegated to repetitious, irrelevant, and eventually unnecessary, activities.

GROUP LEVEL PRACTICE

School psychological services at the group level are less well developed in terms of programs and practices than at the individual level. Furthermore, school psychologists spend less professional time functioning at the group level although, in recent years, the importance of "group work" has become more valued by school psychologists (Bardon, 1982). Group school psychology programs focus on small and large groups of pupils, parents, teachers, and community audiences. Group service includes procedures and programs such as (a) early identification and screening programs designed to identify young children who may be at risk for school maladjustment; (b) group counseling of high school students to improve their social skills; (c) parent education programs to increase parental understanding of drug and alcohol abuse; (d) teacher in-service education to enable classroom teachers to become more proficient in managing use of their instructional time; and (e) presentations to inform community groups about mental health needs of school-aged children. Screening and parent education and training, two of the more commonly used group activities of school psychologists, are discussed below.

Screening
Screening is a process by which the school psychologist attempts to identify, proactively and systematically, groups of children who are experiencing difficulties and who may profit from placement in a particular intervention program. Unless screening programs are tied to intervention, they are of minimal utility. Also, it is assumed that systematic screening will result in earlier, more reliable, and more valid decisions than traditional identification process (e.g., referrals). Finally, early identification and remediation are presumed to be preferable when compared to allowing problem circumstances to persist and deteriorate.

School psychologists contribute to the screening process in a number of ways. For one, they are trained assessment specialists and participate in the selection and use of technically adequate screening devices. Moreover, school psychologists help schools clarify the areas which need to be assessed, by virtue of their familiarity with child development and related literatures. School psychologists are also often trained in program planning and evaluation, and have skills in developing, implementing, and evaluating school projects. These can be of critical importance in managing a screening program.

There is a vast literature on screening from which school psychologists can draw. A recent review (Illback, 1980) has identified available screening procedures in perceptual-motor, behavioral, emotional, social, intellectual/cognitive, language/linguistic, and physical domains, as well as a variety of more comprehensive and/or unique screening programs. By capitalizing on this extensive literature and using their already acquired skills, school psychologists can move beyond the individual level of service delivery to affect groups of children in a positive fashion.

Parent Education and Training
Another group-level approach to the practice of school psychology which has become more prominent is parent education and training. Partly as a function of P.L. 94–142, and partly due to the emerging literature on family dynamics and dysfunction, educators and psychologists have begun to recognize the key role

which families play with respect to learning. Many children with learning and behavior problems experience difficulties in the home setting. Also, having a child who has problems places a great deal of stress on the family as a unit. Thus, a need has been identified to help parents and families cope and interact more effectively, which has led to the development of parent education and training programs.

A good example of such a program is the parent training developed by Gerald Patterson and his associates (1975). In this approach, parents are taught behavior management skills such as systematic observation, behavior recording, contingency contracting, and conflict management. Other programs such as Parent Effectiveness Training (PET), tend to focus more on the affective and relational aspects of parenting (Gordon, 1970). A fairly recent educational development is the systematic use of parents in rewarding school behavior through home-based reinforcement programs, which has demonstrated effectiveness. Also on the market are a broad range of parent information packages, stress management kits, and the like, with new and creative approaches appearing continuously.

School psychologists face a challenge in this area. Many of these materials and approaches are untested and require considerable skill to implement. By virtue of their particular training and expertise, school psychologists are in a unique position to aid in the appropriate training of parents and the evaluation of parent training efficacy. Ultimately, the questions remains: How will these programs impact on the learning and behavior of children?

ORGANIZATIONAL LEVEL PRACTICE

School psychology practice at the organizational level is the least developed area of practice, and the area where school psychology practitioners usually spend the least amount of time. Service at this level is intended to assist in development and improvement of the organization as an educational service delivery system (Maher, Illback, & Zins, 1984).

All school psychologists, however, perform their services in the context of an organization. As previously stated, school psychologists are prone to address problems at the individual level, including assessment, intervention, and consultation functions. It is important to recognize, however, that these problems arise within an organizational context. For example, when a teacher is asked to serve a handicapped child within the regular classroom without receiving necessary additional training (i.e., staff development services), the child's resultant problems can be seen as having an organizational basis (at least to some degree). Thus, it behooves each and every school psychologist to be able to take an *organizational perspective,* in order to both understand the child's problems and help structure appropriate interventions.

Many school psychologists perform explicit organizational-level functions as well as individual-level activities. These may range from helping to plan and evaluate a district-wide screening process for children at high risk for learning problems, to more global administrative/managerial functions. In fact, school psychologists, by virtue of their unique and extensive training, are highly likely to move into leadership positions within the schools, such as Director of Student Services, Special Education Coordinator, Director of Psychological Services, and Director of Research, Planning, and Evaluation.

At the organizational level, a range of activities which are psychologically-based are currently being practiced by school psychologists. For example, psychologists who have responsibility for the coordination of special education and related services must select and supervise staff members, monitor program processes and outcomes, complete state and Federal reports, coordinate the implementation of mandated due process procedures, plan for the allocation of financial resources, "troubleshoot," and a host of related activities. Each of these involves data-gathering, planning, and evaluation; in short, each represents problem solving and relies heavily on the school psychologist's ability to conceptualize about the organization and to translate this psychological understanding into a coherent set of integrated activities which reduce organizational-level problems.

Another component of organizational practice has been termed *program planning and evaluation* (Maher & Kratchowill, 1980; Maher & Bennett, 1984). Here, the emphasis for the practitioner is on the development and improvement of school programs, such as a reading resource room program, the special education program within the district, a district-wide mathematics program, or any other configuration of resources which the school uses to meet identified needs. In reality, a school district is an aggregate of multiple programs, ranging from individual-level programs (e.g., a child's Individualized Education Program) through group-level programs (e.g., a classroom or a building-level instructional approach such as team teaching), to organizational-level programs (e.g., district policies and procedures for mainstreaming, staff development programs, central administrative services). Many school psychologists are now being trained in the emerging principles and methods of program planning and evaluation, and can contribute to the schools' efforts to improve their performance (Maher & Illback, 1982).

A final example of organizational-level practice relates to staff development. With the rapid and escalating emergence of knowledge and technology in education, teacher training becomes quickly obsolete. In fact, there are many educators and other professionals who believe that much of preservice teacher training is irrelevant, given the job requirements of teaching in today's schools. Local school districts are increasingly taking responsibility for the professional development of staff members. In this regard, school psychologists are in a unique position to contribute, given their own extensive training and their unique role within the organization. A prime example is the contribution school psychologists have made as school districts have attempted to respond to recent Federal mandates regarding the "mainstreaming" of handicapped children. For many of these children, placement in regular classes with teachers who have little or no special education training has resulted. Often, these teachers have expressed concerns about their ability to deal with problem children, and have been resistant to the concept. School psychologists have helped by providing training in problem behavior management, by helping regular teachers examine their attitudes and beliefs about handicapped children, and by facilitating communication between regular and special education.

An emerging and extremely promising area for school psychology at the organizational-level is the use of microcomputers. Multiple uses have been suggested for this powerful technology, including computer assisted instruction, computer managed instruction, assessment-related computer functions, and information management systems. However, introducing microcomputers into schools involves a complex series of organizational changes that go far beyond merely understanding how to operate the machines. For example, issues such as staff readiness and skill levels, software availability and constraints, hardware and software allocation, relationship of software of existing curricula, and procedures for collecting and utilizing computer-managed data must all be thought out and resolved. Here again, school psychologists who are organizationally trained can make a meaningful contribution.

ISSUES AND DIRECTIONS IN SCHOOL PSYCHOLOGY PRACTICE

School psychology has had an interesting history spanning the field of education and psychology; it has drawn from many literatures and traditions, which has led to great diversity and richness of ideas. At the same time, significant conflicts remain unresolved, particularly in areas such as role and function, professional affiliation, and education and training.

Role and Function

From the field's inception, the literature has been dominated by articles describing the proper role and function for the school psychologist. At various times, descriptors such as assessment specialist, psychotherapist, psychoeducational therapist, family therapist, psychosituational assessor, curriculum developer, instructional designer, vocational specialist, behavior manager, child advocate, change agent, organizational developer, and a host of others, have been used. The lack of consensus about role has caused great ambiguity and stress within the profession. As a result, school psychologists seem prone to attend to the latest "fads," and role conceptions often change as a function of changing educational priorities and practices, rather than representing a consistent and carefully derived approach to practice, based on a specific knowledge base. In this vein, the newest trends are neuropsychological assessment and computer applications (these topics seem likely to dominate school psychology in the 1980s). While it is important to change with the times, the field must continually integrate new approaches with its tradition, which is systematic psychology and education. Therein lies the vitality and relevance of school psychology as a profession.

Professional Affiliation

The primary allegiance of school psychology has always been at issue. Is the school psychologist a professional psychologist or a professional educator? Answers to this question vary, and reflect a basic polarization of the field. At the risk of overgeneralizing, two major factions seem to be at odds, with many people admittedly somewhere in-between. Professional psychology advocates are more likely to be affiliated with the American Psychological Association (APA), and particularly Division 16 (School Psychology). This group is more prone to believe the doctorate should be the entry level, and that APA training and practice standards should define the profession. Supporters of this position are more likely to be found at universities and in private practice, and tend to hold doctorates themselves.

An alternate view is held by a group viewing specialist training (about 60 graduate hours plus an internship) as the entry prerequisite. This reflects the official position of the National Association of School Psychologists (NASP), which also promulgates training and practice standards. This larger organization encompasses the majority of practitioners, most of whom are nondoctoral.

The differences in the field of school psychology are deep-seated and difficult to resolve. Nevertheless, recent attempts by a joint APA Division 16/NASP Task Force have been promising, resulting in some significant compromises and attempts at joint accreditation of training programs. Should school psychology ever unite as a field, it would quickly emerge as a potent and highly influential force in both psychology and education.

Education and Credentialing

As the previous discussion has indicated, disagreements within the field stem from basic questions about allegiance, knowledge base, and traditions. These disagreements extend to issues such as education and training and credentialing.

The argument over entry level has already been noted. However, the issue goes beyond the doctoral/nondoctoral debate. Patterns and content of training programs are also at issue, including where the program should be housed (e.g., psychology department or education department), faculty composition (e.g., number of faculty, training backgrounds), curricular offerings (e.g., scope and sequence), program focus (e.g., scientist-professional versus practitioner orientation), the role of field experience (e.g., rotational versus extended internships, practicum requirements), and the importance of research. A related issue is whether school psychologists should specialize or whether training should remain generic (some suggested specialities have been preschool education, neuropsychology, and vocational assessment).

Credentialing in school psychology is regulated by two mechanisms. In the public sector (in most states), the credential is given by the state education department as a form of teacher certification. Nearly every state subscribes to a nondoctoral standard, and the recent acceptance of NASP guidelines by the National Council for Accreditation of Teacher Education (NCATE) would seem to insure that school psychology will remain a largely nondoctoral profession. When practiced in the private sector (in most states), The State Board of Psychology regulates practice. Almost always, the doctoral degree is required. The license to practice psychology privately is generic, but there is an expectation that the licensee will only practice in areas in which he/she is competent. There are presently some states which have separate school psychology licensure for private practice, most notably Illinois and Ohio, where large contingents of school psychologists are found.

In general, it appears that uniformity of training standards across states is increasing, primarily through the upgrading of 30-hour, psychometry-oriented programs. State professional organizations have played a large role in these improvements.

RESEARCH IN RELATION TO PRACTICE

Scanning the literature unique to school psychology over its history reveals some interesting trends. Until fairly recently, two major topics predominated, role and function research and research on the technical adequacy of tests. While these aspects remain, a new generation of research and writing has emerged, broadening the scope of the school psychology literature considerably.

The most significant of these new research foci has been consultation. Systematic examinations of consultation processes and products lend great credence to its use by practitioners. A second area is that of assessment and decision making. Here, studies of how individuals and teams make decisions about children have yielded fresh insights into the practice of school psychology, and provoked self-examination by both trainers and practitioners. There is also an increasing trend toward studies of organizational variables which affect children's learning and which impact upon the practice of school psychology.

An exciting development is the increased frequency of outcome studies on a variety of individual, group, and organizational treatment packages. This signals that school psychologists are becoming more sophisticated in their use of evaluation research. In fact, more practitioners seem to be involved in conducting such research, reflected in a trend toward publishing more relevant and practical data. The increased acceptability of single-subject studies and an increased emphasis on program evaluation as practice are related to these trends.

Even within more traditional school psychology research areas, a revolution seems to be in progress. Alternative assessment procedures are being field tested and validated, such as behavioral assessment, dynamic assessment, non-test-based assessment, and criterion-referenced measurement. Clinical and development psychology approaches such as cognitive developmental, neuropsychological, and cognitive-behavioral theory and research, are becoming modified and integrated. And role and function issues are undergoing some basic reformulations to account for current events. All in all, these developments will likely strengthen the profession, and insure its future as the bell weather of psychological and educational change processes.

REFERENCES

Bardon, J. I. (1982). The psychology of school psychology. In C. R. Reynolds & T. B. Gutkin (Eds.), *Handbook of School Psychology*. New York: John Wiley & Sons.

Bellak, L., & Bellak, S. S. (1965). *Manual of instruction for the "Children's Apperception Test."* New York: C.P.S. Co.

Bender, L. (1983). A Visual Motor Gestalt Test and its clinical use. *American Orthopsychiatric Association Monograph,* No. 3.

Bergan, J. (1977). *Behavioral consultation.* Columbus, OH: Merrill.

Buck, J., & Joles, I. (1966). *House-tree-person.* Los Angeles: Western Psychological Services.

Caplan, C. (1970). *The theory and practice of mental health consultation.* New York: Basic Books.

Coles, G. (1978). The learning disabilities test battery. *Howard Educational Review, 48,* 313–340.

Gordon, T. (1970). *Parent effectiveness training.* New York: Wyden Books.

Gray, S. W. (1963). *The psychologist in the schools.* New York: Holt, Rinehart, & Winston.

Illback, R. J. (1980). *The development of guidelines for local school district screening programs: A problem solving approach.* Unpublished doctoral dissertation, Rutgers University.

Kratochowill, T. R. (1982). Advances in behavioral assessment. In C. R. Reynolds & T. B. Gutkin (Eds.), *Handbook of school psychology.* New York: Wiley.

Maher, C. A., & Bennett, R. E. (1984). *Planning and evaluating special education services.* Englewood Cliffs, NJ: Prentice-Hall, Inc.

Maher, C. A., & Kratochwill, T. R. (1980). Principles and procedures of program evaluation: An overview: *School Psychology Monograph, 4,* 1–24.

Maher, C. A., & Illback, R. J. (1982). Organizational school psychology: Issues and considerations. *Journal of School Psychology, 21,* 138–145.

Maher, C. A., Illback, R. J., & Zins, J. E. (1984). Organizational psychology in schools: Perspectives and Framework. In C. A. Maher and R. J. Illback, & J. E. Zins (Eds.), *Organizational psychology in schools: A handbook for professionals.* Springfield, IL: Charles C. Thomas.

Medway, F. J. (1979). How effective is school consultation? A review of recent research. *Journal of School Psychology, 17,* 275–282.

Murray, H. A. (1943). A manual for the Thematic Apperception Test. Cambridge: Harvard University Press.

Patterson, G. R., Reid, J. B., Jones, R. R., & Conger, R. E. (1975). *A social learning approach to family intervention.* Eugene, OR: Castalia Publishing.

Piers, E., & Harris, D. (1969). *The Piers Harris Children's Self Concept Scale.* Nashville: Counselor Recordings and Tests.

Rorschach, H. (1951). *Psychodiagnostics.* New York: Grune & Stratton.

Salvia, J., & Ysseldyke, J. E. (1981). *Assessment in special and remedial education* (2nd ed). Boston: Houghton Mifflin.

Urban, W. (1963). *Draw-a-Person.* Los Angeles: Western Psychological Services.

ADDITIONAL READINGS

Anastasi, A. (1976). *Psychological testing* (4th Ed.). New York: Macmillan.

Atkeson, B. M., & Forehand, R. (1979). Home-based reinforcement programs designed to modify classroom behavior: A review and methodological evaluation, *Psychology Bulletin, 86,* 1298–1303.

Bennett, R. E. (1982). Cautions in the use of informal measures in the educational assessment of exceptional children. *Journal of Learning Disabilities. 15,* 337–339. (a)

Bennett, R. E. (1982). Criterion-referenced measurement in the classroom. *New Jersey Journal of School Psychology,* 1, 3–13. (b)

Cattell, R. B. (1963). Theory of crystallized and fluid intelligence: A critical experiment. *Journal of Educational Psychology, 54,* 1–22.

Guilford, J. P. (1967). *The nature of human intelligence.* New York: McGraw-Hill.

Jensen, A. R. (1980). *Bias in mental testing.* New York: The Free Press.

Oakland, R. (Ed.). (1977). *Psychological and educational assessment of minority children.* New York: Brunner/Mazel.

Piaget, J., & Inhelder, B. (1969). *The psychology of the child.* New York: Basic Books.

Sattler, J. (1982). The psychologist in court: Personal reflections of one expert witness in the case of Larry P. *School Psychology Review, 11,* 306–318.

Spearman, C. E. (1927). *The abilities of man.* New York: MacMillan.

Thorndike, E. L. (1927). *The measurement of intelligence.* New York: Bureau of Publications, Teachers College, Columbia University.

Thurstone, L. L. (1938). Primary mental abilities. *Psychometric Monographs,* No. 1.

LIST OF TEST PUBLISHERS

Consulting Psychologists Press, Inc.
577 College Avenue
Palo Alto, CA 94306
(Frostig)

Psychological Corporation
Division of Harcourt Brace Jovanovich
304 E. 45th Street
New York, NY 10017
(McCarthy, WAIS-R, WISC-R, WPPSI, SOMPA)

Riverside Publishing Company
Subsidiary of Houghton Mifflin Company
Test Editorial Offices
P. O. Box 1970
Iowa City, IA 52240
(Stanford-Binet)

Teaching Resource Corporation
100 Boylston Street
Boston, MA 02116
(Woodcock-Johnson)

University of Illinois Press
Urbana, IL 61801
(ITPA)

Chapter 10

Health Care Settings

Donald Wertlieb

Tufts University

Denise Jones, Ph.D., is Director of Mental Health Services at the Neighborhood Community Health Center, an outreach clinic of the Intown Medical Center. She oversees a staff of professionals and paraprofessionals who provide outpatient psychodiagnostic and psychotherapeutic services to the local community. Some of this staff also serve as regular members of primary care teams in the pediatric, internal medicine, and family practice clinics of the Center. Another project in her department provides consultation and screening services to neighboring schools and daycare centers aimed at identifying children in need of special educational or health care services.

Perhaps a high point of her weekly routine is the Staff Development Seminar, where Dr. Jones and a colleague from the University Public Health School moderate a series of case conferences and didactic presentations on family development and psychosocial factors in health and illness.The Health Center staff, psychology interns, medical residents, social work trainees, and student nurses also look forward to this weekly exchange.

Jeffrey Wallach, Ph.D., Assistant Professor of Behavioral Sciences at State Medical College, devotes much of his time to a very promising and productive program of research on individuals' and families' adaptation to chronic illness. Demonstration projects and intervention evaluation studies based on his more basic research have recently been implemented in the College teaching hospitals. So it is with excitement that he anticipates the refinements of his thinking and research and the contributions to direct patient care likely to emerge from his efforts. His recent publications in the psychosomatics and behavioral medicine journals have been well received by his colleagues. The textbook he is developing is drawn from his experiences teaching second-year medical students at the College and his course in the new interdisciplinary Health Psychology Doctoral Training program conducted by the University's Departments of Psychology, Sociology, and Epidemiology. Students from the Health Psychology program serve apprenticeships with Dr. Wallach, helping with his research as well as executing independent projects on chronic illnesses.

Louise Rubin, Psy.D., works at the Valley Health Plan, a large health maintenance organization (HMO) which provides comprehensive health services to
over 200,000 members on a prepaid basis through contracts with a wide range
of businesses and institutions. Hers is a very busy practice consisting mainly of
diagnostic interviews and brief therapy for individuals and couples. She is
especially gratified by her successful sex therapy with many couples and by
her work with young adults dealing with developmental issues in her short-term
psychotherapy groups. Dr. Rubin trained at an HMO which used a model teaming
the psychologist with the internists and nurse practitioners in primary care
clinics. She prefers the HMO service delivery model at Valley Health Plan because the separate and distinct Mental Health Department allows her more
contact and support from fellow mental health clinicians who share common
interests and training background. Dr. Rubin also enjoys her work in the Health
Education Department of the Health Plan consulting with nurses and nutrition-
ists who run a variety of "lifestyle" groups on topics such as weight control,
smoking cessation, stress management, and coping with single parenthood. She
also maintains a part-time private practice which allows her to see a few clients
in long-term individual psychotherapy.

Jack Latimer, Ph.D., is a pediatric psychologist in practice with a group of
three pediatricians and affiliated with the Western Cancer Treatment Unit and
the Region Rehabilitation Center. His work involves him with a wide variety of
activities ranging from dispensing child development guidance and tips on
toilet training to parents, to helping social workers run a program for families
coping with surviving cancer, to designing psychoeducational programs for
youngsters with congenital or acquired handicaps. Latimer and his pediatrician
colleagues have recently agreed to have their practice serve as a site for a large
epidemiological survey of mental health problems and interventions, and are
collaborating in its implementation.

Dr. Jones, Dr. Wallach, Dr. Rubin, and Dr. Latimer[1] are *health psychologists,*
scientists and practitioners who elaborate our knowledge and skill base and
provide essential services in the health care system. Functions, roles, and skills—
new, old, and in various combinations—basic to the re-emerging field of health
psychology will be articulated in this chapter. A brief sketch of the historical
context will be offered first. Consideration of problems and issues for psychologists in health care settings will then follow.
Recent efforts to define the field of health psychology have encompassed a
broad range of scientific, professional, and educational components based on
the discipline of psychology (Matarazzo, 1980, 1982; Millon, Green, & Meagher,

---

[1] These are fictitious composite sketches offered to illustrate the variety and range of
psychologists' participation in health care settings.

1982; Stone, Cohen, & Adler, 1979; Wertlieb, 1984). A consensus may be emerging around such elements as:

- Psychology's contribution to the treatment and prevention of illness.
- Psychological and behavioral factors in health maintenance and promotion.
- Identification of etiologic and diagnostic correlates or risk factors of health, illness and related dysfunction.
- Analysis and improvement of the health care system including individual behavior, health education, the doctor-patient relationship, service delivery, etc., and
- Health policy formation.

The American Psychological Association Task Force on Health Research (1976) notes that:

> There is probably no specialty field within psychology that cannot contribute to the discovery of behavioral variables crucial to a full understanding of susceptibility to physical illness, adaptation to such illness, and prophylactically motivated behaviors. The areas open to psychological investigation range from health care practices and health care delivery systems to the management of acute and chronic illness and to the psychology of medication and pain. (p. 272).

Thus, health psychology draws quite broadly from psychology and links it to *behavioral medicine,* "the interdisciplinary field concerned with the development and integration of behavioral and biomedical science knowledge and techniques relevant to health and illness and the application of this knowledge and these techniques to prevention diagnosis, treatment and rehabilitation" (Schwartz & Weiss, 1978, p. 250).

The recent re-emergence of health psychology as an organizing discipline is rooted in events and issues as old as psychology itself (Stone, 1979b). The American Psychological Association, founded and incorporated at the turn of the century, held the first symposium on health psychology in 1911, dealing with the role of psychology in medical education. John B. Watson, the father of Behaviorism and, to many, the father of American psychology, wrote in 1912:

> The medical student must be taught that no matter whether he is specializing in surgery, obstetrics, or psychiatry, his subjects are human beings and not merely objects on which he may demonstrate his skill. This shift in his ideas of value will lead him to feel the need of psychologic training and to accept that training. (p. 917)

Even now, training of health care personnel is a major focus of health psychology. Beginning especially in the 1950s, there has been tremendous growth of behavioral science departments and curricula and appointments of psychologists in medical schools and related settings, (Matarazzo, Carmody, & Gentry,

1981; Matarazzo, Lubin, & Nathan, 1978; Matthews & Avis, 1982; Stachnik, 1980; Wexler, 1976). In parallel, there has been wide recognition and participation of psychologists in service delivery, not only in psychiatric or mental health settings, but more broadly in health care settings, as will be elaborated below. Millon et al. (1982) suggest that "it was not until the mid-1970s that psychologists began to be seen not as psychiatry's surrogate, but as independent colleagues and consultants to physicians who worked in nonpsychiatric health settings" (p. 3), and brought important specific skills and orientations to bear upon health and illness. Again, in parallel, was a still-burgeoning array of relevant research conducted by psychologists and documented by the 1976 Task Force cited above (APA, 1976).

A number of more formal milestones mark this re-emergence of health psychology in the past few years. The Behavioral Medicine Branch of the National Heart, Lung and Blood Institute at the National Institutes of Health was formed. The Academy of Behavioral Medicine Research and the Society of Behavioral Medicine as well as a Division of the American Psychological Association (Division 38–Health Psychology) were founded. Several new journals were launched including *Health Psychology, Journal of Behavioral Medicine, Journal of Pediatric Psychology* and *Rehabilitation Psychology*. Millon et al. (1982) point to these developments as evidence that "a scientific foundation is being built to undergird the professional practice of the health psychologist" (p. 3). Indeed, it is the integration of theory, research, and practice so vital in general to the emergence and survival of psychology as a profession and scientific discipline that is a hallmark of health psychology. New hopes and new challenges for the scientist-practitioner ideal are inherent in the re-emergence and revitalization of health psychology. There is sufficient basis for optimism and enthusiasm in terms of employment opportunities (Adler, Cohen, & Stone, 1979).

Who We Are

There has already been allusion to various fields, subfields, and labels related in different ways to health psychology. It is probably important for each individual how he or she identifies one's self at the next level beyond "I am a psychologist." "Behavioral medicine is my field," or "I am a clinical health psychologist" may hold or convey important meaning. A few dimensions of these labels are suggested here (and in Wertlieb, 1984) with the recognition that there is room for diagreement and revision.

A *medical psychologist* is most often a clinical psychologist whose specialization is in serving patients with physical illness, often in hospitals and often as part of a consultation-liason psychiatry service (Wertlieb, 1981, 1984). Though the clinical orientation emphasizes mental health concerns and traditional methods, there is a well-documented context of efficacy of psychotherapeutic interventions in terms of outcome and costs of a variety of physical illnesses (Jones & Vischi, 1979; Mumford, Schlesinger, & Glass, 1981; Olbrisch, 1977; Wertlieb & Budman, 1982).

Medical psychology might also encompass so-called "psychosomatic illness," diseases presumed or demonstrated to be caused or exacerbated by emotional or psychological factors. Increasingly, medicine, in general, and psychosomatic medicine, in particular, are embracing more comprehensive and holistic bio-psychosocial conceptualizations of health and illness. These frameworks attempt to integrate emotional and psychological factors with physical or organic factors in virtually all health or illness (Engel, 1977; Lipowski, 1977a, 1977b; Wertlieb, 1979). Such broadened conceptual frameworks substantiate clinical psychology as a health profession, and may obviate the general subspecialty label of "medical psychology" (Schofield, 1979). Millon, Green, and Meagher's (1982) descriptions of *clinical health psychologists* illustrate related labels, specializations, and identifications. Elsewhere, the mutuality between *consultation–liaison psychiatry* and health psychology have been articulated (Strain, 1982; Wertlieb, 1981).

A *pediatric psychologist* collaborates with pediatricians and allied health professionals around meeting the developmental and health needs of children and their families in service delivery, training, and research domains. As early as 1965, this "new marriage" between pediatrics and psychology was celebrated, heralding the re-emergence of health psychology (Kagan, 1965; Roberts, Maddux, Wurtele, & Wright, 1982; Wright, 1979). At the other end of the developmental spectrum, *geriatric psychologists* address the many and varied health needs of our elderly (Lebray, 1979).

Also among the earlier specialists is the *rehabilitation psychologist* active in serving patients with physical disabilities and chronic disorders. Assessment and counseling are among their important contributions to interdisciplinary collaborations with professionals in rehabilitation medicine and allied health services such as nursing, physical therapy and occupational therapy (Grzesiak, 1981).

Building upon the insights and concerns of both public health and community psychology, newer labels and identifications appear. *Community health psychologists* emphasize preventive over curative approaches and individual models (Iscoe, 1982). *Public health psychologists* and *clinical developmental psychologists* integrate traditional psychological and mental health concerns with broader and innovative conceptualizations and applications in health care arenas (DeLeon & Pallak, 1982; Michael, 1982; Miller, Fowler, & Bridgers, 1982; Singer & Krantz, 1982; Wertlieb, 1979).

Elsewhere I have commented upon some of the important socio-political and economic pressures and motivators related to the re-emergence of health psychology, and noted the interactions and convergence with important conceptual and scientific advances, some of which have just been mentioned (e.g., biopsychosocial perspectives) (Wertlieb & Budman, 1982). A few bear repeating here, to alert us to the important contextural considerations before we focus upon more specific settings, roles, and activities of health care psychologists.

An important guild and scientific issue facing psychology is the preservation of autonomy and appropriate niches in whatever National Health Insurance program ultimately emerges as national poicy. In this regard, health psychologists have been articulating convincing rationales and justification for the essential role of mental health services in the health care system, as well as psychological contributions with other than a mental health service focus. As part of this process, psychologists have become increasingly involved in and appreciative of biomedical and behavioral research which provide the data base for such claims. Meanwhile, the public, its politicians and elected officials, and its bureaucracies clamor for restraint upon the "runaway health care dollar," the health psychologist can offer information, inquiry, demonstration, and direction in these pressing controversies and needs.

Among the conceptualizations and attendant research endeavors reflecting our scientific progress are, for instance, the new "medical model" (Engel, 1977) and new psychosomatics (Lipowski, 1977a, 1977b) which have emerged to explain the "new morbidity" (Haggerty, Roghmann, & Pless, 1975). Health and illness are considered as complex, multifaceted biopsychosocial processes. The insights of these approaches are perhaps best exemplified in the literatures linking stress, social support, and illness (Becker, Haefner, Kasl, Kirscht, Maiman, & Rosenstock, 1977; Cassel, 1977; Cobb, 1976; Coddington, 1972; Cohen, 1979; Eckenrode, & Gore, 1981; Eisdorfer, 1982; Hurst, Jenkins, & Rose, 1976; Lynch, 1977; Rabkin & Streuning, 1976; Rahe & Arthur, 1978; Wertlieb, 1979).

Indeed, "revolution" is a term being used to describe some of the recent advances in understanding health (Michael, 1982; Stachnik, 1980). Health psychologists are among its soldiers and generals.

"The revolution in question is one we are all aware of but seldom articulate: The morbidity and mortality rates of Americans are no longer related to the infectious diseases prevalent at the turn of the century; instead they are related to chronic disorders related to our lifestyles. Influenza, pneumonia, tuberculosis, gastroenteritis and diphtheria have been replaced by heart disease, cerebrovascular disease, respiratory diseases and various cancers—all of which are in part a product of how we live, that is, what and how much we eat and drink, how we exercise, how we deal with daily stresses, whether or not we smoke, and so on. In short, the most serious medical problems that today plague the majority of Americans are not ultimately medical problems at all; they are behavior problems, requiring the attention of characteristic response patterns, and thus fall squarely in the province of psychology" (Stachnik, 1980, p. 8).

Again, the reader is referred to recent, lengthier considerations of these issues by Wertlieb and Budman (1982) and Matarazzo (1982). Several recent major reports or policy proposals reflect related issues; these include the Report of the Select Panel for the Promotion of Child Health (U.S. Department of Health and Human Services, 1981),The National Academy of Sciences Institute of Medicine Report on Stress and Health (Eisdorfer, 1982), the General

Mills American Family Report (Yankelovich, Skelly, & White, 1979), the Carnegie Council Report on Handicapped Children (Gliedman & Roth, 1980), and the Surgeon General's Report on Health Promotion and Disease Prevention (Califano, 1979). These sociopolitical, economic, and scientific contexts must be borne in mind as we now shift our focus to more specific settings, roles, and functions of health psychologists.

Where We Work

There is a tremendous range of settings in which health psychologists provide consultation and service, teach, or carry out research. Recent estimates from the American Psychological Association suggest that about 60% of its membership are health service providers (VandenBos, Stapp, & Kilburg, 1981). Indicated above are the important contributions and potential contributions of researchers in health psychology. Traditionally, medical centers, rehabilitation hospitals, mental health facilities, and their training sites have been populated by health psychologists. Dental schools and settings are also calling upon health psychologists (Sachs, Eigenbrode, & Kruper, 1979; Winer, 1982). Liss-Levinson (1982) describes psychological services in hospices. Increasingly, consultative and staff roles for health psychologists are available in government agencies for health planning and policy development. Business and industry are recognizing the potential contributions of psychologists to employee health enhancement, benefits, and work productivity (Manuso, 1981). The world of "independent" or "private practice" is also being charted and developed in the health psychology framework (Cummings & VandenBos, 1979). Comprehensive review of these myriad settings and models is beyond the scope of this chapter. Rather, using examples of primary health care settings, we will illustrate some of the roles and activities of health psychologists. The reader seeking broader and/or more specific considerations is referred to several recent collections of reports from and by health psychologists (Baum & Singer, 1982; Blanchard, 1982; Budman & Wertlieb, 1979; Millon et al., 1982; Stone et al., 1979).

Primary care settings present some of the newer, most significant, and most promising avenues for health care psychologists. This is by virtue of (a) public policy pressures which emphasize the importance of primary care, (b) practical considerations inherent in these settings being usually the first or entry encounter between an individual and health professionals and serving the largest number of individuals, and (c) conceptual/theoretical considerations which suggest that the health maintenance and enhancement efforts of psychologists may have their greatest impact here. These notions are articulated elsewhere (Wertlieb, 1981, Wertlieb & Budman, 1982).

What We Do

"Primary Care" is the "first contact" level of health services. General practitioners and pediatricians usually are the physicians who provide this care, though other specialists such as obstetrician-gynecologists may also be among those responsible for the continuity, comprehensiveness, coordination, and account-ability inherent in this level of care. "The primary care doctor spends most of his time thinking about the patient and the impact of various forces on his health or illness over a period of time. The secondary or tertiary level doctor spends most of his time thinking about a disease state or a technical skill and how various patients fit into or alter that field of interest over a period of time. For one, the illness is the episode; for the other, the patient is the episode" (Alpert & Charney, 1974, p. 3).

These requirements make such settings especially fertile ground for health psychologists, as is well illustrated in descriptions of health psychologists' roles in Health Maintenance Organizations (Budman, 1981), Neighborhood Health Centers (Marks & Broskowski, 1981) and Family Practice Settings (Bibace & Walsh, 1979). To facilitate an overview of the roles of health psychologists in primary care settings, a schema adapted from Wertlieb (1981) is presented in Table 1 categorizing these activities in terms of diagnostic, treatment, teaching, and research functions and in terms of target or focus. Some of the health psychologist's efforts may be focused upon the patient and/or his or her family, noted as "case-centered." Some activities are directed toward the health care team or "operational group" (Meyer & Mendelson, 1961)—physicians, nurses, or allied health professionals—noted as "consultee-centered." Other functions are "system-centered" and have as their focus change in the health care system, often at a more molar level.

This framework is offered only as a conceptual tool, with the recognition that these differentiations are not mutually exclusive. Indeed, few activities of health psychologists would fit very neatly into only one of these categories. As I have suggested elsewhere, it may be that the capacity to maintain these multiple perspectives on any single function might serve to enhance the psy-chologist's effectiveness. Certainly, any health psychologist might emphasize one or another subset of these functions, or targets (Wertlieb, 1981). The vignettes at the start of this chapter illustrates this. A particular pediatric psy-chologist might be devoted only to direct service functions, diagnosis, and treat-ment. Another health psychologist might restrict his or her functions to a comprehensive program of research on interpersonal processes between patients and physicians related to compliance with medical regimens. It may also be obvious that there might be a less than optimal match between the scopes of current training programs and the demands and potentials charted in Table 1. After elaborating upon the functions using the schema of the Table, we will return to problems such as training.

Diagnosis.   Quality health care relies upon careful and systematic generation and integration of data leading toward a biopsychosocial diagnosis of a patient's illness, disease, or "dis-ease." Components of this diagnostic process are appro-priately expected from the health psychologist. Traditionally and historically, the psychologist's contribution to this process has emphasized the psycho-

TABLE 1. Health Psychologists' Contributions to Primary Care Settings*

Function	Case-centered: patient and family as target	Consultee-centered: health care provider and operational group as target	System-centered: health care system as target
Diagnosis	Contribute to data base and integration of biopsycho-social diagnosis of illness	Encourage and model holistic biopsychosocial approach to patient assessment Interpret patient behavior to primary care team	Implement health assessment and screening to identify patients at bio-psychosocial risk
Treatment	Provide guidance and/or brief psychotherapy Develop and implement management and treatment plans addressing behavioral and psychosocial dimensions of patient care	Encourage and model holistic biopsychosocial approach to patient care Enable communication and teamwork among primary care team Liaison to mental health or other specialty services	Implement psychoedu-cational, lifestyle or health education services, e.g., smoking or weight control

Teaching	Reframe and relate symptoms to lifestyle factors, behavior, stress, etc. at rounds, case conferences, teaching conferences	Didactic interaction regarding doctor–patient relationship, interviewing, diagnosis, and treatment of emotional disorders, human development	Implement integrated behavioral sciences curricula in medical school, teaching hospital or continuing education
Research	Refine diagnostic criteria in a biopsychosocial framework	Identify provider behaviors associated with patient compliance with treatment regimen	Program evaluation
	Basic research in etiology of illness and health	Develop diagnostic and treatment protocols which address biopsychosocial aspects of illness	"Offset" research
			Quality assurance

*From D. Wertlieb, "Mental health providers in primary care settings," pp. 115–135 in *Linking health and mental health*, edited by A. Broskowski, E. Marks, and S. Budman. Copyright © 1981 by Sage Publications. Adapted by permission of Sage Publications, Inc.

logical, psychosocial, or mental health perspectives, potentially reifying a mind-body distinction which must ultimately be overcome. Clinical psychologists and liaison psychiatrists are well aware of the risks involved in "over-psychologizing" the patient's problem or situation.

"The task is to reconcile the medical-biological approach with the psychosocial one and to somehow present this comprehensive (i.e., biopsychosocial) view in a practical and meaningful way in the medical setting" (Brill, 1975, p. 113, parentheses added). Lipowski (1967) offers five categories of differential diagnostic problems faced by primary care teams:

1. psychological presentation of organic disease
2. psychological complications of organic disease
3. psychological reactions to organic disease
4. somatic presentation of psychiatric disorders
5. "psychosomatic" disorders

Discussions by Horowitz (1982), Schontz (1982), and Weiner (1982) amplify these problems. This classification is useful only to the extent that it does not lead the provider (or the patient) to an overly facile, overly simplified, nonintegrated appreciation of the patient's problem. Indeed, "If one views disease from a multicausal point of view, every disorder can be considered psychosomatic, since every disorder is affected in some fashion by emotional factors" (Kaplan, 1980, p. 1973). The health psychologist's role is to foster a comprehensive diagnostic picture relying upon his biopsychosocial perspective on health and illness.

Consultation-liaison psychiatry has traditionally considered development of the psychosocial history as a crucial component of the diagnostic process in primary care (Feldman, 1978; Martin, 1980). "Despite an emphasis on the teaching of the relationship between illness and the patient's emotional status, internists have a tendency to minimize psychiatric issues. Even when significant emotional difficulties are present, physicians tend to place these near the end of their problem-oriented lists. It is common for the internist to note the pain and stiffness of degenerative arthritis, chronic obesity, and other overt symptoms before noting depression or anxiety" (Martin, 1980, p. 2031). The health psychologist calls upon history-taking as well as traditional and innovative screening and assessment instruments to refine diagnosis. Green (1982) discusses several of these instruments and their application in medical settings.

Whether through direct intervention with the patient and family or through indirect consultation with the other members of the health care team, the health psychologist can encourage and model a holistic biopsychosocial approach to patient assessment. Part of this process often involves interpretation of patient behavior to teammates, increasing their awareness of meanings beyond the overt verbal content of the presentation. They can be directed towards greater appreciation of sources of anxiety and depression for the patient and how these may or may not influence his or her illness behavior and complaints. This involves considerably more than identification of so-called psychosomatic or stress symptoms (e.g., tension headache, low back pain). Rather, a biopsychosocial framework for understanding the symptoms, the patient's experience of the symptoms, and the patient's expectations, wishes, and fears within the doctor–patient relationship must be developed via the diagnostic process.

As the kind of diagnostic teamwork suggested above entrenches itself in a setting or system, alterations in the system itself are likley. For instance, prior to such collaboration, descriptions of the patient population served may underestimate the prevalence or significance of depression, anxiety, or other psychosocial or behavioral problems. With such collaborations, these problems may be more accurately recognized and diagnosed, or even overestimated. Depending on the degree of integration and type of care delivery system, one change might be increased referrals to psychiatric or social service components of the system. The health psychologist must maintain such a system-centered focus in order to have a perspective on his contribution to the diagnostic activity of the setting.

Another system-centered contribution by health psychologists in primary care settings is the implementation of health assessment and screening programs aimed at the identification of patients "at risk" for health problems (Wertlieb, 1979; Wertlieb & Budman, 1982). The Kaiser-Permanente Multiphasic Health Appraisal is one program being developed in a health maintenance organization (Harrington, 1978). Such a screening procedure identifying particular behaviors, lifestyle patterns, or other health status indicators allows providers to direct patients toward appropriate preventively oriented intervention programs. Further, identification of at-risk subpopulations within a patient population can focus and foster development of interventions addressing their particular needs. Cigarette smoking, problem drinking, and overeating are among behaviors which should alert the health care team and the system to potential health problems and a need for timely intervention.

Treatment. If one major thrust or implication of these diagnostic issues just mentioned is that there is value in identifying patients "at risk," a corollary assumption and set of activities involves treatment of these patients. It can be argued at a global level that simply presenting one's self in a primary care setting indicates a certain "at risk" status, psychologically, given the high probability of some illness and the actuality of "illness behavior," initial steps in the adoption of a patient role or sick role (e.g., Jacobson, 1979; Mechanic, 1979). Again, the treatment contributions of the health psychologist in primary care settings can be considered from case-centered, consultee-centered, and system-centered perspectives, as suggested in Table 1.

As in the diagnostic process, the treatment process is potentially enhanced by the broadened biopsychosocial perspective fostered by the health psychologist. The primary care team develops and implements treatment and management plans addressing behavioral and psychosocial dimensions of patient care as well as biomedical dimensions. Such treatment has been called "psychomedical treatment," i.e., "the approach that emphasizes the interrelation of mind and body in the genesis of symptom and disorder" (Kaplan, 1980, p. 1973).

That primary care providers are indeed attempting to treat their patients with emotional disturbance is evidenced by the "promiscuous prescription of tranquilizing drugs" (Eisenberg, 1977, p. 240). About 70% of psychotropic drugs are prescribed by nonpsychiatrists (Kline, 1974). Between 29% and 79% of primary care patients, their emotional disturbance diagnosed and undiagnosed, receive a prescription for psychoactive drugs (Hankin, 1979).

The health psychologist in primary care settings is often called upon to provide psychotherapeutic services, not very unlike those traditionally provided in mental health settings. Two major distinctions between traditional psychotherapy and that done in primary care settings present appropriate accommodations to the demands of such settings; a shift toward brief therapies (e.g., Budman, 1981) and an increased use of psychoeducational or guidance interventions (e.g., Wertlieb, 1979; Wright, 1979).

Another accomodation has been the emergence of episodic psychotherapeutic treatment (e.g., Cummings & VandenBos, 1979). Just as the continuity aspect of primary medical care involves relatively brief encounters between patient and primary care providers over a number of years, so too does psychotherapy take shape in such settings. Jacobson (1979) has described this "extensive therapy" and noted the reorientation it requires for the mental health professional. "A successful outcome of speciality mental health service typically has been based on the expectation that the patient will not return after the completion of psychotherapeutic intervention. The definition of successful outcome in primary care is quite the opposite: the primary health care provider assumes that patients will continue to return for health care as needed" ... Thus, the mental health provider "might employ a 'string of beads' approach, in which the patient would work on a theme in a succession of crisis episodes for which he or she would return to the same therapists to pick up the treatment. The treatment course in this approach is not terminated but is considered to have dormant phases" (Institute of Medicine, 1979, p. 126). Advantages of such approaches are a wider availability of such psychotherapy to more people at lower costs. Disadvantages include the relative dearth of training for psychologists and other mental health professionals at this point for such therapy, as well as possible exclusion of patient populations in need of more intensive and extensive services, the chronically mentally ill, for instance. The effectiveness of such brief task-centered treatment remains an important empirical question (Budman, 1981). However, there are significant indications that psychotherapy has an extremely important role to play in the health care system (e.g., Mumford, Schlesinger, & Glass, 1979; Olbrisch, 1977; Wertlieb & Budman, 1982).

Through encouragement and modeling of holistic biopsychosocial approaches, health psychologists can have important impact upon their colleagues on the primary care team. Capitalizing upon his or her training in human relations and interpersonal communication, the health psychologist can enable and facilitate communication and teamwork among the primary care team as well as that between the patient and team.

The modern physician has been criticized as being an impersonal, uncaring, but technically skilled scientist (Martin, 1980). This may be less the case in primary care specialties than in others. Nonetheless, this arena is one of special import for the psychologist in primary care treatment. If it is indeed the case that "90% of curing is caring," as has been suggested, then it is the psychologist who may be in one of the best positions for shifting the attentions of the team to that important "90%." Shared world views or appreciation of biopsychosocial issues may already be in place in primary care, accounting perhaps for these settings being especially hospitable to psychologists (Bibace & Walsh, 1979).

Another, more specific, contribution of the health psychologist to the primary care team can be the by now traditional liaison function. The psychologist is often the key in the identification and facilitation of referral to psychiatric services, or other appropriate services in secondary, tertiary, or other specialty areas of the health care system. This aspect of comprehensive treatment should not be underemphasized. There is considerable evidence that there is great need for improving this component of primary care services (Carey & Kogan, 1971).

Again, proliferation and success of these case-centered and consultee-centered treatment activities can significantly alter the health care system. Further, some activities of health psychologists can begin or focus upon the system level. For instance, given the assessment and screening activities mentioned above, there emerges a need for development and implementation of a range of treatment interventions tailored to address the risk factors identified. Among such interventions are psychoeducational, lifestyle, and/or health education groups centered around issues such as smoking, weight control, relaxation training, and coping with psychosocial stress (e.g., marital separation) (Harrington, 1978; Wertlieb, 1979; Wertlieb et al., 1982, 1984). As will be discussed below, training primary care providers in the provision of such services or appropriate referral considerations, and evaluating such programs, captures a portion of the teaching and research functions of psychologists in primary care settings.

Teaching. Wexler (1976) suggests that the behavioral sciences, particularly psychology, should develop "a model of the doctor's job and clothe it with the basic and essential information required for primary patient care" (p. 275). Again, it is useful to consider direct and indirect teaching services with case-centered, consultee-centered, and system-centered foci.

Though teaching would generally be considered a mutual exchange between psychologists and other primary care providers, there are contributions by psychologists that are more directly centered upon the primary care patient and his or her family. These are generally related to treatment of the patient, but should also be acknowledged as didactic or teaching interventions. For instance, the psychologist on a primary care team may be responsible for helping the patient reframe or relate symptoms to lifestyle factors, behavior, or stress. This same educational effort can be extended by the psychologist in rounds or case conferences centered upon a particular patient, thus providing case-centered teaching to other primary care personnel.

In terms of the consultee-centered focus, that is, teaching functions within the operational group, there has been a traditional and significant reliance upon psychologists' didactic presentations on topics ranging from the doctor-patient relationships to interviewing technique to the diagnosis and treatment of emotional disorders. Much of these contents is presented in handbooks and textbooks appearing on the market (e.g., Bieliaukas, 1982; Billingham, 1982; Counte & Christman, 1981; DiMatteo & Friedman, 1982; Millon et al., 1982; Rosen, Geyman, & Layton, 1980; West, 1979). Matching curricula with the interests and needs of the primary team is a complicated and challenging set of tasks just recently yielding fruitful advances (e.g., Authier, 1979, 1981; Bibace & Walsh, 1979).

Much of this teaching activity occurs in the operational group, i.e., the health care team. However, there is widespread recognition of the need to develop and implement integrated mental health and behavioral sciences curricula throughout the training and service delivery systems, including medical school, teaching hospitals, residency programs, and continuing education settings (e.g., Bibace & Walsh, 1979; Wexler, 1976; Zuckerman, Carper, & Alpert, 1978). Such system-centered work by psychologists may be the most relevant and significant if indeed the primary care mandate is to be met.

Besides these teaching efforts that involve the transmission of the psychologist's perspective and knowledge base to other members of the primary care team, there is a critical mandate for psychologists in the primary care to train members of their own discipline, to enable the next generation of health psychologists to function effectively in primary care settings. Thus, within-discipline teaching at the predoctoral and postdoctoral levels is important.

Research. It is the psychologist's training as a researcher that may make him or her especially needed and valuable to health care systems. In recognition of this specialized contribution, some have argued forcefully and effectively for emphasis of this role in the training and professional practice of health psychologists (Nowicki, 1981; Stone 1979b). It is of interest to note that a similar call for allocation of attention and energy to the research enterprise is implicit and explicit in recent discussions of psychiatry's identity crisis and efforts to reestablish itself as a relevant and mainstream part of medicine (Barksy, 1980; Enelow, 1980; Lipowski, 1974; Shepherd, 1979). An important arena for either conflict or rapprochement between traditionally rivalrous mental health disciplines lies in the broad domain of research activity.

Again, the case-centered, consultee-centered, and system-centered foci each suggest overlapping ranges of research problems and paradigms. A few examples are presented in Table 1 and briefly mentioned here. The APA Health Research Task Force (1976), cited at the opening of this chapter, concludes the numerous specialties within psychology contribute to health psychology and related disciplines.

The Child Stress and Coping Project represents a program of research aimed at refining our understandings of the etiology of illness and health in a biopsychosocial framework (Wertlieb, 1982). In this recently initiated longitudinal study, 200 families with school-aged children are being periodically assessed in terms of their stressful experiences, manner of coping with these experiences, and any relationships of these to a variety of health outcomes including mental health problems, physical symptoms, behavior problems, and use of medical services. Through such prospective mapping and description of stress, coping, and health relationships, as they might emerge over the course of childhood, it is intended that we might better comprehend what is by now a fairly well accepted but poorly understood relationship between stress and illness in adults (Cohen, 1979; Eisdorfer, 1982). Information generated by such research should ultimately be translatable into better diagnostic criteria and more effective interventions effections to address the health needs of our society.

Another example of basic psychological research with important implications for health and health care delivery is the study of developmental progressions and individual differences in concepts of health, illnesses, and bodily functions (Bibace & Walsh, 1981). Through basic research in this area, psychologists can demonstrate how an individual's understanding of his or her health or illness influences how he or she complies (or does not comply) with a treatment regimen. By incorporating such biopsychosocial factors into diagnostic and treatment protocols, health care providers might be aided in maintaining rapport, compliance, satisfaction, and intervention effectiveness.

Other aspects of the patient-provider relationship are being studied in terms of verbal and nonverbal communication processes (Counte & Christman, 1981; DiMatteo & Friedman, 1982; Kagan, 1979). As such processes are better understood, the database for health psychology's contributions to patient care and training of health providers is expanded.

Program evaluation and quality assurance projects are examples of system-centered research activity (Stahler & Tash, 1982). These applied research efforts create feedback loops within the health care system with the potential for stimulating change in the direction of meeting those systems' goals in more timely and efficient ways. "Offset" research is one recent and promising approach to systematically generating valuable information (Jones & Vischi, 1979; Mumford, Schlesinger, & Glass, 1981; Olbrisch, 1977). "The 'offset' paradigm involves the evaluation of a mental health intervention in terms of its impact on medical utilization, i.e., visit to the doctor, lab tests. Thus the 'offset' literature describes outcomes of psychological interventions in terms of decreases, or other alterations in the pattern or rate of use of medical services. Offset research seeks to document and understand these relationships" (Wertlieb & Budman, 1982, p. 71).

Whether at the basic or applied level, whether case-, consultee-, or system-centered, the health psychology researcher faces the full range of methodological and conceptual dilemmas inherent in behavioral science. These problems can be seen as challenges stimulating creative solutions, rather than as insurmountable obstacles making health psychology too complex or too messy.

Problems

Returning now to a more general and pervasive level of problems for the health psychologist, the same strategy of framing challenges might be useful. Each of the activities outlined above has inherent problems and challenges with professional, ethical, political, and conceptual dimensions. Again, a few examples of these issues will be portrayed here, with reference to more comprehensive discussions by Matarazzo (1982), McNamara (1981), Stone et al. (1979), Tefft and Simeonson (1979) and Wertlieb and Budman (1979).

Given the recent reemergence of health psychology, it is only over the next decade that psychologists formally trained as "health psychologists" will take their places in the health care system. Even then, given the diverse and multidisciplinary nature of the field, a range of backgrounds and preparations will be represented. Now and probably in the forseeable future, clinical psychology with its mental health orientation will continue to be a predominant route of entry, especially for direct service functions. Until such time as the biopsychosocial approaches advocated above entrench themselves effectively in the health care system, psychologists are apt to be faced with conflicts and incongruencies. For example, Hoffman (1979) articulates a distinction between medical psychotherapy and psychological psychotherapy, and notes the implications of this distinction for the training and role of the therapist, the contract between patient and therapist, the therapeutic process, and outcome. The health psychologist who may be well trained in mental health service delivery must contend with a new and complex range of considerations and pressures when delivering such services in the context of a medical setting. For instance, comprehensive care of the asthmatic patient presents the health care team with a range of challenges. A movement toward well-defined spheres of responsibility for each profession involved—physicians, nurses, psychologists, etc.—has been proposed as an avenue for addressing some of these pressures (Miklich, 1979). Knowledge of the limits and implications of one's own areas of competence has important implications for care of the patient, collegial relationships, ethical practice, and malpractice risks.

Knapp and Vandecreek (1981) alert us that the psychologist may make himself or herself more vulnerable to criminal and civil liability in health care

settings other than traditional mental health settings. Special features of informed consent, guarantees of cure, duty to refer, and standards of negligence
must all be carefully considered.

The health psychologist may also be at greater risk than other psychologists
in terms of the impact upon professional practice of a number of political and
economic issues. Barsky's (1980) analysis of psychiatry's role in primary care has
analogous implications for psychologists entering the field: "The primary care
movement is itself internally confused and conflicted. Each of the medical
specialties contends for territorial hegemony, while other health professionals
struggle for greater role definition. The organization of practices, the structure
and desirability of teaching programs, and the schemes of financial reimburse-
ment all remain unsettled" (p. 229). Concerns for physician domination, antitrust redress, hospital privileges, professional standards review, national health
insurance, and public health policy take on special and explicit meaning for
many psychologists in health care settings (Clairborn & Stricker, 1979; Dörken &
Webb, 1979; McNamara, 1981; O'Keefe & McCullough, 1979).

Besides these professional and political conflicts and concerns are exciting
conceptual challenges that beg for creative resolution. The potential and actual
"paradigm clash" or incongruence of world view complicates the collaboration
among health care providers. Bibace and Walsh (1979), McNamara (1981),
Tefft and Simeonson (1979) and Wertlieb and Budman (1979) provide numerous examples of conflicting assumptions that guide the work of psychologists
and other health professionals. These "clashes" can be managed and resolved;
among the more promising routes toward these resolutions are the articulation
of shared world views. The biopsychosocial approach and developmental perspectives are examples of arenas where convergence is appearing. And, not
surprisingly, it is in primary care settings, health maintenance organizations, and
multidisciplinary research and service settings that such rapprochement is
making headway.

Training and Resources

Throughout the preceding discussion is implicit and explicit reference to issues
of training. Traditional graduate training in psychology—clinical or otherwise—
is often placed in counterpoint to the more focused and specialized training
experiences considered basic to competence and success in health psychology.
Yet the progress of current health psychologists appears based on traditional
background, and few suggest any wholesale abandonment of traditional training
goals. For some, the scientist-practitioner model of training reemerges as an
ideal, given the demands of health psychology as a discipline. Millon et al.
(1979) have argued that "the burgeoning responsibilities associated with these
roles do not call for discarding familiar skills and techniques, nor do they require
transforming oneself into a totally new professional. The task that faces the
psychologist is to intelligently and creatively refine and extend previously ac-

quired skills to fit these new responsibilities" (p. 529). "National Working Conference on Education and Training in Health Psychology" convened in 1983. Issues of core curricula, standards for internships, retraining, credentialling—many of them controversial—were addressed by the conference and published in the proceedings (Stone, 1983).

In the meantime, a range of courses, seminars, tracks, specializations, internships, programs, joint-programs, fellowships, continuing-education offerings address some of the complex training needs of the field. The University of California-San Francisco began a sepcialized health psychology doctoral program as early as 1970 emphasizing research collaboration with health care providers (Stone, 1979a; Adler et al., 1979). University of Miami has a "Clinical Health Track" in its Psychology Department (Millon, 1982). Drotar (1975) and Kenny and Bauer (1975) describe pediatric psychology training experiences. Gentry, Street, Masur, and Asken (1981) survey programs in medical psychology. Belar, Wilson, and Hughes (1982) describe numerous doctoral training opportunities at 38 different institutions, concluding that "the diversity in training noted is consistent with the diversity of skills, roles and functions of health psychologists today" (p. 297). Given the state of the art in training for health psychologists, discussion of approaches to tapping and orchestrating departmental university and community resources in the service of health psychology training is especially useful, as demonstrated by Olbrisch and Sechrest (1979).

Joint programs and postdoctoral education appear particularly congruent with the current scene in health psychology, both in terms of its young age and complex multidisciplinary foci. The role of public health psychology in preventing disorder, and maintaining and promoting health is the focus of the recently established MPH/Ph.D. program at the University of Alabama (Miller et al., 1982). The University of Hawaii adds business administration training to its public health psychology program (Tanabe, 1982).

These efforts address many of the training issues within psychology, but, as indicated above, there must be simultaneous energizing of training in the allied professions and disciplines. In training medical students and residents, health psychologists must enhance the multidisciplinary perspective and capitalize upon the shared world views via the potential inherent in biopsychosocial and developmental approaches. Authier's (1979, 1981) "integrated medical training with a family focus" demonstrates how this can be accomplished. Similarly, health psychologists must remain open and available for training from their colleagues. For example, the opportunities inherent in a course called "Pediatrics for the Clinical Psychologist" must be enthusiastically embraced and appreciated (Hollen, Ehrlich, & White, 1981).

Both during and after training, the networking, support, and intellectual exchange provided by professional organizations, newsletters, and journals serve to define and strengthen the discipline. Single discipline, multidisciplinary, and interdisciplinary groups and publications abound, several of which were mentioned at the start of this chapter. Recent handbooks and anthologies on health psychology provide extremely useful state of the field assessments (Baum & Singer, 1982; Budman & Wertlieb, 1979; Stone et al., 1979; Millon et al., 1982). Swencionis (1982) lists and describes a selection of 48 journals of general interest in health psychology, providing a very useful orientation to the complicated and diverse literatures which contribute toward the definition of our re-emerging discipline.

SUMMARY

As stated in Weiss's (1982) The Division 38 Health Psychology Presidential Address, "If there ever was a time of opportunity for Health Psychology, that time is *now*! If ever there was a gathering of the multitude of diverse factors and forces that all posit to a new approach to becoming healthy—and staying that way—that time is now! If ever there was the opportunity to put our understanding of behavior and behavior change to work in the service of enhancing the quality of life for all—that time is now!" (p. 81). The optimism and enthusiasm are well founded. The opportunities for psychology and for society inherent in the reemergence of health psychology are impressive. The range of roles, functions, and activities discussed above capture important commitments for diverse groups within the academic and professional field. The numerous problems—or rather, challenges—especially in terms of training are already being addressed in creative and effective ways with many indications that the process should continue and that the discipline will define itself effectively.

REFERENCES

Adler, N., Cohen, F., & Stone, G. (1979). Themes and professional prospects in health psychology. In G. Stone, F. Cohen, & N. Adler (Eds.), *Health psychology*, San Francisco: Jossey-Bass.

Alpert, J., & Charney, E. (1974). *The education of physicians for primary care.* DHEW Publication HRA 74-3113. Washington, DC: Government Printing Office.

American Psychological Association, TASK Force on Health Research. (1976). Contribution of psychology to health research. *American Psychologist, 31,* 263–274.

Authier, J. (1979). The family life cycle seminars: an innovative health care psychology program. *Professional Psychology, 10,* 451–457.

Authier, J. (1981). Integrated medical training: a family focus. In A. Broskowski, E. Marks & S. H. Budman (Eds.), *Linking health and mental health.* Beverly Hills: Sage Publications.

Barsky, A. J. (1980). Defining psychiatry in primary care: origins, opportunities, and obstacles. *Comprehensive Psychiatry, 21,* (3), 221–232.

Baum, A., & Singer, J. (Eds.) (1982). *Handbook of psychology and health* (5 Vols.). Hillsdale, NJ: Erlbaum.

Becker, M., Haefner, D., Kasl, S., Kirscht, J., Maimon, L., & Rosenstock, I. (1979). Selected psychosocial models and correlates of individual health related behaviors. *Medical Care, 15,* 27–46.

Belar, C. D., Wilson, E., & Hughes, H. (1982). Health psychology training in doctoral psychology programs. *Health Psychology, 1,* (3), 289–300.

Bibace, R., & Walsh, M. (1979). Clinical developmental psychologists in family practice settings. *Professional Psychology, 10,* 441–450.

Bibace, R., & Walsh, M. (1981). *Children's conceptions of health, illness and bodily functions.* San Francisco: Jossey-Bass.

Bieliauskas, L. (1982). *Stress and its relationship to health and illness.* Boulder, CO: Westview Press.

Billingham, K. (1982). *Developmental psychology for the health care professionals.* Boulder, CO: Westview Press.

Blanchard, E. (Ed.) (1982). *Behavioral medicine,* Special Issue of *Journal of Consulting and Clinical Psychology.*

Brill, N. Q. (1975). Introduction to psychiatric liaison. In R. O. Posinau (Ed.), *Consultation-liaison psychiatry.* New York: Grune and Stratton.

Budman, S. (Ed.). (1981). *Forms of brief psychotherapy.* New York: Guilford Press.

Budman, S., & Wertlieb, D. (1979). Psychologists in health care settings. *Professional Psychology, 10,* special issue.

Califano, J. A. (1979). *Healthy people: the Surgeon General's report on health promotion and disease prevention.* Washington, DC: U.S. Government Printing Office.

Carey, K. and Kogan, W. (1971). Exploration of factors influencing physician decisions to refer patients for mental health services. *Medical Care, 9,* 55–56.

Cassel, J. Psychosocial processes and stress: theoretical formulation. In R. Kane (Ed.). (1977). *The behavioral sciences and preventive medicine.* Washington, DC: Department of Health Education and Welfare.

Clairborn, W. L., & Stricker, G. (1979). Professional standards review organizations, peer review, and CHAMPUS. *Professional Psychology, 10,* (4), 631–639.

Cobb, S. (1976). Social support as a moderation of life stress. *Psychomatic Medicine, 38,* 300–314.

Coddington, D. (1972). The significance of life events as etiologic factors in the diseases of children. *Journal of Psychosomatic Research, 16,* 205–213.

Cohen, F. (1979). Personality stress and the development of phycial illness. In G. Stone, F. Cohen, & N. Adler, (Eds.), *Health psychology.* San Francisco: Jossey-Bass, 77–112.

Counte, M., & Christman, L. (1981). *Interpersonal behavior and health care.* Boulder, CO: Westview Press.

Cummings, N., & VandenBos, G. (1979). The general practice of psychology. *Professional Psychology, 10,* 430–440.

DeLeon, P. H., & Pallock, M. S. (1982). Public health and psychology. *American Psychologist, 37,* 934–935.

DiMatteo, R., & Friedman, H. (1982). *Social psychology of medicine.* Cambridge, MA: Oelgeschlager, Gunn and Hain.

Dörken, H., & Webb, J. T. (1979). The hospital practice of psychology: an interstate comparison. *Professional Psychology, 10,* (4), 619–630.

Drotar, D. (1975). Clinical psychology training in the pediatric hospital. *Journal of Clinical Child Psychology, 4,* 46–49 (a).

Eckenrode, J., & Gore, S. (1981). Stressful events and social supports: the significance of context. In B. Gottlieb (Ed.), *Social networks and social support.* Beverly Hills, CA: Sage.

Eisdorfer, C. (Ed). (1982). *Stress and health.* New York: Springer.

Eisenberg, L. (1977). The search for care. *Daedalus, 106,* 235–246.

Enelow, A. J. (1980). Consultation liaison psychiatry. In H. Kaplan, A. Freedman, & B.

Sadak *Comprehensive textbook of psychiatry* (3rd ed.). Baltimore, MD: Williams and Wilkins.

Engle, G. L. (1977). The need for a new medical model: a challenge for biomedicine. *Science, 196,* 129–136.

Feldman, A. (1978). The family practitioner as psychiatrist. *American Journal of Psychiatry, 137,* 535–544.

Gentry, W. D., Street, W. J., Masur, F. T., & Asken, M. J. (1981). Training in medical psychology: a survey of graduate and internship training programs. *Professional Psychology,* 12, 224–228.

Gliedman, J., & Roth, W. (1980). *The unexpected minority: Handicapped children in America.* New York: Harcourt Brace Jovanovich.

Green, C. J. (1982). Psychological assessment in medical settings. In T. Millon, C. Green, & R. Meagher (Eds.), *Handbook of clinical health psychology.* New York: Plenum Press.

Grzesiak, R. C. (1981). Rehabilitation psychology, medical psychology, health psychology and behavioral medicine. *Professional Psychology, 12,* 411–413.

Haggerty, R. J., Roghmann, K. J., & Pless, I. B. (1975). *Child health and the community.* New York: Wiley.

Hankin, J. (1979). Literature review on management of emotionally disturbed patients in primary care settings. In *Mental health service in general health care,* Vol. 1. Washington, DC: Institute of Medicine, National Academy of Sciences.

Harrington, R. (interview). (1978, Fall). Balm for the worried well. *Innovations,* pp. 3–10.

Hoffman, I. (1979). Psychological versus medical psychotherapy. *Professional Psychology, 10,* 517–579.

Hollen, L. H., Ehrlich, R. P., & White, S. L. (1981). Integrating mental health training. In A. Broskowski, E. Marks, & S. H. Budman (Eds.), *Linking health and mental health.* Beverly Hills: Sage.

Horowitz, M. J. (1982). Psychological processes induced by illness, injury and loss. In T. Millon, C. Green, & R. Meagher (Eds.), *Handbook of clinical health psychology.* New York: Plenum Press.

Hurst, M., Jenkins, D., & Rose, R. (1976). The relation of psychological stress to onset of medical illness. *Annual Review of Medicine, 27,* 301–312.

Institute of Medicine. (1979). *Mental health services in general health care.* (Vol. 1). Washington, DC: Institute of Medicine, National Academy of Sciences.

Iscoe, I. (1982). Toward a viable community health psychology: Caveats from the experiences of the community mental health movement. *American Psychologist, 37,* 961–965.

Jacobson, A. (1979). The role of the psychiatrist in primary care settings: Issues and problems. In *Mental health services in general health care.* (Vol. 1). Washington, DC: Institute of Medicine, National Academy of Sciences.

Jones, K., & Vischi, T. (1979). Impact of alcohol, drug abuse and mental health care utilization. *Medical Care, 17,* (supplement, December).

Kagan, J. (1965). The new marrage: Pediatrics and psychology. *The American Journal of Diseases of Children, 110* (3), 272–278.

Kagan, N. (1979). Counseling psychology, interpersonal skills and health care. In G. C. Stone, F. Cohen, & N. E. Adler (Eds.). *Health psychology.* San Francisco: Jossey-Bass.

Kaplan, H. (1980). Treatment of psychosomatic disorders. In H. Kaplan, A. Freedman, & B. Sudock (Eds.). *Comprehensive textbooks of psychiatry* (3rd ed.). Baltimore, MD: Williams and Wilkins.

Kenny, J. J., & Bauer, R. (1975). Training the pediatric psychologist: A look at an internship program. *Journal of Clinical Child Psychology, 4*, 50–52.

Kline, N. S. (1974). Antidepressant medications: A more effective use by general practitioners, family physicians, internists and others. *Journal of American Medical Association, 227*, 1158–1160.

Knapp, S., & Vandecreek, L. (1981). Behavioral medicine: Its malpractice risks for psychologists, *Professional Psychology, 12*, (6) 677–683.

Lebray, P. (1979). Geropsychology in long-term care settings. *Professional Psychology, 10*, 375–484.

Lipowski, Z. J. (1967). Review of consultation psychiatry and psychosomatic medicine. II clinical aspects. *Psychosomatic Medicine, 29*, 201–224.

Lipowski, Z. J. (1974). Consultation-liaison psychiatry: An overview. *American Journal of Psychiatry, 131*, 623–630.

Lipowski, Z. J. (1977). Psychiatric consultation: Concepts and controversies. *American Journal of Psychiatry, 234*, 523-528 (a).

Lipowski, Z. J. (1977). Psychosomatic medicine in the seventies: An overview. *American Journal of Psychiatry, 134*, 233–244 (b).

Liss-Levinson, W. (1982). Reality perspectives for psychological services in a hospice program. *American Psychology, 34*, 1266–1270.

Lynch, J. J. (1977). *The broken heart: The medical consequences of loneliness.* New York: Basic Books.

Manuso, J. (1981). Psychological services and health enhancement: A corporate model. In A. Broskowski, E. Marks, & S. Budman (Eds.), *Linking health and mental health.* Beverly Hills, CA: Sage.

Marks, E., & Broskowski, A. (1981). Community mental health and organized health care linkages. In A. Brokowski, E. Marks, and S. Budman (Eds.), *Linking health and mental health.* Beverly Hills, CA: Sage.

Martin, M. Psychiatry and medicine. (1980). In H. Kaplan, A. Freedman, & B. Suddock (Eds.)., *Comprehensive textbook of psychiatry,* (3rd ed.). Baltimore, MD: Williams & Wilkins.

Matarazzo, J. D. (1980). Behavioral health and behavioral medicine: Frontiers for a new health psychology. *American Psychologist, 35*, 807–817.

Matarazzo, J. D. (1982). Behavioral health's challenge to academic, scientific and professional psychology. *American Psychologist, 37*, 1–14.

Matarazzo, J. D., Carmody, T. P., & Gentry, W. D. (1981). Psychologists on the faculties of U.S. schools of medicine: Past, Present, and Future. *Clinical Psychology Review, 1*, 293–317.

Matarazzo, J. D., Lubin, B., & Natham, R. G. (1978). Psychologists' membership of the medical staffs of university teaching hospitals. *American Psychologist, 33*, 23–29.

Matthews, K. A., & Avis, N. E. (1982). Psychologists in schools of public health: Current status, future prospect, and implications for other health settings. *American Psychologist, 36*, 949–954.

McNamara, J. R. (1981). Some unresolved challenges facing psychology's entrance into the health care field. *Professional Psychology, 12* (3), 391–399.

Mechanic, D. (1979). *Future issues in health care: Social policy and the rationing of medical services.* New York: Free Press.

Meyer, E., & Mendelson, M. (1961). Psychiatric consultations with patients on medical and surgical wards: Patterns and processes. *Psychiatry, 24*, 197–200.

Michael, J. M. (1982). The second revolution in health: health promotion and its environmental base. *American Psychologist, 37* (8), 936–941.

Miklich, D. (1979). Health psychology practice with asthmatics. *Professional Psychology, 10*, 580–588.

Miller, H. L., Fowler, R. D., & Bridgers, W. F. (1982). The public health psychologist: An ounce of prevention is not enough. *American Psychologist, 37* (8), 945–948.

Millon, T. On the nature of clinical health psychology. In T. Millon, C. Green, R. Meagher (Eds.), (1982). *Handbook of clinical health psychology.* New York: Plenum Press.

Millon, T., Green, D., & Meagher, R. (1979). The MBHI: A new inventory for the psychodiagnostician in medical settings. *Professional Psychology, 10,* 529–539.

Millon, T., Green, C., & Meagher, R. (Eds.). (1982). *Handbook of clinical health psychology.* New York: Plenum.

Mumford, E., Schlesinger, H., & Glass, G. (1979). Problems of analyzing the cost offset of including a mental health component in primary care. In *Mental health services in general health care* (Vol. 1). Washington, DC: Institute of Medicine, National Academy of Sciences.

Mumford, E., Schlesinger, H., & Glass, G. (1981). Reducing medical costs through mental health treatment. In A. Boskowski, E. Marks, & S. Budman (Eds.)., *Linking health and mental health.* Beverly Hills, CA: Sage.

Nowicki, D. (1981). Problems and prospects in pediatric consultation/liaison. *Division of Child and Youth Services Newsletter, 4,* 5–7.

O'Keefe, A. M., & McCullough, S. J. (1979). Physician domination in the health care industry: The pursuit of antitrust redress. *Professional Psychology, 10,* 605–618.

Olbrish, M. (1977). Psychotherapeutic interventions in physical health. *American Psychologist, 32,* 761–777.

Olbrisch, M. (1977). Psychotherapeutic interventions in physical health. *American Psycholo-training programs. *Professional Psychology, 10,* 589–595.

Rabkin, J. G., & Struening, E. L. (1976). Life events, stress and illness. *Science, 194,* 1013–1020.

Rahe, R., & Arthur, R. (1978). Life change and illness studies: Past history and future directions. *Journal of Human Stress, 4,* 3–15.

Roberts, M. C., Maddox, J. E., Wurtele, S. K., & Wright, L. (1982). Pediatric psychology: Health care psychology for children. In T. Millon, C. Green, & R. Meagher (Eds.), *Handbook of clinical health psychology.* New York: Plenum Books.

Rosen, G. M., Geyman, J. P., & Layton, R. H. (Eds.). (1980). *Behavioral science in family practice.* New York: Appleton-Century-Crofts.

Sachs, R., Eigenbrode, C., & Kruper, D. (1979). Psychology and dentistry. *Professional Psychology, 10,* 521–528.

Schofield, W. (1979). Clinical psychologists as health professionals. In G. Stone, F. Cohen, & N. Adler (Eds.), *Health psychology: a handbook.* San Francisco: Jossey-Bass.

Schontz, F. C. (1982). Adaptations to chronic illness and disability. In T. Millon, C. Green, & R. Meagher (Eds.), *Handbook of clinical health psychology.* New York: Plenum Press.

Schwartz, G. E., & Weiss, S. M. (1978). Behavioral medicine revisited: an amended definition. *Journal of Behavioral Medicine, 1,* 249–251.

Shepherd, M. (1979). Plenary presentation, April 3, 1979. Mental health as an intergrant of primary care. In *Mental health services in general health care* (Vol. 1), Washington, DC: Institute of Medicine, National Academy of Sciences.

Singer, J. E., & Krantz, D. S. (1982). Perspectives on the interface between psychology and public health. *American Psychologist, 37* (8), 955–960.

Stachnik, T. J. (1980). Priorities for psychology in medical education and health care delivery. *American Psychologist, 35,* 8–15.

Stahler, G., & Tash, W. (Eds). (1982). *Innovative approaches to mental health education.* New York: Academic Press.

Stone, G. (1979). A specialized doctoral program in health psychology: Considerations in its evolution. *Professional Psychology, 10,* 596–604. (a)

Stone, G. (1979). Psychology and the health system. In G. Stone, F. Cohen, & N. Adler

(Eds.), *Health psychology*. San Francisco, CA: Jossey-Bass. (b)

Stone, G. (1983) Proceedings of the National Working Conference on Education and Training in Health Psychology. *Health Psychology, 2*, Supplement, pp. 1-153.

Stone, G. C., Cohen, F., & Adler, N. (Eds.). (1979). *Health psychology: a handbook*. San Francisco: Jossey-Bass.

Strain, J. J. (1982). Collaborative efforts in liaison psychology. In T. Millon, C. Green, & R. Meagher (Eds.), *Handbook of clinical psychology.*. New York: Plenum Press.

Swencionis, C. (1982). Journals relevant to health psychology. *Health Psychology, 1* (3), 307-313.

Tanabe, G. (1982). The potential for public health psychology. *American Psychologist, 37* (8), 942-944.

Tefft, B., & Simeonson, R. (1979). Psychology and the creation of health care settings. *Professional Psychology, 10*, 558-570.

U.S. Department of Health and Human Services. (1981). *Better health for our children: a national strategy, the report of the Select Panel for the Promotion of Child Health*. DHHS Publication No. 79-55071.

VandenBos, G., Stapp, J., & Kilburg, R.. (1981). Health service providers in psychology. *American Psychologist, 36*, 1395-1418.

Watson, J. B. (1912). Content of a course for psychology for medical students. *Journal of the American Medical Association, 58*, 916-918.

Weiner, H. (1982). Psychobiological factors in bodily disease. In T. Millon, C. Green, & R. Meagher (Eds.), *Handbook of Clinical Health Psychology*. New York: Plenum.

Weiss, S. (1982). Health psychology: the time is now. *Health Psychology, 1*, (1), 81-91.

Wertlieb, D. (1979). A preventive health paradigm for health care psychologists. *Professional Psychology, 10*, 548-557.

Wertlieb, D. (1981). Mental health providers in primary care settings. In A. Broskowski, E. Marks, & S. Budman (Eds.), *Linking health and mental health*. Beverly Hills, CA: Sage.

Wertlieb, D. (1982). *Stress and illness, coping and health: developmental perspectives*. Unpublished manuscript.

Wertlieb, D. (1984). Health psychology. In R. Corsini (Ed.), *Wiley encyclopedia of psychology*. New York: Wiley.

Wertlieb, D., & Budman, S. (1979). Dimensions of role conflict for the health care psychologists. *Professional Psychology, 10*, 640-644.

Wertlieb, D., & Budman, S. (1981). The mental health linkage: mandates and challenges for program evaluation research. In W. Tash & G. Stahler, (Eds.), *Innovative approaches to mental health evaluations*. New York: Academic Press.

Wertlieb, D., Budman, S., Demby, A., & Randall, M. (1982). The stress of marital separation: intervention in a health maintenance organization. *Psychosomatic Medicine, 44*, 437-448.

Wertlieb, D., Budman, S., Demby, A., & Randall, M. (1984). Marital separation and health: stress and intervention. *Journal of Human Stress, 10*, 18-26.

West, N. D. (1979). *Psychiatry in primary care medicine*. Chicago: Year Book Medical Publisher.

Wexler, M. (1976). The behavioral sciences in medical education. *American Psychologist, 31*, 275-283.

Winer, G. (1982). A review and analysis of children's fearful behavior in dental settings. *Child Development, 53*, 1111-1133.

Wright, L. (1979). Health care psychology: prospects for the well being of children. *American Psychologist, 34*, 1001-1006.

Yankelovich, Skelly, & White, Inc. (1979). *Family Wealth in an Era of Stress*. Minneapolis: General Mills, Inc.

Zuckerman, B., Carper, J., & Alpert, J. (1978). Mental health training for pediatricians. *Journal of Clinical Child Psychology, 7*, 43-46.

PART IV

LEGAL, ETHICAL, & LIABILITY
ISSUES IN THE PRACTICE
OF PROFESSIONAL PSYCHOLOGY

Chapter 11

Licensing

Conrad Lecomte
University of Montreal

Why devote an entire chapter of a book to the subject of licensing? Firstly, because in one way or another, the licensing requirements, such as those in effect in the United States and Canada, run the strong risk of having a considerable influence on the type of psychology being practiced today. In fact, the majority of American states and Canadian provinces are regulated by certain laws which deal either with the psychologist's title or his/her right to practice.

However, the situation becomes even more complex when one realizes that these laws vary from one state to the next. Thus, a licensed psychologist practicing in one state may not be able to do the very same work in another. Moreover, a psychologist trained in experimental psychology may be allowed to offer his/her professional services in yet another state without having had any adequate training. Is there any way out of this maze?

An awareness of the various aspects of licensing may prove to be necessary, not only for the graduate student but for the professional as well. In fact, the many licensing laws can have serious repercussions on one's professional development and identity.

In this chapter, I will try to answer the following questions: Which organizations and statutes affect what psychologists can do and when and where they can do it? What are the specific requirements in terms of degrees, programs, experiences, and supervision for licensing a psychologist? Where can valid information be obtained? It is difficult, if not impossible, to gather all the information available about the laws which affect the psychologist today; this is due to the constant revisions currently in progress. This chapter merely attempts to present an overall view of the latest information that deals with licensing laws in the United States and Canada. Annual revisions may be obtained from the APA Office of Professional Affairs (see address in Appendix C).

WHAT THE TERMS MEAN

The terminology found in the field of licensing can be quite complex and confusing. Literature on the subject overflows with many terms such as "licensure," "certification," "accreditation," "registration," "listing," and "credentialing." How can one differentiate between the various terms?

Firstly, almost all these terms can be grouped under the heading of "credentialing." In fact, by its own definition, "credentialing" generally consists in awarding a particular title to someone, or in recognizing his/her competency. In the universal process known as "credentialing," "licensing" is undoubtedly the term whose definition is the most specific and restrictive. As a matter of fact, the U.S. Department of Health, Education, and Welfare (1977, p. 4) defines "licensing" "as a process for which an agency of government grants permission to an individual to engage in a given occupation upon finding that the applicant has attained the minimal degree of competency required to ensure that the public health, safety, and welfare will be reasonably well protected." These licensing laws are often referred to as "Practice Acts," precisely because of their practical implications. As a result, it becomes illegal for a nonlicensed person to practice any of the activities outlined in the law.

Furthermore, certification is a nonstatutory process in which a governmental or nongovernmental agency allows a person with certain predetermined qualifications to practice a specific occupation or make use of a particular title. However, certification laws do nothing more than protect the title itself. They simply acknowledge the fact that certain individuals have fulfilled certain requirements and are thus allowed to practice a given occupation. Certification, in direct contrast to licensing, does not prevent noncertified individuals from practicing their occupation. It is in this perspective that the APA defines certification.

Beyond these two very fundamental terms which deal with the practice of psychology, one also finds expressions such as "accreditation," "registration," and "listing." The term accreditation can essentially be applied when one speaks of an "accredited program." This describes a program or training course which meets certain requirements and qualifications as determined by supporting documents or a visit from a team of reviewers from a governmental or nongovernmental agency. Finally, because of certain specific qualifications, a number of professionals in the field of psychology are publicly identified in a "listing" or "register," such as the "National Register of Health Service Providers in Psychology" (Council, 1978). This type of public identification is not based on specific requirements, such as an exam, but rather on certain qualifications, for example, recognized internship supervision, etc.

By simply enumerating these various terms, one soon becomes aware of the complexity involved in the field of credentialing. Due to the improper use of these terms, literature on the subject is misrepresentative and filled with many confusing and ambiguous examples.

WHY LICENSING IN PSYCHOLOGY?

Historically speaking, it seems that a monopoly existed for many years: professions were regulated according to the viewpoints imposed by one group upon other groups; this was usually defined in terms of class structure (Ehrenreich

& English, 1973; Gross, 1978). It was only toward the end of the 19th century that a relationship between competency and "licensing" came into being (Tabachnik, 1976).

Today, licensing laws seem to assure the public that a licensed psychologist is indeed competent (Hess, 1977). Because licensing is the most restrictive form of regulation, since it excludes certain individuals from practicing their profession, many feel that licensing protects the public better than any other form of regulation (Gross, 1978). In addition, licensing often guarantees certain economic advantages and social prestige. This comes at a time when one may be eligible not only for third party payments, but possibly for National Health Insurance programs as well.

If one keeps this perspective in mind, then licensure appears to protect the public from incompetent, phoney, and unscrupulous practitioners. Yet this is just one aspect of the situation. In fact, it stands to reason that the possibility of becoming licensed automatically provides the psychologist with public recognition. With this recognition, the psychologist's profession is then protected against individuals who do not possess the academic, professional, or personal qualifications which are considered important. Let us not hide the fact that a psychologist is thus assured of certain economic advantages as well, since a portion of the market is reserved exclusively for him/her. Because a profession regulated by licensing laws has many socio-economical advantages, one can understand the amount of controversy involved, especially from professionals who, for one reason or another, are not allowed to practice their profession.

THROUGH THE PSYCHOLOGY LICENSING MAZE

One might think that it is relatively simple to obtain information about the possibility of becoming licensed. Nothing could be farther from the truth. It is actually easier to understand the laws governing income tax than those pertaining to licensing. What follows is an attempt to clearly examine the licensing laws in effect in most American states and Canadian provinces. I will consider the requirements which pertain to academic, training, program accreditation, and specific experience and supervision.

One must realize from the outset that each American state and Canadian province controls and administers licensing in its own independent way. As a result, since 1978, 50 states, the District of Columbia, and seven Canadian provinces have specific regulations pertaining to the practice of psychology. Each state and province has its own little licensing story to tell.

The mechanisms of licensing are fundamentally assured by a state licensing board or, in the case of Canada, by a provincial licensing board. The members of this board are appointed by the state governor or by the provincial premier. In fact, members are ususally nominated by professional associations and approved by the legislator. Although they claim to be accessible to the public, these boards are actually entrapped by the very profession they are supposed to regulate. The work these examiners do seems to be complex and demanding, especially when one takes into account the fact that they usually deal with the more tedious aspects of the profession, i.e. malpractice, misrepresentation, etc. Generally speaking, the licensing boards should become financially self-sufficient by collecting the money that applicants must pay in order to pass the exams and acquire a license.

On a national level, there are two associations which are closely involved with the development and establishment of regulations pertaining to licensing. They are the APA Committee on State Legislation and the American Association of State Psychology Boards (AASPB).

Since 1950, the APA Committee on State Legislation has been instrumental in determining which criteria regulate the practice of psychology. To a large extent, this committee was the originator of most licensing laws. Moreover, the AASPB was created in order to facilitate the coordination and uniformity of most laws from one state to another. Since then, the AASPB has extended its power and now administers a national Exam for the Professional Practice of Psychology (EPPP). The AASPB also takes care of any legal problems which may arise between professional associations and state psychology examining boards (Carlson, 1978). Since 1979, all states except Arizona have been using or intend to use the EPPP.

It is important for any individual who practices psychology to keep abreast of the continuing developments pertaining to the regulation and professional practice of psychology. The possible availability of National Health Insurance has created a tense atmosphere among psychiatrists, psychologists, and counselors. The APA Committee on State Legislation and the AASPB, while hoping to obtain restrictive licensing laws, are working very hard at assuring psychologists of an exclusive field in which to practice. On one hand, psychiatrists are attempting to broaden their field by reducing the work of psychologists. On the other hand, psychologists, with the help of their two main organisms, are trying to revise the model licensing bill. They hope to further limit the bill to programs of a more psychological nature. This bill would protect the quality of services available to the public, and insure that standards not vary from one state to another. This revision could have serious implications for a large number of counselors, since their perspective may not be psychological enough in nature. There still exists quite a bit of controversy concerning these recommendations (Wellner, 1978). Considerable ambiguity continues to surround what can be referred to as training in psychology or as training which is "primarily psychological in nature."

A revision of this kind is important to note, since it gives new meaning to training in psychology; many practitioners have already expressed a great deal of concern about the matter. It goes without saying that a change in the licensing laws of any given state could have quite an effect on the professional lives of thousands of people.

An overview of current status of state psychology licensing procedures

Providing complete, up to date information on licensing laws is almost an impossible task. In fact, attempts by professional associations to revise the licensing model, combined with legal court proceedings and sunset legislation, result in annual adjustments of the procedures pertaining to licensing in psychology. It is advisable to be aware of all revisions currently in progress; information is available at the APA Office of Professional Affairs. Furthermore, anyone wishing to increase his/her awareness of the procedures pertaining to licensing in psychology can refer to the works of Lahman (1978), the four volumes by Hogan (1974), Fretz and Mills (1980), and the surveys of Bernstein, Lisowski, and Lecomte (1978) and Wayne (1982). For more information, see "Additional References on Current Policies and Procedures" Appendix B.

In order to further clarify the facts about licensing procedures, I have chosen to focus in on certain information which I consider to be the most important for all licensing candidates. I will point out which requirements are usually demanded by the majority of states and provinces (see Appendix B). Let us remember that, above and beyond the specific requirements of each state, most of the states demand that licensing candidates be of good character, be at least 21 years of age, be or intend to be an American or Canadian citizen, and not be engaged in unethical practice.

As of 1978, all 50 states, the District of Columbia, and seven Canadian provinces have enacted laws regulating the practice of psychology. However, it is important to note that, for the past few years, many legislative developments have had a serious effect on professional licensing laws. It seems that the future of licensing statutes appears to be unstable and uncertain.

In 1979, the first important development was the impact of sunset legislation on licensing procedures as a whole. In fact, the sunset provisions, now in effect in 39 states, refer to the legislative revision of professional regulating programs. This revision can go so far as to stipulate that a profession must prove the benefits of licensing laws in a positive and effective manner. According to these requirements, licensing procedures can be temporarily or permanently abolished. It is because of this that, in 1979, the states of Florida, South Dakota, and Alaska lost the right to license psychologists.

There circumstances are very important, since many states will soon come up against the sunset revisions. The effects of these revisions can be positive ones, if the practitioners are prepared to stand up to consumers and legislators alike and demonstrate the beneficial effects of licensing procedures.

What are the specific degree and accreditation requirements for licensure as a psychologist?

This question may appear to have a simple answer. The majority of us undoubtedly think that the requirement for licensure is a doctorate in psychology in an accredited program. Yet this answer would not suit the academic requirements of many states.

As a general rule, one must keep in mind that the licensing board of each state takes many liberties when interpreting and carrying out procedures regarding accreditation, as well as acceptance of academic degrees. Close to 32 states let it be known, explicit or implicitly, that their accreditation and degree requirements depend upon the acceptance of the State Board of Psychological Examiners (Bernstein, Lisowski, & Lecomte (1978).

However, it is obvious that the licensing laws in effect in most states, 38 to be exact, clearly require a doctorate. Only 13 states have certification acts, which really do nothing more than protect the title itself; these are Arizona, Illinois, Indiana, Kansas, Louisiana, Maryland, Mississippi, Nebraska, New Hampshire, New Mexico, New York, Rhode Island, and Wyoming. Moreover, it must be pointed out that 18 states and three Canadian provinces have special conditions allowing them to recognize master's level psychologists. Iowa, Minnesota, Missouri, Pennsylvania, and West Virginia permit individuals with a master's degree to practice a nonsupervised and independent form of psychology. Of these five states, only Iowa groups these psychologists under the heading of "practice of associate psychology." Furthermore, 13 states offer a limited licensing of master's level persons (Arkansas, California, Kentucky, Maine, New Hampshire, North Carolina, Ohio, Oregon, Tennessee, Texas, Vermont, Virginia, Wisconsin). In all of these states, the individual is designated by a title other than psychologist, for example, psychological associate, psychological examiner, or associate psychologist; a specialty, such as educational psychologist or school psychologist, can also be designated. The Canadian provinces of Alberta, British Columbia, and Quebec recognize master's level individuals as psychologists.

In essence, it seems that, in a large number of states, the individual requires a doctorate in order to be licensed, although a minority of important states do recognize the master's degree in some way or another. Yet the matter does not end here; does this mean that one must obtain a degree in psychology before being admitted to licensing? A great deal of controversy surrounds this question. In general, doctorates designated by Ph.D., Ed.D., and Psy.D. are accepted, provided that certain other requirements are fulfilled as well. In fact, only five states (Illinois, Hawaii, Kentucky, Nebraska, and West Virginia) specifically ask for a doctorate in psychology. Other states, such as Louisiana and New Mexico, require a major in psychology; Mississippi insists that the individual specializes in some area of psychology. Thus, it seems that a certain degree of flexibility is demonstrated during the approval of a field of study. In a large number of states, a degree which is primarily in psychology suffices. Recently, the APA recommended that a degree should be recognized irrespective of which school or faculty awarded it—as long as the program leading to the degree was clearly identified and recognized as a program in psychology. It is in this manner that the state of Illinois grants licenses to graduates in its programs in the Department of Guidance and Educational Psychology. Here again, the opinion of the Board of Examiners is often the determining factor.

Regarding program accreditation, most states claim that the program must be accredited by an agency, whether it be national, regional, or other. Only two states, Colorado and Rhode Island, specifically recognize the APA as an accrediting agent. As a whole, one must also remember the tremendous latitude granted to the State Board of Examiners when they deal with accreditation and program requirements.

What are the experience and supervision requirements for licensing as a psychologist?

The states vary considerably in their definition of what constitutes professional experience. For example, most insist that this experience take place after obtaining the doctoral degree and completing the period of internship. Others insist that at least part of this experience be supervised by a state licensed psychologist, or the equivalent.

The states have diverse requirements regarding supervised or nonsupervised experience. In order to simplify the matter, let us examine the most important categories of this procedure. Firstly, it is worth mentioning the states and provinces requiring no experience at all; these are Alabama, Arizona, Nebraska, North Dakota, Wyoming, Alberta, Quebec, and Saskatchewan. Most states (actually 32 states and the province of Ontario) require at least 1 year of experience after the doctorate is obtained and the period of internship is completed. Also, 26 states and 2 provinces (Ontario and British Columbia) demand at least 1 year of experience supervised by a state licensed psychologist, or the equivalent. The majority of other states and provinces require 1 or more years of pre- or post-doctoral, nonsupervised experience. Let us emphasize that the facts which pertain to these requirements are all relative, considering the tremendous latitude granted to each Board of Examiners. As a result, the only subject matter dealing with state licensing laws does not give us a clear enough understanding of what the state requirements are. For example, published laws indicate that only seven states demand supervision by a licensed psychologist, whereas in fact, this requirement is in effect in 26 states. More than 39 states explicitly or implicitly give their Board of Examiners the right to determine supervision requirements.

Let us stress that those states which recognize the master's degree demand an even greater amount of practical experience before licensing. For example, Iowa requires 5 years of experience, 2 of which must be supervised; Minnesota requires 2 years of post-master's experience; Missouri, 3 years of experience; Pennsylvania, 4 years of post-master's experience, 2 of which must be supervised. As far as those states which accept limited licensing, in accordance with titles such as "psychological associate" or "examiner," the number of years required varies between 1 and 4. Finally, the provinces of Ontario, Alberta, and British Columbia recognize the master's without any supervised or nonsupervised experience, with the exception of British Columbia, which requires 1 year of supervised experience.

Reciprocity, examinations, and renewal

In order to become licensed, it is not enough for one to fulfill the requirements pertaining to academic training and professional experience. In all states except Michigan, one must also pass a written and/or oral exam. The only exceptions to this rule are either for diplomates from the American Board of Professional Psychology, or for those who are licensed in another state. In Canada, these exams are only compulsory in Manitoba, New Brunswick, and Ontario.

Problems related to reciprocity further add to the complexity of this situation. Despite the efforts of the AASPB to encourage the use of uniform standards from one state to the other, certain states insist on setting their own rules. This means that being licensed in one state does not necessarily guarantee you the possibility of licensing in another. A large number of states accept reciprocity agreements, but often do so by stipulating a different passing score on the EPPP. Since this situation changes from year to year, it is advisable to verify which of the states recognizes reciprocity of licensing.

Finally, licensing renewal periods vary from 1 to 4 years. Most states advocate an annual renewal system. However, for the last few years, many states insist that a psychologist participates in continuing education courses before being able to renew his/her license. At least 15 states set down the number of hours required in workshops, conventions, professional meetings, etc., in order to be eligible for renewal. Certain states even go so far as to recommend that at least one third of the courses be of an institutional or seminar-type nature.

Who says you're competent?

After fulfilling the various licensing requirements over a period of years, in a multitude of academic and professional ways, are you then ready to be a competent and efficient psychologist? Are you now in a better position to guarantee the protection of the public? Many authors (Bernstein & Lecomte, 1981; Hogan, 1979) have clearly proven that there is little evidence linking licensing and quality of service. In fact, Bernstein and Lecomte (1981) question the postulate which claims that licensure permits better protection of the public. They not only show that the facts reject this postulate; they also suggest that the effects of client deterioration and malpractice suits actually point to the contrary (Gross, 1978; Hogan, 1979). In socio-economic terms, it would appear that licensing protects the psychologist better than the public itself.

The criteria used to define licensing requirements are not based on any facts which support the predictive validity of these measures as related to client outcomes (Shimberg, 1981). In fact, some research (Bergin & Lambert, 1978; Strupp & Hadley, 1979) indicates that the intervention of those other than psychologists can be just as effective in the treatment of clients.

One must also bear in mind that obtaining a license does not necessarily insure competence for life; far from it. There is no guarantee that psychologists will maintain or develop their competence simply because they have participated in certain continuing education courses. In fact, current license renewal procedures do not allow for a formal and valid verification of a psychologist's continuing competence.

As Koocher (1979) points out, the present methods of credentials in psychology are clearly not a very reliable measurement of professional competence. Since, at this time, we have no valid definition of competence in psychology, it is quite difficult to control incompetence.

Furthermore, the state sovereignty emphasis over uniformity is such that the right to practice psychology often differs from one state to the other. One conclusion, when looking at the wide range of licensing criteria in different states and provinces, is that there is no universally accepted definition of what makes a psychologist competent.

In defense of licensure requirements, it may be submitted that there exist very few ways of testing competence, apart from examining actual performance in the field. Although licensure requirements do at least provide some assurance of basic knowledge in a given field of practice, the benefits of these methods can be questioned, since they offer no guarantee with respect to performance.

In summary, present licensing procedures do not seem to offer a useful structure for any kind of effective solution to the problem of providing quality service to the public. In truth, the facts even seem to indicate that licensing better serves the interests of the profession than those of the public. At the present time, it almost seems that licensing protects the psychologist from being accountable for his/her actions. For example, very few licenses were revoked during the last few years (Clairborn, 1982). The methods used to detect incompetence are not clearly defined or implemented very often.

We can therefore conclude that being licensed does not necessarily provide any assurance of one's ability to serve the public interest. Under such circumstances, the value of licensing lies in insuring competence by the self-awareness and conscience of the individual. In fact, a review of all the mechanisms currently, in effect, namely, standards for providers, ethical codes, professional standards, review committees, third party payer quality insurance, state licensing and certification boards, national register, and diplomate status, allow us to conclude that none offers a contextual definition of competence and incompetence in terms of treatment outcomes, relative efficiency of treatments, efficacy of treatments, or treatment plan. These diverse procedures only offer arbitrary standards which are often not indicative of actual performance.

Toward a more responsive system of professional licensure
Present licensing procedures do not seem to insure the psychologist's competence or the protection of the public. In fact, according to Hogan (1979) and Gross (1978), licensing laws are not meant to improve the quality of services or easily determine incompetence. Bearing this information in mind, certain authors (such as Hogan, 1979) recommend that all licensing and related forms of

regulation simply be abolished. Others, such as Illich (1976) go so far as to advocate deprofessionalization. For Matarazzo (1977), experiences pertaining to
licensure are often incestuous acts, performed by members of the same profession who are simply out to protect their own interests.

Nevertheless, it must be stated that, despite these negative opinions, the
licensing process has never really been put to the test in empirical terms before.
Rather than abolish all forms of regulation, the nature of the regulatory process
should be questioned instead, as suggested by Bernstein and Lecomte (1981).

The basic challenge to the entire licensing process relates to its capacity to
define standards of competence which are both acceptable and operational. The
issue is a complex one, since it is difficult to find a method which effectively
deals with unwieldy constructs. It seems, however, that, instead of using ambi-
tious criteria with no valid predictability, it would be more promising to attempt
to base the licensing process on a solid empirical foundation.

The first desirable objective is to try to have licensing procedures clearly
demonstrate a solid correlation with client outcomes. How can this be guaranteed? It is difficult to answer this question. It may be appropriate to attempt to
determine what are the fundamental qualities and skills that a good therapist
must possess, and what is their relation to client outcomes. In the final analysis,
what use is there in fulfilling all sorts of requirements pertaining to degrees,
experience, and supervision, if none of these variables has any significant relation
to client outcomes? It is obvious that we are far from knowing the multitude of
variables which define a successful therapist. However, if we wish to end up with
valid predictability with respect to licensing criteria, we must attempt to isolate
these variables. Thus, in order to encourage positive client outcomes, we must
define the kind of competence that a particular specialist must have.

The increasing tendency towards the use of national standards from the National Commission on Education and Credentialing (Wellner, 1978), as well as
the attempts by the APA to formulate specialization standards, may result in
methods which will better define minimum standards of competence; this will
in turn result in satisfactory client outcomes.

Subsequently, it will be necessary to attack the complex task of measuring
this competence in a valid and reliable way. There are many possible directions.
It seems that it is necessary to provide numerous assessment procedures and
sources from the very beginning, in order to truly reflect the multidimensional
nature of the problem. The detailed evaluation of performance, rather than the
evaluation of information (Bray, 1976), would appear to be a promising direction to take.

Certain experiences currently in progress can already provide us with important information regarding the problems of measuring minimal standards of competence. The experience of peer review systems, such as that of Champus, developed by the APA for the Department of Defense, is a noteworthy attempt to
identify incompetent professional conduct. It may be quite appropriate to think

about the problems which Champus encountered in its attempt to operationalize and measure competence.

Considering the numerous requirements related to licensure, due in particular to sunset legislation, it appears crucial for the profession to clearly demonstrate its ability to be accountable for its competence and to protect the public. With this perspective in mind, it is essential for the profession to work together in order to provide itself with licensing procedures which can have a significant correlation with client outcomes.

To achieve this goal, perhaps it would be advisable to gradually include in licensing criteria only those factors which can actually be used to predict client outcomes. Along these same lines, license renewals might take place according to professional disclosure (Gross, 1978) which would indicate the kind of approach used, the type of problems dealt with, and the clients' improvement rates, as well as information pertaining to professional background. This kind of professional disclosure, added to a clients' self-reported satisfaction over a given period of time, could provide meaningful information about practitioners requesting license renewal.

One of the most interesting methods which can help the psychologist to identify, within his/her own repetoire, the knowledge and skills which are related to positive client outcomes, is the use of systematic programs of self-assessment and self-supervision. Certain programs (Bernstein & Lecomte, 1979; Sulzer-Azaroff, Pottinger, Sechrest, & Kummer, 1981) indicate lists of skills and procedures which may be used to self-assess one's strengths and weaknesses. This method of self-assessment can gradually lead to a process of self-renewal. Lecomte and Bernstein (1978) have suggested that self-supervision, in which the psychologist initiates and implements a set of procedures for reaching self-determined goals, can facilitate the maintenance of professional competence. The integration of self-assessment and self-supervision procedures, within a context of peer evaluation and client self-report, could provide greater professional credibility (Clairborn, Stricker, & Bent, 1982) and promote the development of professional competence.

CONCLUSION

This chapter has attempted to present a general overview of licensing practices in the United States and Canada. An analysis of the various licensing procedures has demonstrated the diversity and multiplicity of requirements from one state to another. In view of the several, apparently unfounded assumptions on which many of the state and provinical regulations appear to be based, it has been advocated that the psychology profession re-examine the value of its licensing procedures so that positive client outcomes become the central criterion for licensing psychologists. Although we now lack the data for more competence-based assessments, appropriate efforts to obtain such data should be made. Unless psychologists collaborate in answering the crucial questions pertaining to competence and the protection of the public, which have been raised by sunset legislation, National Health Insurance, and consumer, the future of credentialing in psychology, and of the profession as a whole, is in jeopardy.

REFERENCES

Bergin, A. E., & Lambert, M. J. (1978). The evaluation of therapeutic outcomes. In S. L. Garfield & A. E. Bergin (Eds.), *Handbook of psychotherapy and behavior change: On empirical analysis.* New York: Wiley.

Bernstein, B., Lisowski, J., & Lecomte, C. (1978, September). *Survey of licensing/certification procedures in the U.S. and Canada.* Paper presented at the meeting of the American Psychological Association, Toronto.

Bernstein, B., & Lecomte, C. (1979). A self-critique competency technique for practicum. *Counselor Education and Supervision, 19*(1), 69–76.

Bernstein, B., & Lecomte, C. (1981). Licensure in psychology: Alternate directions. *Professional Psychology, 12,* 200–208.

Bray, D. W. (1976). The assessment center method. In R. L. Craig (Ed.), *Training and development handbook.* New York: McGraw-Hill.

Carlson, H. S. (1978). The AASPB story. *American Psychologist, 33,* 486–495.

Clairborn, W. L. (1982). The problem of professional incompetence. *Professional Psychology, 13,* 153–158.

Clairborn, W. L., Stricker, G., & Bent, R. J. (1982). Peer review and quality assurance. *Professional Psychology,* 13, 1–166.

Council for the National Register of Health Service Providers in Psychology. (1978). *National register of health service providers in psychology.* Washington, DC: Author.

Ehrenreich, B., & English, D. (1973). *Witches, midwives, and nurses: A history of woman healers.* Old Westbury, NY: Feminist Press.

Fretz, B. R., & Mills, D. H. (1980). *Licensing and certification of psychologists and counselors.* San Francisco: Jossey-Bass.

Gross, S. J. (1978). Professional disclosure: An alternative to licensing. *Personnel and Guidance Journal, 55,* 586–588.

Gross, S. J. (1978). The myth of professional licensing. *American Psychologist, 33,* 1009–1016.

Hess, H. F. (1977). Entry requirements for professional practice in psychology. *American Psychologist, 32*(5), 365–368.

Hogan, D. B. (1979). *The regulation of psychotherapists* (4 vols.). Cambridge, MA: Ballinger.

Illich, I. (1976). *Medical nemesis.* New York: Random House.

Koocher, G. (1979). Credentialing in psychology: Close encounters with competence? *American Psychologist, 34,* 696–702.

Lahman, F. G. (1978). *Licensure requirements for psychologist: U.S.A. and Canada.* Evansville, ID: University of Evansville Press.

Lecomte, C., & Bernstein, B. (1978, March). *Development of self-supervision skills.* Paper presented at the meeting of American Personnel and Guidance Association, Washington, D.C.

Matarazzo, J. D. (1977). Higher education, professional accreditation, and licensure. *American Psychologist, 32,* 856–859.

Shimberg, B. (1981). Testing for licensure and certification. *American Psychologist, 36,* 1138–1146.

Strupp, H. H., & Hadley, S. W. (1979). Specific vs nonspecific factors in psychotherapy: A controlled study of outcome. *Archives of General Psychiatry, 36,* 1125–1136.

APPENDIX A. Statutory Requirements for Licensing

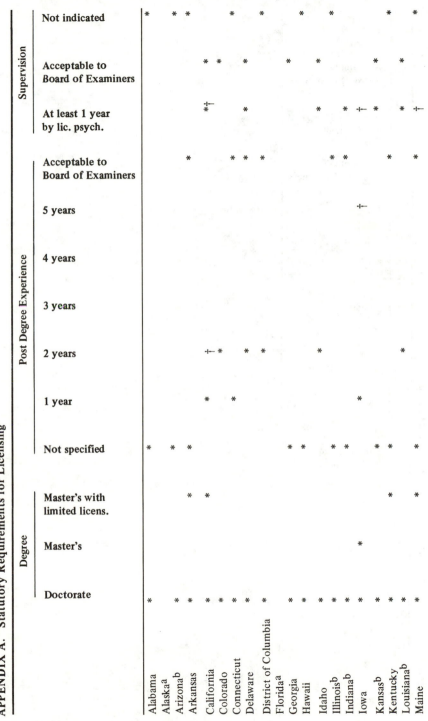

APPENDIX A. Statutory Requirements for Licensing (continued)

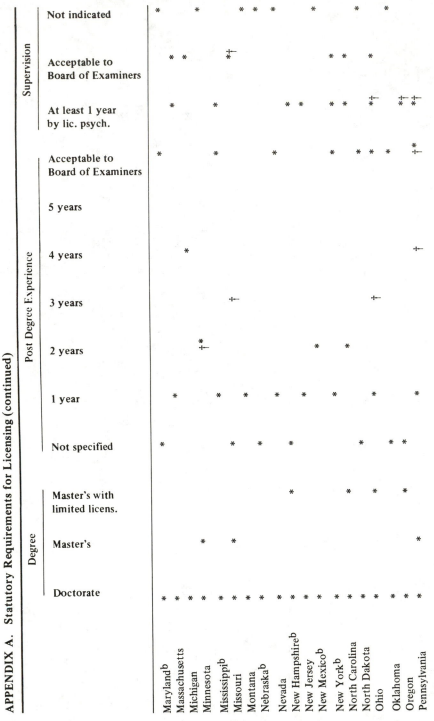

	Degree			Post Degree Experience							Supervision		
	Doctorate	Master's	Master's with limited licens.	Not specified	1 year	2 years	3 years	4 years	5 years	Acceptable to Board of Examiners	At least 1 year by lic. psych.	Acceptable to Board of Examiners	Not indicated
Maryland[b]	*			*									*
Massachusetts	*				*							*	
Michigan		*						*				*	*
Minnesota	*					*†				*	*		
Mississippi[b]	*	*		*	*		†					*†	
Missouri	*			*									*
Montana	*			*	*								*
Nebraska[b]	*			*									*
Nevada	*		*	*	*	*				*	*		
New Hampshire[b]	*		*		*						*		
New Jersey	*			*	*								*
New Mexico[b]	*		*			*					*	*	
New York[b]	*		*	*	*					*		*	
North Carolina	*									*		*	
North Dakota	*		*	*			†			*	*†		*
Ohio	*				*		†			*	*†	*	
Oklahoma	*			*							*†		*
Oregon	*	*	*							*†*	*†		
Pennsylvania	*				*			†		*†	*†	*†	

254

Rhode Island b

South Carolina

South Dakota a

Tennessee

Texas

Utah

Vermont

Virginia

Washington

West Virginia

Wisconsin

Wyoming b

Alberta b

British Columbia b

Manitoba b

New Brunswick b

New Foundland

Nova Scotia

Ontario b

PEI

Quebec b

Saskatchewan b

aLicensing law repealed.

bOnly certification acts are effective

†Specific requirements for master's

Sulzer-Azaroff, B., Pottinger, P., Sechrest, L., & Kummer, T. (1981). *Task force on self-assessment.* Unpublished manuscript.

Tabachnik, L. (1976). Licensing in the legal and medical professions; 1820–1860: A historical case study. In J. Gustle & G. Jacobs (Eds.), *Professions for the people.* Cambridge, MA: Schenkman.

U.S. Department of Health, Education and Welfare, Public Health Services. (1977). *Credentialing health manpower* (DHEW Publication No. 05 77-50057). Washington, DC: Author.

Wayne, G. (1982). An examination of selected statutory licensing requirements for psychologists in the United States. *Personnel and Guidance Journal, 60,* 420-425.

Wellner, A. M. (Ed.). (1978). Education and credentialing in psychology: *Proposal for a national commission on education and credentialing in psychology.* Washington, DC: APA.

ADDITIONAL REFERENCES ON CURRENT POLICIES AND PROCEDURES

American Association for Marriage and Family Therapy. (1979). *Marital and family therapy: State licensing and certification model legislation.* Upland, CA: American Association for Marriage and Family Therapy. (a)

American Association for Marriage and Family Therapy. (1979). *Membership standards brochure.* Upland, CA: American Association for Marriage and Family Therapy. (b)

American Board of Professional Psychology. (1978). Policies and procedures for the *creation of diplomates in professional psychology.* Washington, DC: Author.

American Council on Education. (1979). *Accredited institutions of postsecondary education.* Washington, DC: Author.

American Psychological Association. (1976). *Sourcebook I, education and credentialing in psychology.* Washington, DC: Author.

American Psychological Association. (1977). *Sourcebook II, education and credentialing in psychology.* Washington, DC: Author.

Hollis, J. W., and Wantz, R. A. (1977). *Counselor education directory, 1977: Personnel and programs.* (3rd ed.). Muncie, ID: Accelerated Development.

APPENDIX B: WHERE TO LOOK FOR INFORMATION

Licensing boards addresses for each state may be obtained from the Professional Affairs Office of the American Psychological Association.

American Association of Marriage and Family Therapists
Upland, CA 91786

American Association of Sex Educators, Counselors, and Therapists
5010 Wisconsin Ave., N.W., Suite 304
Washington, DC 20016

American Board of Professional Psychology
2025 I St., N.W., Suite 405
Washington, DC 20006

American Council on Education
One Dupont Circle, N.W.
Washington, D.C. 20036

American Personnel and Guidance Association
Two Skyline Place, Suite 400
5203 Leesburg Pike
Falls Church, VA 22041

American Psychological Association
1200 17th St., N.W.
Washington, DC 20036

Council of Graduate Schools in the U.S.
One Dupont Circle, N.W.
Washington, DC 20036

Council of Postsecondary Accreditation
One Dupont Circle, N.W.
Washington, DC 20036

Council of State Governments
Headquarters Office
Iron Works
Lexington, KY 40578

National Academy of Certified Clinical Mental Health Counselors
10700 62nd St.
Temple Terrace, FL 33617

Professional Examination Service
475 Riverside Dr.
New York, NY 10027

Chapter 12

Professional Liability

R. H. Wright

Long Beach, California

Few areas in the education and training of psychologists (mental health workers generally) are so systematically neglected as is professional liability. (a) Steadily increasing coverage of the consuming public by third party insurers, (b) psychology's successful efforts to become professional service vendors under individual and group health insurance programs, (c) the success of psychology's efforts to gain legal recognition and statutory control, interacting with the increasing sophistication of the American public and the increasing consumption by that same public of mental health services, have resulted in psychological practitioners being held professionally accountable in ways that were literally undreamed of a decade ago.

As late as 1967, the American Psychological Association Insurance Trust could report to APA's Committee on Health Insurance that no claims of malpractice had (to that date) been sustained by the courts; and that the only expenses (to 1967) were those relating to legal and operational expenses of the malpractice program. Concurrent with increased acceptance and consumption of mental health services, the American public became increasing demanding of health service delivery generally and actively litiginous in enforcing such demands. Realistic (and unrealistic) expectations of a personally acceptable "outcome" following the "consumption" of mental health services, encouraged and supported by an excess of attorneys (willing to accept a contingent fee), resulted in significantly increased exposure to allegations of "malpractice" for mental health providers generally, including psychologists.

A recent survey of the APA Professional Liability Program (Wright, 1981a) covering the 5-year period 1976–1980 inclusive revealed that psychological practitioners have been sued for such imaginative reasons as wrong diagnosis; failure to stop clients from smoking; failure to prevent suicides; serving on peer review, ethics committees and/or state licensure boards, etc. Yet, as a group, we are so naive about our vulnerability that, as late as 1981, a major committee of the APA governance took the position that psychologists employed by institutions had no significant vulnerability to legal tests of professional liability for professional services delivered in the context of their institutional employment. However, the facts are that the psychological practitioner is well-advised to assume that, at some time in her/his professional career, she/he is likely to have to defend (hopefully with the assistance of the professional liability insurance carrier's legal staff) against charges of negligence. The reader will note that, thus far, the writer has successfully avoided using (except in the generic sense) the terms "malpractice" and "professional liability."

At the risk of becoming too deeply involved in the specifics of legal theory and/or distinctions between malpractice per se as opposed to a broader range of legal vulnerability subsumed under the heading "professional liability," the following is relevant. Historically, malpractice has been considered a negligence tort (defined as "a civil or private wrong causing damage to a legally protected interest of another") (Simon, 1982, p. 7). Simon further notes "if any of the four elements (i.e., duty, dereliction of duty, damage, and direct causation of damage) is not present, no basis exists for a negligence suit."

Both Cohen (1979) and Simon agree that this historic view of malpractice contemplated a failure on the part of the provider to behave in a way so that the provider's professional service met some generally acceptable standard for care. Simon (1982) concludes that, if the provider "observes a reasonable standard of care in the treatment of his patient, any errors that result will be considered errors of judgment rather than negligence and are not actionable," commenting further, "torts can also be intential, i.e., assault and battery, defamation, the use of threats to persuade a client to accept some modality of treatment, etc." (p. 7). Most actions against psychologists historically have followed the more familiar pattern framing complaints in terms of negligence such as "misdiagnoses, failure to achieve some anticipated or expected outcome, etc." Of late, in certain of the touching therapies, for example, malpractice actions have at least bordered on allegations of intentional damage. Cohen (1979) states that, although legal actions against mental health professionals "have been grounded in tort theory, suits have [also] been brought under the theory of breach of contract as well" (e.g., failure to achieve some designed outcome), and concludes, "suits against mental health professionals will increasingly be brought under contract not tort law" p. 40). He recommends a broader and infinitely more useful definition of malpractice: i.e., "any unreasonable lack of skill or fidelity in the performance of professional or fiduciary duties" (p. 41); i.e., the psychologist is "professionally liable." Psychologists should nevertheless be aware that even such an expanded definition may fail to contemplate the total range of the professional's vulnerability in the delivery of mental health service, which is one of the major reasons why an insurance policy which covers malpractice on the part of the mental health care provider addresses the issue in the broader context of Professional Liability, Premises Liability, etc.

PREMISES LIABILITY

In the context of the foregoing, the psychologist new to independent practice is best advised to consider vulnerability along a number of dimensions. This section will address specifically the nature of one such exposure, and begins literally with the practitioner's office and the arrival of the patient/client.

Human beings in their comings and goings from the psychologist's office can find ways to injure themselves which defy description. Emotionally distressed people laboring under high stress levels stumble on your steps; fall, slip, and/or trip on carpet and rugs; will ignore the exit door placed between adjacent glass panels, and consequently crash through one of the glass panels. They get caught in the doors, slide down parking ramps, trip over electric cords, and so endlessly on. The practitioner's thoughtful eye is invited to study carefully whether or not she/he has been "set up" by personal decorating ideas and/or the imaginative professional services of the interior designer to harvest an abundance of personal injury legal actions attendant on falls, slips, sprains, strains, etc. The psychologist new to independent practice is generally ignorant of the risk because, to this point in her/his career, the practitioner has functioned in an institutional setting under the protection of the "liability umbrella" of the employing institution. There is no such benevolent "big mama/daddy" to protect the independent vendor of professional service.

Whether you (as a provider) are a primary lessee, are subleasing space from fellow practitioners with space to spare, are the building owner, and/or have located your offices in your home, you are equally at risk for any personal injury associated with the premises. If you, as a provider, are renting or leasing space from a rental company, it is likely that they will have a master policy covering the building; but it is nevertheless very likely that in the event of a personal injury on the premises, you will also be named a party to the action. Thus, one of the first exposures for which the service provider needs to procure protection is personal premises liability coverage (in addition to whatever master coverage may be provided by the owning/renting company lessors). In some instances (such as in the APA Professional Liability Policy), premises liability is an included coverage of the professional liability policy; and a provider may (by specifying the address(es) of her/his professional office(s)) protect against such random accidents. However, many professional liability policies do not include the premises liability endorsement (in fact, the APA program has not always included such coverage); and, therefore, the practitioner should be intimately familiar with the various coverage(s) and/or endorsements on the policy(s), so as to be certain of specific coverage for personal injury claims.

If such protection is not included in the overall professional liability program, *the wise practitioner* will obtain specific coverage for his/her premises. Typically, the cost of such coverage is small, and, on an annualized basis is likely to cost less than a "first consultation" with the attorney you will have to retain to defend you in the event you are a party to a personal injury complaint. Reasonable sensitivity to risk management, e.g., the judicious protection of appliance (electrical) cords, plastic inserts for electric wall plugs (especially if you provide service to children), and training office personnel to put away children's toys that may have been scattered about your waiting room, will minimize your exposure and the inconvenience of defending against a personal injury action (even in those instances where you know that the "friendly" insurance company is going to have to handle the complaint and/or pay the judgment).

FEE DISPUTES

One of the most frequent causes (10+%) of malpractice actions originate in fee disputes and/or attempts to collect outstanding bills (Wright, 1981a). The client/patient, perhaps frightened by the "mystery" of a consultation with a "shrink" (but nevertheless desirous of consuming your professional service), will often find it extremely difficult to discuss the fee with you.

The psychologist coming from a training tradition which emphasizes concern for individuals, frequently of "humanistic" philosophic persuasion (with idealistic commitments to and naive notions about human interaction), is also often uncomfortable about discussing fees, consequently overlooking that the delivery and consumption of professional service is a business agreement which has the legal stature of a contract. Thus the client/patient (because of diffidence, megalomania, etc.) and the professional (for reasons of lofty idealism, etc.) conspire to avoid discussing the fee; and/or, if they do talk about it, succeed in "mush-mouthing" to such a degree that the consumer fails to comprehend (or is only partially aware) of the financial aspects of the relationship. Furthermore, at the beginning, it is sometimes difficult to *be* specific in terms of what the consumer can expect relative to cost.

Charges for professional services (and/or the way in which charges are billed) are infinitely variable from one practitioner to another. Some psychologists charge on a straight time basis, irrespective of whether the service to be delivered is "diagnostic" or "therapeutic." Some practitioners use a "sliding scale," attempting to relate charges for the professional service to the client's realistic ability to pay, while other practitioners bill one way for diagnostic time and another way for therapeutic service. Ultimately, it probably makes little difference what procedure is used so long as the consumer is, as early as possible in the process, fully and completely apprised of the *way* in which the services will be billed. Some consumers are sufficiently sophisticated and/or concerned about costs as to be quite straightforward in raising the issue of the fee (often in the initial telephone conversation seeking an appointment). In such cases, and if the provider has a standard fee schedule, a forthright statement can be made as to billing practices, charges per session, etc. Conversely, if the practitioner genuinely follows the "sliding scale" convention, the potential client can be informed of that fact. Although the client/patient may view such an action as an attempt to evade, a straightforward comment to the effect that "until the professional has some knowledge of the individual's circumstances, a realistic fee cannot be established," will often allay such suspicion. It is also frequently helpful to tell inquiring clients that "Generally, fees in this area for this kind of service are *X amount*," so as to give some realistic basis for "guesstimating" the magnitude of the economic commitment.

Whatever the convention followed, failure to address openly the matter of the fee entails the risk that the consumer will interpret the provider reticence in a way useful to the consumer. If the consumer's interpretation is that "the 'pro' doesn't want to talk about fees" (thereby reinforcing the consumer's reluctance to discuss same), important consumer attitudes, feelings, behaviors, etc. may be lost to rational consideration. Consumer interpretation that " the fee is unimportant" may lead to slowness in or failure to pay (or even worse to the consumer fantasy that the "psychologist is so interested in me that money is unimportant").

A related and equally problematic provider behavior is that of tolerating regular and/or substantial accrual of unpaid bills for professional services. Again beguiled by our humanistic concerns (and/or other not so "worthy" motivations), many practitioners allow the patient—in fact, often encourage the patient against the patient's own repeated expression of concern—to accumulate a substantial outstanding balance for professional services. In this writer's judgment and experience, there are relatively few circumstances that justify such a procedure. Occasionally, the client/patient will experience a temporary set-back (such as job-loss, lay-off, or other economic misadventure) warranting the economic support of the psychologist. However, where such situations occur, the professional is best advised to set limits at the outset (as to (a) the length of time, or (b) the maximal sum of money to be accrued, or both) that will be tolerated. Therapeutic strategy (as in the case of substantial under- or nonemployment) may also dictate some deviation from the foregoing, as in the case of a passive acceptance of job termination, a firing, extended unemployment, or where an individual is chronically underemployed. Such a person may benefit from the support of an explicit agreement which says: "Okay, for X number of weeks and/or months, I will see you (a) so long as you are actively involved in seeking employment (more renumerative employment), and/or (b) are actively getting your economic house in order. However, as of X date, I expect that you will again regularly begin to pay the monthly billing."

The risk of engendering troublesome transference responses is still present; but so long as such agreements are (a) reasonably limited as to duration and amount, and (b) are specifically an acknowledged part of the therapeutic plan, the risk may be justified. At least, under these circumstances, emerging transference attitudes can be dealt with and counter-transference behaviors eliminated or contained. In circumstances where the consumer cannot realistically handle the financial responsibility of consuming psychological services, it is probably better for both provider/consumer to recognize that fact and desist from initiating a professional relationship and/or work toward early transfer of the consumer to a more appropriate facility. For the psychologist to encourage unrealistic consumption minimally will result in complicating the consumer effort to cope with reality, and additionally runs the risk of exposing the consumer to what can ultimately become potentially overwhelming debt. The resulting guilt and/or trauma frequently finds expression in a malpractice action.

Given any of the foregoing and the extremely complex nature of psychologist/client interaction, the professional who allows an ever-mounting outstanding balance to accrue is, at the very least, creating the possibility of a client/patient interpretation: "I am so special that she/he will indulge me by continuing to allow me to consume services even if I don't pay for them." Though such "special status" may be very gratifying to the client/patient, the suspicion must exist (for the individual receiving such "preferred treatment") that it is at the price of conformity. Therefore, the consumer may well be unable to express negative feelings, hostility, aggression, etc. either toward the therapist or toward authority figures generally (because of the risk of losing "specialness") or may conversely displace and discharge such feelings in inappropriate (but related) circumstances. At the point where the indulgence is discontinued (i.e., when the psychologist says: "Your balance is now so-and-so; I expect you to pay it"), the patient may feel betrayed, robbed of special status, abused, etc., and will often retaliate by retaining an attorney with the (unconscious) motive of "getting back" at the therapist for the withholding of the previously extended indulgence. Unfortunately, the professional (often unconsciously) provokes and/or encourages such consumer acting-out. Unconsciously, the practitioner will expect gratitude, conforming behavior, etc. (on the part of the client/patient), and, if it is not forthcoming, counter-transference reactions from the therapist are all too frequently a not too surreptitious part of the transaction—provoking the consumer into even further excesses. The ultimate provider response is often self-righteous indignation at consumer ingratitude culminating in a "legal" (malpractice) resolution of transference and/or counter-transference behaviors (with substantial "loss" to everyone involved).

DIAGNOSTIC SERVICES

Diagnostic services are, by their very nature, not easy to specify in advance of the time involved, with the result that a convention covering billing for such services may be less easily defined. Many psychologists simply bill for the amount of time involved (after the fact), feeling that to do otherwise would be to unfairly penalize someone whose diagnostic problem is reasonably straightforward and/or for whom the delineation thereof does not require extended expenditures of time and effort. Other psychologists incline to the view that the consumer is not contracting for time, but rather for a procedure wherein the diagnostic instrument is the professional. From such a perspective, it is relatively easy to say to the consumer, "The procedure is as follows: there is an initial interview followed by a basic diagnostic test battery including evaluations of overall intellectual/emotional functioning, etc., consuming a minimum of X amount of time and including a 'summing-up' reporting session of at least X amount of time for which the total fee will be X dollars."

Such a procedure has the advantage of specifying, from the outset, what the total cost of the process will be; and, by "out-front" procurement of consumer concurrence, minimizes a subsequent consumer complaint of "failure to understand" or "misconception." The disadvantage of this approach is that, in extremely complex or difficult cases, copious amounts of provider time may be required to establish the diagnostic or evaluative formulations (time that the professional will have to absorb). It has been the writer's experience that, where the concept of a basic battery (as further detailed below) is adhered to, unreasonable and/or excessive time demands occur infrequently. The advantage of being able to specify "up-front total cost" offsets those infrequent occasions when the billing inadequately covers the provider's time and service. Conversely, where one uses the "open-ended" approach of charging only for the time which is actually utilized, my experience has been that, if the concept of a basic battery is adhered to, the savings for any individual consumer are likely to be modest; whereas the exposure to charges of excessive testing to "pad" the bill and subsequent legal actions, etc., are all too readily available to an unhappy consumer. Again it must be emphasized that, irrespective of the convention followed, the critical factor is full and complete disclosure to the consumer of what is being done and why it is being done, accompanied by an explicit and constant appreciation of the consumer's right at every step in the process to make the ultimate decision as to proceeding or terminating.

The psychologist performing any evaluative function must be acutely and continually aware that, for the client/patient, something is always "at-risk" in the diagnostic/evaluative process. The results of psychodiagnosis, psychological testing, psychological evaluation (whatever term one prefers) are put to a variety of uses, many of which may be inimical to the participant's perceived interest. Whether the client is a parent concerned about a child's poor school performance, an executive being evaluated for a promotion, a patient suspected of a brain tumor, parents squabbling over the custody of a child, or an individual being evaluated for potential probation or parole, something of substantial value to the individual is potentially in the balance.

In many of the above contexts, the question of "Who is the client?" is also an open-ended one. In the case of a parent concerned about an under-achieving youngster, the question "Who is the client?" appears easily answered: "The concerned parent who is paying the bill." The precautionary phrasing "appears easily answered" is here appropriately used in that, at least professionally, there is an equal responsibility to the child. Unless the child can be reasonably assured that the provider recognizes and respects that responsibility, less than complete cooperation will be forthcoming.

In any of the other examples, the answer to the question "Who is the client?" is a very complex and difficult one from either the standpoint of good practice or professional liability. In instances such as a pre-employment or promotional evaluation, a legal proceeding, etc., the question may be further contaminated by the fact that the agency paying for the professional service (be that agency an employing company, the courts, one or the other contending attorneys) may have interests—if not directly opposed—at least in potential conflict with that of the individual being evaluated. All too frequently, psychology has tended traditionally (and in an over-simplified way) to answer the question of "Who is the client?" with the phrase "the person who pays for the service." Such a presumption is likely to occasion an ultimate court appearance by the unquestioning and/or incautious practitioner. The fact is that practically everyone involved is "the client." The individual being evaluated is certainly "a client," as is the agency paying for the professional service. Failure to recognize the foregoing frequently results in the professional giving "short shrift" to one or more of the "clients," and can provoke hostile, retaliatory legal actions by the offended client. In view of the fact that the individual being evaluated may have a greater "stake" in the outcome than the agency paying for the evaluation, it is not surprising that diagnostic/evaluative activities are one of the major contributors to the totality of malpractice actions against psychologists.

Because of the frequency of the threat, the enormity of the responsibility involved, etc. and as a defense against such exposure, many psychologists ultimately turn away from the stimulation and challenge of the evaluative process. This is doubly unfortunate, in that (a) it often denies society important and needed information and (b) it denies to the psychologist that which is unique to the psychologist's functioning: the diagnostic tools and procedures psychology has developed to allow us to assess human behavior.

In spite of very real vulnerability, the thoughtful psychologist can minimize exposure to legal actions by recognizing the importance to the individual of the outcome of the evaluative process. Unlike the therapeutic relationship (where the consumer of service generally has repeated exposure to the provider and, thereby, the opportunity to refine perceptions of provider interjections, commentary, evaluations, etc.), the evaluative process, by its very nature, is a highly time-delineated one. Therefore, it is up to the practitioner to provide the "client" with every opportunity to understand the provider's ultimate findings and recommendations. To the person being evaluated (especially where something of consequence is denied as a result of the outcome of the evaluation), it is all too easy to deny personal responsibility by externalizing the problem, and conceiving it instead as one of professional incompetence, lack of sensitivity, lack of exhaustiveness of evaluative measures, etc. To the individual denied custody, probation/parole, vocational advancement, etc., it is all too easy to discredit the process rather than to view the outcome as a realistic reflection of some limitation within one's self. In an appalling number of cases, the individuals undergoing the evaluation process first learn of the psychological practitioner's findings and recommendations in a formal arena (hearing, etc.) in which the evaluated individual is denied custody, denied parole/probation, or denied a job or a promotion, on the basis of a cold reading of some sentence or comment abstracted from the psychologist's report.

Good professional practice dictates that, from the outset, the psychologist will refuse to undertake the evaluative procedure unless time can be scheduled for the professional to reveal to the individual involved the findings of the psychologist. Even if the findings are negative (in the sense that they go against the individual's perceived wish/interest), the fact that the psychologist is willing to face the consumer's displeasure and/or give the individual a chance to interact with and ventilate feelings about the findings and recommendations (prior to the formal procedure in which the findings/recommendations become institutionalized) goes far towards averting an ultimate denial by the individual of personal responsibility, and/or frequently forestalls an attempt to externalize the disappointment, rationalizing it by complaints of professional negligence, insensitivity, lack of comprehensiveness, etc. culminating in a legal action.

The problem of "unacceptable outcome" is especially frequent in child custody cases, and has resulted in many psychologists refusing to play the parental "good guy/bad guy" game. Many practitioners refuse to become involved in the custody process unless both parents are willing to agree in advance that the responsibility of the psychologist is to the child, and that both parents will be bound by the psychologist's recommendations. In order to procure such agreement, it is necessary for the psychologist to assure both attorneys and both parents about (a) the objectivity of the psychologist and (b) the psychologist's commitment to the child's ultimate welfare. If such a commitment cannot be obtained prior to initiating the procedure, it is unlikely that psychological services (no matter how well performed) will be of significant value in the custody determination.

THE DIAGNOSTIC/EVALUATIVE INSTRUMENT

The selection(s) of the test instrument (to be used in the evaluative process) is also a frequent contributor to the psychologist's discomfort when the day comes that the professional must defend his findings and recommendations. Psychology's long-standing "love affair" with "science," and/or our need to "objectify" the evaluative process, has resulted in an endless proliferation of psychological tests designed to perform all kinds of diagnostic and/or evaluative functions. In a feature article in a recent edition of the *APA Monitor*, a respected senior colleague long experienced in the field of industrial and organizational psychology exhorted colleagues to select the "right test" for the job. Publishers of psychological tests are many, and, at the slightest indication of the professional's interest, will inundate the psychologist with catalogues describing an almost endless array of test instruments, including cursory data on their validity, reliability, standardization process, etc., while extolling the virtues of one test instrument as opposed to another.

For many providers undertaking some aspect of evaluation, the task then becomes one of "fitting" the particular test (instrument) to the question to be answered, as our "teachers"—(themselves often relatively inexperienced in either the evaluative *or* the legal process)—exhort us to do. Keeping in mind that the outcome of the evaluative process is as likely to deny something that a client wants as it is to grant that desire, and given the current litigious state of the American public, the psychodiagnostician and/or psychological evaluator (following such "cook book" procedures) can then look forward to spending considerable time in a courtroom, defending the choice of a particular test instrument and discussing learnedly (with opposing counsel) those very procedures of test standardization, reliability, and validity studies, etc.

For those interested in such pursuits, Dr. Theodore Blau (1976) has recorded a series of tapes covering his informed and charming lectures on forensic psychology. The sophisticated psychologist will not only review Dr. Blau's tapes but will dig out long-unused textbooks on research design, statistical methodology, reliability and validity studies, etc., for one can be assured that, before the psychologist's day in court is completed, these matters will be discussed with such depth, vehemence, and attention to detail as was not even witnessed in one's long ago classroom encounters with the mysteries of reliability, validity, test design, etc.

Another extremely helpful volume with which the psychologist should be intimately knowledgeable (prior to going to court) is Jay Ziskin's (1976) thoughtful volume, *Coping with Psychiatric and Psychological Testimony*. For those who do not find such legal material fascinating reading, be advised of the high probability that opposing counsel (who is out to discredit you) will have most assuredly—and with ecstatic attention—devoured the contents of the referenced volume.

For those who take the view, "I'm a clinical psychologist and I don't want to become an expert in test design, construction, and standardization," is there an alternative? The answer is a somewhat qualified "yes." However, let me hastily add a cautionary note; there is no way (except the ineptitude of the opposing attorney) for the psychologist to escape the necessity of justifying his professional procedures and judgments (after all, the function of the court is to "discover truth"—or the nearest approximation thereto). For many psychologists, the decision to utilize an alternative (to "scientific justification") is a relatively easy one; because, when one honestly reviews published data, it is the exception where reported reliability, validity, and/or standardization studies give the practitioner the degree of confidence in the instrument most professionals would desire.

The alternative to the "let's use Test A for Purpose A" approach is to conceive of *the psychologist* as the *test instrument*, and of the psychological "test(s)" as providing a standardized situation in which the professional (as the instrument) can make reasonably systematic, objective and valid observation(s) (about client/patient behavior) *in that standardized setting.* Such an approach also argues secondarily for the concept of a basic battery (discussed immediately below).

Few, if any, "tests" in the writer's experience have the degree of specificity of purpose and/or level of validity and reliability to make them easily defensible in a courtroom. However, if the professional is, instead, defending personal observations and judgments based on long experience with the particular test instrument, the professional is, in the main, dealing with variables relevant to professional service delivery rather than esoteric standardization, reliability, or validity studies. Practitioner comfort and ease in explaining professional behavior is likely to be much greater where the preferred findings, recommendations, etc. are based on long, intense experience with a particular test or tests. From this perspective, many psychologists have found that the selection and routine use of a so-called basic battery of tests not only reflects well on their professional expertise (when that expertise is being challenged in a courtroom), but at the same time offers an exceptionally worthwhile benefit in that it will considerably enhance the professional's evaluative and/or diagnostic skills.

Unfortunately, many training programs and many colleagues appear to have had relatively little interest in evaluative procedures, and/or little systematic exposure (in the training process) to the acquisition of such skills. Consequently, in many offices, the evaluative functions are performed by clerks or psychological assistants, with only minimal (if any) involvement of the professional psychologist. Where such involvement exists, it is often only at the level of cursory review. Such an approach will, frequently, ultimately "bite" the practitioner who must defend such slipshod or unprofessional service in a courtroom.

It is difficult for this writer to conceive of any evaluative process which would rule out the use of a so-called basic battery. Such a battery should, of course, contain a good test of intellectual functioning, (preferably of the individually administered type, e.g., WISC, WAIS, etc.) backed by paper-and-pencil screening tests of intellectual function (such as the Shipley-Hartford). Tests of visual perceptual-motor integration and function are extremely helpful in such a battery, as are such widely used paper and pencil instruments as the Proverbs, human figure drawings, etc. Tests of personality such as the Minnesota Multiphasic Personality Inventory are often included, although the writer finds the MMPI less helpful (for the amount of time invested) than such devices as a good sentence completion test, the human figure drawings, House-Tree-Person tests, etc. In specific instances, so-called "deep tests" of personality function such as the Rorschach or Thematic Apperception Test may add additionally valuable dimensions in the clinician's understanding of the client's/patient's overall functioning. As noted above, such a basic battery is applicable to almost any type of evaluative situation; and, where carefully administered by and/or under the ongoing scrutiny of the psychologist, will not only provide valuable behavioral data (helpful in understanding client's functioning), but will also identify areas where specialized tests are called for (i.e., disturbances in block design, Bender, and/or House-Tree-Person drawings may suggest the need for specialized tests such as the Reitan or Rorschach, TAT, etc.).

Again, it is probably that the specific tests used in the basic battery are not as consequential as the fact that they are routinely used by the clinician (because it is the intimate, repeated familiarity with the particular instrument that heightens the value of the clinician's perception almost beyond the value of standardized or derived score). The ability of the psychologist to say in court, "I have given this test battery approximately 500 times and, based on my experience, I made the following judgments" is likely to be far more convincing to judge and jury than some objective test score from a test which "everybody knows doesn't measure much of anything anyway."

The psychologist can always shift the professional role so that it is the reliability and validity of the test that is at issue in a court of law. However, it is likely to be far more meaningful and carry much greater credibility when the issue is the professional's work. It is critical to add that the conception of the psychologist as "test instrument" in no way relieves the practitioner of the professional obligation to utilize psychological tests only in their prescribed or standardized fashion. I have repeatedly made the astonishing observation that many licensed and experienced psychologists administer standardized tests in "nonstandard" ways. Of late, it is the exception to encounter clinical psychologists familiar with and/or using the standardized language prescribed for test presentation (e.g., the "scripted" language specified by the individual subtests of the various Wechsler tests), and/or observing the protocol for presentation of test parts and subparts to the person being evaluated. It is even more appalling to discover the number of practitioners totally unaware that their "nonstandard" presentations completely violate the integrity of the test instrument (and the observations associated therewith) or that their test presentations have made highly suspect (if they have not invalidated) any "objective" scores derived from such "nonstandard" presentations. Psychologists should be advised that there is a high degree of probability that they will be asked (in that courtroom) to demonstrate one or all of the tests administered precisely as administered (while the plaintiff's attorney and/or associated counsel are carefully checking adherence to test procedures by comparing the psychologist's every move to the test manual). The psychologist found deviating from standard will experience a dramatic, sobering, and sudden learning experience—for the net effect of such "nonstandard presentation" may well be to have one's credibility totally destroyed and/or one's testimony literally "thrown out."

Finally, the importance of refusing to undertake any diagnostic or evaluative functions without (a) a very careful intake interview (covering the nature of the individual complaint and/or the individual's perception of the situation), (b) a careful history, and (c) an opportunity for the person (undergoing the experience) to make available to the psychologist any data felt relevant by that individual cannot be over-emphasized as a defense against ultimate legal embarrassment. As noted earlier, the importance of a closing interview in which full disclosure is made of findings and recommendations, including time and an opportunity for the client to act and react with the psychologist is also a very valuable way of avoiding the summons to defend one's self against allegations of malpractice.

THERAPEUTIC ACTIVITIES

Conventional psychotherapeutic activities, except in certain specialized contexts, are a relatively infrequent contributor to the malpractice experience of psychologists (Wright, 1981a). That is not to say that clients are not frustrated, that their expectations (realistic and unrealistic) are not met, and that these attitudes, behaviors, and experiences do not lend themselves to an ultimate resolution in a malpractice action; but rather that such "legal resolutions" occur, with relatively lesser frequency than in the diagnostic/evaluation areas.

Undoubtedly, the fact that the psychotherapeutic relationship is, in general, an ongoing one offering repeated opportunities for exchange between the professional and the consumer, accounts in large measure for the foregoing observation. Good judgment, sensitivity to both transference and counter-transference issues, strict adherence to ethical standards, and, above all, the utilization of plain good sense are the best defense against an ultimate malpractice complaint centering on some therapeutic misadventure. Often, psychologists in their enthusiasm for some new technique or approach fail to use good sense in the utilization of the technique. For example, the use of the styrofoam bat, certainly an innocuous enough and apparently harmless device, has, in one instance, resulted in a significant eye injury and a subsequent malpractice action against the psychologist conducting the group. In another instance, the same device was being so enthusiastically employed by participants in the group that one client/patient (when hit by the "bat") slipped on an unattached throw rug and sustained significant bodily injury (ultimately culminating in a malpractice suit alleging negligence, assault, battery, bodily injury, etc.)

It would seem almost unnecessary to admonish psychologists *not* to become sexually involved with their clients. Yet it is unfortunately the case that historically approximately 10 to 15% of malpractice actions and/or complaints to licensing boards feature allegations of sexual misconduct (Wright, 1981a). Psychologists using "aversive" conditioning techniques have been sued for "wrongful death" and/or homicide in instances where patients were encouraged to consume such excessive amounts of water as to occasion complete disruption of the patient's internal environment, allegedly resulting in the patient's demise.

Most psychologists would not accept a style of "defensive practice" in which the capability of the professional is severely limited by concerns about malpractice exposure. At the same time, it is frequently the case that we become so enamored of the "worth" and/or "good intent" of what we are doing that we overlook the critical challenge; i.e., "Does this make good sense?" If, with relative comfort, one can contemplate a "reasonable" defense of some technique or procedure in an open "forum," it seems obvious that the professional has a fair chance of "justifying" the use of the procedure. However, the practitioner must never forget that the burden of proof to justify the utilization of *any* procedure is heavily on the utilizing professional.

GENERAL OFFICE/BUSINESS PROCEDURES

Admonitions to psychologists to maintain carefully detailed records would seem unnecessary. Yet professional health practitioners generally and psychologists particularly, are notorious for the informality of their record-keeping. Many psychologists' poor record-keeping tendencies have been additionally reinforced by having served in institutional settings in which "security" and/or "confidentiality" of client/patient records was of concern. From the "malpractice" perspective, what in one context may be a laudable concern about privacy may result in an inability to document adequately the basis for professional judgment, interventions, and/or procedures. As a consultant on professional liability exposure, I have seen offices in which record-keeping procedures are so informal that diagnostic protocols and/or evaluations (spanning several days in time) are undated, so that it was subsequently impossible to ascertain on what day (in the time span or in what sequence) a particular test was administered. Routine matters like being sure that the patient's name and the date is on each and every piece of paper associated with the evaluation (if for no other reason than as a means of identifying the random page that falls out of the folder) are precautions all too infrequently observed by far too many colleagues.

It is even more incredible to find that substantial numbers of professionals do not cover their professional liability exposure with insurance. In many instances, there is the mistaken belief that, because one is member of a staff of an institution, one does not "need" professional liability (malpractice) insurance. Perhaps this misconception is carried forward into independent practice. For whatever reason, it is a regrettable and unfortunate fact that many psychologists are practicing without insurance coverage in situations in which malpractice judgments can run into hundreds of thousands of dollars. As psychologists more routinely employ various kinds of physical and chemical interventions in psychological practice, the "at risk" vulnerability will increase, as will the magnitude of "damages" sought and/or "judgments" rendered. Such coverage is economically very reasonable, the cost amounting to (literally) pennies per day. To be without such coverage may well border on the economically (and psychologically) self-destructive, and, from the perspective of economic redress of consumer grievance, is most assuredly professionally and socially irresponsible.

During the writer's tenure as the Chair of the Professional Liability subsection, the APA Insurance Trust offered (for the first time) specific coverage for students and supervisors in training settings, a type of protection that all too few teachers or students know is available, or *that they need*. The minimal cost of such coverage, measured against the magnitude of risk, argues that such coverage is a good investment for anyone involved in the training enterprise. Students and teachers assume immunity or institutional coverage for allegations of malpractice. Legal actions against those "in-training" and their "trainers" have to date been relatively infrequent occurrences. However, the increasing prevalence of professional schools, and psychology's aforementioned move into physical and chemical intervention strategies, argue that the "immunity of invisibility" (enjoyed in the past by participants in the training enterprise) is becoming part of history.

Early on, it is also important for the new practitioner to establish lasting relationships with the professional cadre in the area where one practices. A professional relationship with a good attorney is very important, because attorneys are increasingly high utilizers of psychological services in their practice of law, and are therefore good sources of referrals, and because the expertise of an attorney well-versed in business procedures and/or health care delivery is a decided advantage in reviewing procedures and forms (in such areas as confidentiality, patient privilege, billing procedures, etc.). In the unhappy event that the psychologist does face civil (malpractice) litigation (even assuming that the bulk of the defense will be carried by attorneys supplied by the insurance carrier), it is unfortunately true that, at the moment of litigation, potential conflict of interest between the insuror and the insured can occur. The interest of the insurance company is in settling the case at the least possible cost, whereas the interest of the insured practitioner may lie in legal vindication of professional integrity and/or the salvaging of professional reputation, etc. Expert guidance from one's own personal attorney (advocate), devoted to one's personal and professional interests, will assist in insuring that the activities of the insurance company attorney are as devoted to the insured's welfare as they are to the financial balance sheet of the insurance company.

Other important professional relationships to be established are those with other health care professionals within the community, as potential referral sources, and also as resouce people/collaborators (whose unique expertise can enhance the quality of all health care delivery) and as a means of reducing our exposure to allegations of malpractice.

Perhaps because of anxiety, inexperience, or excessive defensive concern about infringing on "medicine's" turf, many psychologists require a medical evaluation before initiating the delivery of psychological services; others work in physical or close collaboration with physicians; and others refer to medical colleagues on an "as needed" basis. All such procedures "spread the risk" in the event that the plaintiff's attorney attempts to imply that the psychologist is "practicing medicine without a license." However, operating strictly from the legal perspective that the psychologist is only culpable for a reasonable standard of care as provided by other *psychological* practitioners in the community, elaborate procedures such as requiring routine physicals and/or routine medical consults are *not* inevitably a necessary or desirable part of the delivery of good psychological services. In reality, such techniques probably serve more to allay the psychologist's anxiety than to reduce that professional's "at-risk" status. However, the availability of knowledgeable, sophisticated, and experienced specialists in internal medicine, neurology, pediatrics, OB-GYN, etc. with whom one can work in a truly collaborative fashion (when such additional professional services are indicated) can only enhance the quality of all health care delivery of whatever persuasion.

An often overlooked and decided aid in dealing with a practice inadvertency, etc., which might ultimately culminate in a malpractice action is an ongoing relationship with a senior psychologist in the provider's community. As professionals, we like to feel that, with the granting of our license, the completion of internships, etc., we are now full-fledged members of the "lodge." The fact is that we have really only taken the first qualifying step along what is, hopefully, a life-time of learning about what we do. No one, no matter how well-trained in whatever discipline, is truly completely knowledgeable about the infinite range and complexity of human behavior or professional service thereto. Specific recourse to professional consultation from an established psychologist, perhaps even of a different theoretical orientation or persuasion, can be an extremely helpful way of learning more about the practice of psychology, and certainly will result in an enhancement of the quality of the psychological health care service we provide. The senior practitioner's greater experience and knowledge can be very helpful in managing some of the practice problems or "crises" that, if maladroitly handled, can eventuate in a malpractice action. Certainly where an "incident" occurs (which has implicit within it a basis for subsequent civil litigation), a *paid* and formal consultation with such a senior colleague can not only make *confidentially* available to us greater experience/ knowledge, etc.; but can also provide trained (and *protected*) emotion assistance to the "at-risk" professional in a moment of personal emotional crises.

Finally, it is worth noting again that law is an ever-expanding body of theory, technique, and procedure (as is our own profession), with the consequence that the degree of professional exposure can be expected to expand also. Idealistically, we might hope that no psychologist would ever face the enormous personal, emotional, and economic crisis or threat that comes with a malpractice action; but such can never be. One of the best ways to minimize the impact of such an experience (since it is literally impossible to preclude the possibility of the experience) is to try to anticipate the areas of our exposure and to attempt systematically to reduce our vulnerability. In another context, Wright (1981a,

1982b) has summed up (a) the major causes of malpractice actions and (b) the major issues involved in the actual experience of malpractice litigation. These articles contain a "survivor's checklist" (Wright, 1981b, p. 1541), a handy listing of do's and don'ts for the practitioner confronted with the possibility or reality of a malpractice proceeding.

REFERENCES

Blau, T. H. (1976). *The psychologist as expert witness.* Garden Grove, CA: Infomedix.

Cohen, R. J. (1979). *Malpractice: A guide for the mental health practitioner.* New York: Free Press.

Simon, R. I. (1982). *Psychiatric intervention and malpractice: A primer for liability prevention.* Springfield, IL: Charles C. Thomas.

Wright, R. H. (1981). Psychologists and professional liability (malpractice) insurance: A retrospective review. *American Psychologist, 36,* 1485–1493. (a)

Wright, R. H. (1981). What to do until the malpractice lawyer comes: A survivor's manual. *American Psychologist, 36,* 1535–1541. (b)

Ziskin, J. (1976). *Coping with psychiatric and psychological testimony.* Beverly Hills, CA: Law and Psychology Press.

Chapter 13

Legal Issues

Gerald Cooke

Plymouth Meeting, Pennsylvania

INTRODUCTION

In recent years, psychologists have found an increasing need to be aware of legal issues affecting their practice. This need arises for several reasons, including protection of the patient's rights, providing the most appropriate treatment for the patient, protection of the psychologist, and preparation for legal testimony. The chapter topic, "Legal Issues," is intertwined with ethical issues, malpractice law, licensing or certification laws, and courtroom testimony. Because these areas are covered in other chapters in this text, the attention to them will be de-emphasized in this chapter. However, the reader should be aware that this in no way implies that these areas, particularly eithical considerations, are unimportant.

The following areas will be covered in this chapter:

1. Privileged communications;
2. Informed consent;
3. Access to records;
4. Issues relating to hospitalization of patients;
5. The patient's right to treatment and right to refuse treatment;
6. Legal issues in research.

PRIVILEGED COMMUNICATION

The *ethical* principle guiding the psychologist with respect to release of information about clients is called *confidentiality*. According to the American Psychological Association's Ethical Principles of Psychologists (1981), information is to be revealed "only with the consent of the person or person's legal representative, except in those unusual circumstances in which not to do so would result in clear danger to the person or to others" (p. 636). The ethical concept of confidentiality is often confused with *privilege*. Privilege is a *legal* concept. Privilege is usually defined by statute, though it may be modified, limited, or expanded by case law. The definition of privilege varies from state to state and under federal law. In some states, it is defined in the psychologist's licensing or certification act. In others, it is subsumed under the physician–patient privilege or in a general context referred to as psychotherapist–patient privilege. However, in some states there are no specific statutes granting privilege to the psychologist's clients.

Psychologists often mistakenly talk about privilege as if it belongs to them. There have been a number of cases in which therapists have refused to release information, despite requests by their patients to do so. These therapists claimed that the privilege was theirs. The courts have been very clear on this matter: the privilege belongs to the patient, not to the mental health professional (e.g., in Re Lifshutz, 1970). With a few well-defined exceptions to be discussed below, the patient has the right to have his/her information released by the psychologist or to prevent the psychologist from releasing it. This extends to testimony in court, release to parents, release to spouses, or release to other third parties such as insurance companies.

There are also variations from jurisdiction to jurisdiction regarding who is covered by privilege. Where statutes exist, an individual patient *in treatment* is always covered. However, some states distinguish between treatment, where privilege exists, and *evaluation*, where privilege may not exist. In the latter case, there are often other alternatives to the psychologist–patient privilege. For example, if the evaluation is at the request of the person's attorney, then the psychologist is acting as an agent of the attorney and the relationship is covered by the attorney–client privilege.

A major dilemma arises when more than one person is involved in therapy. This occurs in couples therapy, family therapy, and group therapy. Central to this dilemma is the question of who is the client. Is each individual the client, or is the couple, family, or group as a unit the client? Psychologists often assume, and communicate to the persons involved, that what goes on in couples, family, or group therapy is confidential. But this is a tenuous assumption. Courts have traditionally limited the expansion of privilege because privilege allows important information to be kept from the court. Also, in some jurisdictions, when privileged information is revealed to a third party, the privilege is lost, and this may apply even though the patient and the "third party" are both members of the same family or group in therapy. Numerous cases have arisen in which a married couple was seen in therapy and, later, as part of a divorce or custody matter, one spouse requested that the therapist testify regarding the other spouse. In most states where these cases have arisen, the statute did not adequately address the issue of privilege in marital therapy. The tenuousness of the assumption of privilege is underscored by the fact that some of the judges in these cases decided the privilege did exist, and others did not and ordered the therapist to testify. This clearly illustrates that one may not assume that privilege exists in family, couples, or group therapy unless the state statute explicity indicates that it does exist.

Another issue regarding privilege involves situations where it either does

not exist or rnay be waived. As already discussed above, depending on jurisdiction, privilege may not exist in an evaluation or in a situation where more
than one person is in treatment. Privilege also does not exist when an evaluation, and possibly even treatment, is ordered by the court. In such cases,
the psychologist has the responsibility to inform the patient that privilege
does not exist and that a report will go to the court and may become a matter
of public record. This is true not only in criminal cases, but also in family
cases, (e.g., custody) and some civil cases. Whether or not court-ordered treatment (e.g., as part of probation or parole, or in mediation of divorce or custody), as opposed to evaluation, is covered by privilege varies from jurisdiction
to jurisdiction, judge to judge, and even by the nature of the problem. For
example, in some jurisdictions, treatment of drug and alcohol problems, treatment of persons charged with sexually or physically abusing children, etc.,
are governed by special statutes which provide that privilege does not exist
in that treatment relationship.

Two other situations lead to the waiver of privilege. When the patient him-
self/herself raises the issue of his/her mental status in a criminal, civil, or domestic relation matter, he/she is assumed to have waived the privilege. That is, the
patient gives up the privilege when he/she decides to use his/her mental condition as a basis of a defense in a criminal case, in a claim for damages in a civil
case, (because he/she is mentally unable to work), or as part of a claim (e. g.,
for alimony) in a domestic case. The other situation is one which gained notoriety through the Tarasoff case (1974). In this case a man in therapy informed
the therapist that he intended to kill Miss Tarasoff. Though an attempt was
made to detain him, he was released and 2 months later, he did kill her. Her
parents bought a suit for "wrongful death," and the court was forced to address
the issue of privilege in psychotherapy. While the decision has been oversim-
plified and does have a number of fine points and implications, it basically
states that "private privilege ends where public peril begins." That is, where the
psychologist determines that the patient poses a danger to a third party, the
psychologist has a "duty to warn" the intended victim.

To summarize regarding privileged communication, the psychologist needs
to know that it represents a conversion of the ethical principle of confidentiality
into a legal definition. This legal definition varies from jurisdiction to jurisdiction and situation to situation. The psychologist should become acquainted
with the specific statutes and cases in the jurisdiction where he/she practices.
This can be accomplished by obtaining a copy of the Psychologist Licensing Act
from the Department of Licenses, and the Mental Health Act from the State
Department of Public Welfare. Another source of both federal and local cases
and new statutes is *The Mental Disability Law Reporter*, which is published bi-
monthly by the American Bar Association (see additional readings for address)
and presently costs $50.00 per year.

INFORMED CONSENT

Informed consent refers to the psychologist's responsibility to provide the patient with sufficient information for the patient to make a judgment concerning whether he/she wishes to participate in the particular treatment. When applied to psychotherapy, this means that the individual should be told:

1. The procedures, goals, and possible side-effects of therapy;
2. The qualifications, policies, and practices of the therapist or agency; and
3. Available means of help other than therapy with that practitioner.

Some psychologists and attorneys have even suggested that the therapist and patient enter into a written contract, though most therapists tend not to do this. The process of providing information to the patient should also include the limitations of privilege, as discussed in the previous section.

Another aspect of informed consent involves obtaining the permission of the patient before releasing any information to third parties, including to insurance companies. Most insurance companies have their own release of information forms which the patient signs and which accompanies the insurance form. The psychologist should retain a copy of this for the files. Some psychologists are content to receive verbal permission to release information. If this is done, either face-to-face or by phone, it should be documented in the patient's record, along with the date, time, and nature of the discussion. However, it is much more prudent to obtain written consent which is then placed in the patient's file.

ACCESS TO RECORDS

Many psychologists performing evaluations or providing psychotherapy feel that it may be deleterious to the patient to see reports on him or herself. Also, therapists often feel similarly regarding therapy notes, which reflect the therapist's observations and interpretations. Whether or not the therapist feels this way, psychologists should recognize that, with a few exceptions, the Freedom of Information Act (1972) guarantees to patients the right to read the medical records. This right has been reiterated in the Federal Mental Health Systems Act (1980), which has a section entitled "A Patient's Bill of Rights" which contains the right of access to information. The patient may also make notes based on his/her reading of the records. However, the psychologist or agency is not required to give the patient copies of the records. The distinction is a fine point: the records themselves belong to the psychologist or agency; the information in the records belongs to the patient.

Though the psychologist is required to give the patient access to the records, several limitations are considered to be justifiable. First, the psychologist has the prerogative of first removing any statements about the patient which are made by a third party, such as a parent or spouse. Second, the psychologist or agency may require that the records be read in the presence of a clinician, administrator, or other appropriate person. This serves two purposes: it protects the records, and also affords to the patient the opportunity to have technical terms, statements of dynamics, etc., explained.

Patient access to records is not the only issue concerning recordkeeping. Insurance companies may also require access to the records. This has been discussed partially in the section on Informed Consent. Most insurance forms request only basic data such as diagnosis, type of treatment, dates of treatment, and date first consulted. Some may require a prognosis or an anticipated date of completion of treatment. Occasionally, however, additional data is requested. If this happens, the nature of the requested information should be discussed with the patient in specific detail. A patient has the right to choose to take the choice of losing insurance coverage rather than disclosing certain information. In my experience, this most often occurs in cases where a person with a responsible job has been charged with a crime, such as exposing himself, and has been allowed to pursue treatment as an alternative to prosecution. Naturally, in such cases, the patient would rather not take the chance of having the diagnosis or nature of the problem appear on an insurance form. There are, however, some ways of providing the patient with treatment and insurance coverage without compromising his/her confidentiality. For example, where appropriate, a diagnosis such as Adjustment Reaction of Adult Life could be listed rather than a diagnosis of Sexual Deviation.

There are occasions where other third parties may also request access to patient records. This may include parents, probation or parole officers, child-care caseworkers, etc. If such a request is anticipated from the beginning of the treatment, then informed consent discussions with the patient should include how such requests would be handled and what information would be provided. This may sometimes require that all three parties (e.g., psychologist, patient, probation officer) meet together and enter into an agreement. It may also be helpful to have the patient's attorney present. The agreed-upon information may range from a minimum of dates of attendance in therapy to a detailed description of what occurs in therapy and the therapist's interpretation and opinion regarding the patient's behavior. The general guideline is that protection of privilege requires release to third parties of the minimal possible information. Such reassurance to the patient is also likely to make for more efficacious therapy.

A related issue is the giving of patient names to an attorney or collection agency when the patient has failed to pay outstanding bills. I usually precede any such action with increasingly strong letters, including a final, registered letter, usually after about 1 year has passed, threatening legal action. The release of names for this purpose is, from a legal perspective, permissible because the patient has, by not paying, caused a breach of contract. Thus, it is a matter of weighing one legal issue against another, and privilege cannot be used as a shield against breach of contract. However, the principle of "need to know" would apply, and only minimal information, such as name and amount owed, should be released.

These issues of access of records raise a related issue: what information should the psychologist place in records, whether these be evaluation reports or therapy notes? There is some disagreement on this issue. Some psychologists feel that their records should contain only basic data and a little of the substance of what goes on in therapy. Others feel that all information should be included, no matter how sensitive. What is to be included in the records may be a matter of agency policy or in the individual practitioner's preference. However, many psychologists agree that three classes of data should generally be excluded. The first of these is statements by others about the patient. This has been discussed earlier. The second class involves criminal activities. Contacts with the law enforcement agencies should be included only if directly relevant to the issues at hand. For example, if the patient is being evaluated for a recommendation on disposition of a present criminal charge, the past criminal record is very relevant. But, on the other hand, if a patient who had a criminal charge many years ago is in evaluation and/or treatment for an anxiety problem, then such information should probably not be included. Even more important is the issue of criminal activity that the patient tells the psychologist about for which he/she has never been arrested. This is most common with persons with drug problems who have frequently sold drugs, committed burglaries, etc., in order to support their habit, but have never been arrested for many of these crimes. Such information is not already a matter of public record, is self-incriminating, is not evidence of a potential danger to others, and may be extremely harmful to the patient if it becomes known. There is little justification, therefore, for recording such information. An analogous situation arises with the third class of material: information on sexual behavior. If the person has a sexual problem, such information is relevant. If this is not the case, including in the records such items as an extramarital affair, a past homosexual experience, etc., serves little purpose and can cause great harm.

What goes in the records should also be taken very seriously for another reason. I have seen numerous cases where the records of an individual who was incarcerated or hospitalized indicated he was assaultive, suicidal, psychopathic, or sexually aggressive. At times, a review of the files on these people reveals that such descriptive terms were based on previous reports in which those terms were, in turn, based on earlier reports, and so on. As the description is traced back to its origin, it is sometimes found that the use of the term was inappropriate from the beginning. Often, the origin of such terms lies in test responses or a clinical impression which may suggest such characteristics, but occurs in the absence of any actual overt behavior. At other times, there may have been an isolated incident under highly specific conditions which then became the basis of a generalized statement about personality. This tendency for terms which have little or no behavioral correlate to be transmitted repeatedly should lead to great caution in including such terms in notes or reports, unless there is a firm behavioral basis for these terms. This is related to an important issue in psychology at the present time: the prediction of dangerous behavior. Research on the prediction of dangerous behavior indicates that such prediction is extremely difficult even when there is a history of prior dangerous behavior, but that a prediction of dangerous behavior is totally unwarranted when there is no prior behavioral history. Also, the psychologist should question the use of such statements in prior reports and be careful about including them in his/her notes or reports unless a behavioral basis is discovered.

The psychologist, either in an agency or in private practive, may receive a subpoena for records. Most agencies have a policy for handling such subpoenas and have access to legal counsel where necessary. For the psychologist in private practice, several issues must be considered. The first question should be whether the subpoena is accompanied by a timely written release of information by the patient. If not, two steps should be taken. The psychologist should contact the patient and ask if he/she is aware of this subpoena and its purpose. If so, a written release should be requested. The other step is to contact the attorney who sent the subpoena to determine the purpose. If the patient is unwilling for records to be released, ti is permissible to inform the attorney requesting them that the records will not be released without a court order to do so. In my experience, if the request was improper in any way, that will be the last that is heard of it. Even in the event that the psychologist is ordered to appear in court with records, there is a step that can be taken. Many psychologists unfamiliar with the courtroom feel intimidated by it. However, the great majority of judges are supportive of mental health professionals. When such a request has been made, I have frequently turned to the judge with a phrase such as "I would like to request the court's guidance." I then explain whatever issues of privilege or other law which I feel should prevent me from releasing information. Judges usually listen carefully and have sometimes even recessed court to research the issue before they reach a decision. Judges do not want to be reversed and, rather than being angered by such a request, they are usually glad that the issue has been raised.

ISSUES RELATING TO THE HOSPITALIZATION OF PATIENTS

On occasion, a patient being seen as an out-patient may require hospitalization. This presents both practical and legal issues. The agency or private psychologist should be aware of commitment procedure as contained in the state Mental Health Law. Most private hospitals require that a doctor with staff privileges make the admission. The private psychologist who does not have staff privileges should make such an arrangement when he/she embarks on his/her practice, rather than waiting until an emergency presents itself. The other option is commitment to a state, veteran's, or emergency facility. At such facilities, a patient merely needs to request hospitalization and then will be evaluated by the on-call staff, who determine the appropriateness of hospitalization. With the patient's permission, the treating psychologist may provide information to the evaluation team.

Greater difficulties arise when the patient does not see the need for hospitalization, and an involuntary commitment is required. This raises legal as well as treatment issues. Until the 1970s, there were few procedural safeguards in cases of involuntary hospitalization. This was because of the doctrine of parens patria, which held that hospitalizing a mentally ill person for his/her "own good" was a legitimate power of the state and did not require the same legal safeguards as incarcerating a person charged with a crime. A series of legal cases have altered that standard (e.g., O'Connor v Donaldson, 1975). At present, most statutes embody, in some form, the concept that mental illness alone is not grounds for involuntary commitment. The individual must be both mentally ill and imminently dangerous to himself/herself or others. When possible, the psychologist should inform the patient of his/her opinion that hospitalization is required, and try to convince the patient to hospitalize himself/herself voluntarily. If this cannot be done, the psychologist may request a relative or other interested party to initiate commitment or, as a last resort, the psychologist may initiate it himself/herself. The actual procedure for this varies from jurisdiction to jurisdiction. The procedure usually involves calling a speical crisis intervention team or community mental health center. Where such special arrangements are not available, the only alternative is to contact the police. The committing party will usually have to appear before the hearing officer and provide evidence of not only mental illness, but also of imminent danger to self or others based on threats and/or overt behavior. During the hearing, the patient has the right to present independent evidence as well as having other legal safeguards.

A recent case (Addington v Texas, 1979), has established that the standard for ordering commitment to a mental hospital must be "clear and convincing evidence," which is the middle of the three stages of legal proof (the least demanding being "a preponderance of the evidence" and the most demanding, used in criminal cases, being "beyond a reasonable doubt"). If the person is hospitalized, then treatment must be provided. Also, this treatment must be in the least restictive, appropriate setting.

THE PATIENT'S RIGHT TO TREATMENT AND TO REFUSE TREATMENT

Beginning in 1966, there were a series of legal cases establishing that involuntarily committed patients have a right to treatment (e.g., Rouse v Cameron, 1966; Wyatt v Stickney, 1972; Donaldson v O'Connor, 1974). These cases also increasingly set guidelines for what was to be considered adequate, minimal facilities and treatment. Hospitals were required to upgrade their facilities, their treatment teams, and their procedures in order to meet these guidelines. Out of this emerged the patient's bill of rights referred to earlier. Recent cases have outlined a bill of rights for out-patient care in the community as well (Dixon v Weinberger, 1975).

An interesting and important derivative of the right to treatment is the right to refuse treatment. The concern leading to the right to refuse treatment cases originally came from situations in which legally competent persons were not allowed to participate in the choice of treatment and were sometimes treated against their will. This is a particularly important issue with so-called "intrusive" treatments, such as electro-shock, medication, and some behavioral modification procedures. The analogy has often been made to the medical situation: someone who is competent, and has cancer, is told to undergo radiation treatment, though the treatment may be noxious and the outcome may be doubtful. If this person in the medical situation were to refuse such treatment, is it likely that the person would be involuntarily hospitalized and subjected to treatment against his/her will? When expressed this way, the idea of such involuntary treatment is repugnant to most people. Yet such is precisely what was done to mentally-ill persons for many years. Two 1979 cases (Rogers v Okin, 1979 and Rennie v Klein, 1979) stated that competent patients have a right to refuse medication except in an emergency situation where they are potentially dangerous to themselves or others. Several cases followed which extended this right even to mentally incompetent persons (In Re Roe, 1981, and Addington v Texas, 1979). Under these decisions, if the person was incompetent, then the court would make the decision as to whether he/she should be subjected to the treatment. The Roe decision concerned noninstitutionalized incompetent persons, so the rulings relate to out-patients as well as to in-patients.

But the issue is far from resolved. In Youngberg v Romeo (1982), the court gave signs of turning the responsibility for medication back to psychiatrists, without legal intervention. And in Mills v Rogers (1982), the Supreme Court remanded back to the circuit court the issue of whether involuntarily committed mental patients have a constitutional right to refuse treatment with antipsychotic drugs. Apparently, it will be some time before this issue is resolved. Though medication is a psychiatric, rather than a psychological issue, the same guidelines are likely to be extended at least to any treatment considered "intrusive," and possibly even to nonintrusive treatment.

LEGAL ISSUES IN RESEARCH

The American Psychological Association's *Ethical Principles of Psychologists* (1981) formulates guidelines for psychologists conducting research with human participants. Several of these reflect issues discussed earlier: privilege and confidentiality, informed consent, and access to records. But there are several other important guidelines as well. Psychologists are exhorted to plan the study weighing the scientific contribution against the dignity and welfare of the subjects. The rights, as well as the safety, of the patients must be guarded, and the subject must be allowed to refuse to participate or to withdraw at any time. There are also guidelines on deception. An added concern, not covered sufficiently in the Ethical Principles, is that in-patients, prisoners, or even persons attending (and dependent upon) out-patient clinics, may be subtly coerced by the implication of the withholding or limiting of services. Such practices are unethical, and if services are actually withheld, the practice would be illegal as well.

SUMMARY

Few psychologists, except those specializing in forensic psychology, are likely to have an in-depth knowledge of statutory and case law. However, it is easy for the psychologist to include a few important reference sources in his/her library:

1. The State Psychology Licensing Law;
2. The American Psychological Association publication, *Ethical Principles of Psychologists*;
3. The State Mental Health Act.

In addition, there are some basic guidelines:

1. When in doubt, get it in writing and/or document it with notes;
2. Don't be afraid to ask an attorney or even a judge for guidance.

The law is ever-changing, and even existing law is subject to interpretation; that is why there are judges. Judges have legal immunity; psychologists do not. If the psychologist's action, in questionable cases, is based on a judge's order, then two needs are served: the protection of interests of the patient, and the protection of the psychologist.

REFERENCES

Addington v Texas, 441, U.S. 418, 1979.
American Psychological Association. (1981). Ethical principles of psychologists. *American Psychologist, 36,* 633–638.
Dixon v Weinberger, 405 F. Supp. 974, D. C. Cir. 1975.
Donaldson v O'Connor, 493, F. 2d, 507, 5th Cir. 1974.
Federal Mental Health Systems Act of 1980, Pub. L. No. 96–398, 94 Stat. 1564, 1980.
Freedom of Information Act, Act 5 UCS Sect. 552, 1972.
In Re Lifschutz 85, Cal. Rep. 829, 476, P2d, 557, 1970.
In Re Roe, 421, M. E. 2d, 40 Mass. Sup. Jud. Ct., 1981.
Mills v Rogers, 50 U. S. L. W. 4676 U. S., 1982.

O'Connor v Donaldson, 422, U. S. 563, 1975.
Rennie v Klein, 62 F. Supp. 1131, D. N. J., 1979.
Rogers v Okin, 478 F. Supp., 1342 D. Mass., 1979.
Rouse v Cameron, 373 F. 2d, 451, D. C. Cir., 1966.
Tarasoff v The Regents of the University of California, et al., 529 P 2d, 533, Ca., 1974.
Wyatt v Stickney, 325 F. Supp., 381, M. D. Ala., 1972.
Youngberg v Romeo, 50 U. S. L. W. 4681, U. S., 1982.

ADDITIONAL READINGS

American Bar Association. *Mental Disability Law Reporter* (MDLR), Commission on the Mentally Disabled, American Bar Association, 1800 M St., N. W., Washington, D. C. 20036–5886.

Cooke, G. (1980). *The role of the forensic psychologist.* Springfield, IL: Charles Thomas.

Hare-Mustin, R., Maracek, J., Kaplan, A., & Liss-Levinson, N. (1979). Rights of clients, responsibilities of therapists. *American Psychologist, 35,* 3–16.

Margolin, G. (1982). Ethical and legal considerations in marital and family therapy. *American Psychologist, 37,* 788–801.

Meyer, R. G., & Smith, S. R. (1977). A crises in group therapy. *American Pscychologist, 32,* 638–643.

Sadoff, R. L. (1982). *Legal issues in the care of psychiatric patients: A guide for the mental health professional.* New York: Springer.

Steadman, H., & Cocozza, J. (1974). *Careers of the criminally insane: Excessive social control of deviants.* Lexington, MA: Lexington Books.

Chapter 14

Ethical Issues

Rosalea Ann Schonbar

Teachers College, Columbia University

Recently, an aide in a psychiatric hospital was reported as having had sexual contact with a female patient. Although the hospital was ready to fire the aide, the union contract required that an arbitrator decide the issue. The arbitrator found that the sexual encounter had been "consensual," and recommended a 2-month suspension. This decision was upheld by a judge. Had the aide been a psychologist, he would have violated *Principle 6a* of the ethical code of the American Psychological Association (1981). He would have been subject to a hearing and probably dismissal from the APA, and to the loss of his license to engage in the practice of psychology. It is even possible that, had the aide been a psychologist, the arbitrator and the judge would have rendered a harsher decision.

One of the hallmarks of a profession is, or ought to be, its willingness to demand high and public standards of practice and responsibility. Whereas the goal of a union is the protection of the rights of its members, a major goal of an association of professionals in the human services field must be the protection of the rights of the people they serve.

In the case of the profession of psychology, the definition of those rights is also informed by the kinds of services we perform and the kinds of understanding our own profession yields. In the case cited above, for example, the unequivocal proscription of sexual intimacies with clients arises to some extent from our knowledge concerning relationships of unequal power and our understanding of the force and functioning of transference, both of which make impossible a truly "consensual" sexual liaison between psychologist and patient.

The Preamble to the most recent revision of the APA *Ethical Principles* (1981)[1] states the following:

> Psychologists respect the dignity and worth of the individual and strive for the preservation and protection of fundamental human rights. They are committed to increasing knowledge of human behavior and of people's understanding of themselves and others and to the utilization of such knowledge for the promotion of human welfare . . . They use their

---

[1]Material quoted from the APA *Ethical Principles* by permission of the publisher. Copyright © 1981 by the American Psychological Association.

skills only for purposes consistent with these values and do not knowingly permit their misuse by others. While demanding for themselves freedom of inquiry and communication, psychologists accept the responsibility this freedom requires: competence, objectivity in the application of skills, and concern for the best interests of clients, colleagues, students, research participants, and society. (p. 633)

The *Ethical Principles* themselves set forth the details of the implementation of the values of Preamble. In order for the profession to be in a position to regulate itself, a procedure exists for the investigation of formal reports of violation of the code, and, in cases where these reports are found to have had substance, to make decisions about the response of the profession to the violator and the violation.

Thus, it is clear that certain values are expected to play a major role in the professional behavior of psychologists. In a sense, the stated values of any individual or group define that individual or group. For this reason, it is important that graduate programs in psychology start early and continue to instruct their students in these values and their implementation, whether in the classroom, the lab, or the clinic. This is so, not only because students are expected to be guided by these *Principles*, but also because, whatever view one takes of "professionalization," the goal of such socialization is the continued awareness of the consensually arrived-at values and responsibilities of the profession, so that decision-making can occur more easily within their context.

THE DEVELOPMENT OF THE PRINCIPLES

When certain behaviors are described as desirable and others as unethical, it is legitimate to ask that the origin of these judgments be identified. Thus, it is important to point out that the current statement of these principles has evolved over the years since their first publication in 1953 out of an empirically determined set of concerns and several mandated reviews.

When, after World War II, clinical psychology became a formal specialization backed by government support, it was from within psychology itself that the impetus came for definition, regulation, and responsibility. Two outcomes of this impetus were the beginnings of the push toward licensing and *legal* recognition (and responsibility) on the one hand, and the creation of ethical standards on the other. Today, these standards are used by licensing agencies themselves as the criterion for acceptable professional behavior for psychologists.

In 1948, with the help of a grant from the Rockefeller Foundation, the American Psychological Association began the task of developing a set of ethical standards . Because of psychology's commitment to empiricism, this set of standards was compiled by means of asking all 7500 APA members "to describe a situation they knew of first-hand, in which a psychologist made a decision having ethical implications, and to indicate what the correspondents perceived as being the ethical issues involved" (APA, 1953, p. vi). The more than 1000 replies were then sorted into several categories, and the ethical commitments stated or implied in the incidents were embodied into a set of principles. The initial and ensuing drafts were submitted for discussion and modification to other APA committees and boards, presented at panels, symposia, and other meetings, and distributed to state associations and university psychology departments. This procedure took 4 years and is believed to have actively involved at least 2000 psychologists. The standards, thus created, were adopted at an APA Council of Representatives meeting in 1952. Built into the procedure was a mandated periodic review and revision; the latest of these was passed, after 3 years of similar review, at a January 1981 meeting of the Council, and was published in 1981.

It can therefore be seen that these standards were not imposed on psychologists from outside by any arm of government, or from inside by a select committee. They were created by ourselves to govern or guide our own professional decisions and behavior, and they therefore express the values and "the ethical aspirations" (APA, 1953, p. v) we hold as psychologists.

The 1953 publication of the standards is, in some senses, a research report; it contains a selection of the critical incidents from which each of the principles was derived, and it differentiated between matters which were clearly unethical and those which constituted courteous professional behavior. It was 179 pages long. Succeeding versions have presented only the principles, condensed to capture the most important issues as unambiguously as possible. From the onset, it has been clear that ethical decisions in psychology arise mainly from interpersonal relationships in various professional contexts, and these contexts form the structure or categories within which the principles are presented.

THE ETHICAL PRINCIPLES OF PSYCHOLOGISTS (1981)[2]

Principle 1. Responsibility

> In providing services, psychologists maintain the highest standards of their profession. They accept responsibility for the consequences of their acts and make every effort to ensure that their services are used appropriately. (p. 633)

The major thrust of the six principles implementing this general statement is the necessity for the avoidance of any kind of pressure to distort or suppress research findings, to slant teaching, and to influence clinical judgment and impact. It is thus a statement that psychologists value objectivity and that all aspects of our professional activities demand that objectivity.

Of perhaps the greatest interest are Principles *1a* and *1f*. Principle *1a* states that, in research, psychologists

---

[2]Unless otherwise indicated, all page references in this section are from the 1981 *Principles*.

provide thorough discussion of the limitations of their data, especially
when their work touches on social policy or might be construed to the
detriment of persons in specific age, sex, ethnic, socioeconomic, or other
social groups . . . they never suppress disconfirming data. (p. 633)

Principle *1f* concerns psychologists as practitioners, urging alertness to "personal, social, organizational, financial, or political situations and pressures that
might lead to misuse of their influence" (p. 633).

These caveats recognize not only the abstract value of conscious responsibility, but implicitly also recognize the existence of such issues as the experi-
menter effect in research and countertransference in the clinical enterprise.
These principles appear to recognize that objectivity is difficult in an inevitable
social context and that conflicts of interest are difficult to avoid, and therefore
urge continual awareness to insure the possibility of maximum objectivity.

Another, though possibly less far-reaching principle (*1a*) is that, in research,
psychologists, unlike members of some other professions, "take credit only for
work they have actually done" (p. 633), and detailed guidelines for distributing
credit among contributors are offered under *Principle 7, Professional Relationships.*

Principle 2. Competence

The maintenance of high standards is a responsibility shared by all psychologists . . . Psychologists recognize the boundaries of their competence
and the limitations of their techniques. They only provide services and
only use techniques for which they are qualified by training and experience. . . . (p. 634)

The detailed spelling out of what seems to be a statement so obvious as to be
unarguable touches upon situations and decisions which can nevertheless be very
troublesome when they arise. Principle *2a*, for example, states that "Psychologists accurately represent their competence, education, training, and experience" (p. 634). Let us consider three fairly common situations in which this
principle is frequently tested:

1. The following quotations are excerpts from statements by two recently
licensed psychologists in response to a question about any ethical conflicts they
had experienced:

. . .the question of accepting referrals prior to licensing is one of the more
painful acts of abstention I can recall . . . During that time I was getting a
number of testing referrals. I was also doing full-time testing on my ward
so the licensing question seemed even more incongruous. I did turn down
the referrals and some referring physicians treated me as an odd duck because I wouldn't go ahead and do the same work I was doing in the hospital.

In thinking about your questions concerning ethical issues for the psychologist in training, the one that most plagued me during my last year

of graduate school was the problem of beginning to see private patients before the dissertation was finished (and during the period before state licensing was obtained). In (city where respondent was working) there seemed to be a rather laissez-faire attitude towards this dilemma with the idea that as long as you were in supervision and did not call yourself a psychologist, etc., you were adequately meeting the ethical standards of your profession.

Both of these statements deal with engaging in the independent practice of psychology before being licensed to do so. This is, of course, a legal as well as an ethical issue. However, since licensure is designed to certify and communicate to the public a certain standard of competence for which members of the public may hold the practitioner responsible, then clearly the psychologist who offers such services before licensure is presenting himself or herself at a level of defined competence beyond his or her status at the time.

The second of the two excerpts refers also to the issue of independent practice before the actual attainment of the doctorate. This is a problem many graduate programs face. At Teachers College, we take very seriously the principle that independent professional practice in an area in which one is still in formal training is a clear and serious ethical violation; each student, therefore, receives a letter elaborating this view, defining independent practice, and informing the student that the local consequence for violation is expulsion from the Department.

2. Since most internships are in medical settings, interns are often pressed to use the title "Doctor." This is, of course, very tempting, especially in a setting where that title represents the highest authority, and where "bucking the system" as a trainee is difficult anyway. It also violates this Principle. Even with the doctorate, the title can sometimes be misleading, as indicated by a young licensed psychologist working in an inpatient setting:

. . . Does one volunteer to patients and families that one is a *psychologist* doctor, as patients assume one is an M. D. doctor? I now routinely introduce myself as a *psychologist*.

3. In times when universities and research-supporting agencies are retrenching financially, some psychologists see some form of direct service as offering an alternative. Generic licensing means that a psychologist is not licensed in a specialty area, and most of our licenses are of this type. Nevertheless, a licensed psychologist whose training was in physiological or social psychology, for example, may be no more competent to engage in the practice of assessment, psychotherapy, or counseling than is a person untrained in any psychological specialty. The APA has a carefully developed procedure for retraining, which guarantees the supervised acquisition of new competencies. Simply hanging out a shingle violates the principle.

Principle 2f is of special interest. It states that, since "personal proble
conflicts may interfere with professional effectiveness," psychologists

> refrain from undertaking any activity in which their personal problems are
> likely to lead to inadequate performance or harm to a client, colleague,
> student, or research participant. If engaged in such activity when they
> become aware of their personal problems, they seek help to determine
> whether they should suspend, terminate, or limit the scope of their pro-
> fessional and/or scientific activities. (p. 634)

While it is probably true that those personal problems which are likely to result
in harmful behavior are usually not consciously recognized, this principle implicitly calls attention to the desirability of some kind of continuing supervision or
formalized collegial contacts for the mutual monitoring of our impact on those
we work with; in this regard, it may be recalled that Freud (1937/1964) recommended periodic reanalysis for practitioners of psychoanalysis. It also allows
Ethics Committees to prescribe remedial rather than punitive action for colleagues in this situation.

Principle 3. Moral and Legal Standards

> Psychologists' moral and ethical standards of behavior are a personal matter
> to the same degree as they are for any other citizen, except as these may
> compromise the fulfillment of their professional responsibilities or reduce
> the public trust in psychology and psychologists. Regarding their own be-
> havior, psychologists are sensitive to prevailing community standards and
> to the possible impact that conformity to or deviation from these stan-
> dards may have on the quality of their performance as psychologists. Psy-
> chologists are also aware of the possible impact of their public behavior
> upon the ability of colleagues to perform their professional duties. (p.
> 634)

The specific principles, for the most part, flesh out this theme in terms of hu-
mane and sensitive professional behavior. However, the general statement itself
goes somewhat beyond the scope of professional behavior into the arena of
"public behavior" even of a nonprofessional character. Moreover, *Principle 3d*
states in part that, "In the ordinary course of events, psychologists adhere to
relevant governmental laws and institutional regulations in their professional activities" (p. 634). Both of these issues seem to me to go beyond the scope of a
code of professional ethics. On the other hand, the General Principle is worded
in such a way as simply to urge careful thought in decision-making. In the instance of adherence to laws and regulations, there is elaboration to the effect
that, in situations in which those laws and regulations conflict with Association
standards and guidelines, we make known our adherence to the latter and "work
toward a resolution of the conflict." In any case, we involve ourselves in the creation and modification of such laws and regulations wherever possible, in ways
which "best serve the public interest."

I know a psychologist who worked in a Community Mental Health Clinic to which the Community Mental Health Board, consisting of mental health professionals and laymen, was scheduled to pay a visit. Continued funding was at stake. As part of their evaluation procedure, the Board was accustomed to selecting case records from the files and reviewing them. Dr. R., the psychologist, let it be known that this procedure violated the ethical standards of his profession (*Principle 5, Confidentiality*), and that he would not participate in the procedure, mandated or not. Eventually, a compromise was developed in which preselected case records were presented after all identifying details had been deleted.

There are other places where the issue of differentiating between ethical and legal matters arose as a problem in creating this revision of the *Principles*.

Principle 4. Public Statements

This Principle states that announcements of services, advertising, promotional activities, and appearances in the media "serve the purpose of helping the public make informed judgments and choices" (p. 634). To this end, many of the specific operational principles detail the limitations and guidelines which assure that such statements and behaviors provide relevant and accurate information. The Principle also deals with "public statements providing psychological information or professional opinions or providing information about the availability of psychological products, publications, and services" (p. 634), reminding us to base such statements on evidence and to recognize and communicate the limitations of that evidence. Of note is the statement (Principle *4j*) that one has the responsibility to correct misstatements made by others about his/her qualifications, affiliations, and the like. Young psychologists in particular sometimes find it difficult to exercise the obligation not to overstate certain professional affiliations which might make them seem to be somewhat more experienced and qualified than they are, and to correct such statements about themselves when made by others in the professional arena.

Principle 5. Confidentiality

Psychologists have a primary obligation to respect the confidentiality of information obtained from persons in the course of their work as psychologists. They reveal such information to others only with the consent of the person or the person's legal representative, except in those unusual circumstances in which not to do so would result in clear danger to the person or to others. Where appropriate, psychologists inform their clients of the legal limits of confidentiality. (p. 635)

This Principle seemingly needs little elaboration. It is seen as the linchpin of clinical functioning; it is complemented in some state licenses by the granting of "privileged communication" to the clients of psychologists.

Nevertheless, there are interesting and important issues here, centering particularly around the definition of "clear danger" and possible legal complications. In the relatively few instances where laws have been enacted limiting the psychologist's ability to observe this Principle legally, the courts are defining "clear danger" by their decisions in individual cases. Nevertheless, in instances in which actual physical harm is not an issue, this definition will probably remain a matter of professional judgment and conscience and will necessitate attempts to resolve conflicts case-by-case with the judiciary. Subpoenas of records and of the psychologist's testimony (in, for example, custody cases) lead at times to such conflicts.

Although it is not explicity stated here, it is the psychologist who is responsible for maintaining confidentiality, and this responsibility cannot be delegated; secretaries, assistants, receptionists, and the like, must be carefully trained, but violations on their parts are violations on the psychologist's part.

> A psychologist in a training clinic interviewed couples in a room with a one-way vision wall, from behind which his students observed the interviews. It was left to the receptionist to obtain signatures on an informed consent form for the observation. On a particular day, the receptionist failed to do so, and the couple discovered that they had been observed only after the interview was completed. They sued the psychologist and the university for malpractice. A settlement was made out of court, because the psychologist (not the receptionist) had been so clearly delinquent in the exercise of his responsibility.

In this regard, it is also customary in training clinics that the patients be apprised of the sharing of their material in the supervisory process, and that they give signed permission for recording and possible observation.

Storage and disposal of patient records must be done in such a way as to protect confidentiality (5c).

Principle 5b deals with the responsibility to obtain permission for presentation of "personal information during the course of professional work in writings, lectures" (p. 636), etc. The alternative to permission is adequate disguise, but, in practice, disguise is considered essential, even with permission. Such information obtained from research subjects is also to be treated confidentially; this is stated explicitly in *Principle 9, Research with Human Participants.*

Principle 6. Welfare of the Consumer

> When conflicts of interest arise between clients and psychologists' employing institutions, psychologists clarify the nature and direction of their loyalties and responsibilities and keep all parties informed of their commitments. Psychologists fully inform consumers as to the purpose and nature of an evaluative, treatment, educational, or training procedure, and they freely acknowledge that clients, students, or participants in research have freedom of choice with regard to participation. (p. 636)

The operating Principles here have ramifications in many areas of professional work. One (6d), for example, prohibits fee-splitting for referrals and asserts the psychologist's responsibility to devote some part of his/her professional services for low or no fee. Another (6e) cites the responsibility to terminate a relationship from which the client in receiving no benefit and to help him or her to "locate alternative sources of assistance" (p. 636).

The most serious of the operating Principles (6a) recognizes the power position of the psychologist in a myriad of relationships—with students and clients, for example—and the possible exploitation inherent in such relationships. In addition to the general proscription of any such exploitation, the Principle concludes: "Sexual intimacies with clients are unethical" (p. 636). This statement, referred to in the opening section of this chapter, is the shortest and most emphatic statement in the code; implicitly, it recognizes that *any* such behavior represents taking advantage of a position of power.

Interestingly, in attending to the issue of power relationships, the framers of the language of the general principle seem to me to have inadvertently set up an unacceptable situation in stating that, after having informed students of "the purpose and nature of an . . . educational or training procedure," psychologists "freely acknowledge that students . . . have freedom of choice with regard to participation" (p. 636). This implies that there can really be no required courses or practicum supervision in a graduate program. Since APA itself mandates some of these courses, this statement will undoubtedly have to be changed in the next revision.

Principle 7. Professional Relationships

Psychologists act with due regard for the needs, special competencies, and obligations of their colleagues in psychology and other professions. They respect the prerogatives and obligations of the institutions or organizations with which these other colleagues are associated. (p.636)

Here the psychologist is reminded of his/her obligation to help clients to obtain the services of appropriate representatives of other professions when this is in the client's interest. Suggestions are offered for dealing with instances in which a person seeks services from a psychologist which he/she is also receiving elsewhere; offering or seeking to offer services under these conditions is proscribed. Psychologists are described as having the obligation to facilitate the professional growth of trainees under their supervision. "Psychologists do not exploit their professional relationships with clients, supervisees, students, employees, or research participants, sexually or otherwise," nor do they "condone or engage in sexual harassment" (7e, pp. 636-637). Again, the potential dangers in a power position are recognized.

It is within the context of this Principle that psychologists are informed of the behavior expected of them when they become aware of unethical behavior on the part of another psychologist. The recommendation, particularly if the violation is not major, is that a direct, informal approach to the violator be made, and that reports to the Ethics Committee of the State Association or the APA be made only for serious violations or when the informal approach does not work. I have found that the informal approach can be very effective.

Principle 8. Assessment Techniques

This principle deals primarily with the psychologist's responsibility to afford full explanations of the purposes of the techniques and of any limitations to the validity and/or reliability of the results. The necessity for the avoidance of misinterpretations and misuse of findings is noted. In addition, psychologists are admonished against supporting in any manner the use of these techniques by "inappropriately trained or otherwise unqualified persons through teaching, sponsorship, or supervision" (p. 637). Thus, classes in projective techniques are usually limited to doctoral students in appropriate psychology programs. Ethical concerns and professional standards having to do with assessment techniques are discussed in more detail in other APA publications.

Principle 9. Research With Human Participants

> ... the psychologist carries out the investigation with respect and concern for the dignity and welfare of the people who participate and with cognizance of federal and state regulations and professional standards governing the conduct of research with human participants. (p. 637).

The psychologist is responsible for the ethical treatment of subjects by any of the persons who are involved in the research. Except in "minimal-risk" research, the potential subject is informed of the research procedures, especially any elements which might (negatively) influence the decision to participate; the subject is also informed of the right to withdraw at any time. Evidence of informed consent is necessary. Psychology professors who have required their students to serve as subjects in order to receive credit have had to change their procedures. The use of concealment or deception is acceptable only when there are no methodological alternatives, and the subject must be debriefed as soon as possible. The subject must be protected by the psychologist from physical and mental discomfort, harm, and danger. Should there be undesirable consequences to any subject, the psychologist is to make himself or herself available for whatever may be required "to detect and remove or correct these consequences, including long-term effects" (p. 638). This does become necessary from time to time; I was collecting people's reports of their dreams as part of a research project once, and one of the subjects, possibly as a result of his greater attention to his unconscious conflicts, became suicidal. I saw the person until the crisis was alleviated; later this relationship developed into a longer-term therapy situation.

> With regard to the obtaining of informed consent, psychologists doing research in medical settings are likely to find that they are tempted to by-

pass these requirements because of the attitude of some medical colleagues that they are unnecessary. One psychologist in such a situation refused to participate in the research, and the physician eventually gave up his position that the potential subjects' patient status in the hospital made the informed consent procedures unnecessary. Here the psychologist not only insisted that the research be ethically conducted, but may even have made some policy impact on research in that hospital.

Principle 10. Care and Use of Animals

An investigator of animal behavior strives to advance understanding of basic behavioral principles and/or to contribute to the improvement of human health and welfare. In seeking these ends, the investigator ensures the welfare of animals and treats them humanely. Laws and regulations notwithstanding, an animal's immediate protection depends upon the scientist's own conscience. (p. 638)

SOME FINAL COMMENTS

Because of the policy of periodic revision, the *Ethical Principles* are frequently referred to as "a living document." Nevertheless, despite the passage of time and societal changes, as well as the condensation and clarification of language, the changes in the code since its first publication 30 years ago are remarkably minor. Because of rulings by the Federal Trade Commission, advertising, proscribed in the original, is now permissable, but only within the context of offering accurate public information. Attention to an issue like sexual harassment reflects a new focus of concern in society itself, but it does not indicate any change in the direction of humanitarian concerns since 1953. No doubt changes in the sexual mores of our society and the greater incidence of court cases (although these do not usually involve psychologists), as well as the relatively small but possibly increasing number of sexual contacts between therapist and patient admitted to in research, have made the explicit prohibition of such behavior necessary. Even without the *explicit* statement, however, this behavior would have been considered unethical under any of the earlier versions. Thus, the *Principles* appear to represent a relatively constant set of values and concerns within which only certain highlighted issues or somewhat changed implementations vary. It is a tribute to all the psychologists who participated in the original formulations that a much larger APA, split so frequently as it is by geographical, speciality, and other parochial issues, can continue to agree that those formulations represent our ethical aspirations and define us as a profession.

REFERENCES

American Psychological Association. (1953). *Ethical standards of psychologists.* Washington, DC: Author.

American Psychological Association. (1981). Ethical principles of psychologists. *American Psychologist, 36,* 633–638.

Freud, S. (1964). Analysis terminable and interminable. In J. Strachey (Ed. & Trans.), *The standard edition of the complete psychological works of Sigmund Freud* (Vol. 23, pp. 209–255). London: Hogarth Press. (Original work published 1937)

Author Index

Subject Index